MW01484333

Studies in Jewish Culture and Society

A SERIES OF THE

CENTER FOR ADVANCED JUDAIC STUDIES

UNIVERSITY OF PENNSYLVANIA

CONTRIBUTORS

ISRAEL BARTAL Hebrew University of Jerusalem

MALACHI BEIT-ARIÉ Hebrew University of Jerusalem

YAAKOV ELMAN Yeshiva University

DAPHNA EPHRAT Open University of Israel and Tel Aviv University

ISRAEL GERSHONI Tel Aviv University

JEFFREY GROSSMAN University of Virginia

MOSHE IDEL Hebrew University of Jerusalem

MARTIN S. JAFFEE University of Washington

PAUL MANDEL Haifa University

MARC SAPERSTEIN George Washington University

ELLIOT R. WOLFSON New York University

EDITED BY YAAKOV ELMAN
AND ISRAEL GERSHONI

Transmitting Jewish Traditions: Orality, Textuality, and Cultural Diffusion

Yale University Press/New Haven & London

Printed in the United States of America.

Library of Congress Cataloging-in-Publication Data

Transmitting Jewish traditions : orality, textuality, and cultural diffusion / edited by Yaakov Elman and Israel Gershoni.
p. cm.—(Studies in Jewish culture and society)
Includes bibliographical references and index.
ISBN 0-300-08198-7 (alk. paper)
1. Tradition (Judaism)—History. 2. Transmission of texts—History. 3. Jewish learning and scholarship—History.
I. Elman, Yaakov. II. Gershoni, I. III. Series.
BM529 .T73 2000
306'.089'924—dc21
00-023049

A catalogue record for this book is available from the British Library.

The paper in this book meets the guidelines for permanence and durability of the Committee on Production Guidelines for Book Longevity of the Council on Library Resources.

10 9 8 7 6 5 4 3 2 1

For Herbert D. Katz and Eleanor Meyerhoff Katz

Contents

Foreword

This fascinating volume of essays on the subject of learning, orality and literacy, and the transmission of knowledge in the Jewish tradition represents the second in our series *Studies in Jewish Culture and Society.* It brings together a rich sampling of the scholarly work accomplished during the academic year 1995–1996 among some twenty fellows from around the world invited by the University of Pennsylvania's Center for Advanced Judaic Studies to reflect on this broad theme from a variety of perspectives and disciplines. The group consisted of scholars who worked on the Hebrew Bible and Jewish literature of the Hellenistic-Roman period, Midrash and Talmud; historians of Christianity and Islam; specialists in medieval Jewish philosophy and kabbalah; historians of Jewish culture and society in early and modern Europe; and experts on Zionism and Eastern European Jewry, German and Yiddish literature, Jewish musicology, and the modern Arabic world. This diverse group was joined by a variety of guest speakers during their weekly seminars and for the conference which closed the year. Two distinguished historians of literacy and the history of the book, Brian Stock and Roger Chartier, made several presentations to the group and stimulated a remarkable cross-cultural and comparative dialogue. These intense oral encounters can hardly be distilled into a short volume such as this one. Nevertheless, it is our hope that these important contributions offer a broad spectrum of the scholarship conducted during that year and present a major contribution to a subject of inquiry still very much in its infancy within the fields of Judaic studies. Although many of the other significant papers and presenters could not be represented in this volume, some of them have appeared elsewhere and those that are represented clearly reflect the collective wisdom emanating from the remarkable discussions of the entire fellowship.

A third volume of our series is now in press, tentatively entitled "Divergent Centers: Jewish Cultures in America and Israel in the Twentieth Century." Two additional volumes on "Text, Art, and Artifact in Ancient Israel and the Middle East," and "Dialogues Between Past and Present" on the cultural interactions of Jews in medieval Spain, Renaissance Italy, and Enlightenment Germany and Eastern Europe are in preparation.

I would like to thank all the fellows who worked at the Center for Advanced Judaic Studies in 1995–1996 for their rich intellectual contributions and for their willingness to engage in so meaningful a conversation. Yaakov Elman and Israel Gershoni worked tirelessly to conceive and shape this volume. David Goldenberg, editor of the *Jewish Quarterly Review,* again supervised the process of editing and preparing the manuscript for publication. Adam Shear copyedited the volume, and Tamar Kaplan prepared the index. Charles Grench, the executive editor of Yale University Press, offered his usual sage counsel and encouragement. My sincere gratitude to all of them. A special thank you is offered to Martin D. Gruss for his generous and continuous support of the annual Gruss Colloquium and of this volume which has emerged from it.

This volume is dedicated to Herbert D. Katz and Eleanor Meyerhoff Katz. Both of these generous and caring individuals were primarily responsible for the creation of the program in Modern Jewish History at the University of Pennsylvania. Rather than resting on his laurels, Herbert Katz also assumed the chairmanship of the Board of Overseers of the Center for Advanced Judaic Studies three years ago. Under his remarkable leadership the Center has become a unique intellectual treasure that energizes and stimulates Jewish learning both within the academic community as well as throughout the larger culture of American Jewry. This written record of part of the Center's learning experience is offered to Herb and Eleanor with our sincere appreciation of their magnificent commitment to this endeavor.

David B. Ruderman
Director, Center for Advanced Judaic Studies
University of Pennsylvania

INTRODUCTION

Transmitting Tradition: Orality and Textuality in Jewish Cultures

YAAKOV ELMAN AND ISRAEL GERSHONI

Nineteenth-century Jewish scholars were preoccupied with uncovering areas of history and culture previously ignored, neglected or otherwise lost ("the hunting and gathering" approach to cultural studies), and, with a few notable exceptions, much of the effort of twentieth-century Jewish cultural studies has been devoted to texts and textual changes, without much consideration of their wider cultural context. Understandably, even those exceptions — the work of Gershom Scholem and his successors comes to mind — had not until recently come to terms with the effects of changing modes of cultural transmission on the sum and substance of Jewish culture.

The following essays constitute an attempt to survey some of the ways — conscious and unconscious — in which the transmission of various cultural elements is affected by the mode of transmission. In particular, the larger part of this volume will focus on the ways in which oral and written transmission of those cultural elements interact within a context in which written transmission is more or less readily available. The last three papers focus on the methods by which written transmission allows the selection and shaping of the tradition which is transmitted, and thus provides a useful contrast to the earlier studies of various forms of mixed oral/written transmission.

Although our primary concern will be with texts transmitted *over time,* several papers deal with transmission in space as well, that is, the transformation of traditions in their travels from one (contemporaneous) cultural context to another. Several features distinguish such "synchronic" transmission from "diachronic" transmission, that is, transmission over time. Those who translate texts from one existing cultural context to another can exercise more precise control of the process, since they have a better idea of their intended audience. However, since all diachronic transmission must begin synchronically—a parent to a child, a teacher to students—this is not an essential difference. In cross-cultural synchronic transmission, the transmitter stands athwart the two cultures, attempting to bridge the gap, while in diachronic transmission the tradent and receptor ostensibly share a common culture. The future comes imperceptibly, by the slow accretion of minor changes. Often, and this was certainly so in the past, the transmitter may even believe that he is working in a static environment. But despite his best efforts, the transmitter is ineluctably tied to his time, which is different from that of the would-be receptor, though perhaps only in subtle ways. Indeed, when we deal with past societies, such subtleties may be beyond our detection; we thus speak of "static" societies when such a creature is all but impossible, and we should know better.

The difficulty of detecting change over the span of one historic generation makes one subset of synchronic studies, those which are focused on cross-cultural transmission in our own time, most important. Here the data for a full exposure of cultural contexts is available to a much greater extent than for the past, and may generate paradigms which may aid our study of the past.

Though chronologically arranged, the studies included in this volume may be conveniently divided into two parts. The first great divide in the (barely) recoverable history of human cultural transmission is that precipitated by the invention and spread of writing. Oral transmission requires great expenditures of energy, and despite the striving for fixity, inevitably brings with it unconscious and unexpected reshaping.[1] While rabbinic culture never existed in such a world, important elements of rabbinic teaching do approximate certain characteristics of oral cultures. The reason for this seems to have been twofold: the strictures against the writing of legal traditions and analyses, which was in force at certain times and places, limited the recourse to written records of this material, and, after a certain point, the sheer technical difficulties of reducing this mass of tradition to writing, tended to discourage such attempts.

With the coming of writing, the range of such unanticipated change narrowed, and the opportunities for conscious control of the text expanded. A written text can be edited in ways that memorized, or even "recreated" texts, cannot. Studies of written transmission must be sensitive to a wider range of conscious change. Thus, the studies included in the first part (chapters 1–6) will deal with the various stages in the long transition from mixed oral-written cultures to ones in which written transmission is not only dominant, but all but exclusive.

This long period, and the essays devoted to it, may be subdivided into two parts; one in which, at least among the rabbinic elite of late antiquity, orality predominated, and one in which medieval Jews used the ideology of orality in order to introduce and spread mystical teachings among the rabbinic elite.

In contrast to the diachronic studies in this first part, the remaining essays consider "synchronic" transmission. Among the modes of such transmission are anthologizing, which is inevitably accompanied by the need to shape and select the material to be included (and the formation of any canon involves such a process); translation, which requires sensitivity on the part of the translator to both the cultural context in which the text originated, and to that of the target audience; and teaching or sermonizing. Indeed, the latter two require the ability to bridge the gap between the culture of the (secondary) elite and that of two quite disparate audiences. Disciples or students are of course prospective members of the elite, while those who come to hear a sermon are not at all interested in such membership. To some extent, therefore, students—at least before the modern era of mass education—could be expected to share the teacher's values to a greater extent than the audience at a sermon could be expected to share those of the preacher. The preacher's shaping of his texts should therefore teach us more about the target audience and its values; the study of such transformations deserves, perhaps, more attention than has been paid to it.

Thus, the second part of our volume (chapters 7–10) deals with some of these processes as manifested in Italian-Jewish society of the sixteenth century, nineteenth-century Jewish culture in Eastern Europe as it influenced both the cultural formation of modern Israeli society (in anthologizing rabbinic sources for Eastern European consumption), and as it attempted to influence Western European Jewry (in the translation of Y.L. Perets from Yiddish to German), and the attempt to transform twentieth-century Egyptian elite culture of the 1920s and 1930s. All these studies deal with cultural contexts which date long after the transition to written and print culture had taken place.

ORALITY AND TEXTUALITY

Rabbinic Judaism has from its inception insisted on the authority and authenticity of its oral teachings, which constitute a revelation coeval with that of the Pentateuch, the Written Torah. Josephus refers to such a claim; early rabbinic literature itself bears the traces of rejection of such claims by the Sadducees; the Damascus Covenant of the Dead Sea sect also seems to contain such a rejection.[2] Indeed, the consolidation of Rabbinic Judaism's authority in the Jewish community of Babylonia in the early geonic period (seventh–eighth centuries) was followed not long after by the growth of the Karaite movement that rejected both the authenticity and the authority of the "rabbanite" Oral Torah.

The debate, transmuted into historical and cultural research, continues to this day, and casts its shadow on contemporary scholarship. Ironically, however, until recently this debate was carried out without reference to study of oral literatures carried out by folklorists and other since the eighties of the last century. Thus, within Jewish studies, those fields which deal with the Jewish cultures of late antiquity and the High Middle Ages, when oral transmission was valorized, privileged and at times pervasive, existed in isolation from the various schools devoted to the study of oral tradition, oral composition and orality as a general cultural phenomenon.

The ignorance was mutual. Aside from the few landmark studies of classic rabbinic texts which faced the issue squarely,[3] Jewish philological and cultural studies continued in the tradition of the nineteenth and early twentieth centuries. Moreover, with one exception, no detailed attention was given to the ways in which oral transmission affected the texts so passed on. It is thus no wonder that the general field of orality had little to say about any Jewish texts but the Bible.

The modern study of early Jewish literature matured in a century which began with Hermann Gunkel, continued with the Scandinavian school of the 1930s, the studies of Parry and Lord et al., which became extremely influential in the 1960s, and the more recent work on orality associated with Walter Ong and Jack Goody, each proceeding in his own way, and more recently Brian Stock. All this activity has had little influence on the study of classic rabbinic texts, which until comparatively recently proceeded along lines set out by biblical studies of the 1880s.

The irony inheres more particularly in the fact that classic rabbinic literature presents us with the elements of a theology of oral learning which served to shape the transmission of rabbinic learning to as late as the tenth century, at least. One would have thought that Jewish studies could not fail to be enriched by insights from the study of other oral literatures.

Though long delayed, such cross-fertilization is beginning, in particular in this country. Alongside the "theory of oral composition" and the study of oral transmission has grown up a cognate field, that of the study of orality in its broader sense, the study of the sociology of knowledge in societies in which writing is either entirely absent, rare, or, in its infancy, together with the study of the impact of increasing literacy as time passes. Brian Stock has dubbed the two approaches which have emerged within literary and anthropological circles as the "strong" and "weak" approaches to the place and influence of orality within cultures into which literacy is introduced. In the former, "changes in mentality may be the result of bringing reading and writing to a society for the first time."[4] Clearly, the strong approach is inappropriate for rabbinic literature, since even when its oral component was strong or even pervasive, writing was well known and highly valued, and recourse to Scripture was fairly easy.

> The weak thesis is somewhat different: it attempts to account for the interaction of the oral and the written after the initial step is taken. . . . Therefore, cognitive change cannot be based on a straightforward transition from nonliteracy to literacy. This is not even the central issue. The focus of interest lies in the way in which speech and writing answer to different social priorities. . . . One must also look at geographical, linguistic, economic, and political factors.[5]

The picture is still more complex, since there was no one uniform "rabbinic culture" in this respect, as in others. Palestinian rabbinic society differed from that of Babylonia; in the latter, a culture of pervasive orality was the norm for even elite rabbinic society, with writing playing an important, but marginal role, restricted primary to scriptural texts, deeds and documents, and amulets — to the exclusion of the (orally transmitted) legal texts and analyses which were the warp and woof of rabbinic learning. Whatever reports we have of written notes — even in the Babylonian Talmud — refer to Palestinian venues.[6] Thus, while literacy was universal within rabbinic circles, a scholar could function without having to commit his work to writing.

Within this context we may understand why the work of the Parry-Lord school provides many insights into the structure of classic rabbinic texts. However, the meaning of the parallels which exist is under debate. While some contemporary scholars point to the presence of features commonly recognized as characteristic of oral transmission, namely, ring structures (the structuring of narrative elements in chiasmic patterns and the like), the use of symbolic numbers to organize heterogeneous data, recurrent phrases and distinctive syntax, as well as the formulaic use of language in the major classical rabbinic texts — the Mishnah and the two Talmuds, others insist that these forms cannot be viewed as more than stylistic survivals from an earlier era, and that these texts were composed and transmitted in written form.[7]

In contrast, the Palestinian Talmud shows much less of such a character, especially when originally Palestinian texts are compared with their later Babylonian parallels. However, it has become clear that the issue is hardly one of either/or, but rather the exact point at which we must place the interface of orality and textuality. As noted, classic rabbinic culture—from the second to the tenth centuries CE—may be considered a "mixed" society, with oral transmission playing an important role within an essentially literate society. As Martin Jaffee put it in a recent issue of *Semeia* devoted to such issues, "there is an increasing appreciation of the interpenetration of both cultural registers at all levels of the compositional and transmissional processes. . . . But the overall assessment of orality in the cultural life of early rabbinism is still in its infancy."[8]

In a recent reprint of her classic *Oral Poetry: Its Nature, Significance and Social Context,*[9] Ruth Finnegan reflects on developments in the field since the original publication of the work in 1977:

> There is now a general development across a number of disciplines away from older views of text as hard-edged, spatial, fully comprised by its verbal components, existent independent of its performance, analysable separately from other texts or other aesthetic media, or finally, as *the* form in which artistic expression quintessentially exists and should be analysed. How, for example, can we explore the complex relation between 'texts' and 'textuality' on the one hand and specific performances or events on the other (if indeed this is a proper distinction)? . . . Questions also arise about the place of 'intertextuality' in oral poetry, of the unfixedness of what were once regarded as definitively established genres, and about how far a concept of text as emergent process may throw more light on oral (and perhaps written?) poetry than the older model of finalized a-social product.[10]

And somewhat later:

> Following on the same lines there is now also a deepening understanding of the interaction of oral and written forms as a regular and unsurprising process across a multi-dimensional continuum, rather than as something which involves bridging some deep divide. . . . It can be a limiting vision just to highlight the poles of 'oral' and 'written' as if this verbally based model comprised the whole gamut of poetic communication; and, second, . . . even the term 'interaction' can itself be

> misleading. For it may not so much be a question of the meeting or blending of, as it were, two naturally separate or pure types but of whole sets of communication dynamics in which there may be at any one time creative usage of a series of different media and processes—spoken, written, printed, sung, gestural, artifactual, recorded, enacted. . . .[11]

Since our focus is on the pre-modern period, our task is both simpler and more difficult. On the one hand, the very lack of technical development narrowed the range of choices available to transmitters; on the other, for students of Jewish cultures, the exigencies of persecution and expulsion have impeded the survival of anything but (in the main) elite literature in the form of legal codes and discussions, commentaries on sacred and standard legal and theological works, and independent legal and theological works. Still, as John Miles Foley has remarked, writing and literacy are hardly monolithic, but "complex technologies."[12] Amazingly, despite this limitation, the pervasive emphasis given to the importance of oral transmission, both ideologically and practically, provides us with a window in which to view the very meeting and blending that Finnegan notes.[13]

Students of ancient rabbinic culture are fortunate in having at their disposal texts which, while clearly transmitted in oral form, or at least strongly influenced by a preceding oral culture, exist in alternate recensions which in some cases can be dated. Material which makes up the early rabbinic compilation now known as the Tosefta[14] in essence exists in two versions, one redacted before the middle of the fourth century, and one in hundreds of independently transmitted parallels in both Talmuds. To our great fortune, each can be dated on either side of the linguistic divide constituted by the change from what is known as Middle Hebrew I to Middle Hebrew II. Moreover, the talmudic versions were transmitted within a strongly oral culture, at least in Babylonia.

The Toseftan recension serves to anchor our studies of the talmudic versions, and a comparison of the two illustrates the ways in which oral transmission can alter and shape the texts thus transmitted.[15]

Beyond that, the case of Tosefta illustrates the fact that a text may exist in both oral and written form simultaneously. The Tosefta's written *ur-*

exemplar was almost certainly in existence before the fourth century in Palestine, at least as an archival copy. But from the evidence of both the Palestinian and Babylonian Talmuds, it did not circulate as such; instead, parts of it, perhaps even parts of the antecedent collections from which the Tosefta itself was redacted, were transmitted orally.[16] In modern times there are examples of rabbinic *printed* texts which were copied by Yemenite Jews who could not afford the cost of the "original" printed copy; a number of Yemenite "manuscripts" have turned out to be dependent on printed editions! Thus, even in modern times, printed and handwritten copies coexisted. In talmudic times it would seem that texts in oral and written transmission coexisted.

Beyond that is the wider issue of the place of orality in ancient rabbinic culture. Though the rabbinic elite was certainly highly literate, their literacy was partial, and did not in the main extend to the scribal arts, at least not among the Babylonian scholars of the third through the sixth centuries.

Nevertheless, despite this dual oral and written transmission of the same texts in the rabbinic world, we ought to beware of speaking in too facile a manner of the "interface" between the two. Generally speaking, the two forms of transmission did not exist side by side within the same cultural context. In Babylonia, where orality predominated, transmission of texts was oral; even when written exemplars were available, as in the case of Scripture, much was quoted by heart. Reports of *megillot setarim,* private notes, all refer to the situation in Palestine;[17] recently, Yeraḥmiel Brody expressed skepticism as to their use in Babylonia.[18] Again, aggadic/midrashic texts seem to have achieved written form earlier in Babylonia than did halakhic, or legal ones.[19]

Since the rabbis were themselves aware of the hazardous nature of such transmission, they often bring to such texts a relatively sophisticated approach. Thus, for example, the redactors of the Babylonian Talmud regularly register variants in the names of tradents and in traditions regarding essential legal points. These variants, which are almost all the creation of errors of association or hearing, rather than "scribal" in nature, also allow us to gauge the affect of such transmission. Recently, A. N. Doane and Katherine O'Brien O'Keeffe have called attention to the scribal "recreation" of traditional texts in Anglo-Saxon culture. O'Keeffe writes:

> Whenever scribes who are part of the oral traditional culture write or copy traditional oral works, they do not merely mechanically hand them down; they rehear them, "mouth" them, "reperform" them in the act of writing in such a way that the text may change but remain authentic, just as a completely oral poet's text changes from performance to performance without losing authenticity.[20]

Alternatively, as the work of Shamma Friedman has suggested for rabbinic texts, Dundes and Person for biblical ones, and Doane and O'Keeffe for Anglo-Saxon ones, scribal activity produces similar variants as well—but by intentional scribal editorial activity.[21] Martin Jaffee's study of one Greco-Roman paradigm of oral/written transmission in this volume provides yet another explanation for the pervasive variation found in parallel rabbinic texts by drawing on models from the rhetorical literature of Late Antiquity in order to shed light on the mutual interaction of oral and written texts within the process of traditional learning, in the hope that they will illumine for us the parallel processes which took place within Palestinian rabbinic culture, the circles that gave rise to the Palestinian Talmud (the Yerushalmi) in the third to the fifth centuries.

Jaffee takes as his model the exercises in textual manipulation contained in the textbooks on rhetoric of the first and second century sophists, who emphasized the importance of "the various exercises by which orators may appropriate the text of a *chreia* [the Greco-Roman equivalent of the rabbinic short, concise statement, the *memra*], working it orally through a series of grammatical and rhetorical transformations, [beginning with] the mastering of the memorized text itself."[22] These transformations generally begin with relatively simple grammatical changes, shifting number and case, and continue with the addition of rationales to the original statement, or analogies, examples, support from statements by other authorities, or exhortations.

Jaffee applies this model to a case in the Yerushalmi in which the latter seems to have drawn on the information contained in earlier compilations, and have recycled them in its own way, with the addition of one crucial element, the investigation of the scriptural sources for the rabbinic statements. The essential point of his exercise is to demonstrate that "the existence of an exclusively oral tannaitic literary tradition [of the second and early third centuries] is neither likely in light of parallel Greco-Roman oral-educational settings, nor necessary in order to explain the presence of multiple versions of tannaitic textual tradition. Moreover, when seen in broader comparative context, the Yerushalmi's exegetical engagement with the Mishnah seems aware of both written and orally transmitted sources."[23] However, while the rhetors were quite open on the need for flexibility in the reworking of traditions, explicit rabbinic teaching emphasized the need to transmit teachings of the masters in their own words, without change. Though the practice may have fallen well short of the ideal, the very distance between the ideals of the rhetors and those of the rabbis suggests that such material must be used with care.

Nevertheless, Jaffee's study illustrates the difference between Palestinian and Babylonian rabbinic cultures, a difference which has become more and more apparent in recent years. The prohibition of recording rabbinic legal tradition in writing was much more stringently observed in Babylonia than in Palestine, as noted above. Moreover, it has long been noted that the Yerushalmi's citation of antecedent texts is much looser than the Bavli's.[24] Jaffee's observation may be yet another example of this difference.

Also from the Greco-Roman sphere, in this case specifically the Byzantine, Paul Mandel's study of the two versions in which a rabbinic midrash on the biblical book of Lamentations was transmitted sheds more light on the subject, and, as important, coheres with recent investigations of the history of the oral and written transmission of the Babylonian Talmud in the seventh through the tenth centuries. Just as the materials which make up the Tosefta have come down to us in two versions, one a compilation which descends from Palestinian examplars from before the fourth century, and the other imbedded piecemeal in the two Talmuds, so too *Lamentations Rabba*. Mandel's detailed studies of the two versions of the manuscript material and *testimonia* indicate that one version represents the original Palestinian tradition, originally oral and then written, while the other "is the result of a previously fixed text . . . which has *re-entered* the sphere of oral transmission. The reason for this re-entry would seem to be related to the activity of the scholarly academies and study circles in Babylonia, where the ancient traditions of oral study of fixed texts continued."[25] Indeed, the increasing evidence in regard to the Babylonian Talmud itself, where the manuscript material for certain tractates reflect two ancient versions, one fuller and one less developed, may also point to a similar process in that transmission.[26] Nevertheless, Mandel's examples illustrate another important aspect of rabbinic textual transmission: the relation of the amount of variation to the genre of the text, both in parallels and in the manuscript traditions. Tradents seem to have recognized three *genres* of rabbinic material in regard to textual inviolability: (1) strictly legal materials, where the range of permitted variation is relatively narrow,[27] (2) talmudic dialectic, where greater freedom is permitted, and (3) anecdotal and narrative material, which is handled with much greater freedom.

However, all these studies indicate that extreme care must be taken in making statements regarding the orality or textuality of these compilations. While written transmission was predominant in the Byzantine cultural sphere, and oral transmission in the Babylonian, the oral/written ratio varied with genre and time and, undoubtedly, with the individual or with the particular rabbinic circle in question. As to genre, aggadic texts were transmitted in written form even in Babylonia at a time during which oral transmission was privileged for legal texts. On the other hand, during the earlier period (third–fourth centuries) in Palestine, oral transmission was the rule, while such transmission continued to as late as the tenth century in Babylonia.

Daphna Ephrat and Yaakov Elman investigate yet another aspect of orality, one which carries through into the medieval period in Europe: oral transmission as a source of authority. Their joint chapter on Jewish and Islamic institutions of elite education in the eleventh and twelfth centuries in Iraq attempts to appraise the effect of the increasing availability of writing on the organization of learning within the central institutions of the religious elites which flourished in early Muslim Iraq, the Jewish geonic yeshiva and the Islamic madrasa. On the Jewish side, writing was considered a threat to the elites' authoritative access to the tradition and therefore held at bay; on the Islamic side it was domesticated by providing an oral venue for the written transmission of authoritative texts by means of *i'jaza*. Indeed, in part the differing strategies of the Islamic and geonic elites mirror the different stakes they had in the institutionalization of their traditions;

Islamic jurisconsults always had less at stake than the embattled rabbinic elite of Islamic Babylonia, which faced dissent within (the Karaites) and an at best neutral, and at times hostile, surrounding culture. Official and non-official support for Islamic studies was easily available; the Geonim had to find support where they could, and, as time went on, that support came from abroad, chiefly North Africa. Their only hope, as they saw it, was to serve as the repository of rabbinic culture, maintaining a hold on its authoritative transmission.

ORALITY AS PRIMARILY IDEOLOGICAL

Indeed, even later, when one might suppose that the domination of the written text was all but assured, the separate studies of the spread of Jewish mystical traditions by Moshe Idel and Elliot Wolfson demonstrate that orality is an *ideologically charged strategy of transmission* and was still influential as such well into the medieval period, and that it still represented *the authoritative mode of transmission* of esoteric knowledge.

However, despite their agreement on this essential point, their view of the implications of the reports of such traditions differs quite a bit. Idel holds the view that such reports, against the backdrop of rabbinic culture, constitute a bid for authority, and served a primarily conservative function; for him, Moses Naḥmanides' (1194–1274) insistence on the importance of such oral traditions, and the continuance of his kabbalistic school virtually unchanged for a century and a half while other schools produced innovation after innovation, demonstrates this fact.

In contrast, Wolfson discerns a good deal of original kabbalistically oriented exegetical work on Naḥmanides' part, and attempts to demonstrate the ways in which the ideology of oral transmission served the purposes of that elite committed to *developing* as well as transmitting its mystical teachings. The essential function of claims for, and employment of, oral transmission, was to underline the esoteric nature of lore being disseminated. The ideology of orality, deployed in the service of textuality, facilitated the development of a self-conscious elite, a version of Brian Stock's "textual community," conversant with the esoteric lore which was withheld from others.[28]

As noted above, in geonic times in Babylonia the maintenance of a policy of oral transmission served the purpose of maintaining the geonic elite's monopoly and authority over rabbinic tradition. However, if Wolfson is correct, the example of the dissemination of esoteric lore by Spanish mystics within the "book culture" of thirteenth-century Europe shows that insistence on orality alone, without the full substance of it, can also succeed in promoting the elite's ideas, and furthering its influence.

Nevertheless, a basic distinction must be drawn between these oral "snippets" within a predominantly book culture, and the orally transmitted texts of the rabbinic period. The latter texts betray their oral origins, or at least their origins within an oral context, by their use of organizing devices common to oral literatures, as noted above. These have not been shown to be characteristic of orally transmitted kabbalistic esoterica. Orality in the later period is thus a *claim* rather than reflecting an organized practice for the transmission and dissemination of a large body of esoteric material. The kabbalists of the thirteenth century committed their teachings to writing; they composed and disseminated volumes of kabbalistic teachings, even while insisting on the essential oral modes of transmission by which these teachings reached them.

Generally, the history of orality within the rabbinic cultures of late antiquity and medieval times provides a striking contrast with the Latin Christian developments that are discussed in the empirical studies of Brian Stock. After the end of antiquity, new forms of orality, hitherto unknown in Western Europe, made their appearance owing to immigration by peoples whose laws, institutions, and cultural traditions were based on the spoken word. In the subsequent centuries, these oral traditions were transformed and assimilated, initially producing a hybrid culture in which oral and literate traditions often functioned side by side. However, beginning as early as the Carolingian revival of the ninth century, and continuing through the church reforms of the eleventh and twelfth centuries, Europe gradually began to move away from its early medieval interdependency with oral traditions of law, religion, and literature. An increasingly literate and self-conscious elite, composed initially of the clergy but later including lay men and women as well, began to explore such questions as the relationship of text to reality, the meaning of ritual, the ways of explaining historical changes, and the like.[29] One of the chief focuses of debate took place between the *antiqui* and the *moderni,* who differed in their attitudes toward tradition but shared the belief that increases in literacy were linked to social and intellectual progress.

These developments contrast with the attitudes of Jewish thinkers in the same periods, who were heirs to a culture in which literacy, in whatever restricted terms it is to be understood at various times, was always an option. Judaism had in general left behind what its thinkers considered to be an archaic world of ritual and feeling long before the end of antiquity, and in this sense medieval Europe was catching up with what had taken place more than a thousand years previously, just as, in philosophy and theology, European thinkers were slowly beginning to assimilate the Platonic and Aristotelian heritage of ancient philosophy. Perhaps as a result of this much earlier period of change, medieval Jewish thinkers, at least those working outside Christian influences, were less likely to connect literacy, progress, and modernization than monastic and scholastic authors in the Latin West. Jewish authors also appear to have been less concerned with the debate between the ancients and the moderns.[30] Even the Tosafists only "rediscovered" dialectic—they did not invent it, as H. Soloveitchik remarked more than a decade ago.[31]

AUTHORSHIP, TEXTUAL AUTHORITY, AND PERSONAL AUTHORITY

On the other side of the oral/written divide, Malachi Beit-Arié investigates the implications of the book culture of the Jewish Middle Ages for the question of transmission. In particular, he raises a question which becomes central to the study of written transmission, the attempt of the transmitters to control the texts they promulgate, and their own awareness of the limits of such control. As Beit-Arié concludes, those Jewish manuscripts produced after the middle of the thirteenth century "present texts not only corrupted by the accumulation of involuntary copying errors, but also distorted by editorial or even redactional reconstruction, by contamination from different exemplars and versions, and by the deliberate integration of related texts. . . . Chirographic and visual texts were as flexible as oral ones."[32]

In other words, the concept of authorship does not yet—and will not for many centuries to come—develop to the point of conceding to the author of a work complete control over its contents. As Roger Chartier pointed out, copyright was a problematic concept in the eighteenth century precisely because authorship was still viewed as a relatively inchoate, communal process rather than an individual, creative one.[33] Again, as Mary Carruthers noted, while the importance of creativity was not altogether negated in medieval times, the emphasis was on erudition and the arts of memory rather than on creativity.[34]

> Historians of literacy have been concerned with normative channels of communication in societies. An "oral" society is thus one in which communication occurs in forms other than written documents, and in which law and and government are conducted on the basis of orally-preserved custom. . . . Because oral cultures must obviously depend on memory, and hence value memory highly, such valorization has come to be seen as a hallmark of orality, as opposed to literacy. This has led to the further assumption that literacy and memory are *per se* incompatible, and that a "rise of literacy" will therefore bring with it a consequent devaluing and disuse of memory. It is this assumption that my study calls particularly into doubt.[35]

Does this malleability of the medieval written text then break down the oral/chirographic divide? Both are subject to change; both tend to become communal productions in some sense. Certain considerations impell a negative response to this question. While oral texts were also subject to some "editing" of the sort that Beit-Arié traces in medieval manuscripts, the sheer effort involved in oral transmission insured that involuntary changes would predominate, and that these occur in relatively mechanical ways, analogous to scribal error, while the coming of writing inaugurates an era in which conscious shaping would predominate. Again, as Elman has shown elsewhere, oral change tends to shorten texts, while written editing tends to lengthen them.[36] If this seems counterintuitive to our contemporary Westernized, chirographically-shaped sensibilities, we need look no further than both the medieval Christian, and medieval Jewish/Muslim worlds for the proof. In the first case, Mary Carruthers' work provides much food for thought, beyond her own program. The valorization of memory is one thing; its failings, as contrasted to written transmission, quite another. And while scribal error may be analogous to failures of memorization, editorial intervention is certainly less difficult in the one than in the other.

Nevertheless, the cultural component must not be ignored. Though Beit-Arié carefully provides examples of the openness of the medieval Hebrew book "to correct, emend and add to authorial texts" from all eras and areas of medieval Jewish culture, this tendency was particularly pronounced in Germany, and much less so in Spain. Thus, for example, it was considered proper in Germany to alter a text in order to make it conform to popular custom; this was not the case in Spain. As a consequence, as has long been noted, Spanish manuscripts are superior in their fidelity to their original texts.[37] As I. Ta-Shema notes, this freedom extended to the legal sphere: German and Northern French authorities upheld local custom against codified law, something that was unimaginable in Provence.[38] Similarly, and even more remarkable, as H. Soloveitchik has pointed out in a number of detailed studies, this mindset extended to the interpretation of talmudic texts.[39] Thus, in its heyday, French Jewry, quite unlike that of Spain, resisted efforts at codification. Within limits, local religious practice, with its baggage of cultural accommodation, won out over traditional texts.

The Spanish tradition generally harks back to geonic Babylonia, and that of Ashkenaz to Palestine. Even at its most pliant, however, the geonic tradition upheld the supreme authority of its Talmud to the end, as we might have expected. Nevertheless, Babylonian Jewish culture, with its thousand-year history, had in the course of time developed a rich substratum of heterogenous local traditions, not only centered in the two geonic academies, but reflecting true local differences, both linguistic and cultural. In response, one of the last and greatest of the Geonim, Rav Hai, promoted the authority of local custom.[40]

In the case of the medieval Muslim and Jewish worlds, there is some indication of the close interrelationship between oral and written texts between the covers of the present volume. To add one note which was not included in the chapter on the geonic *yeshiva* and the Islamic *madrasa,* a recent study of talmudic variants which appear in geonic texts indicates that the essential structures of the complex talmudic discussions are hardly ever affected by the frailties of human memory, despite the minimum of five hundred years of oral transmission which these texts underwent.[41] On the other hand, on the textual level, oral transmission continued to produce minor variants, by the mechanisms noted above. Ultimately, it appears that we must look to a combination of the two to account for all these variants.

This dual transmission of rabbinic texts in oral and written form in the classic rabbinic period continued, *mutatis mutandis,* beyond the classic rabbinic period in yet another way. Institutionalized teaching remained (and remains) essentially oral. Marc Saperstein's study illustrates the point. Saperstein's study of the sermons of Saul Levi Morteira, a seventeenth-century preacher of the Portuguese community in Amsterdam, reveals something of the timeless nature of that interface. In both cases, the teacher attempts to present the tradition in a way that is acceptable to his listeners, but the differences between the two venues is also striking. As we shall see, the preacher has much greater control over the material than does the classroom teacher, since the preacher's audience has little opportunity for direct response, or immediate reference to the texts the preacher cites and interprets. In the more spontaneous atmosphere of the classroom, the future may impinge more directly on the past, and the teacher must face the challenge it presents in a more immediate way, especially since, to some extent, the texts studied are available to the students. The result may be unpredictable.

Moreover, the preacher's "text" is often highly stylized, employing time-honored devices which are ever to be found in oral performance. In the sermon studied, Saperstein notes Morteira's use of a ring structure which encloses the entire sermon, where the sermon ends as it began, thus enabling the preacher to open with a prefiguration of his theme, and to leave his audience with that theme once again fresh in their minds. However, because this oral performance is situated within a highly literate culture, the preacher is able to play on his listeners' expectations of the constraints of specific chirographic genres—and reverse them. Thus, Morteira refers to the respected if not quite hallowed *responsa* literature, ordinarily the domain of arcane legal argumentation, the preserve of scholars and thus removed from public scrutiny, though hardly unknown as a genre to his audience. In a masterly inversion, Morteira employs the data presented in this literature—which was certainly not available in oral form—not only as a source of discussions of legal and ritual matters, but also as a source for his charges of moral deficiencies of various sorts over the centuries. In other words, the revered authorities of earlier times can be brought to testify to the failings of the Jews of their times. Against the background of the regnant doctrine of the "devolution of the species," these earlier generations—the *antiqui*—were certainly superior in intellect, learning and moral fiber to Morteira's audience's own self-perception. And yet, the leaders of these superior generations testify to the contemporaries' faults. How much greater, so would his audience understand, were their own failings. Thus, the interplay of oral and written elements in a literate culture can thus be made to yield rich rhetorical fruits. And, of course, with the coming of printing, the publication of originally orally presented sermonica allowed the perpetuation in frozen form of those rhetorical strategies originally formulated for oral presentation.

TRANSLATION AND ANTHOLOGY

At the opening of this essay we spoke of other transmissional contexts which involve transmission within a unified time-frame—anthologizing, translation, teaching or sermonizing. We have seen that the shared cultural context in which sermonizing takes place allows the preacher to proceed from the known and accepted in order to engage the unknown and uncertain—the problems which face his audience. When this shared base is lacking, and communication takes place across cultural boundaries, either contemporaneously or retrospectively, the transmitter must reformulate his tradition in light of the needs and expectations of his prospective recipient(s) to a much greater extent than is done in oral contexts. Two of these agencies of cultural change, translation and anthologizing, are examined in three papers. Both translation and anthologizing, the latter of which may be accompanied by the former, are means by which works produced in one cultural matrix are transmitted and transformed when transferred into another.

The mere possibility of computer-assisted teaching in our own time, and especially interactive teaching programs, points to the difficulty that such cultural agents—translators and anthologists—have in addressing a conjectural audience which is foreign to the original culture which they must re-present and represent. Cyberlearning also serves to return the transmission of knowledge to its essentially malleable base, where the tradition is modified in an echo-chamber effect at its very point of transmission. The concept of a fixed tradition, itself the effect of the introduction of writing, may give way to a process by which the fluidity of oral transmission is combined with the historical memory of a recorded text. This perspective allows us an insight into the difficulties that cross-cultural transmission by written text involves. How does an anthologizer or translator retain enough of the original cultural weight of a text in its new cultural context? And how can such recontextualized material serve its new home most efficiently? Several papers deal with this issue in diverse ways and for different contexts.

Jeffrey Grossman's study of the shaping of German translations of the stories of the Yiddish writer Y.L. Perets illustrates in exquisite and illuminating detail the concerns which go into the reconstitution or the representation of one culture into another. The fact that these two cultures, the Yiddish-Polish one and the German-Jewish one, are formally related makes the considerations which governed the amplification of some cultural elements, and the supression of others, all the more striking. We may call the result not so much representation as reconstitution. The problem of continuity and discontinuity has seldom been more stunningly but subtly illustrated.

However, Grossman's enlightening study serves to highlight yet another aspect of specifically written transmission. In oral performance, the audience's likes and dislikes, and its knowledge of the tradition, directly affect the content and delivery of the substance of the performer's art. While this is true to some extent of written and printed texts, the translator, who moves from one culture, or subculture, to another, may select the mode by which he or she will bridge the gap between the two. He or she may present both, by glossing the elements foreign to the target audience, either in footnotes or in a glossary. He or she may suppress those foreign elements entirely or in part. Thus, in the case study presented by Grossman, the Eastern European contrast between the rebbe and the rabbi, which was crucial in the Eastern European Jewish culture and crucial to Perets' original, is muted to varying degrees in the German translations. The conflict, so deep and pervasive in Poland, even in Perets' own time, was simply irrelevant in Germany.

There is another aspect to the matter as well. Translation in this case involved a conscious attempt to modify the existing "canon" of German-Jewish literature, and thus, ultimately, to influence the culture of German Jewry. This could only be accomplished by this means in an era of print culture and mass literacy. This was not the first time that printing had influenced the reshaping of a cultural canon; as Elchanan Reiner has shown, the success of Hebrew publishing in the sixteenth century had promoted the widespread dissemination of Spanish legal and philosophical works in Poland, leading to a thoroughgoing confrontation of Ashkenazic and Sephardic elite cultures. While the religious challenge of philosophical texts was eventually suppressed in Poland and Middle and Eastern Europe with the victory of Lurianic kabbalah, this penetration of philosophical ideas and texts left its mark on Polish Jewry and its descendents.[42]

Israel Bartal's survey of the *kinnus* ("in-gathering, collection") project provides us with the model of a highly motivated attempt to reshape traditional Jewish culture so as to serve the cultural needs of a modern national-group-in-formation. It began in the pre-nationalistic movement of "the Science of Judaism," inaugurated in the early nineteenth century and concerned primarily with preservation rather than renewal, and was continued within the Zionist movement of the nineteenth and early twentieth centuries. The *kinnus* movement was to be dedicated to the "collection, editing and preservation of the nation's cultural creative assets"—chiefly in textual form. In this respect it resembled *Wissenschaft des Judentums,* but explicitly added another dimension: publishing and disseminating these texts so as to "influence the new life being fashioned in Palestine." As the activities of "collection and editing" became the province of the Academy as embodied in the Hebrew University of Jerusalem, matters became, as we might have expected—more academic and disengaged. Though at the beginning there was some overlap in personnel, after the thirties most activities of the "in-gatherists" took place outside the university, where a "cautious scholarly 'objectivity'" reigned.

However, it may be doubted that the exclusively textual and informally "academic" basis of the movement could have succeeded, even with academic support. A national culture built up of those texts which are grist for the academic mill is an anemic entity at best—even when the collection and editing of folkloric material is included. Even the highly text-centered society of the traditional Jewish societies of Eastern and Central Europe contained a strong folk-component. Israel Gershoni's study of an Egyptian parallel is instructive in this regard.

A reconstitution of Egyptian national culture, in this case as a response to colonialism, was attempted by successive generations of intellectuals in the first half of twentieth-century Egypt. First, Egyptian national culture was portrayed as heir to a supposed "Pharonic" legacy, and then, reconstituted as an Islamic and Arab culture. Gershoni provides us with the other half of the coin; while Grossman works in miniature, Gershoni gives us a macro-vision of a similar process. Remarkably, the studies of Bartal and Gershoni, though at first blush so divergent, have some urgent points of contact. In both cases a highly sophisticated secondary elite aspired to lead their people into modernity by shaping for them a "national culture" and thereby transforming them into a modern nation. For that purpose, they attempted to select those elements of the past which presumably most effectively would connect the historical heritage with their vision for the future. The historical projections suggested by this elite did not become generally accepted, and were overtaken by more popular nationalist trends, which attempted to reproduce the national culture in a more nativist fashion.[43]

NOTES

1. Much has been made of Walter Ong's characterization of oral cultures as "conservative" precisely because of this expenditure of energy, and his statement has aroused a fair amount of opposition, but, as noted, the difficulty of oral transmission cuts both ways; see Walter J. Ong, *Orality and Literacy: The Technologizing of the Word* (London, 1982), 33–36.

2. The literature on this topic is immense, but Gerhardsson, *Memory and Manuscript: Oral Tradition and Written Transmission in Rabbinic Judaism and Early Christianity* (Upssala, 1961) is still useful, as is Jacob Neusner's introduction to the recent reprint edition (Grand Rapids, 1998). For another approach, see

E.P. Sanders, "Did the Pharisees Have an Oral Law?," in his *Jewish Law From Jesus to the Mishnah: Five Studies* (London, 1990), 97–130, and for an attempt to bring insights from the Ongian school to bear on the question, see Albert I. Baumgarten, *The Flourishing of Jewish Sects in the Maccabean Era: An Interpretation* (Leiden, 1997), esp. 114–136, "Literacy and Its Implications."

3. Lieberman, Gerhardsson, and Neusner.

4. Brian Stock, *Listening for the Text* (Baltimore, 1990), 5.

5. Ibid., 5–6.

6. See Elman's forthcoming "Orality in Talmudic Babylonia," *Oral Tradition* 14 (in press). In contrasting these two contemporaneous exemplars of rabbinic culture one is reminded of Brian Stock's apt warning "not to use *literacy* (and, by implication, *orality*), in an unqualified manner" (*Listening for the Text,* 143).

7. Here too the literature is immense, and a forthcoming issue of *Oral Tradition* will be devoted to the subject of orality in rabbinic literature. In one case, a later Babylonian version of an originally Palestinian text indicates that the earlier Palestinian text underwent a thorough reworking in the pervasively oral cultural context of Babylonia.

8. Martin S. Jaffee, "Figuring Early Rabbinic Literary Culture: Thoughts Occasioned by Boomershine and J. Dewey," *Semeia* 65: *Orality and Textuality in Early Christian Literature,* ed. J. Dewey (Atlanta, 1995), 67–74.

9. Bloomington, 1992.

10. Ibid., x–xi.

11. Ibid., xiii.

12. *Singer of Tales in Performance* (Bloomington, 1995), 79.

13. Naturally enough, the Bible continues to be a major focus of attention, as is evident in two works which have recently appeared, Susan Niditch's *Oral World and Written Word* (Louisville, 1996) and Alan Dundes' *Holy Writ As Oral Lit: The Bible As Folklore* (Oxford, 1999). The primary purpose of the latter is to insist on defining the Hebrew-Christian scriptures as "folklore" (or, more precisely, "oral traditions written down") inasmuch they contain the characteristics of "multiple existence (=versions)" and "variation" (18–20). Interestingly enough, Raymond F. Person, Jr., in a recent article in the *Journal of Biblical Literature* 117 (1998) 601–609, basing himself on Niditch, Doane, and O'Brien O'Keefe (see below), suggests that Israelite scribes acted as "performers" in pursuing their craft. As the present volume demonstrates, rabbinic texts, unpoetic and un-"literary" as they may be, have their own contribution to make to the field.

14. A parallel and complementary text to the Mishnah, the earliest collection of

rabbinic law available. The latter dates to the first quarter of the third century; the former, somewhat later.

15. See Yaakov Elman, *Authority and Tradition: Toseftan Baraitot in Talmudic Babylonia* (New York, 1994), and *idem,* "Orality in Talmudic Babylonia," *Oral Tradition* 14 (in press), and "Yerushalmi Pesaḥim, Tosefta Pisḥa and the Problem of Orality," in Harry Fox, ed., *Toseftan Relationships* (Hoboken, N.J., 1999).

16. See *Authority and Tradition,* 275–281, and E.S. Rosenthal, "Ha-Moreh," *PAAJR* 31 (1963) 56 (Hebrew numbering).

17. See Shlomo Na'eh, "The Structure and Division of *Torat Kohanim* (A): Scrolls" (Hebrew), *Tarbiẓ* 66 (1997) 505–512.

18. Yeraḥmiel Brody, "Sifrut ha-Ge'onim veha-Teqst ha-Talmudi," *Meḥqerei Talmud* I, ed. Yaakov Sussman and David Rosenthal (Jerusalem, 1990), 281, n. 180.

19. See Naḥman Danzig, *Introduction to Halakhot Pesuqot with a Supplement to Halakhot Pesuqot* (Hebrew) (New York, 1993), 3–8.

20. From her *Visible Song: Transitional Literacy in Old English Verse* (Cambridge, 1990), 80–81, quoted in John Miles Foley, *The Singer of Tales in Performance,* 74–75. Doane's article, "The Ethnography of Scribal Writing and Anglo-Saxon Poetry: Scribe as Performer," *Oral Tradition* 9 (1994), 420–439 makes some of the same points, but with different emphasis. See also Foley, p. 75, n. 31.

The reader may wonder at our acceptance of a methodology drawn from the study of poetry and epic to the somewhat more prosaic world of rabbinic legal and ethical texts. The reason is that classic rabbinic literature as embodied in the collections of the third–eighth centuries bear all the "earmarks" of oral transmission—formulaic language, mnemonics as part of the text, ring-cycles, chiastic structures of various sorts, the use of the number "three" as an organizing principle, etc. In addition, the two Talmuds are themselves cast in the form of unending dialogue, a testimony to Ong's insistence on the "agonistic" nature of oral societies (Ong, *Orality and Literacy,* 43–44).

21. S.Y. Friedman, "Le-Hithavvut Shinnuyei ha-Girsaot ba-Talmud ha-Bavli," *Sidra* 7 (1991), 67–102. As has been noted in the study of ancient Near Eastern literatures, scribal activity tends to be cumulative, oral transmission tends to condensation; comparing Babylonian texts of Tosefta to the earlier Palestinian version yields, in the main, the latter sort of example. See *Authority and Tradition,* 81–92. Moreover, since these texts exist in differing forms in differing compilations, the variants cannot be the result of scribal activity *per se,* but rather of (in the case of the later inclusions in the two Talmuds) independent transmission.

22. Jaffee, pp. 33–34. Jaffee's paper is reprinted from Peter Schäffer, ed., *The Talmud Yerushalmi and Graeco-Roman Culture* (Tubingen, 1998); our thanks to

author, editor and publisher to reprint this valuable study so pertinent to the issues that generated the present volume.

23. Jaffee, p. 44.

24. See, for example H. Albeck, *Meḥqarim bi-Varaita ve-Tosefta* (Jerusalem, 1969), 95, n. 3.

25. Mandel, p. 99 below.

26. See now Paul David Mandel, "Midrash Eikhah Rabbati: Mavo, u-Mahadurah Biqortit le-Parashah Shelishit," Ph.D. diss., Hebrew University, 1997, 1: 160–178; English summary, x–xiii.

27. See *Authority and Tradition,* 18, n. 25.

28. See Stock's highly influential *The Implications of Literacy: Written Language and Models of Transmission in the Eleventh and Twelfth Centuries* (Princeton, 1983), 4–10, 42–59, and his "Textual Communities," in *Listening for the Text,* 140–158.

29. Brian Stock, *The Implications of Literacy,* 12–18, 46–51, 326–328, 517–521, 523–525, 529–530. We would also like to thank Brian Stock for his discussion of these issues with us in a personal communication.

30. As in the rise of concern with the plain sense meaning of Scripture in northern France; the classic example of this new mentality is to be found in the remarks of R. Samuel b. Meir in his comments to Genesis 37:2.

31. See H. Soloveitchik, "Rabad of Posquieres: A Programmatic Essay," in *Studies in the History of Jewish Society in the Middle Ages and in the Modern Period.* Festschrift for Jacob Katz, ed. E. Etkes and Y. Salmon (Jerusalem, 1980), 14.

32. Beit-Arié, pp. 236–237 below.

33. Roger Chartier, *The Order of Books: Readers, Authors, and Libraries in Europe between the Fourteenth and Eighteenth Centuries* (Stanford, 1994), "The Figure of the Author," 24–59.

34. Mary J. Carruthers, *Book of Memory: A Study of Memory in Medieval Culture.* Cambridge Studies in Medieval Literature 10 (Cambridge, 1990), 1.

35. Ibid., 10–11.

36. *Authority and Tradition,* 83, n. 35, and 71–140.

37. As a particularly egregious example of the freedom some Ashkenazic scribes allowed themselves, see Y. Sussman, "'Yerushalmi Ketav-Yad Ashkenazi' ve-'Sefer Ashkenazi'" *Tarbiẓ* 65 (1995), 37–63, and the text publication in *Qovetz 'Al Yad: Sidra Ḥadashah* 12 [22] (1954), 1–120.

38. See Ta-Shema, *Minhag Ashkenaz ha-Qadmon* (Jerusalem, 1992), 103–105.

39. See especially his *Halakhah, Kalkalah ve-Dimmuy 'Atsmi* (Jerusalem, 1985), 111–112.

40. See Ephrat and Elman's chapter on geonic policy in this volume, and see also Ta-Shema, 28.

41. See Brody, "Sifrut ha-Geonim veha-Teqst ha-Talmudi," 275, based on the examination of variants on 269–275.

42. See Elḥanan Reiner, "Temurot bi-Yeshivot Polin ve-Ashkenaz be-Me'at ha-16–ha-17 veha-Vikku'aḥ 'al ha-Pilpul," in *Ke-Minhag Ashkenaz u-Polin: Sefer Yovel le-Ḥone Shmeruk, Qoveṣ Ma'amarim be-Tarbut Yehudit,* ed. I. Bartal, C. Turniansky, and E. Mendelsson (Jerusalem, 1993), 9–80; for the century before, contrast Joseph M. Davis, "Philosophy, Dogma, and Exegesis in Medieval Ashkenazic Judaism: The Evidence of *Sefer Hadrat Qodesh,*" *AJS Review* 18 (1993), 195–222.

43. The contributors to the volume and we are grateful to the staff of the Center in 1995–1996 for their assistance—Sheila Allen, Aviva Astrinsky, Bonnie Blankenship, Sam Cardillo, Sol Cohen, Elizabeth Fattah, Ettie Lassman, and Judith Leifer. We would also like to thank the participants in the symposium whose papers were not able to be included in this volume, in particular, Alon Confino, Tamar El-Or, Ruth Katz, and Ronit Meroz, for their input and observations.

ONE

The Oral-Cultural Context of the Talmud Yerushalmi: Greco-Roman Rhetorical Paideia, Discipleship, and the Concept of Oral Torah

MARTIN S. JAFFEE

INTRODUCTION: THE TALMUD YERUSHALMI AND RABBINIC ORAL CULTURE

The present essay attempts to make some progress in clarifying the role of writing in the transmission of early rabbinic learned tradition.[1] This attempt is nourished by a growing body of comparative studies focused upon the nature of scribal texts produced in cultures that preserve rich oral-traditional milieus.[2] In such cultural settings, the expression of communal literary tradition in writing does not necessarily establish a radical discontinuity from the orally rooted tradition. Rather, the written form enters the life of the oral tradition, each register of tradition modulating the other in diverse ways.[3]

Texts composed in oral performance, to be sure, often undergo dramatic reformulation as they enter written tradition. But the relative "fixity" of written texts in comparison to their oral versions is often overstated, as if the canonical orthography of many scriptural texts exhausted all possible models of writing.[4] Written representations of orally grounded literary tradition are normally transmitted in multiple textual versions and commonly preserve stylistic residues of oral-performative settings. Moreover, in their role as mnemonic aids, written texts commonly shape further performances within the tradition, producing an oral tradition deeply imprinted by written forms.[5] Finally, it is increasingly acknowledged that even scribal copies of texts from manuscript retain intertextual signs of orally mastered versions of the text. The oral life of a text in scribal cultures can be assessed in diverse manuscript traditions as the written text is expanded or modified in light of emerging traditions of public reading or recitation.[6]

The rabbinic culture of late antiquity was, obviously, such a scribal culture, one in which the memorization and oral delivery of scriptural and rabbinic textual material represented a fundamental cultural performance. The surviving compilations of rabbinic literary tradition, therefore, are rich sources for exploring the nature of writing that is produced under the impact of a culturally-prestigious oral tradition. Among these compilations, the Talmud Yerushalmi is especially significant. As a collection of literary texts distinct from mishnaic tractates, but organized around their structure, it represented a major innovation in third–fourth century Galilean rabbinic literary culture.[7]

By selecting the Mishnah-text attributed to R. Judah the Patriarch as its organizing set of textual cues, the Yerushalmi's compilers drew an analogy between this prestigious recension of tannaitic tradition and that of the paradigmatic subject of commentary in Judaic culture, Scripture.[8] The Yerushalmi's form as a companion to the Mishnah also encouraged (if it did not itself create) incipient distinctions within the inherited tradition of tannaitic teachings. With the Mishnaic redaction of tannaitic tradition central to its own structure, the Yerushalmi's literary form encouraged the construction of reified taxonomies distinguishing the emerging bodies of tannaitic tradition. In light of the growing prominence of "our Curriculum" (*matnytyn*), other recensions of orally-mastered tradition (*matnyt'a*) cited in rabbinic discussions came to appear as supplemental (*toseft'a*) or external (*barait'a*) to the primary collection.[9]

In this sense, the Yerushalmi attests to a moment in which the generic boundaries of tannaitic literary tradition were solidifying and rough compilations of specific traditions were taking shape. In addition to providing rich attestations of the emerging shape of tannaitic literary traditions from a point close to their own chronological and geographic origins, the Yerushalmi's discourses are dotted with literary representations of the amoraic social and institutional settings in which tannaitic textual traditions of diverse sorts were mastered, discussed, and transmitted. Such representations—when employed in a critical and comparative spirit—can guide efforts to contextualize the Yerushalmi's society of learning within the larger non-rabbinic cultural settings in which that learning thrived. They enable us to appreciate ways in which the literary culture reflected in the Yerushalmi was part of the broader literary life of its era.

Such contextualization is, in fact, the primary contribution of this essay. It uncovers no new "facts" about the Yerushalmi, but rather attempts to freshly illumine what has long been observed by others. Accordingly, the first part of the essay focuses on ways in which the relation of written texts to oral performance in the Greco-Roman rhetorical schools of the second–fourth centuries might illumine literary phenomena common in the Yerushalmi. Surviving handbooks on rhetorical education from this period describe the use of written texts to train orators for extemporaneous oral delivery of complex discourses. One common exercise in memorization is particularly illuminating, for it was designed to produce disciplined oral variants of written sayings of famous teachers. I shall argue that this intentional production of oral versions of stabile written sources may lead us to a similar mnemonic practice among the Galilean Sages. In order to illustrate the hermeneutical possibilities of the hypothesis that Galilean Sages used written sources as mnemonic preparation for orally performed discourses, I offer an analysis of a set of tannaitic variants that underly one of the Yerushalmi's typical contributions to mishnaic exegesis.

The second part of the study moves the question of oral and written tradition from the mnemotechnical to the ideological level of inquiry. We ask how the Yerushalmi's representations of rabbinic tradition as a body of unwritten, memorized teachings might be connected to institutional settings in which written texts of rabbinic tradition were shared and mastered. This question, like the mnemotechnical one that preceded it, benefits from a contextual approach. We begin, then, by drawing parallels between—and distinctions among—the rabbinic communities of third–fourth century Galilee and other contemporary philosophical or religious communities grounded in close discipleship to explicators of venerated texts.

This will help place in context the Yerushalmi's conception of the decisive role of face-to-face encounters in the shaping of disciples—and the concomitant ideologically-motivated rejection of written texts as legitimate sources for rabbinic instruction. What the Talmud Bavli later designates as "Torah in the Mouth,"[10] that is to say, has its social and cultural roots in the Yerushalmi's conception of the exclusively oral transmission of a rabbinic tradition "that had already been disclosed to Moses from Sinai" (yMeg 4:1, 74d) and, as "tradition (*halakhah*) of Moses from Sinai" was already "embedded in the orally-mastered Curriculum (*mishnah*) (yPe'ah 2:6, 17a). In what follows we explore how such a conception of the oral origins of rabbinic teaching was generated by, even as it reflected and sustained, the social forms of the Galilean discipleship circles among which the Yerushalmi as a whole took shape.

GALILEAN AMORAIC LEARNING IN GRECO-ROMAN CONTEXT

The very earliest examples of written versions of rabbinic texts are fragments that can be dated no earlier than the seventh century.[11] Barring future discoveries of an as yet unknown cache of early rabbinic writing, therefore, it is unlikely that we will ever have firm empirical grounds for distinguishing between written and oral sources that might have supported the composition and transmission of such early rabbinic compilations as the Mishnah, the Tosefta, or the various midrashic collections ascribed to tannaitic authority. The consensual opinion among historians of rabbinic literature, however, is that versions of these compilations reached at least preliminary form in the Galilee sometime between 220 and, perhaps, 400.[12] The shaping of the tannaitic tradition, therefore, overlaps geographically and chronologically with the literary work that reached its completion by 375–400 CE in the Yerushalmi.

This is why the study of tannaitic literature must proceed in close association with the Yerushalmi. In addition to preserving important versions of independently compiled tannaitic texts, the Yerushalmi offers crucial insight into the social settings and functions of the traditions preserved in the tannaitic compilations. Of particular importance for study of the oral and written foundations of tannaitic tradition is the educational setting in which its texts were mediated. While historians have for some time recognized the similarity of rabbinic educational methods and institutions to those of the surrounding Greco-Roman environment,[13] the relevance of the Greco-Roman material for interpreting the role of writing in rabbinic culture has yet to be fully explored. Here we reflect upon some aspects of Greco-Roman rhetorical education in particular that may help us to think about the role of oral and written texts in the education of rabbinic disciples.[14]

THE PROGYMNASMATA AND THE MNEMONIC BASIS OF TANNAITIC TRADITION

The rabbinic movement of Roman Galilee was not equivalent in all respects to a rhetorical or philosophical academy. Yet an important body of recent scholarship shows that it nevertheless bore important functional similarities to such schools.[15] Like the training offered by Sophists, rabbinic training bore a strong scholastic orientation, focused on guiding young men in the mastery of a literary tradition whose values they would personally embody. Like these men, rabbinic students were preparing in many cases for lives of public service in political, judicial, or ecclesiastical institutions. Finally, like the students of the rhetorical schools, many of those who studied in the rabbinic beit midrash would make their professional mark beyond it through skilled, effective public speech. As we shall note momentarily, such similarities extended beyond the institutional settings themselves. They are apparent as well in traits of literary style and substance.[16]

In third–fourth century Galilee, non-Jewish political and social elites committed the advanced education of their male children to professional practitioners of the Greco-Roman rhetorical tradition. This tradition was available in two primary forms. The older of these, just beginning a long, slow decline from the heights of its second- and early third-century dominance of Greek and Latin literary culture, was the tradition of classical literary education fostered by the rhetoricians of the Second Sophistic.[17] The younger, beginning a path which would lead it to dominance in the fourth and fifth centuries, was the tradition of Christian preaching, teaching, and exegetical scholarship fostered by the Church's growing cadre of priest-intellectuals.[18]

Sophistic or Christian, rhetorical education was preparation for a life of public service. And such a life—as a lawyer, academic scholar, or other public official (in Christian circles, as a functionary in the Church hierarchy)—demanded skill in elegant, persuasive, oral address. What made an oral presentation elegant was its ability to cite or allude to well-known classical texts in the process of the speaker's development of his own thought. The orator's persuasive power was in part bound up with the weight of classical diction he could support without apparent effort; it was also dependent upon the apparently spontaneous organization of fresh ideas into well-known and easily-recognizable patterns of presentation and argument. The psychological pressure of the rhetorical address, the subject of some sardonic humor,[19] proceeded from this insistence that something new be said within forms of speech venerated by centuries of literary tradition—and that it be said in such a way so as to appear to come from the top of one's head.

This illusion of effortless public performance was enabled by an education that stressed the rote memorization and recitation of written literary texts of diverse kinds. Homeric texts or those of the great dramatists, for example, had to be summoned accurately and on cue in order to appropriately set off a particular turn of thought. Speeches of the Greek orators, such as Demosthenes, were memorized and performed as a prelude to the analyses of the structural principles that provided them their power. Moreover, teachers of rhetoric would commonly make available to students written copies of their own oral discourses for study. All of this training in memorizing the written word repaid itself in the characteristic possession of the trained orator—the capacity to deliver, at length and with captivating effectiveness, a memorized composition without resorting to written mnemonic cues.[20]

Textbooks on rhetoric, produced between the first and sixth centuries in Greek and Latin, are useful sources for illustrating the relation of written and oral discourse in rhetorical training. These works, called by the generic title of Progymnasmata, amply illustrate the intertwined nature of written texts and oral discourse in rhetorical education. In such textbooks we can see how memorized written literary sources nourished the education of orators, as well as the ways in which the mobilization of memorized written texts in oratory reconfigured those texts into fresh patterns.[21]

Our illustrations are drawn from the ways in which the authors of Progymnasmata instructed their readers in the nature and use of one of the most common literary forms of Greco-Roman tradition, the *chreia.*[22] Written collections of *chreiae* circulated widely and constituted the basic store of wisdom and values that public speakers could assume they shared with their audiences. Not uncommonly, a single *chreia* might be ascribed to more than one authority, as the same text became naturalized in traditions with differing intellectual lineages. This malleability of transmission is part of the testimony that the circulation of a *chreia* in written form was only one aspect of its textual life. The *chreia,* as a cultural possession, was experienced in oral presentations of artistic speech.

As described by Theon of Alexandria, a first-century Sophist commonly considered to have composed the first rhetorical textbook, the *chreia* is "a concise statement or action which is attributed with aptness to some specified character or to something analogous to a character."[23] The main business of Theon's introduction is to flesh out this spare definition with the analysis of numerous examples. Among them is the following, ascribed here to Isocrates. Its evaluation of the relative importance of parents and teachers will figure in our discussion at a later point: "Isocrates the rhetor used to advise his students to honor their teachers before their parents, because the latter are the cause only of living, while teachers are the cause of living nobly."[24]

Much of Theon's discussion is concerned with typological analyses of various *chreia*-forms. These are distinguishable from each other by, for example, varying emphases on indirect discourse as opposed to direct discourse, privileging of action over discourse, the kinds of situations to which the hero of the chreia responds, and so forth. Of interest from the perspective of understanding the oral life of the written *chreia,* however, is Theon's careful exposition of various exercises by which orators may appropriate the text of the *chreia,* working it orally through a series of grammatical and rhetorical transformations. The foundational act of this performance is the mastering of the memorized text itself well enough to "report the assigned chreia very clearly in the same words or in others as well."[25] Upon this basis, the budding orator proceeds then to a series of revisions of the text.

The simplest of these is an exercise in restating the memorized text in terms of number. In the instance of the following *chreia,* "Isocrates the rhetor used to say that gifted students are children of gods," Theon instructs:

> we inflect in this way: singular to singular, for example, "Isocrates the rhetor used to say that the gifted student is a child of gods." Dual to dual: "The two rhetors named Isocrates used to say that the two gifted student students are two children of gods." Plural to plural: "The rhetors named Isocrates used to say that gifted students are children of gods."[26]

Such an exercise would not, of course, ever gain reflection in a public oration. It was purely preliminary, part of the discipline of rooting the text firmly in the mind by running it, so to speak, through its paces.

More complex inflections involved grammatical cases. These require the rewording of the *chreia,* usually transmitted in the nominative case, in terms of other cases. Thus:

> In the genetive case we will inflect in this way. If it is a sayings-*chreia,* we will add to it "the statement is remembered" or "the saying is recalled of the one speaking." It is good style to add the former after the recitation of the whole *chreia.* For example: "Isocrates the rhetor's statement, when he said gifted students are children of gods, is remembered.[27]

Or, again:

> In the accusative case we will generally add to any *chreia* the words "they say," "it is said." For example, "They say (or it is said) that Diogenes the Cynic philosopher, on seeing a rich young man who was uneducated, said: 'This fellow is silver-plated filth.' "[28]

In both of these examples, the written text is worked through the memory by disciplined exercises in recasting its language. The product of this exercise is knowledge of the text as a multi-form literary reality. The written version retains its form as transmitted, but it is malleable in light of the needs of the rhetorical situation. The text is at once its written version and the possibilities of its oral transformations.

Theon's discussion became foundational to the entire genre of Progymnasmata, and was cited (explicitly or by allusion) and amplified by later Sophistic teachers. A particularly important example is that of the late second-century Sophist, Hermogenes of Tarsus. His discussion of the forms of the *chreia* and its inflections is much briefer than Theon's, but he introduces a subject of great relevance to our discussion of the interplay of oral and written texts. With marvelous theoretical rigor, he describes the manifold ways in which the public speaker may interweave *chreiai* into his discourse and adapt for his own purposes stories or epigrams widely known to his audience.

Hermogenes identifies this rhetorical practice as "elaboration" (*ergasia*) and defines it in terms of eight specific procedures: Praise (*enkomion*); Paraphrase (*paraphrasis*); Rationale (*aitia*); Statement from the Opposite (*kata to enantion*); Statement from Analogy (*ek paraboles*); Statement from Example (*ek paradeigmatos*); Statement from Authority (*ek kriseos*); Exhortations (*paraklesis*). These rhetorical procedures introduce the audience to the wisdom contained in the *chreia* and unfold the implications and authority of the *chreia* in a disciplined, easily followed manner.

Taking as his text the *chreia*, "Isocrates said that education's root is bitter, its fruit is sweet," Hermogenes illustrates these procedures as follows. The report of the *chreia* (step 2) is actually only a single element of a complex discourse to which it is structurally central:

(1) Praise: "Isocrates was wise," and you amplify the subject moderately.
(2) Then the chreia: "He said thus and so," and you are not to express it simply but rather by amplifying the presentation.
(3) Then the rationale: "For the most important affairs generally succeed because of toil, and once they have succeeded they bring pleasure."

(4) Then the statement from the opposite: "For ordinary affairs do not need toil, and they have an outcome that is entirely without pleasure; but serious affairs have the opposite outcome."

(5) Then the statement from analogy: "For just as it is the lot of farmers to reap their fruits after working with the land, so also is it for those working with words."

(6) Then the statement from example: "Demosthenes, after locking himself in a room and toiling long, later reaped his fruits; wreaths and public acclamations."

(7) It is also possible to argue from the statement by an authority. For example, Hesiod said: "In front of virtue gods have ordained sweat" . . .

(8) At the end you are to add an exhortation to the effect that it is necessary to heed the one who has spoken or acted.[29]

Hermogenes' method of elaboration supplements Theon's inflections as a further example of how rhetorical training was devoted to the oral transformation of written texts. In elaboration, the *chreia*'s text (step 2) serves as the springboard of a discourse that moves back and forth between the text itself and other cultural intertexts (steps 3–8), weaving the whole into a morally compelling rhetorical tapestry. Here, instead of changing the words of the text itself (as in Theon), the *chreia*'s meaning is enriched by weaving it into an expanded rhetorical fabric.

Discussions such as those of Theon and Hermogenes lend some nuance to our conception of the nature and purpose of textual memorization in Greco-Roman rhetorical culture. They show that memorization of a written text was compatible with, and indeed encouraged, the existence of the same text in a variety of orally presented versions. The written record of a text was itself a version, whose literary purpose was fulfilled in the oral variations played upon it by the orator. In other words, the variations of the text are not the result of erroneous transmission; rather, they are the intentional result of mastering a fixed written version for the purpose of communicating its meaning in diverse performative settings. At issue for us now is the degree to which the dialectical relation of written and oral textual versions cultivated in rhetorical paideia can illumine textual phenomena familiar from the early rabbinic literature.

THE RHETORICAL BACKGROUND OF MISHNAH EXEGESIS IN YERUSHALMI YOMA 4.6

Of particular interest, in this regard, are the ways in which the diverse tannaitic traditions, especially those containing reports of tannaitic sayings, came to be transmitted in several versions in different literary settings. Among scholars committed to exclusively oral models for the transmission of rabbinic tradition, such variation has normally been interpreted as evidence for the fluidity of purely oral literature prior to its reduction to writing.[30] In light of the Progymnasmata, it is possible to explore the degree to which such variety may be as well explained by the hypothesis that amoraic rhetorical education, including the intentional oral reconfiguration of written tannaitic material, may lie behind diverse transmissional variations of such literary units.

Let us look at a representative case in which the Yerushalmi engages an array of tannaitic variations of a single textual substrate. Our example focuses upon a very brief unit of tannaitic tradition in mYom 4.6 and the exegetical contribution of yYom 4.6, 41d. The mishnaic passage is part of a larger discussion, mYom 4.4–6, that draws a series of distinctions between the daily Temple sacrificial procedures (Lev 6:1 ff.) and those prescribed for Yom Kippur (Lev 16:1 ff.). The entirety of mYom 4.4–6 is structured by a single mnemonic pattern: "on every day/but this day." The specific passage discussed below concerns a difference of opinion among mid-second-century Tannaim concerning the number of altar pyres lit for the liturgical needs of each day:

M. YOMA 4.6[31]

בכל יום היו שם ארבע מערכות והיום חמש, דברי רבי מאיר. רבי יוסי אומר: בכל יום שלש, והיום ארבע. רבי יהודה אומר: בכל יום שתים, והיום שלש.

On every day there were 4 pyres, but this day 5—words of R. Meir.

R. Yose says: On each day 3, but this day 4.

R. Yehudah says: On each day 2, but this day 3.

Y. YOMA 4.6[32]

מה טעמה דרבי מאיר והאש על המזבח תוקד בו לא תכבה. זו מערכת קיומי אש וביער עליה הכהן —זו מערכת איכול איברין ופדרים. וערך עליה העולה —זו מערכה גדולה. והקטיר עליה חלבי השלמים —זו קטורת. ולית לרבי יוסה מערכת איכול איברין. ולית לרבי יהודה מערכת קיומי אש. מה מקיים רבי יהודה — אש תמיד? אש שאמרתי לך תהא תמיד, לא תהא אלא על מזבח החיצון . . . מניין למערכת יום הכיפורים. ר׳ ירמיה בשם ר׳ פדת גחלי מה תלמוד לומד אש שהיא בטילה על גבי גחליה.

1. What's the source behind R. Meir?

   —"And the fire on the altar shall burn on it and not go out" (Lev 6:5)—this refers to the pyre for maintaining the fire.

   —"and the priest shall burn upon it" (Lev 6:5)—this refers to the pyre for consuming limbs and innards.

   —"and he shall arrange the burnt offering on it" (Lev 6:5)—this refers to the large pyre.

   —"and he shall burn on it the fat of the whole offerings" (Lev 6:5)—this refers to the incense pyre.

2. And R. Yose does not count the pyre for consuming limbs and innards.

   And R. Yehudah does not count the pyre for maintaining the fire.

3. How does R. Yehudah apply "a perpetual fire (Lev 6:6)?"

   The fire that I specified as "perpetual" shall only be on the outer altar. . . .[33]

4. And where do we know about the pyre for Yom Kippur?

   R. Yirmiyah in the name of R. Pedat: "Coals of fire" (Lev 16:12)—Why does the Teaching specify "fire"? For it is insignificant compared to the coals. . . .

The Yerushalmi appears to supply a relatively straightforward exegesis of the Mishnah. Its basic interest is to define scriptural sources for R. Meir's view (1, 4). Stichs 2–3 play a secondary role, with 2 explaining the deviating positions of R. Yose and R. Yehudah, and 3 amplifying the minimalist view of R. Yehudah in particular. We shall see momentarily, however, that this simple exercise in mishnaic exegesis is grounded in complex set of intertextual references that link the mishnaic text and the Yerushalmi to textual sources now preserved in the written redactions of other compilations.

There are, in fact, three primary sources that must be considered in reconstructing the matrix of yYom's comment in a spectrum of oral and written literary tradition. Two sources are now found in extant tannaitic compilations, the Tosefta and Sifra; a third is the foundation of the discussion of mYom 4.6 in the Talmud Bavli. Here are the texts.

T. YOMA 2.11[34]

בכל יום היו שתים מערכות שם והיום שלש. אחת למערכה גדולה, ואחת למערכה שנייה, ואחת שמוסיפין לקטרת של לפני לפנים, דברי ר׳ יהודה, ר׳ יוסה מוסיף אהת לקיום האש, ר׳ מאיר מוסיף אחת לאברים ופרדים שלא נתעכלו מבערב.

On every day there were 2 pyres there, but this day 3.
1 for the large pyre
and 1 for the second pyre
and 1 they added for the incense of the innermost chamber—
words of R. Yehudah
R. Yose adds 1 for maintaining the fire.
R. Meir adds 1 for limbs and innards unconsumed from evening.

SIFRA, TZAV PER. 2.11[35]

רבי יהודה אומר שתי מערכות בכל יום ושלש ביום הכפורים ר׳ יוסי אומר שלש בכל יום וארבע ביום הכפורים אחת מערכה גדולה, זאחת מערכה לקטורת ואחת לקיום האש, ואחת שמוסיפים ליום הכפורם, רבי מאיר אומר ארבע מערכות בכל יום וחמש ביום הכפורים אחת מערכה גדולה ואחת לקטורת ואחת לקיום האש ואחת לאיברים ופדרים שלא נתעכלו מבערב, ואחת שמוסיפים ליום הכפורים.

R. Yehudah says: 2 pyres on every day, and 3 on Yom Kippur
R. Yose says: 3 on every day, and 4 on Yom Kippur.
1 for the large pyre
and 1 for the incense pyre
and 1 for maintaining the fire
and 1 they added for Yom Kippur

R. Meir says: 4 on every day, and 5 on Yom Kippur
1 for the large pyre
and 1 for the incense
and 1 for maintaining the fire
and 1 for limbs and innards unconsumed from evening
and 1 they added for Yom Kippur

B. YOMA 45a[36]

תנו רבנן בכל יום היו שתים מערכות והיום שלש אחת מערכה גדולה ואחת מערכה שניה של קטורת ואחת שמוסיפין בו ביום דברי רבי יהודה רבי יוסי אומר בכל יום שלש והיום ארבע אחת של מערכה גדולה ואחת מערכה שניה של קטורת ואחת של קיום האש ואחת שמוסיפין בו ביום רבי מאיר אומר בכל יום ארבע והיום חמש אחת של מערכה גדולה ואחת של מערכה שניה של קטורת ואחת של קיום האש ואחת לאיברים ופדרים שלא נתעכלו מבערב ואחת שמוסיפין בו ביום.

On every day there were 2 pyres, but this day 3
1 for the large pyre
and 1 for the second pyre of incense
and 1 they added on that day—
words of R. Yehudah
R. Yose says: On every day 3, but this day 4
1 for the large pyre
and 1 for the second pyre of incense
and 1 for maintaining the fire
and 1 they added on that day
R. Meir says: On every day 4, but this day 5
1 for the large pyre
and 1 for the second pyre of incense
and 1 for maintaining the fire
and 1 for limbs and innards unconsumed from evening
and 1 they added on that day

These texts bear complex relationships to each other as well as to mYom. Let's summarize them briefly before reflecting on their connections to the

Mishnah exegesis at yYom. We will then illumine these relationships in light of the model of oral permutations of a written textual source found in the Progymnasmata.

MYom differs from its parallel sources in two respects. The first concerns a mnemonic matter. M. lists its distinctions between daily liturgy and Yom Kippur in descending numerical order (Meir–4/5, Yose–3/4, Yehudah–3/2), while all the parallels reverse the mnemonic, moving in ascending numerical order from Yehudah through Meir. The second obvious difference is that all the parallel passages contain material absent from mYom, but crucial to grasping its implications—that is, only the parallels enumerate the precise sorts of pyres assumed by Meir, Yose, and Yehudah.

So the tannaitic parallels together share traits that distinguish them collectively from the Mishnah. They also differ from each other, primarily in their economy of supplying the information missing from the Mishnah. TYom offers a complete list of pyres only for Yehudah's view, and then specifies the further pyres Yose and Meir would add. Sifra and bYom, for their part are progressively more ample, the former supplying complete lists for Yose and Meir, the latter supplying them for all three authorities.

As renderings of tannaitic tradition, all the pericopes are textually distinct from yYom, but they fall into two basic groups. BYom and Sifra, organized for mnemonic convenience, represent versions of a single textual tradition, while tYom, composed without mnemonic requirements in mind, represents an independent way of organizing the same information. The same mnemonic patterning in Sifra and bYom indicates that both are closer than tYom to the mnemonically arranged textual tradition of mYom. They merely reverse the order of mYom's mnemonic cues and fill in mYom's gaps, while tYom shows no attempt to follow the mishnaic mnemonic at all.

Let us now reflect upon this complex set of literary relations with the help of the model offered by Greco-Roman rhetorical practice. In that setting, we recall, the disciplined transformation of memorized texts was a routine aspect of rhetorical training that prepared students to deploy texts in various versions in their spoken and written discourses. Moreover, the transformation of such texts involved not only expansive elaboration (as in Hermogenes) but also exercises in simple grammatical reconstructions of the core text (as in Theon). There are instructive analogies to such transformations in the tannaitic texts before us.

Surely, it is not difficult to order mYom, Sifra and bYom as a single pattern of transformations. All share an identical mnemonic (albeit in reverse order), and the latter two texts seem to expand M. Yet one must ask: is this expansion "exegetical" in the sense that it supplies information needed by a textual exegete to interpret the Mishnah? Or does it simply give textual expression to knowledge the mishnaic tradent already assumed on the part or students? I suggest the latter. MYom could hardly have conveyed much useful information at all unless its audience was already familiar with the kinds of pyres used in daily and festival liturgy.

The Mishnah is, in fact, formulated with such information in mind. In order to yield to the rigor of its overall mnemonic program (mYom 4.4–6), M. 4.6 has simply omitted what its framers assumed could be taken for granted. Sifra and bYom, from this perspective, are not "commentaries," supplying by exegetical ingenuity information wholly independent of the text it cites. Rather, they restore to the text the oral audience's implicit referential system.[37] MYom, then, is bound up with Sifra and bYom in an oral-performative hermeneutical circle that appears impossible to open from our own historical distance. On what grounds might we determine that the mishnaic form is textually primary and the others secondary or, to the contrary, that the Mishnah formulates in its own way material already known in the forms preserved in Sifra and bYom? Here, it would seem, lies the one crucial difference between the example of the Progymnasmata and the tannaitic examples. While the rhetoricians supply us with the written versions of the *chreiae* that serve as the basis of mnemono-technical exercises, there appears little hope in the rabbinic case of firmly determining which text—if any—is the "base" and which the "transformation."

In this particular case, however, there may be a way out of the echo chamber of oral tradition. The key lies, perhaps, at tYom. This toseftan pericope contains all the information of its tannaitic companions, identifying the various pyres and linking them to the appropriate Tannaim. Moreover, its listing of the sequence of Tannaim (Yehudah–Yose–Meir) conforms to that of Sifra and bYom, in opposition to that of mYom. Its fundamental deviation from all the other tannaitic sources, as we have already observed, lies in T.'s lack of a clearly recognizable mnemonic pattern for the effective recall and transmission of the information. How, then, does tYom fit into the textual complex of the mnemonically managed traditions with which it shares much content but little form?

The rhetorical model of the Progymnasmata, which prescribes the recycling of written texts into oral versions, suggests a way of imagining what is before us. TYom may indeed preserve a version of the written textual source standing behind the renderings of mYom, Sifra, and bYom. The latter three, that is, may be read as rhetorically guided transformations of tYom, reshaping its written text for the oral-performative instructional setting in which tannaitic traditions would be transmitted and analyzed. On this reading, mYom, Sifra, and bYom represent diverse oral-performative transformations of a foundational written text that happens now to be preserved in the version of tYom.[38]

This reconstruction of the oral-written continuum, of course, suggests that mYom 4.6 does not stand at the origins of the larger stream of tradition it itself exemplifies. Rather, M. assumes T.'s information on the nature of the pyres and the sources of the various opinions and organizes T. mnemonically for use in a larger literary setting in which the mnemonic "every day/this day" defines the formulation of the material. Sifra and bYom, by contrast, preserve T.'s order of authorities and information on the pyres, but reorganize the information in light of the Mishnah's creation of a mnemonic mattern of paired numbers in sequential order.

This is the situation of tradition into which the composer of yYom 4.6 entered. His exegesis of mYom is deeply intertwined with the tannaitic materials we have just examined. Indeed, his own exegetical language echoes each of his sources so subtly that the literary critic has no grounds for isolating any single textual version as the primary source of the exegete's tradition. Nevertheless, the exegete's work is distinguishable from his tradition in a crucial respect: his main contribution to M., the elucidation of the scriptural foundation of the tannaitic opinions, is fresh with his own enterprise. He comes to answer, in fact, the one question that the antecedent tradition has left unexplored—the scriptural foundations of the opinions.

Let us at this point stress the modesty of our claim about the role of written sources in the transmission of tannaitic tradition. As indicated in the introduction to this part of our discussion, reconstructive work with medieval manuscripts of rabbinic literature cannot offer definitive proof that writing was used in the construction and preservation of tannaitic textual tradition.[39] Neither, however, can it prove the absence of written sources. Our goal is simply to show that the existence of an exclusively oral tannaitic literary tradition is neither likely in light of parallel Greco-Roman oral-educational settings, nor necessary in order to explain the presence of multiple versions of tannaitic textual tradition. Moreover, when seen in broader comparative context, the Yerushalmi's exegetical engagement with the Mishnah seems aware of both written and orally-transmitted sources.

But as soon as we make this point, its significance must be assessed. Written texts of tannaitic tradition may have existed in the Galilean community, but the surviving literary sources yield the impression that such texts were neglected in formal instructional settings. At least in mid-to-late-third-century circles associated with R. Yohanan, R. Shmuel b. Nahman and others (yMeg 4.1, 47d/yPe'ah 2.6, 17a; bGit 60b/bTem 14b), use of such texts in public instructional settings was condemned on halakhic grounds.[40]

In this instance, halakhic judgments surely underlie the rabbinic depiction of the origin and transmission of Sages' traditions. For the nascent historical representations of rabbinic tradition insist repeatedly that writing had played no role whatever in the transmission of a tradition that began with an unwritten revelation to Moses on Sinai. In the following section of this essay we attempt to reflect on the significance of such claims. We move from the role of written texts in the mnemotechnics of rabbinic tradition to a discussion of the ideological significance of the rabbinic privileging of oral instruction.

AMORAIC ORAL INSTRUCTION IN GRECO-ROMAN CONTEXT

Scholars have recognized for some time that rabbinic references to the unwritten character of rabbinic tradition served a variety of ideological or apologetic functions within the emerging movement.[41] As a jurisprudential tool, the distinction between scriptural and scribal-rabbinic Torah is already assumed in the Mishnah (e.g., mOrl 3:9), where it articulates a theory regarding the sources of halakhic norms and their relative legal authority.[42]

Additionally, by the close of the sixth century, the unwritten character of rabbinic tradition figured significantly as a topos in rabbinic polemics defending the authority of rabbinic teachings from Christian theological critics (e.g., Tanḥuma Ki Tissa 34 and parallels).[43]

Be that as it may, we shall see momentarily that the Yerushalmi's conception of orally transmitted tradition is neither a development of pure jurisprudential theory (as found in the Mishnah) nor a polemical idea originally framed in conflict with non-rabbinic Jewish or Christian outsiders. To the contrary, the Yerushalmi's ideological commitment to the concept of an unwritten rabbinic tradition is thoroughly explicable as a way of framing and celebrating the distinctive social form of rabbinic community—the master-disciple relationship.

In this section of our inquiry, accordingly, we offer an experiment in imagining the salience of the concept of unwritten Torah in the Galilean amoraic community that surely served as its formative social matrix. The experiment begins with a descriptive summary of the oral-learning setting as assumed in the Yerushalmi's literary representations of learning sessions. Then we place this setting in the larger context of the role of written texts and face-to-face tutelage in discipleship training in the Greco-Roman world.

ORAL LEARNING AND THE WRITTEN TEXT

While tannaitic materials might circulate in written form, they were mastered in memory and integrated into the substance of an oral academic performance. This was so not only of the Mishnah-text, ascribed to the editorial activity of Rabbi, which ultimately became the mnemonic spine of the Yerushalmi. It held true as well for many tannaitic traditions beyond the formal mishnaic curriculum. Text-fragments referred to variably as *matnyt'a, halakhah,* or *toseft'a* are routinely represented as having been cited from memory by Sages and disciples in the course of analytical exercises.[44]

With the exception of official text-memorizers, however, who mastered entire corpora of tannaitic tradition verbatim, there seems to have been little value placed on extended renditions of, say, an entire tractate for its own sake.[45] While descriptions of students repeating their *mishnayot* and *halakhot* are common, such acts of memorization were not ends in themselves. They belonged, rather, to the preparation for the oral-analytical interchange before a Sage. In this sense, the performance setting of tannaitic tradition was not comparable to the recitation of a poetic epic or a piece of classic oratory. Rather, on the model of rhetorical training such as those described in the Progymnasmata, students would deliver their citations of tannaitic material as part of their larger give and take with teachers and other students.

The Yerushalmi is rich in representations of analytic interchanges in which two or more colleagues, or teachers and students, are portrayed in dialogical analysis of shared orally reported texts.[46] Commonly, such dialogues include ample citation of tannaitic material. These, of course, represent masters and disciples interpreting previously memorized texts. In others, of even greater interest to us, the entire analytical interchange concerns texts that are only alluded to metonymically but are never actually cited. The success of such a literary representation depends upon the presence in the audience's memory of at least the conceptual substance, of not the precise wording, of the appropriate tannaitic intertexts, for without them the discussions themselves are unintelligible.

Such examples illustrate from another perspective what we have seen earlier in yYom 4.6. Memorization of texts was more than a cultural ideal valorized in the literary representation of learning; it was, rather, taken for granted as part of the cultural competence of the audience exposed to those representations and assumed to be capable of decoding them. What J.M. Foley has observed in the oral-performative setting of poetic narrative, and what W. Kelber has found in regard to primitive Christian traditions about Jesus, has its rabbinic expression in the academic literary traditions of the Galilean Amoraim as well. That is, the performative success of the eliptical oral text depends upon the audience's repeated experience of earlier performances/hearings of various versions of the text currently before it (see n. 37).

A typical example appears in yPes 4.1, 30d, framed—at least at the outset—as a comment on mPes 4.1. The Mishnah acknowledges a diversity of local practices concerning the time that people cease their labors on Passover Eve. In the Gemara, R. Yohanan and R. Shimon b. Laqish debate the grounds upon which the Mishnah permits such potentially divisive variations in custom:[47]

ר״ש בן לקיש שאל לר׳ יוחנן ואינו אסור משום בל תתגודדו. א״ל בשע׳ שאילו עושין כב״ש ואילו עושין כבית הלל. ב״ש ובית הלל אין הלכה כבית הלל. א״ל בשעה שאילו עושין כר״מ ואילו עושין כר׳ יוסה ר״מ ור׳ יוסי אין הלכה כר׳ יוסי. א״ל תרי תניין אינון על דר״מ. ותרין תניין אינון על דר׳ יוסי. א״ל הרי ראש השנה וי״ה ביהודה נהגו כר׳ עקיבה. ובגליל נהגו כר׳ יוחנן בן נורי. א״ר שנייה היא שאם עבר ועשה ביהורה כגליל ובגליל כיהודה יצא. הרי פורים הרי אילו קורין ב״ד ואילו קורין בט״ו. א״ל מי שסידר את המשנה סמכה למקרא משפחה ומשפחה מדינה ומדינה ועיר ועיר.

1. R. Shimon b. Laqish asked R. Yohanan: And isn't [such customary diversity] proscribed by the injunction "do not fall into sects" (cf. Deut 14:1)?[48]
2. He replied: [That Scriptural injunction applies] when some follow Bet Shammai and others follow Bet Hillel [but this is not the case here].

   [R. Shimon b. Laqish challenged this view: How can the Scriptural proscription be at all relevant, for in disputes between] Bet Shammai and Bet Hillel, doesn't the norm accord with Bet Hillel?
3. [R. Yohanan] replied: [If so, it applies] when some follow R. Meir and others follow R. Yose.

   [R. Shimon b. Laqish challenged: In disputes between] R. Meir and R. Yose, doesn't the norm accord with R. Yose?
4. [R. Yohanan] replied: There are two Tradents who transmit regarding [the traditions of] R. Meir and two Tradents who transmit regarding R. Yose [and in light of the resulting confusion in such cases, we apply the principle of Deut 14:1]
5. [R. Shimon b. Laqish] replied: What about [blowing the Shofar during the Royal Blessings of] the New Year and the Day of Atonement?[49] For in Judah they do it, in accord with R. Akiva; while in Galilee they do not do it, in accord with R. Yohanan b. Nuri![50]

   [R. Yohanan] replied:[51] That's a different case, for one who had already acted in Judah in accord with Galilee, and in Galilee in accord with Judah, has fulfilled his obligation.
6. [R. Shimon b. Laqish] replied: What about Purim? Surely, some read [the Esther Scroll] on the 14th of Adar and others on the 15th![52]

> [R. Yohanan] replied: The one who formulated this tradition (*mišnah*) found Scriptural support: "by every family, every province, and every city" (Es 9:28).

Stichs 1–4 represent R. Yohanan's responses to his colleague's persistant challenge of his own explanations of the Mishnah's underlying principle. In stichs 5–6, however, R. Shimon b. Laqish shifts the terms of debate, extending the search for a comprehensive explanation of the Mishnah to comparison with diverse customs concerning Rosh Hashanah and Purim.

The orally grounded assumptions of this representation of amoraic learning are most evident in stichs 5–6. Note that the customs discussed in these stichs are not explicitly explained, but are rather referenced by allusion. In stich 5, mention of the autumn festivals establishes a metonymic reference to the principal issue—the nature of the Royal Blessings—which is itself explicitly discussed at mRH 4.5. So, too, in stich 5, mention of R. Akiva and R. Yohanan b. Nuri recalls the explicit formulation of the rule at tRH 2.11. Finally, reference to the two dates in Adar at stich 6 cues the audience to mMeg 1.1's fuller discussion of the practice of reading the Scroll on Purim.

We should not dismiss these as off-handed allusions to what "everyone knew," for just how "everyone knew" this is the whole point. The editor's portrayal of his disputants as working without consulting written texts assumes that those who study his text will have a rich body of cultural competence to bring to it. He requires them to consult their own memories of texts, supplemented by their prior experience as participants in the community's ritual life, for recovering the details of his intertextual allusions. Thus his representation of oral textual mastery is dependent for its pedagogic purpose upon a similar capacity in his audience.[53]

In this example, as in nearly all others, written texts of tannaitic tradition play little discernible role. But this representation of the norm is belied by at least one clear discussion of a written halakhic source. It is worth taking a look at how yMa'as 2:4, 49d cites the halakhic notebook (*pinkas; pinax*)[54] of Hilfai (early fourth century), which contained, among other things, versions of material now compiled in the Tosefta:[55]

הלוקח תמרים והוא עתיד לדורסן גרוגרו׳ והוא עתיד לדושן אסור לוכל מהן עראי. מתקנן דמאי דברי ר׳ מאיר. וחכמים אומרים אוכל מהן עראי ומתקנן ודאי דברי ר׳ יוסי. ר׳ הילא ר׳ לעזר בשם חילפיי א״ר יונה אשכחון כת׳ בפינקסיה דחילפיי אוכל מהן עראי ומתקנן ודאי. וקשיא אם אוכל מהן עראי מתקנן ודאי. אם מתקנן דמאי יהא אסור לוכל מהן עראי. ר׳ יוסי בשם רבי הילא אוכל מהן עראי משום דבר שלא נגמרה מלאכתו. ומתקנן ודאי מתוך שיודע שביתו טובל אף הוא מפריש תרומה משעה ראשונה.

1. *One who purchases dates that he intends to mash and dried figs that he intends to press* — . . .
   Sages say: He makes a random snack of them and removes the offerings as produce that is certainly untithed (cf. tMa'as 2:3)
2. R. Yose, R. Hela, R. Lazar in the name of Hilfai:
3. Said R. Yonah: They found this written in the notebook of Hilfai: *He makes a random snack of them and removes the offerings as produce that is doubtfully tithed.*
4. Now, here is a difficulty: for it is reasonable to assume that a person making a random snack of produce will eventually remove offerings as produce that is certainly untithed; but if he removes offerings as for doubtfully tithed produce, he should be forbidden from making a random snack.
5. R. Yose in the name of Hela: He makes a random snack of it on the grounds that it is in completely processed, yet he removes the offerings as doubtfully tithed produce.
6. The reason is—since it is clear that entry into the home renders the produce forbidden for untithed use, even he will separate heave-offering as early as possible.

This passage offers a literary representation of an analytical exercise that would normally have been mounted in oral exposition of a tannaitic source (1). But it differs from most others in the Yerushalmi in two key respects. First, Hilfai's written version of that source (3) is cited as a serious challenge to the orally delivered version. More crucially, it is subjected to an analytical interchange (4–6) that provides cogent grounds for accepting the version recorded in the notebook. One can only guess, in light of the overall silence of the Yerushalmi on written tannaitic sources, how many other alternative readings for such materials had their basis in written versions of texts meant for oral delivery.

There is, indeed, one other clear citation of a written halakhic tradition that may have important implications for addressing this question. YKil 1.1, 27a attributes to R. Hillel b. Alas[56] the habit of recording halakhic traditions on pinaxes and even walls, and cites one of his texts. There, too, his text is introduced by the identical citational formula found in yMa'as 2.4: *'ashkekhon ketiv befinkasei d-* . . . A key figure in the tradental chain of both texts is the leading mid-fourth-century Tiberian master, R. Yonah. This inkage of a specific transmissional formula with a key Tiberian master of the mid-fourth century suggests, in the first place, that written rabbinic texts circulated among important groups long after the late third-century prohibitions against citing them. It also suggests that before us is at least one literary formula for citing such written materials. These two examples, therefore, may be the only survivors of a larger body of unpreserved Tiberian traditions that acknowledge citation from written sources.

The point for us is simple. Rabbinic disciples were exposed to written materials and might refer to them in case of need. But we must accept the overwhelming representation of the Yerushalmi that resort to such writings was ancillary to preparation for a learned performance in which such written sources were accessed only through memory. This was the oral examination before a Sage in which the disciple was expected to have extensive tannaitic sources at his fingertips, available for accurate citation and rigorous exposition. The learning-exchange, that is, constituted a social space that privileged orality as expressed in a give-and-take structured by a ritualized protocol of questions and answers.

We shall discuss before long how this setting of instruction served as the social matrix that supported ideological conceptions about the exclusively oral sources of the entire rabbinic tradition, from its point of Sinaitic origins. But it will be helpful first to make a comparative detour and to explore the degree to which the rabbinic privileging of orality compared to that of other Greco-Roman settings in which written texts yielded to living teachers as repositories of wisdom.

WRITTEN WORD AND LIVING PRESENCE IN THE MASTER-DISCIPLE RELATIONSHIP

We may start with the already-familiar Greco-Roman rhetorical school. We noticed earlier, in a *chreia* attributed to Isocrates, that the bond of the rhetor and his student might be represented as displacing even that of parent and child. The point is a common one in rhetorical literature. Philostratus, the principal historian of the Second Sophistic, describes relations between a second-century Sophist, Favorinus, and his student as follows: "[Favorinus] was very intimate with Herodes the Sophist who regarded him as his teacher and father, and wrote to him: 'When shall I see you, and when shall I lick the honey from your lips?' Accordingly at his death he bequeathed to Herodes all the books that he had collected, his house in Rome, and [his slave,] Autolecythus."[57] Here the disciple, like a son, inherits the teachers worldly possessions. And, more importantly for us, the *words* of the father-teacher, in a learned allusion to Aristophanes, are likened to honey.[58]

This intimate bond of teacher and student was cemented through common devotion to a world of learning. Such bonds forged in study were not unique to rhetorical education in antiquity, in which paideia commonly represented a path of personal cultivation in the venerable ways of tradition. It was common as well to a host of Greco-Roman instructional settings, collegia, in which the study of great works of the past served to solidify and further shape students' embrace not only of ideas but of the patterns of life that embodied them. The international Greco-Roman philosophical schools were not bastions of unfettered intellectual curiosity. Rather, they placed a great premium on an emotional attachment to canonical ideas akin, in its way, to conversion.[59]

Philosophical training involved, of course, intellectual mastery of the writings or orally transmitted teachings of philosophical founders.[60] But the primary goal of such study was not merely to master knowledge discursively. Rather, the goal was to be transformed by that which one possessed. The privileged path to such transformation lay in emulating the living embodiment of that knowledge in the writings and deeds of one's teachers, and their teacher's teachers. In the person of the philosophical sage, the instructional text came alive.

Pursuit of intimate discipleship in shaping a life of transformative piety played a crucial role as well in emerging Christian culture in the Roman Empire. Writings in—and well-beyond—the Christian scriptural canon routinely represent disciple-communities, grounded in the oral transmission of redemptive teachings, as the primitive form of the Church.[61] More importantly, the commitment to discipleship-training in the formation both of Christian intellectual elites and ascetic communities became, if anything, even stronger in the third–fourth century milieu in which Galilean Sages shared living space—and intellectual traditions—with a growing body of Christian clerics and holy men.[62]

In addition to witnessing the development of a distinctive Christian rhetorical paideia as an integral part of the life-path and professional advancement of the cultivated Christian son,[63] these centuries provided the framework for the emerging Egyptian, Palestinian, and Syrian ascetic communities.[64] The latter in particular placed an absolute premium on intimate service of the ascetic master as a prerequisite for the soul's transformative quest.[65] Moreover, they produced an impressive literary tradition in the form of gnomological collections, philosophical writings, and hymnody designed to transmit the wisdom of living and departed masters.[66] Preservation of such written compositions subserved a broader pursuit of a life-discipline grounded in emulation of living masters.

Judaic traditions of discipleship in Second Temple priestly, scribal or prophetic settings surely preceded the engagement with these deeply hellenized forms of discipleship.[67] Yet it is also clear that, by the turn of the Common Era, the social and intellectual forms of Judaic discipleship-communities were deeply colored by centuries of immersion in the Greco-Roman social and cultural milieu.[68] This background of a culture-wide pursuit of transformative knowledge, bound up with an energetically embraced discipline of life, is the proper setting for appreciating the fundamental traits of rabbinic discipleship in all of its diverse manifestations.[69] The tannaitic literature, from the Mishnah on, is rich in depictions of learned fellowship as grounded in the personal relationship of disciples and Sages,[70] and the

Yerushalmi's Amoraim preserve and amplify these tannaitic traditions as legitimizing models for their own communities.

In addition, the Galilean Sages of the third–fourth centuries contribute their own share of literary representations of the life of discipleship. Among these are such common narrative settings as interchanges delivered while sitting before the Sage in instructional session, in the course of judicial deliberations, at meals, during a journey, while attending the Sage's personal needs, or at his deathbed.[71] These stock-settings remain remarkably stable throughout the literature from the third through the sixth century. They testify, at the very least, to the high evaluation of discipleship as the normative setting in which to pursue the transformative life of Torah.[72]

This broad similarity of rabbinic disciple-communities with those in the larger Greco-Roman cultural sphere might be useful in helping us to interpret the privilege placed in rabbinic schools on oral mastery of the Sages' traditions. Philosophical collegia, patristic schools, and early monastic communities clearly prized the intimacy of the knowledge gained by service to the master as the sine qua non for living the life he taught. While collections of the master's own sayings, or those of earlier teachers, might circulate in manuscript, these were imperfect representations of what he alone could impart in living relationship. Written sources might serve as aids for memorizing teachings, but they in no sense displaced the primacy of the living teacher as a source of knowledge. We find an entirely congruent picture in the Galilean rabbinic communities of our period.

DISCIPLESHIP, IDEOLOGY, AND THE MEDIA OF RABBINIC TORAH

Galilean Sages of our period claimed access to revealed knowledge that could be learned only in discipleship. They made this claim, to be sure, in an idiom of their own; but the claim itself marked the Sages' position within a larger Greco-Roman conversation. At stake were the relative merits of knowledge gleaned from books as opposed to knowledge gained from the embodiment of books in the intimate knowledge of one's teacher.[73]

The earliest and most well-known rabbinic engagement with this opposition even precedes the development, in Babylonia, of a formal distinction between a *torah shebikhtav* (Written Torah) and *torah shebe'al peh* (Oral Torah). It is found, of course, in tractate Avot's depiction of the Torah's transmission from Moses, through a series of prophets, on to the Second Temple teachers and the great tannaitic masters (mAvot 1.1–2.8).[74] This text is commonly read as prefiguring or encapsulating the earliest form of what became a fully articulated theory of the oral transmission of rabbinic tradition. Such a reading appears to be an overinterpretation, an imposition onto Avot of later developments in the rabbinic ideology of revelation. The claim that rabbinic tradition originates in oral teachings received from Moses at Sinai is neither latent nor manifest in this text's enumeration of its chain of authorities. The fundamental claim, expressed in the key verbs, *qbl* and *msr*, concerns the means of continuity: knowledge of Torah may be gained only through the transmission made possible by personal discipleship. For Avot, it is not the medium of the Sages' knowledge that is crucial, but its mediation through an unbroken chain of tradition.[75]

The development, no later than the fourth century, of a formal terminology distinguishing scriptural revelation in writing from knowledge transmitted solely in a memorized oral tradition reinforced Avot's emphasis upon the primacy of discipleship in the pursuit of Torah.[76] Moreover, this self-consciousness regarding the two media of tradition elevated to a new level the primacy of the Sage as mediator of transformative knowledge.[77] As such, his own acts and teachings were apprehended in a dual aspect—as impartings of unbroken traditions stemming back into the past and as disclosures of how that tradition might attain authoritative expression in the present.[78] Since such a body of knowledge was perpetually in process, one could master it only by placing oneself directly in its path—by attending the Sage in whose life the tradition was embodied.[79]

In basic structure, then, the rabbinic model of oral tradition recapitulated—and drew to their ultimate conclusions—the pedagogical assumptions of non-rabbinic, Greco-Roman predecessors and contemporaries. The transformative power of the Sage's teachings depended upon more than his personal charisma. It could become effective only to the degree that it carried forward an unbroken line of transmission within a privileged community of traditional learning. Those who might read the texts of rabbinic teaching in isolation from the discipleship experience had neither the complete text nor any Torah. For properly transformative knowledge could not be gained by discursive understanding of any text on its own — not even that of the Torah inscribed in Scripture. Rather, it was won existentially by living a life open to dialogue with the Sage, in whom Torah was present as a mode of his embodied existence. For Torah to be present the Sage must be present as its unmediated source and embodiment in word and deed.

The Galilean Amoraim's insistence upon the exclusively oral nature of their tradition, therefore, is thoroughly intelligible on the basis of the internal needs of their own discipleship circles. That is, the jurisprudential utility of the distinction between scriptural and scribal-rabbinic legal traditions, and its power in polemically defending the hermeneutical foundations of rabbinic halakhic norms, were rhetorically grounded in a more fundamental concern to explain and celebrate the radical change of life demanded by discipleship to the Sage. If the purpose of the concept of "Torah transmitted orally" was to legitimate proscriptions against the writing of such Torah, we have seen that it was a failure. But if the concept emerges to ideologically enhance the centrality of the Sage as a vessel of Torah, the concept was a brilliant success.

It explained, first of all, how the discipleship community's attachment to the Sage offered a way of life distinct from (and more authentic than) other forms of Jewish community from which disciples had been drawn. The answer was that the covenantal imperative inscribed in the Scriptures bequeathed to all Israel could be embodied only by a life emulating the Sage's way. Thus, the arduous service of the Sage received its fundamental theological legitimation. More importantly, perhaps, it was necessary to privilege the living presence of the Sage as a source of transformative instruction over against any written versions of his teaching that, by virtue of being permanently inscribed, could be freed from the hermeneutical authority of his own presence or that of disciples, who might further extend his teaching by virtue of their embodied extension of his presence. The efforts to suppress the use of written texts in the transmission of rabbinic Torah are, therefore, eloquent expressions of the desire to preserve the living Sage's transformative teaching-presence as the crucial element in amoraic paideia. Torah came from the mouth, even if that mouth sounded out the silent syllables first inscribed in texts.

SUMMARY AND PROSPECT

As I have stressed throughout this discussion, the proper question regarding the role of writing in the Yerushalmi's literary tradition is not whether it figured in the composition or transmission of rabbinic teachings. The use of written versions of rabbinic texts in third- and fourth-century Galilean Amoraic circles in both compositional and transmissional contexts is—while "unprovable" on the basis of surviving documents—nevertheless beyond serious doubt. Instead of devising new proofs for such use, scholars should rather attempt to assess its significance for interpreting the oral-cultural context in which they functioned. How might enhanced appreciation of the complex relationship of written and oral habits of composition or transmission shape critical scholarship's interpretations of rabbinic texts and the ideological structures that mediate their form and content?

The present essay has attempted to model strategies for such critical engagement. From a literary perspective, we must be alert to ways in which the habits and constraints associated with writing may have shaped the composition, transmission, and compilation of the oral-performative texts that now survive as the written record of the Yerushalmi. Similarly, it is important to explore how the pressures of the oral-performative interchange with the rabbinic master shaped the written literary renderings of such interchanges.

To this end, I have attempted to find appropriate comparative models from Greco-Roman late antiquity that, because they offer explicit pictures of the penetration of oral and written media in the process of traditional learning, might illumine the shadows within which the pedagogy of the Galilean beit midrash lies hidden. At the very least, the Progymnasmata suggest how memorized written texts routinely lived their cultural lives in integral connection to oral-performative settings that encouraged variety in the transmitted forms of the texts even as their content was preserved. I fully acknowledge the dangers of moving from the relative clarity of the Second Sophistic's materials to the as-yet-obscure setting of the rabbinic beit midrash. Only further work in defining the various connections of broadly parallel materials in the tannaitic corpus and the Yerushalmi can suggest the degree to which methods of Greco-Roman rhetorical training can broadly serve as analogical models for explaining transmissional variations in rabbinic materials. The parallels, however, are suggestive enough to justify further work by those whose facility in the Greco-Roman literary tradition far exceeds my own.

In addition to such literary questions, the ideological dimension of orality in rabbinic culture still requires reflection. We must press further to unravel the complex puzzle of the *Sitz im Leben* of the emerging historical image of rabbinic tradition as originating in orally preserved revelations from Sinai. Rabbinic tradition surely inherited from various streams of Second Temple Judaism a rich oral-traditional culture that had manifold connections to the canonical and non-canonical writings of Israel. But there is an enormous cultural difference between inheriting or possessing an oral-traditional culture and the development, among the Galilean Amoraim, of an ideologically legitimated discipline of transmitting specialized knowledge in ritualized oral-instructional settings.

The key contribution of the foregoing discussion in this regard has been to recontextualize the usual ways of imagining the legitimating function of the idea of an orally transmitted Torah. The fact that appeals to oral transmission from the primordial moment of revelation served, especially in post-Talmudic times, to defend the authority of rabbinic tradition before Christian or Karaite opponents explains neither the origins of the idea of Oral Torah nor its primary ideological force. I have suggested, rather, that the ideological privileging of oral transmission — and its cultivation in public instructional performance — may be more readily explained by attending to the internal dynamics of power and authority that shaped the lives of masters and disciples in rabbinic communities. Accordingly, a richer examination of the Yerushalmi's constructions of mastership and discipleship, informed by all the critical strategies offered by literary and cultural studies, ought to be a fundamental program of research.

NOTES

This essay was first published in *The Talmud Yerushalmi and Graeco-Roman Culture,* ed. Peter Schäfer (Tübingen: J.C.B. Mohr [Paul Siebeck], 1998). It is reprinted here with permission of Mohr Siebeck.

1. The most influential presentations of the view that writing was used from an early point to preserve mishnaic and other literary traditions are those of Z. Frankel, *Darkhei ha-Mishnah, ha-Tosefta, Mekhilta, Sifra, Sifrei* (repr. Tel Aviv, 1923), 228–231 and Y.N. Epstein, *Mav'o la-Nusaḥ ha-Mishnah,* 2nd ed. (Jerusalem, 1964), 692–706.

Surveys of the evidence for the use of writing in various genres of rabbinic tradition are: S.W. Baron, *A Social and Religious History of the Jews,* 2nd ed. (New York, 1958), 6:156–159; and G. Stemberger, *Introduction to The Talmud and Midrash,* 2nd ed., trans. M. Bockmuehl (Edinburgh, 1996), 31–37.

For discussions of the function of written non-scriptural texts in the early rabbinic community, see Stemberger, 38–44; J. Faur, *Golden Doves With Silver Dots: Semiotics and Textuality in Rabbinic Tradition* (Bloomington, 1986), 84–113; J. Neusner, "Oral Torah and Oral Tradition: Defining the Problematic," in his *Method and Meaning in Ancient Judaism* (Missoula, Mont., 1979), 59–75; Neusner, *Oral Tradition in Judaism: the Case of the Mishnah* (New York, 1987), 133–160; P. Alexander, "Orality in Pharisaic-Rabbinic Judaism at the Turn of the Eras," in *Jesus in the Oral Gospel Tradition,* ed. E. Wansbrough (Sheffield, 1991), 159–184; and M.D. Swartz, *Scholastic Magic: Ritual and Revelation in Early Jewish Mysticism* (Princeton, 1996), 33–50.

2. In classical studies, see: R. Thomas, *Literacy and Orality in Ancient Greece* (Cambridge, 1992), 74–127; K. Robb, *Literacy and Paideia in Ancient Greece* (Oxford, 1994), 99–124; and G. Nagy, *Poetry as Performance: Homer and Beyond* (Cambridge, 1996), 153–206.

In Hebrew Bible and New Testament studies, see: M. Fishbane, *Biblical Interpretation in Ancient Israel* (Oxford, 1985), 23–88; S. Talmon, "Oral Tradition and Written Transmission, or the Heard and Seen Word in Judaism of the Second Temple Period," in *Jesus in the Gospel Tradition,* 121–157; E. Tov, *Textual Criticism of the Hebrew Bible* (Minneapolis, 1992), 164–197; H. Gamble, *Books and Readers in the Early Church: A History of Early Christian Texts* (New Haven, 1995), 42–143.

In medieval tudies, see: B. Stock, *The Implications of Literacy: Written Language and Models of Interpretation in the Eleventh and Twelfth Centuries* (Princeton, 1983), 12–87; D.A. Troll, "The Illiterate Mode of Written Communication: The Work of the Medieval Scribe," in *Oral and Written Communication: Historical Approaches,* ed. R. Enos (Newbury Park, 1990), 96–125; and M. Carruthers, *The Book of Memory: A Study of Memory in Medieval Culture* (Cambridge, 1990), 189–220.

Although students of rabbinic literature have only recently begun to drawn explicitly on the above scholarly currents, they have long appreciated the decisive role of the oral-traditional milieu in shaping the work of copyists of rabbinic texts. See, for example: A. Shinan, "Sifrut ha-Agadah: Bein Higud 'al Peh u-Mesoret Ketuvah," *Jerusalem Studies in Jewish Folklore* 1 (1981), 44–60; E.S. Rozental, "Toledot ha-Nusaḥ u-Va'ayot Arikhah be-Ḥeqer ha-Talmud ha-Bavli," *Tarbiẓ* 57 (1987), 1–36; Y. Zussman, "Kitvei Yad u-Mesorot Nusaḥ shel ha-Mishnah," *Proceedings of the Seventh World Congress of Jewish Studies: Talmud, Halakhah, Midrash* (Jerusalem, 1981), 215–250; Zussman, "Kitvei Yad Leiden shel ha-Yerushalmi: Lifanav u-Le'aḥarav," *Bar Ilan Annual* 26–27 (1995), 203–220; Zussman, "Pirqei Yerushalmi," in *Talmudic Studies,* ed. D. Rozental and M. Bar-Asher (Jerusalem, 1994), 2:220–283; A. Rozental, "Li-Mesoret Girsat ha-Mishnah," in *Saul Lieberman Memorial Volume,* ed. S. Friedman (New York, 1993), 29–48; S. Reif, "Aspects of Mediaeval Jewish Literacy," in *The Uses of Literacy in Early Medieval Europe,* ed. R. McKitterick (Cambridge, 1990), 134–155; S. Friedman, "Le-Hitḥavut Shinuei ha-Nusḥa'ot be-Talmud ha'Bavli," *Sidra: A Journal for the Study of Rabbinic Literature* 7 (1991), 62–102; and most recently, the excellent collection of essays in P. Alexander & A. Samely, eds., *Artefact and Text: The Re-Creation of Jewish Literature in Medieval Hebrew Manuscripts = Bulletin of the John Rylands University Library of Manchester* 75 (1993).

3. The pre-eminent contemporary theorist of the mutual relations of oral and written literary traditions from a cross-cultural perspective is John Miles Foley. See his recent *The Singer of Tales in Performance* (Bloomington, 1995), esp. 60–98.

4. The assumption of a profound, almost ontological, distinction between written and oral texts flawed much of the earlier work in cultural studies of orality. See, for example, the groundbreaking article of J. Goody and I. Watt, "The Consequences of Literacy," in *Literacy in Traditional Societies,* ed. J. Goody (Cambridge, 1968), 304–345. For a recent estimate of the "great divide" between orality and literacy, see J. Halverson, "Goody and the Implosion of the Literacy Thesis," *Man* ns. 27 (1992), 289–303.

5. This issue is illuminated in particular by anthropologists such as R. Finnegan,

Literacy and Orality: Studies in the Technology of Communication (Oxford, 1988), 110–122. Her insights have proved particularly useful in rabbinic studies as applied by Y. Elman, *Authority and Tradition: Toseftan Baraitot in Talmudic Babylonia* (Hoboken, NJ, 1994), 71–111. See also the important comments of J. Rovner on the role of oral memory in the written composition of the Talmud Bavli: "Rhetorical Strategy and Dialectical Necessity in the Babylonian Talmud: The Case of Kiddushin 34a–35a," *Hebrew Union College Annual* 65 (1994), 184–187, 217–219.

6. The degree to which rabbinic compilations ought to be conceived as "works in progress" or as relatively fixed compositions with more or less canonical literary boundaries is a core issue frequently debated. See J. Neusner, *Canon and Connection: Intertextuality in Judaism* (Lanham, Md., 1987), 15–92; P. Schäfer, "Research into Rabbinic Literature: An Attempt to Define the *Status Quaestionis*" *Journal of Jewish Studies* 37 (1986), 139–152; C. Milikowsky, "The *Status Quaestionis* of Research in Rabbinic Literature" *Journal of Jewish Studies* 39 (1988), 201–211; P. Schäfer, "Once Again the *Status Quaestionis* of Research in Rabbinic Literature: An Answer to Chaim Milikowsky," *Journal of Jewish Studies* 40 (1989), 89–94; P. Alexander, "Textual Criticism and Rabbinic Literature: The Case of the Targum of the Song of Songs," in *Artefact and Text*, 159–173.

With particular relevance to the question of the Yerushalmi's lack of closure as a literary work, see G. Wewers, *Probleme der Bavot-Traktate* (Tübingen, 1984), 9–11, 289–307 and the statement of principles underlying the Yerushalmi edition of P. Schäfer and H.-J. Becker, eds., *Synopse zum Talmud Yerushalmi*. I/1–2: Ordnung Zera'im: Berakhot und Pe'a (Tübingen, 1991), vii–viii.

7. Here I disagree with Neusner's characterization of the Tosefta as the "Mishnah's first commentary," in terms of which the Yerushalmi and the Bavli are modelled (J. Neusner, *The Tosefta: An Introduction* [Atlanta, 1992], xvii). Even if we accept for argument's sake Neusner's contention that the Tosefta is redacted to serve as an exegetical companion to the Mishnah, the Tosefta's literary tradition shares similar patterns of formulation and diction as that of the Mishnah, despite its rather more chaotic organization. The Yerushalmi, by contrast, is constructed of materials that self-consciously distinguish themselves from all tannaitic literary tradition, including the Mishnah's. Approaching the mishnaic text from a rhetorical position beyond tannaitic discourse, the Yerushalmi displays a consciousness of the Mishnah as a cogent source, a literary "voice" distinct from its own. Such a consciousness is nowhere evident in the Tosefta.

For further discussion of the Mishnah-Tosefta relationship, see Y.N. Epstein, *Mevo'ot la-Sifrut ha-Tannaim* (Jerusalem, 1957), 241–262; B. Bokser, *Post Mish-*

naic Judaism in Transition (Chico, Calif., 1981), 443–447; Stemberger, *Introduction,* 153–156; Elman, *Authority and Tradition,* 1–46; S.M. Friedman, "Tosefta atiqt'a (1): Le-yaḥas maqbilot ha-Mishnah, veha-Tosefta—Kol Kitvei ha-Qodesh," *Tarbiẓ* 62 (1993), 313–338; Friedman, "Toseft'a atiqi'a (2): Le-yahas Maqbilot ha-Mishnah veha-Tosefta," *Bar Ilan Annual* 26–27 (1995), 277–288; and the forthcoming doctoral dissertation of E. Shanks, under the direction of S. Fraade (Yale University).

Earlier in this century, Moses Zuckermandel sought to prove that the Mishnah as a whole is a Babylonian condensation of an original Palestinian work represented by the Tosefta (M.S. Zuckermandel, *Gesammelte Aufsaetze: Erster Teil. Zur Halachacritik* [Frankfurt a. M., 1911], 86–87). While his argument is untenable, it is likely that more than a few passages of the received Mishnah represent developments or condensations of materials now found in the Tosefta.

8. On the significance of scriptural midrash as a model for constructing a literary companion to the Mishnah, see J. Neusner, *Midrash in Context: Exegesis in Formative Judaism* (Philadelphia, 1983), 53–110 and Bokser, *Post Mishnaic Judaism,* 461–484.

9. The significance of the terminological distinction between *matnyt'a* and *matnytyn* is clarified by W. Bacher, *Tradition und Tradenten in den Schulen Palaestinas und Babyloniens* (repr. 1966), 20–21, and Epstein, *Mav'o,* 2:813–814. For *toseft'a,* see Epstein, *Mevo'ot,* 88. For *barait'a,* see H. Albeck, *Mav'o le-Talmudim* (Tel Aviv, 1969), 19–20. These distinctions are tacit and unsystematic in the Yerushalmi, but are taken for granted in the Bavli.

10. *Torah shebe'al peh* or *torah sebefeh* (e.g., bShab 31a/ARNa15 [b29]; bGit 60b, bTem 14b) are usually rendered in English as "Oral Torah." On the term, see W. Bacher, *Traditionen und Tradenten,* 22–24; Y. Blidstein, "Le-Korot ha-Munaḥ Torah Shebe'al Peh," *Tarbiẓ* 42 (1973), 496–498.

11. On the version of yDem/yShevi represented on the seventh-century mosaic-tile floor of the Rehov synagogue, see J. Sussmann, "The Inscription in the Synagogue at Rehob," in *Ancient Synagogues Revealed,* ed. L. I. Levine (Detroit, 1982), 146–151 and the additional comments of G. Stemberger, *Introduction,* 37. Normally, it seems that scrolls, rather than codices, served as the earliest forms for preserving large rabbinic manuscripts. See M. Bregman, "Qet' a Qadum shel Avot de-Rabi Natan Mitokh Megilah," *Tarbiẓ* 52 (1983), 201–222; and S. Friedman, "An Ancient Scroll Fragment (B. Hullin 101a–105a) and the Rediscovery of the Babylonian Branch of Tannaitic Hebrew," *Jewish Quarterly Review* 86 (1995), 9–51.

12. See Stemberger, ibid., for discussions of the dating of the Mishnah (133–

140), Tosefta (152–153), the Mekhiltas (254–256, 260), Sifra (262–264), Sifre Numbers (268), Sifre Zutta (271), and Sifre Deuteronomy (273–274).

13. See the excellent collection of essays on this topic gathered by H. Fischel, *Essays in Greco-Roman and Related Talmudic Literature* (New York, 1977) and Fischel's "Prolegomenon," which includes a comprehensive bibliography, xiii–lxxvi. Useful observations may also be found in S. Lieberman, *Hellenism in Jewish Palestine* (New York, 1950), 20–114; B. Gerhardsson, *Memory and Manuscript: Oral Tradition and Written Transmission in Rabbinic Judaism and Early Christianity,* trans. E.J. Sharpe (Lund, 1961), 59–66; A. Wasserstein, "Greek Language and Philosophy in the Early Rabbinic Academies," in *Jewish Education and Learning,* ed. G. Abramson and T. Parfitt (Chur, Switzerland, 1994), 221–231.

14. Introductions to aspects of rhetorical education in the Greco-Roman world may be consulted in H. Marrou, *A History of Education in Antiquity* (London, 1956), 194–226, 284–298, and S.F. Bonner, *Education in Ancient Rome* (London, 1977), 65–96, 250–287. For a broader overview of the entire range of educational institutions and relationships in Greco-Roman culture, see L.C.A. Alexander, "Schools, Hellenistic," in *The Anchor Bible Dictionary,* ed. D.N. Freedman (New York, 1992), 5:1005–1011.

15. The most comprehensive discussion of all aspects of the rabbinic movement in third–fifth century Galilee within the comparative perspective of the Roman social and cultural setting is that of L. Levine, *The Rabbinic Class of Roman Palestine in Late Antiquity* (Jerusalem, 1989).

Specific institutional comparisons between the rabbinic beit midrash and other Greco-Roman educational settings are complicated by the difficulty in distinguishing the specific amoraic Galilean institution from Palestinian rabbinic predecessors or later Babylonian transformations. See, for example, M. Schwabe, "On the Jewish and Greco-Roman Schools in the Days of the Mishnah and the Talmud" (in Hebrew), *Tarbiẓ* 21 (1949), 112–123; B. Gerhardsson, *Memory and Manuscript,* 123–130; D. Goodblatt, "Sources Concerning the Origins of Organized Jewish Education in the Land of Israel," *Studies in the History of the Jewish People in the Land of Israel,* ed. B. Oded vol. 5 (Haifa, 1980), 83–103; A.I. Baumgarten, "The Politics of Reconciliation: The Education of R. Judah the Prince," in *Jewish and Christian Self-Definition: Volume Two. Aspects of Judaism in the Greco-Roman Period,* ed. E.P. Sanders (Philadelphia, 1981), 213–225; M. Goodman, *State and Society in Roman Galilee A.D. 132–212* (Totawa, NJ, 1983), 71–81; P. Alexander, "Quid Athenis et Hierosolymis? Rabbinic Midrash and Hermeneutics in the Graeco-Roman World," in *A Tribute to Geza Vermes: Essays on Jewish and Christian Literature and History,* ed. P.R. Davies and R.T. White (Sheffield, 1990),

101–123. An important methodological model is the essay of S.J.D. Cohen, "Patriarchs and Scholarchs," *Proceedings of the American Academy for Jewish Research* 48 (1981), 57–85.

16. Comparisons of rabbinic literature with diverse aspects of Greco-Roman literary culture that have an important bearing upon the present essay's discussion include: A. Kaminka, "Les rapports entre le rabbinisme et la philosophie stoicienne," repr. in Fischel, *Essays,* 23–42; E. Bickerman, "La chaine de la tradition pharisienne," repr. in ibid., 127–137; D. Daube, "Alexandrian Methods of Interpretation and the Rabbis," repr. in ibid., 165–182; Daube, "Texts and Interpretation in Roman and Jewish Law," repr. in ibid., 240–255; Daube, "Rabbinic Methods of Interpretation and Hellenistic Rhetoric," *Hebrew Union College Annual* 12 (1949), 239–264; H. Fischel, "Story and History: Observations on Greco-Roman Rhetoric and Pharisaism," repr. in Fischel, *Essays,* 443–472; Fischel, "Studies in Cynicism and the Ancient Near East: The Transformation of a Chria," in *Religions in Antiquity: Essays in Memory of Erwin Ramsdell Goodenough,* ed. J. Neusner (Leiden, 1968), 372–411; Fischel, *Rabbinic Literature and Greco-Roman Philosophy* (Leiden, 1973); R. Birchman, "Rabbinic Syllogistic: The Case of Mishnah-Tosefta Tohorot," in *Approaches to Ancient Judaism: Vol. V. Studies in Judaism and Its Greco-Roman Context,* ed. W.S. Green (Atlanta, 1985), 81–98; B.L. Visotzky, "Jots and Titles: On Scriptural Interpretation in Rabbinic and Patristic Literatures," in his *Fathers of the World: Essays in Rabbinic and Patristic Literatures* (Tübingen, 1995), 28–40; P. Alexander, "Quid Athenis et Hierosolymis?"; A. Avery-Peck, "Rhetorical Argumentation in Early Rabbinic Pronouncement Stories," in *Semeia 64: The Rhetoric of Pronouncement,* ed. V. Robbins (Atlanta, 1994), 49–69.

17. For general discussion, see G. Bowersock, *Greek Sophists in the Roman Empire* (Oxford, 1969); Bowersock, *Approaches to the Second Sophistic* (University Park, PA, 1969); G. Anderson, *The Second Sophistic: A Cultural Phenomenon in the Roman Empire* (New York, 1993); G.A. Kennedy, *A New History of Classical Rhetoric* (Princeton, 1994), 201–256.

18. An instructive cultural portrait of this group, with particular attention to the role of rhetorical education in its larger political and religious aspirations, is now provided by P. Brown, *Power and Persuasion in Late Antiquity: Towards a Christian Empire* (Madison, 1992), especially 35–70.

The rhetorical traditions cultivated in the sophistic and patristic schools should be considered as a single tradition, albeit borne by politically antagonistic and socially distinct communities. Indeed, long after the non-Christian schools of rhetoric passed into oblivion, patristic education perpetuated the Sophists' high regard for allusive rhetorical eloquence grounded in mastery of a canon of Greek and Latin literary texts that extended well beyond the normative Christian scriptures (G.A. Kennedy, *Classic Rhetoric and its Christian and Secular Tradition From Ancient to Modern Times* [Chapel Hill, 1980], 120–160). Accordingly, for our purposes here it is convenient to ignore the mutual ideological contempt in which representatives of the Sophists and the Church held the other and focus upon the models of rhetorical education they held in common.

For a bibliographical overview of the rich scholarship on the connections between rabbinic and patristic literary culture, see J.R. Baskin, "Rabbinic-Patristic Exegetical Contexts in Late Antiquity: A Bibliographical Reappraisal," in Green, *Approaches,* 53–80. Recent studies of the rabbinic-patristic discussion over scriptural interpretation in particular include Visotzky, *Fathers of the World* and M. Hirshman, *A Rivalry of Genius: Jewish and Christian Biblical Interpretation,* trans. B. Stein (Albany, 1996).

19. For example, "[The Sophist, Polemo,] . . . on seeing a gladiator dripping with sweat out of sheer terror of the life-and-death struggle before him, . . . remarked: 'You are in as great an agony as though you were going to declaim.'" Cited in Philostratus, *Lives of the Sophists* 541 in Philostratus and Eunapius, *Lives of the Sophists,* trans. W.C. Wright (Cambridge, Mass., 1921), 129–131.

20. Even where texts were composed in writing prior to performance, the performance had to appear extemporaneous. See Kennedy, *A New History,* 83–84.

21. My discussion of the Progymnasmata depends entirely upon the collection of translated texts and comments compiled in R.F. Hock and E.N. O'Neil, eds., *The Chreia in Ancient Rhetoric. Volume I: The Progymnasmata* (Atlanta, 1986). See their introduction to the genre, 3–58. See also Kennedy, ibid., 202–217.

22. See the works of Fischel and Avery-Peck, "Early Rabbinic Pronouncement Stories," (n. 16) for basic studies of rabbinic literature's heavy dependence upon the *chreia.*

23. Hock and O'Neil, *The Chreia,* 83.

24. Ibid., 91. The privileging of the teacher over the parent is, of course, a commonplace of rabbinic literature as well, e.g.: "[Where a disciple finds] a lost object of his father's and a lost object of his master's, [the return of] his master's takes precedence, for his father brought him into This Aeon, but his master, who has taught him wisdom (*ḥokhmah*), brings him into the Coming Aeon" (mBM 2.11; cf. tBM 2.30, tHor 2.5).

The Mishnah's placing of the fruits of wisdom in an eschatological framework is, perhaps, a reflex of its rabbinic milieu; the elevation of the teacher of wisdom (*ḥokhmah/sophia*) over the parent is thoroughly harmonious with the Greco-

Roman philosophical tradition. The toseftan textual witnesses seem troubled by the appearance of *ḥokhmah* (wisdom) where *torah* is to be expected, but they nevertheless attest the Mishnah's choice. Cf. the toseftan version cited at bBM 33a and the comments of S. Lieberman, *Tosefta Ki-fshuta: A Comprehensive Commentary on the Tosefta. Part IX. Order Nezikin* (New York, 1988), 168.

25. Hock and O'Neil, 95.

26. Ibid.

27. Ibid., 97.

28. Ibid.

29. Ibid., 177. See Avery-Peck, "Early Rabbinic Pronouncement Stories," 67, for a catalog of rabbinic *chreiai* that conform to the patterns outlined here by Hermogenes. Avery-Peck's concern is to demonstrate rabbinic use of rhetorical patterns known also to the Second Sophistic; my own interest, to the contrary, concerns the light that sophistic usage of written texts, as demonstrated in the oral deployment of memorized *chreiai*, sheds on the mnemonic practices of the Amoraim.

30. See, for example, L. Finkelstein, "Studies in the Tannaitic Midrashim" and "The Transmission of the Early Rabbinic Traditions," both now collected in his *Sifra on Leviticus* (Jerusalem, 1991), 5:151*–190*, 224*–244*; S. Safrai, "Oral Tora," in *The Literature of the Sages. First Part: Oral Tora, Halakha, Mishna, Tosefta, Talmud, External Tractates* (Philadelphia, 1987), 52–72; and D. Zlotnick, *The Iron Pillar-Mishnah: Redaction, Form, and Intent* (Jerusalem, 1988), 51–71.

Perhaps the most important full-scale "oralist" study of rabbinic literary tradition is that of Gerhardsson, *Memory and Manuscript*. Gerhardsson's model is a subtle one, in which orally formulated texts in fixed forms served as the foundation of more fluid secondary textual forms, corresponding roughly to "Mishnah" and "Gemara" (see 19–84 and 122–170). While Gerhardsson acknowledges that some rabbinic material was written, he follows Lieberman (*Hellenism*, 83–99) in discounting the possibility that writing played more than an episodic role at best in preserving tannaitic literary tradition.

31. Cited from H. Albeck, ed., *Shishah Sidre Mishnah: Seder Mo'ed* (Jerusalem, 1973), 235.

32. Cited from the Krotoschin edition, checked against MS Leiden.

33. Here and at stich 5 I have deleted material that does not affect the present discussion.

34. Cited from S. Lieberman, *The Tosefta: According to Codex Vienna, With Variants from Codices Erfurt, London, Genizah MSS. and Editio Princeps*. Vol. 2, Mo'ed (New York, 1962), 236.

35. Cited from *Sifra (Torat Kohanim), with Commentaries of R. Shimshon of Sens and R. Avraham b. David* (Jerusalem, 1959), 32a.

36. R. Rabbinowicz, *Sefer Diqduqei Soferim* (repr., New York, 1976), 1:24–25 records no significant textual variants of this passage in the manuscript tradition of the Bavli.

37. My discussion here depends upon the important contributions of John Miles Foley to the interpretation of the "metonymic" capacity of the orally performed text. In his view, the oral text's economy of expression is integral to its capacity to convey meaning, for it testifies to the performer's ability to depend upon his audience's memory of past versions to fill in his own omissions and allusions. See Foley, *Singer*, 2–7.

Foley's conception of oral-performative metonymy has been taken up with particular effectiveness in W. Kelber's notion of the "biosphere" of tradition: "Tradition in this encompassing sense is a circumambient contextuality or biosphere in which speakers and hearers live. It includes texts and experiences transmitted through or derived from texts. But it is anything but reducible to intertextuality" (W. Kelber, "Jesus and Tradition: Words in Time, Words in Space," in *Semeia 65: Orality and Textuality in Early Christian Literature,* ed. J. Dewey [Atlanta, 1995], 159).

38. This conclusion supports, from a different point of view, Y. Elman's recent argument that a written compilation of tradition analogous to the Tosefta circulated in amoraic Palestine. See Y. Elman, *Authority and Tradition,* 73–74.

39. At this writing, Y. Elman's *Authority and Tradition* offers the strongest argument for the presence, at least in Palestine, of written versions of the Tosefta. For a much briefer inquiry into the role of writing in mishnaic composition, see M. Jaffee, "Writing and Rabbinic Oral Tradition: On Mishnaic Narrative, Lists and Mnemonics," *Journal of Jewish Thought and Philosophy* 4 (1994), 123–146.

40. For a survey of the texts and scholarly discussion, see Stemberger, *Introduction,* 32–34 and Safrai, "Oral Tora," 45–52.

41. See, for example: S. Kaatz, *Die Mündliche Lehre und ihr Dogma,* vol. 1 (Leipzig, 1922), 4–15, and vol. 2 (Berlin, 1923), 44–59; J. Neusner, "Oral Torah and Oral Tradition," in *Method and Meaning in Ancient Judaism,* 59–75; P. Schäfer, "Das Dogma von der Mündlichen Torah im Rabbinischen Judentum," in P. Schäfer, *Studien zur Geschichte und Theologie des Rabbinischen Judentums* (Leiden, 1978), 153–197; D. Kraemer, "On the Reliability of the Attributions in the Babylonian Talmud," *Hebrew Union College Annual* 60 (1989), 175–190; S. Safrai, "Halakhah le-Mosheh mi-Sinai: Historyah 'o Teologiah?" in *Talmudic Studies,* ed. Y. Zussman & D. Rozental, vol. 1 (Jerusalem, 1990), 11–38; A. Rozen-

tal, "Torah she'al Peh ve-Torah mi-Sinai: Halakhah u-Ma'aseh," in *Talmudic Studies,* ed. D. Rozental & M. Bar-Asher vol. 2 (Jerusalem, 1994), 448–487; M. Jaffee, "Halakhah in Early Rabbinic Judaism: Innovation Beyond Exegesis, Tradition Before the Oral Torah," in *Innovation in Religious Traditions: Essays in the Interpretation of Religious Change,* ed. M. Williams, C. Cox, and M. Jaffee (Berlin, 1992), 109–142; Jaffee, "Halakhah as Primordial Tradition: A Gadamarian Dialogue with Early Rabbinic Memory and Jurisprudence," in *Interpreting Judaism in a Postmodern Age,* ed. S. Kepnes (New York, 1996), 85–117.

42. For discussion, see Jaffee, "Primordial Tradition," 99–102 in particular.

43. In Midrash Tanḥuma, Ki Tissa 34 (repr., standard edition with commentaries of Ets Yosef and Anaf Yosef, p. 127), the oral tradition (*mishnah*) is represented as a "mystery" (*mistoryn*) reserved for Israel alone, as opposed to the written Scriptures that have been appropriated in translation by other nations. For discussion, see E.E. Urbach, *Ḥazal: Pirqei'Emunot ve-De'ot* (Jerusalem, 1973), 271, Safrai, "Oral Tora," 47 and M. Jaffee, *Early Judaism* (Upper Saddle River, NJ, 1997), 222.

44. For collection and discussion of the principal literary evidence, see Gerhardsson, *Memory and Manuscript,* 93–170; Safrai, "Oral Tora," 60–77. These portrayals require refinement in light of methods that provide a critical basis for evaluating the relation of the various tannaitic and amoraic various sources to particular chronological or institutional settings.

45. The sources describing the official "repeater" (*tanna*) are discussed in Epstein, *Mav'o,* 673–690 and S. Lieberman, *Hellenism,* 88–91. See also S. Gandz, "The Robeh," in *Exploring the Talmud,* ed. H.Z. Dimitrovsky (New York, 1976), 262–269. For a general appreciation of the constructed literary character of Rabbinic representations of academic debate and their value in reconstructing actual processes of learning, see Bokser, *Post Mishnaic Judaism,* 471–473.

46. These dialogues are presented, literarily, in spare formal terms. Commonly the introductory settings employ forms of the verb "sit," *ytv* (e.g., yTer 43c: Rabbi X and Rabbi Y *havun yatvin 'amrin;* yHag 77a: Rabbi X and Rabbi Y. *havun yatvin la'ayin be'orait'a*). With the introductory context established, the resulting dialogue is normally framed with the simple verb "say," *'mr:* he said to him (*'amar leh*) . . .; he replied . . . (*'amar leh*); he replied . . . (*'amar leh*), and so on. Another verb commonly used to introduce a depiction of a learning session is "ask" (*s'l*), as in the passage we shall examine in a moment.

For discussion of these formulaic terms, see W. Bacher, "Zur Geschichte der Schulen Palaestina's im 3. und 4. Jahrhundert. Die Genossen," *Monatsschrift für die Geschichte und Wissenschaft des Judentums* 43 (1899), 345–346; M. Gewirtsmann,

"Ha-Munaḥ Yetiv u-Mashma'uto," *Sinai* 65 (1969), 9–20. The most exhaustive study, unfortunately, concerns the formulaic use of these terms in the Bavli; see D. Goodblatt, *Rabbinic Instruction in Sasanian Babylonia* (Leiden, 1975), 199–259.

47. My citation is based upon ed. Krotoschin, with reference to MS Leiden. See the fuller discussion of the text in B. Bokser, trans., *The Talmud of the Land of Israel: A Preliminary Translation and Explanation. Vol. 13. Yerushalmi Pesahim* (Chicago, 1994), 154–155.

48. *lo titgodedu:* literally, "do not make incisions." I render the passage, following Bokser, ibid., in accord with the sense assumed in the Yerushalmi.

49. mRH 4.5 in the Albeck edition, Seder Mo'ed, 322, reads as follows. I have italicized the disputed material assumed in Y.:

(1) The order of blessings [in the Tefillah of Rosh Hashanah]:

(2) *He recites "the Fathers," and "the Powers," and the "Sanctification of the Name," and includes the "Royal Blessings" with them, but does not sound the Shofar; [he continues with] the "Sanctification of the Day" and sounds the Shofar; [he continues with] the "Remembrance Blessings" and sounds the Shofar;* [he continues with] the "Sounding Blessings" and sounds the Shofar; and he recites the "Liturgy," and the "Thanksgiving," and the "Priestly Benediction"—words of R. Yohanan b. Nuri

(3) Said to him R. Akiva: If he doesn't sound the Shofar at the "Royal Blessings," why does he mention them?

(4) *Rather, he recites "the Fathers," and "the Powers," and the "Sanctification of the Name," and he includes the "Royal Blessings in the "Sanctification of the Day," and sounds the Shofar . . .*

50. I cite the text from Lieberman, Tosefta: Mo'ed, 316:

"In places where they are accustomed to teach in accord with the views of R. Akiva, they teach in accord with the views of R. Akiva; in places where they are accustomed to teach in accord with the views of R. Yohanan b. Nuri, they teach in accord with the views of R. Yohanan b. Nuri. . . ."

51. So MS Leiden, as opposed to Krotoschin's: "Said Rabbi." See the commentary of *Pnei Moshe.*

52. mMeg 1.1, in Albeck, Seder Mo'ed, 355, reads as follows. The italicized material is alluded to in the Yerushalmi:

1. The Esther Scroll is read on the eleventh [of Adar], the twelfth, the thirteenth, the fourteenth, the fifteenth—not less and not more.
2. Towns surrounded by a wall from the days of Joshua b. Nun read on the fifteenth.

3. *Villages and large cities read on the fourteenth, yet villages may advance [the reading to take advantage of larger crowds] on days of congregation.*

53. This model of metonymy and oral-cultural competence is fruitful as well in explaining the phenomenon of partial citations of tannaitic texts in the Yerushalmi. See L. Moskovitz, "Od al ha-Baraitot ha-Ḥaserot bi-Yerushalmi," *Proceedings of the American Academy of Jewish Research* 61 (1995), 1–20.

54. For discussion of the *pinax* in rabbinic culture and the larger Greco-Roman world, see Lieberman, *Hellenism,* 203–208.

55. The citation is from MS Leiden, compared against textual witnesses gathered in P. Schäfer & H.-J. Becker, *Synopse* I/6–11, pp. 176–177. At stich 2, delete "divrei." At stichs 3 and 5 correct *wdyy* > *dm'y.* See also S. Lieberman, *Tosefta Kifshuta: A Comprehensive Commentary on the Tosefta. Part II Order Zera'im* (New York, 1955), 678–79.

56. Variants: R. Hillel b. Alem, R. Hillel b. Vale(n)s. See Schäfer & Becker, *Synopse* I/3–5, pp. 96–97.

57. Philostratus, *Lives* 490, p. 25.

58. The homoerotic implications of this passage are obvious. In this paper I make no claim that rabbinic discipleship involved such relationships, although these were common in other Greco-Roman settings. For a rich discussion of the matter of Greco-Roman pedagogical homoeroticism, see R. Valantasis, *Spiritual Guides of the Third Century: A Semiotic Study of the Guide-Disciple Relationship in Christianity, Neoplatonism, Hermetism, and Gnosticism* (Minneapolis, 1991), 63–104. An assessment of the implications of pedagogical homoeroticism for understanding discipleship in rabbinic communities is available in M.L. Satlow, "'They Abused Him Like a Woman': Homoeroticism, Gender Blurring, and the Rabbis in Late Antiquity," *Journal of the History of Sexuality* 5 (1994), 1–25.

59. On the theme of philosophical conversion, see: A.D. Nock, *Conversion: The Old and New in Religion From Alexander the Great to Augustine of Hippo* (London, 1933), 164–186; R.L. Wilken, "Collegia, Philosophical Schools, and Theology," in *The Catacombs and the Colosseum,* ed. S. Benko & J. O'Rourke (Valley Forge, PA, 1971), 268–291; M. Hengel, *The Charismatic Leader and His Followers* (Edinburgh, 1981), 27–33; I. Hadot, "The Spiritual Guide," in *Classical Mediterranean Spirituality: Egyptian, Greek, Roman,* ed. A. H. Armstrong (New York, 1986), 436–359; P. Hadot, "Forms of Life and Forms of Discourse in Ancient Philosophy," *Critical Inquiry* 16 (1990), 483–505.

60. See D. Aune, "Prolegomena to the Study of Oral Tradition in the Hellenistic World," in *Jesus in the Oral Gospel Tradition,* 87–90 and R. Valantasis, *Spiritual Guides of the Third Century,* 35–61.

61. On the first-century setting, see, e.g.: Gerhardsson, *Memory and Manuscript,* 324–335; Hengel, *The Charismatic Leader and His Followers,* 38–83; W.H. Kelber, *The Oral and the Written Gospel: The Hermeneutics of Speaking and Writing in the Synoptic Tradition, Mark, Paul, and Q* (Philadelphia, 1983), passim; T. Boomershine, "Jesus of Nazareth and the Watershed of Ancient Orality and Literacy," in *Orality and Textuality,* 7–36. For a comprehensive study of the role of discipleship in shaping the nature of the Jesus-sayings traditions in particular, see S. Byrskog, *Jesus the Only Teacher: Didactic Authority and Transmission in Ancient Israel, Ancient Judaism and the Matthean Community* (Stockholm, 1994).

62. On the sharing of such traditions, see Visotzky, *Fathers of the World,* passim.

63. Brown, *Power and Persuasion,* 3–34.

64. On the role of personal relationships in the shaping of ascetic Christian piety, see: P. Rousseau, "The Spiritual Authority of the Monk-Bishop: Eastern Elements in Some Western Hagiography of the Fourth and Fifth Centuries," *Journal of Theological Studies,* n.s. 23 (1971): 380–419; Rousseau, *Ascetics, Authority, and The Church in the Age of Jerome and Cassian* (Oxford, 1978), 9–76; R. Kirschner, "The Vocation of Holiness in Late Antiquity," *Vigiliae Christianae* 38 (1984), 109–114; and works cited in n. 66 below.

65. See R. Valantasis, *Spiritual Guides of the Third Century,* 13–33.

66. See, e.g., the Apothegmata Patrum in the translation of B. Ward, *The Desert Christian: The Sayings of the Desert Fathers* (New York, 1975) and R.A. Edwards & R.A. Wild, trans. and eds., *The Sentences of Sextus* (Chico, Calif., 1981). Valantasis, *Spiritual Guides of the Third Century,* 47–54, 100–102, and 147–149, offers particularly rich discussions of the way the reading of traditional texts and the composition of new ones functioned in the spiritual formation of disciples in contemporaneous non-Christian Neoplatonic and Hermetic communities.

67. For useful essays that place ancient Israelite discipleship communities in helpful Mediterranean and Mesopotamian cultural context, see J.G. Gammie & L.G. Perdue, eds., *The Sage in Israel and the Ancient Near East* (Winona Lake, Wisc., 1990).

68. The penchant, therefore, of Josephus and Philo for describing Jewish communal associations in terms of philosophical discipleship need not be entirely beside the mark. The point has been made quite sharply by S. Mason, "Philosophia as a Group-Designation in Graeco-Roman Society, Judaism, and Early Christianity," in J. Neusner, *Approaches to Ancient Judaism,* ed. J. Neusner, n.s., vol. 4 (Atlanta, 1993).

It is frequently observed that the actual social and ideological constitution of

Jewish groups such as Philo's Therapeutae and Josephus' Pharisees, or of each author's Essenes, may be irrecoverable behind the work of cultural translation that motivated the Philonic and Josephan accounts. Nevertheless in the one case where a group's own writings are available for examination, the parallels to collegia are rather clear. The community rules of the Dead Sea Yaḥad testify to the ways in which discipleship under a regime of religious transformation or conversion, closely akin to contemporary Hellenistic associations, played a crucial role in at least one form of Second Temple Jewish piety that regarded itself as vigorously opposed to the Hellenistic milieu. See H. Stegemann, "The Qumran Essenes—Local Members of the Main Jewish Union in Late Second Temple Times," in *The Madrid Qumran Congress: Proceedings of the International Congress on the Dead Sea Scrolls,* ed. J.T. Barrera & L.V. Montaner (Leiden, 1992), 83–166 and M. Klinghardt, "The Manual of Discipline in Light of Statutes of Hellenistic Associations," in *Methods of Investigation of the Dead Sea Scrolls and the Khirbet Qumran Site,* ed. M. Wise et al. (New York, 1994), 251–270.

Important comparative discussions of discipleship patterns in early Judaism from the perspective of the transmission of teaching-traditions may be consulted in Hengel, *The Charismatic Leader and His Followers,* 16–60 and Byrskog, *Jesus the Only Teacher,* 35–196. See also the illuminating discussion of Greco-Roman philosophical discipleship in L.C.A. Alexander, "Schools, Hellenistic," 1007–1009.

69. For an explanation and application of the term "transformative knowledge" to the study of Judaism in the Greco-Roman setting, see Jaffee, *Early Judaism,* 213–243.

The most comprehensive collection of source-material on the master-disciple relationship in rabbinic circles is, unfortunately, marred by an ahistorical tendency to posit a single pattern of discipleship throughout the tannaitic and amoraic communities. See M. Averbach, *Ha-Ḥinukh ha-Yehudi bi-Tequfat ha-Mishnah veha-Talmud* (Jerusalem, 1983), 93–212.

70. See the sources and analyses in J. Neusner, *Rabbinic Traditions About the Pharisees Before 70,* vols. 1–3 (Leiden, 1971). For synthetic treatments of the tannaitic discipleship-communities, see S. Fraade, "The Early Rabbinic Sage," in *The Sage in Ancient Israel,* 417–436; S.J.D. Cohen, "The Place of the Rabbi in Jewish Society in the Second Century," in *The Galilee in Late Antiquity,* ed. L. Levine (New York, 1992), 157–173; and S. Byrskog, *Jesus the Only Teacher,* 89–98.

71. See Levine, *The Rabbinic Class,* 59–69.

72. I elaborate on this point in an essay entitled "A Rabbinic Ontology of the

Written and Spoken Word: On Discipleship, Transformative Knowledge, and the Living Texts of Oral Torah," to appear in the *Journal of the American Academy of Religion*. Compare S. Byrskog, *Jesus the Only Teacher*, 96–98.

73. See, for example, R. Valantasis, *Spiritual Guides of the Third Century*, 35–61 and 147–155 and L.C.A. Alexander, "The Living Voice: Scepticism Towards the Written Word in Early Christian and in Graeco-Roman Texts," in *The Bible in Three Dimensions: Essays in Celebration of Forty Years of Biblical Studies in the University of Sheffield*, ed. D.J.A. Clines, S.E. Fowl, S.E. Porter (Sheffield, 1990), 221–247.

74. Studies of this passage from the perspective of its ideological message include: Bickerman, "La chaine de la tradition," 128–137; M.D. Herr, "ha-Retsef sheba-Shalshelet Mesiratah shel ha-Torah," *Sinai* 44 (1979), 14–56; J. Neusner, *Torah: From Scroll to Symbol in Formative Judaism* (Philadelphia, 1985), 31–56; M. Jaffee, "Oral Torah in Theory and Practice: Aspects of Mishnah-Exegesis in the Palestian Talmud," *Religion* 15 (1985), 387–394, S. Fraade, *From Tradition to Commentary: Torah and Its Interpretation in the Midrash Sifre to Deuteronomy* (Albany, 1991), 70–71, A. Wasserstein, "Greek Language and Philosophy," 225–226. See also nn. 41 and 75.

75. J. Neusner, "Oral Torah and Oral Tradition," and A.I. Baumgarten, "The Pharisaic *Paradosis*," *Harvard Theological Review* 80 (1987), 63–77 have made complementary arguments that the earliest pharisaic antecedents of Avot's concept of the transmission of tradition had no particular investment in proposing the oral nature of the *masoret/paradosis*. At issue, rather, was its reliability as an authoritative transmission of ancient teachings "from the fathers" over against the public priestly traditions in particular. The opposite position, arguing for the privileging of orality in early pharisaic circles, is best represented by J.M. Baumgarten, "The Unwritten Law in the Pre-Rabbinic Period," *Journal for the Study of Judaism in the Persian and Hellenistic Period* 3 (1972), 7–29. See n. 74 for further bibliography.

76. The earliest references to a formal terminological distinction between Torah in written form and Torah in oral form (*shtei torot . . . 'aḥat befeh ve'aḥat bikhtav*) occur in the tannaitic midrashic compilations, Sifre Deuteronomy, no. 351 (ed. Finkelstein, p. 408) and Sifra, Beḥuqotai 8:12. Other passages in Sifra, Sifre and Mekhilta d'Rabbi Ishmael link Scriptural terms for law, e.g., *miṣvot, mišpatim, ḥuqim*, etc., to various aspects of the rabbinic academic curriculum. I discuss these latter in Jaffee, "Halakhah in Early Rabbinic Judaism," 129–132. On the dating of Sifra, Sifre Deuteronomy and Mekhilta, see n. 12 above.

For a discussion of the impact of the distinction between written and oral tradition upon the conceptualization of tradition in later Talmudic and Hekhalot literatures, see Swartz, *Scholastic Magic,* 175–186.

77. For discussion of how the representation of the orality of tradition enhances the figure of the Sage and the value of discipleship, see S. Fraade, *From Tradition to Commentary,* 13–23, 69–121.

78. I discuss the innovative nature of the Sage's halakhic ruling in the context of received tradition in Jaffee, "Halakhah in Early Rabbinic Judaism," 113–125.

79. Service to the Sage, which provided the opportunity to observe first-hand his embodiment of Torah, is portrayed in tannaitic texts as a sine qua non for the preservation of tradition in its pristine form. Lapses in service, correspondingly, are portrayed as the cause of dispute and social fragmentation.

The classic source is tHag 2.9/Sot 9.9: "With the increase of disciples of Hillel and Shammai who served insufficiently (*sl' smsw kl srkn*), disputes increased in Israel, and two Torahs resulted" (Lieberman, Tosefta: Mo'ed, p. 384).

The versions transmitted in ySan 1.4, 19c and yHag 1.2, 77d differ from each other, and from T., in minor ways, but each shares a common amplification of the Toseftan version: "who served their masters (*rbyhn*) insufficiently." Thus the Yerushalmi's appropriation of the tannaitic passage renders explicit what is already implicit in its source—the primacy of the master.

For textual discussion see Lieberman, *Tosefta Ki-fshuta*: Part V, pp. 1298–1299. Broader discussion of the role of emulation and personal service to the Sage in the shaping of rabbinic disciples may be found in Averbach, *Ha-Ḥinukh ha-Yehudi,* 94–99, and Jaffee, "A Rabbinic Ontology."

TWO

Between Byzantium and Islam: The Transmission of a Jewish Book in the Byzantine and Early Islamic Periods

PAUL MANDEL

I

We are standing in front of a good library of Jewish texts from the rabbinic period, which include the Mishnah, the Tosefta, the Palestinian and Babylonian Talmuds, and the many midrashim. How did these works come to us in the form in which they appear on this shelf? Of course, the various printed editions go back to the earliest printings from the turn of the sixteenth century, which were themselves based on manuscripts. The manuscripts, in turn, were copied one from another. It is a rather straightforward procedure to follow the works back in time, and the classic tenets of text criticism—palaeographic and codicological analyses of the manuscript evidence, as well as consideration and analysis of the large amount of textual *testimonia* accessible through citations in medieval rabbinic literature—aid in establishing lines of descent of the works. During this period, the many rabbinic works were transmitted in writing—not by the *scriptoria* so much in use by non-Jewish circles, but by individual scribes writing for their own and others' benefit.

The written transmission of the works comprising the rabbinic corpus is attested by the relative stability of these texts in our extant manuscript traditions, as well as by the close agreement in the citations of these works by the medieval authors. It is clear, even in cases where these authors' texts do not conform with that of the manuscripts, that their citations are based on written records, which were paraphrased, conflated or otherwise manipulated.

However, in our travel back in time, we hit a virtual wall at around the ninth century, at the time of the earliest fragments known to us. Apart from quotations of the Babylonian Talmud in responsa and legal compendia produced by the Babylonian scholars of the geonic period from the eighth century on, there is an almost complete dearth of direct witnesses—either manuscript or testimonial—for the ancient rabbinic works. It has been suggested that this absence is related to the relatively late appearance of the codex form, adopted by Jews perhaps only after the Arabic conquest, or as late as the eighth or ninth century.[1] Be that as it may, we have virtually no knowledge of the transmission of ancient texts during this period, at least from direct sources.

At this point, it must be emphasized that, regarding most of these works, their origins betray an *oral mode of transmission of linguistically fixed units of discourse.* This is evident, first and foremost, by the textual context of the individual elements of these works, which are largely made up of a collection of independently attributed sayings, introduced by phrases such as "Rabbi X says," "Rabbi X says in the name of Rabbi Y," "It is told," "It is taught." It is borne out by the literary nature of the elements themselves, which are most often written in language of a highly terse, cadenced character. And it is reflected in the modes of composition of the works: Editing of materials within chapters of the Mishnah or sections of a midrash is often carried out along lines of linguistic association, a device which aids memorization of large blocks of text.[2]

Indeed, in a now classic paper, Saul Lieberman delineated the original oral nature of the publication and early transmission of the Mishnah, the first edited work of the rabbinic corpus.[3] While it is true that students and teachers of the mishnaic period possessed private written records of the sayings and *dicta* of the earlier Sages, what Lieberman clarified was the *oral nature* of the publication of the mishnaic work as whole. Never during the subsequent periods was a written record of the Mishnah consulted; rather, it was the job of the *Tannaim*—the official reciters of the study circles and academics—to memorize the chapters and tractates of the Mishnah and other tannaitic collections, and "play back" relevant passages during the legal discussions.[4]

This norm of oral transmission did not cease with the completion of the Mishnah in the third century. The often long strings of names of tradents which precede most sayings from the subsequent amoraic period—R. So-and-so said in the name of Rabbi So-and-so, etc.—show that oral transmission of short, easily memorizable sayings continued to be the norm. Even when, during subsequent periods, these sayings were attached together, and molded into longer legal discussions, their early oral nature seems to be preserved. Thus, during this period we see the beginning of the existence, in the legal literature of the Talmuds, of *sugyot,* self-enclosed units of legal discussion, usually centered around a collection of early sayings, comparing them with other material and raising relevant questions and answers. These *sugyot* are the basic building blocks of the talmudic discussions of the Mishnah, and may be seen as a method for organizing orally transmitted material in a cogent way, easily memorized and accessible.

Another important indication of the more fluid mode of transmission usually associated with orality is the existence of numerous parallel passages in the rabbinic corpus: entire units of sayings are found to exist, with considerable variation, in widely different texts. While some variants are clearly the result of a conscious re-editing of earlier material, many variants seem inconsequential, and reflect an unconscious variation typical of an oral retelling of a previously memorized text. The extent of variation between two parallel texts is often a function of the relative distance of time and place of the two works in which each is imbedded. Thus, while parallel *sugyot* are cited practically verbatim within a work such as the Palestinian Talmud, they vary slightly more among works belonging to the same cultural milieu, such as the Palestinian Talmud and the later, Palestinian-redacted midrashim. When a Palestinian *sugya* is found paralleled, however, in the Babylonian

Talmud, one finds that there often exist points of contact and even similar stages of discussion, but not, in general, an exact parallel of words, and often significant changes of names, sayings and events occur. These variations are just the type to be expected as the legal traditions are transmitted over time and space, to new cultural and scholarly milieus.[5]

Such processes apply as well to the nonlegal, or *aggadic,* traditions of rabbinic material. Many stories, parables and scriptural comments are repeated in the numerous midrashic and aggadic works, redacted in the postmishnaic period, and these parallel passages often vary in details large and small. Among the parallel historical tales, variations in plot, in structure and even in the historical backgrounds of the story abound. And here, too, variations multiply and expand as the transmitted material spans greater measures of time and space.[6]

Now this fluidity of form, betraying a freer, presumably oral mode of transmission, seems to contradict the existence of fixed written texts — texts whose language, orthography and structure imply an ancient written exemplar which underlies our known texts. The contradiction is resolved, however, by acknowledging a major characteristic of Jewish study in the premedieval period. Even if and when written exemplars of a text were available,[7] it is not the text existent as a separate "work" which is recognized and cited in the ancient academy or study session, but the individual element — be it *baraita,* rabbinic comment, parable or anecdote — which is the subject of study and discussion, in a predominantly *oral* setting. Thus, nowhere in any work of the classic rabbinic corpus is any rabbinic citation preceded by an indication of the source of the text; rather, passages are introduced by such phrases as "it is taught," "Rabbi X said," "they said," etc. The tannaitic material (i.e. from the first two centuries CE), which enjoyed hightened authority and achieved semi-canonical status, is distinguished by special forms of introduction (*tanni, tanya, matni,* all derived from the Aramaic verb *t-n-y,* meaning 'to recite').

However, it is evident that the extant written documents representing the works of the rabbinic corpus derive at some time from early *written* records. Thus, these works span the "great divide" of Jewish book transmission. On the one side of this divide, during the talmudic period and shortly thereafter (roughly, until the fourth–fifth centuries CE), as evidenced from the form and content of the various works, exist traditions of short, easily memorized sayings, transmitted separately and in larger contexts, retained and passed on by the students and teachers of the period. On the other, from the early ninth century, exists a full library of written works, transmitted from then on almost exclusively in written form by scribes and scholars. What happened in the intervening period? When did the presumed orality of the former period stop, and to what extent did it leave its imprint on the subsequent periods of creativity? A partial answer to these questions — as they relate to one work of the rabbinic corpus — will be discussed in the following pages.

II

The work which we shall investigate is the midrash to Lamentations (also named Lamentations Rabbati = LR; in Hebrew: Ekha Rabbati), assumed to have been redacted in Palestine after the compilation of the Palestinian Talmud, roughly around the fifth century CE. Like the other classical midrashim,[8] LR reflects in its language the Palestinian dialect of Aramaic (as opposed to the eastern, Babylonian dialect), and it bears strong affinities to other Palestinian works, and less to parallels in the Babylonian Talmud. Since the publication of the *editio princeps* of this midrash, along with the midrashim to the other "scrolls" (Song of Songs, Ruth, Qohelet and Esther), around 1514, the work had been known in essentially one version.[9] In 1899, Solomon Buber edited a new version of the midrash, which reproduced the text found in a manuscript of the Casanata library in Rome.[10] As Buber took pains to point out, the text of the midrash in this manuscript, although undoubtedly reflecting the same work, differs considerably from that of the printed editions. In copious notes to the text, as well as in his detailed introduction, Buber directed attention to the fact that many medieval authors and commentators seem to consistently cite this manuscript version of the midrash, in places where the text differs from that of the printed editions. Upon perusal of the list of citations and *testimonia,* Alexander Marx (in a short review of Buber's edition) discovered a most significant fact. The scholars who cited the text according to Buber's Casanatense manuscript were from France, Germany and Italy, while the Spanish scholars cited generally the version represented by the printed edition. Thus

Marx concluded that the two versions may be seen to represent a Franco-German, or Ashkenazic, recension, and a Spanish recension.[11]

In a detailed study of all known manuscripts and *testimonia* to this midrash, I have been able to show that, indeed, all known textual witnesses to our midrash can be collated either with Buber's manuscript or with the *editio princeps*. That indicates that indeed, Lamentations Rabbati existed—from some indeterminate time on—in (only) two distinct text-types, or recensions, reflected by the two published representatives of the midrash. Moreover, Marx's suggestion that these two text-types were known in separate geographic areas is borne out by the numerous medieval citations of the midrash, as well as by the provenance of the manuscripts themselves. Specifically, the manuscripts and *testimonia* which conform to Buber's text have their origins in Italy, France, Provence or Germany, while all Spanish texts and *testimonia*—including also fragments from the Cairo Geniza, as well as a text transmitted in Yemen—present the text as found in the *editio princeps*.[12]

A further analysis of the texts, including a paleographic analysis of the early Geniza fragments (which go back to the beginning of the tenth century), shows that the division into two recensions could not have originated in medieval Europe, and that, in fact, both texts were already known in the East prior to the tenth century. It seems plausible to suggest that the Spanish-North African recension originated in Babylonia, and is connected to the Jewish cultural center there, whose sphere of influence spread especially throughout the lands under the Islamic empire, whereas the Ashkenazic-European recension has its origins in a Byzantine milieu. Indeed, the roots of much of Ashkenazic literature and culture can be traced, through Italy of the ninth–tenth centuries, to Byzantium, and, ultimately, to origins in the Palestinian Jewish culture of the Byzantine period.[13]

The variants between the two textual traditions are many, and are of different types: changes in wording, in language (a passage appearing in Hebrew in one recension may be presented in Aramaic in the other), and in the order of the sayings. The nature of the variants precludes the supposition that one text is original and the other a later copy of it. In fact, the wide divergence has led one scholar to claim that "the differences between the versions are extensive and no-one would claim they are the same work. . . .

They are simply two separate entities known as Ekha Rabba, which had a complex joint history up to a certain point, though unfortunately this joint history cannot be reconstructed by philological techniques."[14]

This textual situation is, in effect, a conundrum. The relationship between individual elements in each manuscript tradition seems to be the same as that which is attested between separate works of the rabbinic corpus, and would thus reflect the more fluid, oral transmission typical of the early period. A reasonable assumption holds that "anyone who *copies* a written text would not switch terms, changes details and their order, or stylize the text anew."[15] If so, then these apparently unconscious variants—attested now in separate textual traditions of one work—could be seen to be the result of different, creative, and fluid oral performances of the stories and sayings.[16] One scholar of aggadic texts has in fact suggested that "variants between manuscripts of one work [may] reflect . . . variant active "performances" of the text," and that these may be seen to hark back to the prior, but on-going, tradition of oral transmission of these individual passages.[17] A more extreme position questions the very existence of a separate redactional entity referred to by the name "book" in such instances: "The variations [between the manuscripts of a given midrashic work] are sometimes so great that the redactional identity of the work is debatable. Is it meaningful to speak of one work at all, or rather of various recensions of a work? But then . . . are [these] different versions of one and the same text . . . or are they autonomous to a certain extent, and is [the work] merely an ideal or fictitious entity?"[18] This approach leads to the conclusion that what we call the "works" of rabbinic literature "are artificial products which at best mirror the historical reality of the last redactor, and at worst, the historical reality of the modern, "critical" editor."[19]

Nonetheless, a comparison between the two manuscript traditions of LR demonstrates that they constitute exactly the same work. Almost all passages found in one recension are found in the other, in *similar* language, and in *approximately* the same order, but with no discernible reason for the variations. The forests are identical, but the trees differ by varying amounts. What model of transmission can explain such a division, which, it would seem, occurred during that very gap of textual transmission described above?

In what follows, we shall examine a number of passages from LR, paying close attention to the divergence between the two recensions of the text. Since we shall be concerned with the question of the authenticity of parallel versions of a passage, I will preface our study with one example (out of many) where both recensions of LR present a unified version of an anecdote which appears in a slightly different form in an earlier work. Having seen an example of the relationship between two works, we shall then proceed to investigate examples where the texts of the two recensions of LR differ from each other. Through an analysis of these differences, I believe it is possible to learn something about the way this work was transmitted during the formative period from its initial redaction until the beginning of the "manuscript era."

III

A. The following anecdote appears in a collection of "dream" stories in the Palestinian Talmud (= PT), Tractate *Ma'aser Sheni* 4.9 (Venice edition, p. 55b):[20]

> A man came before R. Yose b. Halafta.
> [The man] said: "I saw in my dream [that I] was wearing an olive-wreath."
> [Rabbi Yose] said: "[This means:] that you will be elevated."
> After a time, another [man] came.
> He said: "I saw in my dream [that I] was wearing an olive-wreath."
> [Rabbi Yose] said: "[This means:] that you will be lashed."
> [The man] said: "To that man you said ". . . you will be elevated,"
> and to me you say, ". . . you will be lashed"?!"
> [Rabbi Yose] said: "That one [saw it] in the blossoming [stage]; [but] you [saw it] at the beating [stage]."

The success of this anecdote lies in the tension created by the story-teller between the apparently identical nature of the two dreams, and the very different interpretations given to them by Rabbi Yose. Rabbi Yose's interpretations are dependent, of course, on details of the dreams themselves:

The blossoms of the olive tree – one of the early blossoming fruit trees in the Land of Israel, already visible in March – prophecy the imminent "blossoming" of the dreamer, while the beating of the olive tree – the common method of harvesting the olives at summer's end – mirrors the beating which is in store for the second dreamer. However, until the last line the descriptions of the two dreams are undifferentiated, and we know only that the second dreamer came "after a time," telling the same dream. Rabbi Yose's insight involved his recognition of the differences between the two dreams. This may be interpreted in two ways: either Rabbi Yose discovered that the dreams were not identical, perhaps through an "anamnesis" (much like the psychological analysis of dreams in therapy), which the story-teller left unsaid; or Rabbi Yose deduced the difference between the types of olive-trees from the season in which each dream was told. Either way, the story-teller has succeeded, through the classic device of literary restraint, in allowing us, the readers, to identify with the second dreamer's astonished objection.

Still unresolved, however is a more subtle, underlying question: Is the second dreamer's "punishment" of lashes a reflection of his character or deeds? The story-teller indicates that this may be the case, for while we are not told of any connection between the two dreamers, and supposedly Rabbi Yose knows of no such connection, we are surprised to learn that the second dreamer knows about the first dream and its interpretation. This leads to the supposition that the second dreamer is actually a liar. Unlike the first dreamer, who has come with an authentic dream, the second dreamer has come to Rabbi Yose knowing that a dream told about olive-wreaths has led to a very positive interpretation. We may assume that not only does the second dreamer know of the interpretation, but he most likely has witnessed its realization. This is intimated by the words, "after a time," that is the second dreamer has come to tell his dream after enough time has gone by to validate Rabbi Yose's interpretation of the first dream. Rabbi Yose, however, is wise enough to see through the ruse, and cleverly predicts this "dreamer's" downfall, based on the very "dream" which he had hoped to use to his advantage.

The entire collection of dream stories found in PT is recorded also in the beginning of LR, albeit in a slightly different order, with variant readings. Our anecdote appears there as follows:

Another [man] came and said to [Rabbi Yose]:
"I saw in my dream an olive tree at the time of blossoming."
[Rabbi Yose] said to him: "You will see great light."
Another [man] came and said to [Rabbi Yose]:
"I saw it at the time of beating."
[Rabbi Yose] said to him: "You should prepare yourself for lashes."
[The man] said to [Rabbi Yose]: "Rabbi! To him you said thus, and to me—thus?!"
[Rabbi Yose] said to [the man]:
"That one [saw it] at the time of blossoming,
and you—at the time of beating!"

In comparing this version with that of PT, it becomes clear that the pointed aspect of the anecdote has been lost in the retelling. In his desire to make everything clear, this story-teller has provided us immediately with the information necessary to understand Rabbi Yose's interpretations, thus eliminating the literary tension we noted above. He has further ruined the balance created by the first story-teller, by leaving out the seemingly innocuous words, "after a time." This not only deprives us of the possibility of understanding the significance of the second dreamer's retelling, but also reduces Rabbi Yose's dream-interpretative skills.

In this example, the two recensions of LR preserve essentially the same text; it can be assumed that this text reflects that of the original LR. The relationship between this version and that of the Palestinian Talmud is typical of parallels between the two works: the original pointed and polished story in PT becomes flattened through its retelling in LR. The second story-teller, in his (unconscious?) desire to expound and explain, has focused on the story-line, without regard for the nuances of language in the original story.

B. We now turn to a passage in which the two recensions of LR present different but seemingly equally authentic texts. Here, a popular Aramaic proverb is used as illustration of the midrashic interpretation of the verse in Lamentations 3:20, (זכור תזכור ותשיח עלי נפשי), wherein Israel is portrayed as wasting away while God bides his time in punishing the nations of the world for their sins against Israel.[21]

VERSION A	VERSION B
'ad de 'aviah qaten, nafshet deqetina	*'ad deshemina ḥashikh, ḥashikha mait*

While the fat one gets thin, the thin one dies!

The two proverbs, while identical in structure and meaning, employ different idioms: Version A uses the pair *'avi/qatin* for "fat"/"thin," while Version B uses the pair *shamin/ḥashikh*; the verb "to die" is the usual *mit* in version B, and the much rarer *nefaq nafsha* in version A. Clearly, this is not an example of *scribal* emendation, whether conscious or unconscious. Rather, it would seem that the two recensions reflect separate "live performances," or *oral versions*, of the original proverb, which somehow became incorporated in the two recensions of LR. We shall return to this example later on.

C. Further study of the relationship between the two recensions of LR uncovers a series of anomalies in one version, which are missing in the other. The following story appears in the Palestinian Talmud, in the same collection as the story in example A above, and in the early midrash, Genesis Rabbah.[22] The major difference between these versions is the addition in Genesis Rabbah of the middle section:

GENESIS RABBAH	PALESTINIAN TALMUD
A man came to R. Yose ben Halafta. He said, "Someone told me in a dream: 'Go fetch your father's property (*po'ala*) in Cappadocia.'"	A man came to R. Yose ben Halafta. He said, "I dreamed that someone said to me: 'Go to Cappadocia, and you will find your father's property (*madela*).'"
[R. Yose] said to him, "Did your father ever go to Cappadocia?" [The man] said, "No."	[R. Yose] said to him, "Did you father ever go to Cappadocia?" [The man] said, "No."
[R. Yose] said, "Go count twenty beams (*kšwryn*) in the roof of your house, and you will find it."	[R. Yose] said, "Go and count twenty beams (*šryyn*) in your house, and you will find your father's property (*madela*)."

[The man] said, "And if there are not twenty?"
[R. Yose said,] "Count from their beginning to their end and from their end to their beginning—until you find twenty, you will find it."
He went and did so, and found [it].
And from where did R. Yose ben Halafta learn this?
From "*Kappa*"—"*doqaia.*" "*Kappa*"—"*de-qoraia.*"

The essence of this story is the discovery of the symbolic meaning of the name of the city, Cappadocia, for the dreamer. Rabbi Yose interprets the name paronomastically, breaking it up into two Greek words: *kappa,* the Greek letter whose numerical value is twenty; and *dokos,* or, in its Aramaicized plural form, *dokaia*—beams of wood, or tie-beams, used primarily to support the roof.[23] And so, he tells the dreamer that the money left to him by his father will be found in the twentieth beam of his house. In the version of the story in Genesis Rabbah, the dreamer suggests that there are not twenty beams in his house, to which Rabbi Yose instructs the dreamer to count forwards and backwards, until he reaches the twentieth beam. The brevity of the story in the Palestinian Talmud emphasizes the anecdotal nature of the tale. The important point here, as in the rest of the "dream" stories in this collection, is the ability of Rabbi Yose to interpret the dream. The tale in Genesis Rabbah, on the other hand, extends the anecdote by including the complication raised by the dreamer. This "literary" character is reflected additionally in the inclusion of the concluding statement which relates that the dreamer did as he was told, and indeed found the treasure.

In the parallel version of the story in LR, the two recensions seem to preserve these two separate versions of the story: Version B presents the shortened variant (akin to the version of the Palestinian Talmud), while Version A includes the middle section, as in Genesis Rabbah:

VERSION A	VERSION B
A man came to R. Yose ben Halafta. He said, "I dreamed that they told me, 'Go to Cappadocia, and you will fetch your father's property (*po'ala*).'"	A tale told of a man who went to R. Yose ben Halafta. He said, "I saw in a dream: 'Go to Cappadocia, and you will find your father's property (*po'ala*).'"
[R. Yose] said to him, "Has your father ever gone to Cappadocia?" [The man] said, "No."	R. Yose said to him, "Did your father ever go to Cappadocia?" [The man] said, "No."
[R. Yose] said to him, "Go and count twenty rows (?)[24] in your house." [The man] said to him, "There aren't twenty." [R. Yose] said to him, "Go and count from the top to the bottom and from the bottom to the top, and at the place where you finish counting twenty beams — there you will find it." He went and did so, and found his father's property (*po'ala*), and became rich.	[R. Yose] said to him, "Go and count twenty beams, and you will find your father's property (*po'ala*)."
And from where did R. Yose learn it? "*Kappa*" — "*doqaia*" (*Kappa* in Greek is twenty; *doqaia* in Greek are beams.)	From where did R. Yose ben Halafta learn it? From "*Kappa*" — "*doqaia*."
He did so, and found it.	He went and did so, and found his father's property (*po'ala*).

At first glance, the two versions of LR again seem to reflect two separate traditions of this story, both of which are already represented in the earlier collections. A closer look, however, makes it clear that Version A is an interpolated text, influenced, apparently, by the text of Genesis Rabbah, but not a scribal copy of that text. The interpolated nature of Version A is betrayed by the inclusion in the middle section of the statement describing the denouement of the tale ("He went and did so, and found his father's property") — a statement reappearing at the tale's end. It would seem that the middle section has been "lifted" from the Genesis Rabbah version of the tale. However, a comparison of the language of Version A with that of Genesis Rabbah shows that parts of the former have been freely recast into a dialect of Aramaic which is not that of the Palestinian midrashim and the Palestinian Talmud, but rather reflects Babylonian Aramaic influences.[25]

Neither can Version B be seen as a simple copy from the text of the Palestinian Talmud. What distinguishes the PT version from that of Genesis Rabbah is not only the addition of the possibility that there are less than twenty beams in the roof, but also the use of the Aramaic term for "possessions." While the PT version uses the word *madela,* Genesis Rabbah uses the term *po'ala*. Both versions of LR, however, use the term *po'ala*; thus, a simple copy from PT in Version B is ruled out.

Most importantly, however, is the fact that Version A reveals a mistaken understanding of the anecdote. In Palestine, beams — that is, long wooden beams — were found primarily in the construction of the roof, the walls being made of stone. Thus, the "beams," referred to in the story can only be those making up the construction of the roof of the house, as is explicitly mentioned in the Genesis Rabbah version. Therefore, the dreamer is told to continue counting from beginning to end and back again to the beginning (that is, where he started counting). But the storyteller in Version A of LR specifies that the counting should be done from "top" to "bottom", and from "bottom" to "top"! The redactor of this version apparently misunderstood the word *shraiin* "beams" as *shurayya* "rows" (of bricks?!). Such architecture was common in Mesopotamian houses, but not in Palestinian ones.[26]

Thus, the two recensions of LR do not reflect at this point two equally authentic traditions of the tale. It may be assumed that Version B is the authentic version of LR, and displays the usual variant readings from the earlier Palestinian Talmudic texts indicating a free (oral?) transmission of the tale. Version A, on the other hand, seems to graft a reading of the tale as found in Genesis Rabbah onto the original text of LR, although in language which betrays Eastern Aramaic influences.

D. In the following passage, we compare a midrashic comment in Version B of LR (in a comment to Lamentations 1:2) to a similar midrashic exegesis in Genesis Rabbah, both utilizing the same verse from Isaiah (33: 7):

GENESIS RABBAH 56.5[27]

"And he bound Isaac his son" (Genesis 22: 9) –

Now when our father Abraham stretched out his hand to take the knife to slaughter his son, the ministering angels wept. As it states: "The [angels] shouted *ḥutsa,* the angels of peace wept bitterly" (Isaiah 33: 7) What is *ḥutsa*? Rabbi Azariah said: "*ḥitsa*" – He is determined to slaughter his son!

In the biblical passage, Abraham's actions in binding his son in preparation for his slaughter are followed immediately by God's intervention, through an angel from heaven (Genesis 22: 9–11). The midrash here focuses on the actions of the host of angels at that moment before the slaughter, quoting the verse from Isaiah. Rabbi Azariah reads the word "*ḥutsa*" from that verse according to its *written* consonantal form in the Masoretic Text: *ḥet–tsade–heh*: When pronounced with a short vowel (*ḥitsa*), we have the Palestinian Aramaic word meaning "urgent, determined." Thus, the angels cry out – perhaps to God himself, urging him to take action soon, lest it be too late – "Abraham is determined – *now* – to slaughter his son!"

In LR, Rabbi Azariah's comment on this very same verse from Isaiah is cited in the context of a midrashic comment to Lamentations 1:2 – *bakho tivkeh balaila* – where the doubling of the verb "to cry" is seen to indicate that not only is Zion crying over her destruction but this cry contagiously causes the angels themselves to cry along with her. In their cry, the angels express their despair over God's *determination* to destroy the Temple (in keeping with the context of the verse in Isaiah):

LAMENTATIONS RABBATI, VERSION B

"She greatly weeps at night" (Lam 1: 2) –
She [Zion] weeps, and makes the ministering angels weep with her.
As it states: "The [angels] shouted *ḥutsa,* the angels of peace wept bitterly."
What is *ḥutsa*? Rabbi Azariah said: *He is determined* to destroy the [Temple]!

One may assume that the original exegesis was re-applied in creative fashion here by the re-teller of this midrash.

Version A of LR, as Version B, includes the exegesis on the verse from Isaiah; although in the name of "R. Zeira" (!). However, the content of the exegesis does not fit the context of LR, but rather that of Genesis Rabbah:

LAMENTATIONS RABBATI, VERSION A

"She greatly weeps at night" (Lam 1: 2) –
She [Zion] weeps, and makes the ministering angels weep with her.
As it states: "The [angels] shouted *ḥutsa,* the angels of peace wept bitterly."
Rabbi Zeira said: It is written "*ḥitsa*"; he is determined to sacrifice him!

The exegesis of Genesis Rabba has again been grafted in Version A onto the text of LR, but in this case completely supplanting the exegesis indigenous to LR!

E. Our final example involves a tannaitic text cited in LR, appearing also in the Tosefta, Berakhot 4.8. We shall first look at the text in its context in Tosefta, which discusses the proper protocol at a formal banquet.

TOSEFTA BERAKHOT 4.8

What is the order of the banquet?

The guests enter [the ante-room] and sit on benches and chairs, until all have entered.

[When] they give them [water for] their hands, each one washes one hand.
[When] they pour the cup [of wine] for them, each one recites the blessing by himself.
When they bring before them *parparaot,* each one recites the blessing by himself.

[After the guests have] gone up [to the dining room], they recline [to dine].
[When] they give [water for] their hands, even though he has washed one hand [he now] washes both hands. [When] they pour the cup [of wine] for them, even though he recited the blessing over the first [cup of wine], he recites the blessing over the second [cup of wine].
[When] they bring before them *parparaot,* even though he recited the blessing over the first [*parparet*], he recites the blessing over the second [*parperet*];
and one recites the blessing for all.

One who comes after three *parparaot* has no permission to enter.
Rabbam Shimeon ben Gamaliel said:
"This was a great custom in Jerusalem:
[They] draped (*porsin*) a napkin (*mitpaḥat*) over the door.
As long as the napkin is draped, guests [may] enter.
When the napkin is removed (*nistalqa*), the guests have no permission to enter."

The statement of Rabban Shimeon ben Gamaliel is to be understood in the context of the preceding passage, and is related to the final sentence of that passage, which forbids entry to guests coming to a banquet-hall after three *parparaot*[28] have been served. Rabban Shimeon ben Gamaliel notes that the customs of (the aristocratic society of) Jerusalem prevented such a situation from ever occurring: The guests were duly warned that the banquet had begun by the absence of the napkin draping the door. The laconic quality of the Tosefta text, which does not specify what door is being discussed and who the guests are, is a result of the appearance of Rabban Shimeon's statement as an appendix to the preceding passage.

This *baraita* is cited in LR as one of several examples of the "precious" nature of Jerusalem society at the end of the Second Temple period (appended to an understanding of Lamentations 4:2—"*benei Tsiyon hayeqarim*"):

VERSION A	VERSION B
Rabbam Shimeon ben Gamaliel said: "This was a great custom in Jerusalem:	Rabban Shimeon ben Gamaliel has taught: "There was a great custom in Jerusalem:
	When one of them would enter a banquet
[They] draped (*porśin*) a napkin (*mitpaḥat*) over the door.	**the host would** hang (*toleh*) a napkin (*mappa*) on **his** door.
As long as the napkin is draped, guests [may] enter.	As long as the napkin was draped, the guests would enter **his house.**
When the napkin is removed (*nistalqa*), the guests have no permission to enter **except until three parparaot.**"	When he withdrew (*he'evir*) the napkin, there was no permission **to any of them** to enter."

The citation of this *baraita* in LR, *without* the preceding context, requires the introduction of explanatory material. This is duly given in Version B, which explicitly mentions the banquet, the host, the host's house and door, and the guests (note passages in bold typeface in Version B)—all missing from the toseftan version. This is an additional example of the natural changes due to (oral?) transmission of early textual materials, exemplified also by variant terms for the napkin (*mappa* as opposed to the toseftan *mitpaḥat*;[29] attested also in the parallel in the Babylonian Talmud, Bava Batra 93b), and for the verbs describing its hanging (*toleh* as opposed to *porsin*) and its withdrawal (*he'evir* as opposed to *nistalqa*).

The version of A, however, mirrors *exactly* the text of the *baraita* in the Tosefta, without including the necessary referands which make the context clear. The identity of language of a toseftan *baraita* quoted in a later source is highly suspect. The spurious nature of Version A is further indicated by the addition of the last line: "[When] the napkin is removed, the guests have no permission to enter *except until three parparaot.*"[30] The mention of the *parparaot* makes no sense in its context here: The removal of the napkin from the door was undoubtedly an unambiguous sign that further guests were not allowed in; why, then, would the serving of the *parparaot* make a difference? Indeed, it would seem that this custom was instituted in Jerusalem as a preventive measure (to avoid embarassment), and supplants the formerly mentioned protocol related to the serving of the *parparaot*.

This line in Version A is undoubtedly a mistaken textual "slip," influenced by the line immediately preceding Rabban Shimeon ben Gamaliel's statement as cited in the toseftan context. The author of this passage in Version A was thus intimately aware of the toseftan text (that is, the *baraita* as cited in its context in the Tosefta), and has grafted the last line of the protocol mentioned there onto the end of Rabban Shimeon ben Gamaliel's statement, either through an unconscious mental slip due to the similarity of language, or as a conscious attempt at harmonizing the two texts, disregarding the incongruity which thus ensues.[31]

IV

We may summarize as follows: While it would seem at first that LR appears in two equally fine recensions, presenting parallel material which might be considered to originate in early, oral presentations of these passages, on closer view it becomes apparent that Version A is actually a strange, hybrid text. This recension has evidence of literary interpolations, of contamination from parallels or near-parallels from other texts, of affinities to dialects of Eastern Aramaic (Syriac and Babylonian Aramaic), and of a number of misconceptions and misreadings.

How could such a recension come about? While the variants of Version A certainly do not reflect a "natural" oral transmission of these passages, such as is evident in the relationship between the text of Version B of LR and earlier redacted texts, it is also evident from the many, wide-ranging variants that they are not the result of scribal mistakes in copying, nor can they be easily explained as a fully conscious, written re-edition of the original version of LR. The numerous small changes in wording and in style are not indicative of the type of variants which are introduced as a result of a written contamination of the textual tradition, such as is often found in written transmissions through the mistaken inclusion of marginal notes into the text, or through a conscious conflation of two readings. Such textual emendations do show up in the textual tradition of LR, but only within each recension, and they are clearly the work of medieval scribes. Note that even when Version A is seen to "copy" a text found in an earlier work (as in example C above), the text may undergo a free transformation of language or structure, untypical of scribal interpolation.

A solution to this problem is as follows: Lamentations Rabbati is indeed one text, and was edited, in Palestine, in one linguistic form. I assume that sometime after the completion of the text—whether still in oral form or already in written form—this text was brought, along with other Palestinian texts, to scholars at the academies in Babylonia. As mentioned, in these academies there were official "reciters," the *Tannaim,* whose job it was to recite entire works from memory. We have incontrovertible evidence that these *Tannaim* could recite entire portions of the Mishnah by heart, and that the Tosefta was also committed by them to memory.[32] Similarly, it is now recognized that the Babylonian Talmud was learned, transmitted and recited in the academies primarily by heart.[33] This is not to say that there were no written records; there undoubtedly were. But their status as records of the text had nowhere near the status of authority that we invest in written records today. On the contrary, the scholars in the academy put greater trust, on the whole, in the official reciters of the material than in written records, as is evident from numerous passages by the Geonim in their responsa.

My suggestion is that, in addition to these texts—Mishnah, Tosefta, and Talmud—which were undoubtedly part of the curriculum of the yeshiva, there also existed *Tannaim* of the other texts of the Rabbis: the midrashim and aggadot, even those long books which seem to us today to be nearly impossible to memorize. These *Tannaim* might or might not have been part of the academy. But they committed these texts to memory in similar fashion to the other texts which were studied regularly.

However, the very nature of these texts—the many parallel versions, their language which was in a dialect different than the one spoken by the Babylonians themselves—and the fact that these texts were not part of the yeshiva curriculum, meant that it was not so simple and straightforward to keep them in one's memory. Many checks had to be carried out, and other Tannaim of this literature had to be sought out for possible corrections. It therefore happened often that a text was "corrected" in accordance with a parallel passage in another midrash, or in the Palestinian Talmud, or in a Tosefta text, or even in accord with the Babylonian Talmud's parallel passage. So too, sometimes "Babylonianisms" would creep in, "supercorrections" would be made, which would reveal the spoken language of the reciter. And so certain harmonizing tendencies would appear, where phrases original in one place would be grafted, unconsciously, onto other, similarly worded passages.

This hypothesis can account for certain variants between Versions A and B which are difficult to explain otherwise. I will mention a few:

It is very common to find several similar stories, parables or sayings grouped together as a commentary or expansion of a verse in LR, as in other midrashim. In such groupings, Version A will often differ from version B in the order of the sayings or stories. Such variations in order are a hallmark of oral transmission of collections of passages.

There are several passages in LR where two proverbs are mentioned; one prefaced by the words רבנין דתמן אמרין "the Rabbis of there [i.e. the Babylonians] say"; and the other by the words רבנין דהכא אמרין "the Rabbis of here [i.e. the Palestinians] say."[34] But in Version A the order is reversed! There would seem to be no reason why such a reversal would take place consistently, as it does in our texts, if we were to assume a simple written transmission. But if a reciter of this obviously Palestinian text is living and reciting the text in Babylonia, he would, upon hearing "there," i.e. Babylonia, correct the reading to "here" (and vice versa), because he is reciting to a particular audience, and he conditions his recital to that audience.

Additional evidence is found in the orthography of both recensions. Version B preserves, in its better manuscripts, a very fine original Palestinian orthography of Hebrew and Aramaic, as well as some original linguistic forms; these are missing from even the best manuscripts of Version A. It would seem that, at least in its better witnesses, Version B is one link in a chain of a written transmission of the text, starting perhaps from Palestine of the fifth century, while Version A was copied in a milieu which had not preserved the exact Palestinian orthography.

Related to this is the tendency of Version A to write Greek words, which are frequent in LR, in a singularly unusual way. As an example, the name of the Roman emperor, Trajan, in its Greek form — Traianus — appears in Version B, as it does in the Palestinian Talmud and other Palestinian texts, with an intervocalic *gimmel* (טרגיינוס), reflecting the Byzantine pronunciation *Tragianus*. In Version A — and only in Version A of LR — this *gimmel* becomes consistently a *kaf* (טרכיאנוס).[35] The change from *gimmel* to *kaf* cannot be due to graphic considerations; it is explained rather by a common phonetic shift of the soft *g* of *Tragianus* to a hard *k*.

The above-mentioned affinity to and influence of Syriac, as well as Babylonian Aramaic, on Version A is attested in several passages, and readily explains those variants for which no other reason can be found. Such is the explanation for the variants in example B above: While both pairs of synonyms for fat / thin — *'avi/qatin* and *shamin/ḥashikh* — are attested in Western (Palestinian) Aramaic, only the first pair (of Version A) is attested in Syriac. Thus, it is reasonable that a reciter of LR, whose linguistic milieu is dominated by Syriac or another Eastern Aramaic dialect, would, during his recital of the parable, replace — perhaps unconsciously — the unusual forms of *shamin* and *ḥashikh* with terms with which he is familiar.

And finally, proof of the secondary nature of Version A, and an indication of the period of its redaction, is found in a list of the four nations which ruled over the Jews throughout its early history. These are typically given in rabbinic literature as the Babylonians (*Bavel*), the Persians (*Paras*), the Greeks (*Yavan*) and the Romans (known by the biblical name of Esau, *Edom*). In a passage in LR (to verse 1:14; ed. Buber, p. 77), each of these nations is paired with a synonymous name: *Bavel* and *Chasdim*, *Paras* and *Madai*, *Yavan* and *Makedonia*, *Edom* and *Se'ir*. In Version A, the final pair is listed as *Edom* and *Ishma'el*. There is no doubt that the substitution of *Ishma'el* for *Se'ir* reflects the contemporary subjugation to Islam, and is thus a sure indicator that this recension originated during a period subsequent to the Islamic conquest!

Is it plausible to suggest that such large works such as the classical midrashim were indeed committed to memory and recited? While this is exactly what has been posited for the transmission of the Mishnah, the Tosefta, and the Babylonian Talmud,[36] it can be claimed that these works, being the central texts of the halakhic enterprise, naturally were recited in the yeshiva. But why should the aggadic texts be so recited?[37]

The answer to these questions lies in an understanding of a dominant mode of transmission of books in the Islamic East during the early part of the Islamic period, and it is to this matter which we now turn.

V

For many years there has been an ongoing debate about the place of orality in the transmission of early Islamic texts. While it is well-known that early pre-Islamic poetry was recited by the *rawi,* who could memorize many texts, and while it was traditionally claimed that all early texts—especially the Qumran and the *ḥadith,* but also other redacted works—were memorized in Islam, many scholars of Islamic texts pointed out that this picture was at times over-idealized. Scholars have taken sides on this issue, some claiming orality and others emphasizing the written aspects of the text transmission.[38] Many scholars of Islamic literature have pointed out the very fluid nature of these texts, with many widely-diverging variants between texts.[39] However, a solution to the problem of variants in the *ḥadith* compilations, as well as those found in clearly redacted, fixed texts, has been proposed by scholars of this literature. The solution is based on a consideration of the mode of study in Islamic scholarly circles, which took place in a study hall, either in a mosque or in a private home. The *shaikh* would lecture to a group of students in a "learning circle," the *ḥalqat.* The *shaikh*'s lecture would then be memorized by the students, the best of whom would be privileged to recite back to the *shaikh* the memorized text, who would provide corrections, and, finally, issue a permit to the specific student, an *ijaza,* which would authorize that student—and him only—to transmit the lecture-text further. What is fascinating is that this procedure was maintained not only when the content of the lecture was the *ḥadith,* which naturally would be preserved in a fixed, oral fashion, but also in cases when a previously written book was being transmitted. Thus, books were "published" through these semi-public lectures, or "hearings" (*sama'*). To be sure, the *shaikh* may lecture from memory or from a written text, and the students as well may simultaneously make a written record of the text. But the evidence shows that the written text was only used as an *aide-mémoire,* to abet a failing memory, while the major emphasis was on the memorization of the text. In this manner, the text goes through a process of memorization, correction, and rewriting in collective learning sessions, which ultimately changes the fixed nature of the text, and allows for variants, corrections and even super-corrections. The written textual witnesses extant today reflect, in their variants and even in their structure, this process of oral recitation of a fixed text.[40]

These works, once learned and memorized by a student, then became the "possession," as it were, of the new scholar. In such a situation, of course, not everybody could "take possession" and receive an *ijaza* for all works. And so, each scholar had his own specialty, and certain scholars were sought out for recitations of particular works. And, it stands to reason, if several scholars "possessed" the same work, that they could collate such a work among themselves, one scholar correcting his (memorized) text according to the reading of his fellow.[41]

I would like to claim that in this milieu, it was only natural that the Jewish scholars in Islamic societies—and especially those living in or near the Islamic scholarly centers in Baghdad—would preserve and transmit their textual material in similar fashion. With all the precautions necessary in drawing analogies, and without wishing to make any claim concerning origin or direct influence of such methods, it would seem to be as natural to a Jewish scholar living in Babylonia to memorize fixed texts and transmit them orally as it is natural for us to copy and transmit texts today on computers and other electronic media. In each case our scholarly customs simply reflect those of the ambient scholarly community, in particular, and, in general, the technological culture of which we are a part.[42]

In Byzantine circles during the fifth to ninth centuries, however, the learning process was very different. Here, the "supreme source of education" was from books.[43] Here, too, as in the Islamic scholarly milieu, we see circles of students surrounding their teacher, and even memorizing texts. But the authority rested with the book, as it had for centuries in the Greco-

Byzantine world. The students invariably had the text in front of them; "the Byzantines wrote text-books for every conceivable study."[44] Many of the numerous studies made of literacy in Byzantium try to correct an overly idealized picture of the availability of books in the Byzantine empire, showing the relative scarcity of the books and literacy during most of the periods among laymen.[45] But we are not interested in laymen here, but in the scholarly circles themselves, and what becomes clear again and again in Byzantine studies is the high place accorded the written text in Byzantine society. One study mentions how the Iconoclastic councils of the eighth century centered around the collection and reading of early Patristic texts:

> We cannot help noticing the extreme bibliographic accuracy that was observed during the proceedings. In each case *the actual codex was produced* before the assembly; the lector usually started with the *incipit* and then went on to read the relevant passage.[46]

In her book *Christianity and the Rhetoric of Empire,* Averil Cameron states, "Christianity early became a religion of books . . . Christians . . . gave their written texts a special status. . . ."[47]

I propose, therefore, that the written transmission of the text in "the West," i.e. Palestine, is quite in keeping with a generally high regard for the codex[48] (or scroll) and its authority; while in Babylonia the tendency among scholarly circles to emphasize memorized knowledge reflects the practice of the surrounding non-Jewish scholars. While direct influence of one culture on the other may not be ruled out, I wish here only to draw attention to parallel lines of scholarly activity taking place in the same locale.

In fact, a careful reading of geonic responsa provides direct evidence of the type of oral transmission of fixed aggadic texts of which I have been speaking. Besides the citation in these responsa of talmudic texts which are clearly marked as being transmitted orally,[49] there is also evidence of the similar recital of nontalmudic texts. One reads of "*mishnayot of aggadot,*" said of works which we know of as written, aggadic volumes, which would seem to refer to orally transmitted works of aggadah, since the verb *sh-n-h* in geonic texts is consistently applied to the oral recitation of texts. This would seem to imply that these works were, indeed, known and recited orally.[50]

VI

We have seen that the two recensions of Lamentations Rabbati cannot have preserved equally authentic textual passages, which somehow echo and reflect early oral presentations. One recension, Version B, originating most probably in Byzantine circles, may be the result of an unbroken chain of written transmission—subject to all the contingencies of scribal activity—from the time when this midrash was first put to writing, presumably not long after (or perhaps concurrent with) its composition in Palestine during the fifth century CE. The other version, while indeed reflecting elements of orality which have changed the text, is the result of a previously fixed text (which may or may not be equivalent to that of Version B) which has re-entered the sphere of oral transmission. The reason for this re-entry would seem to be related to the activity of the scholarly academies and study circles in Babylonia, where the ancient traditions of oral study of fixed texts continued throughout the geonic period. This practice, attested both within and without the Jewish scholarly world, utilized the capacity of human memory to preserve long sections of text. While the primary texts to be memorized were no doubt those in constant use in the academies, such as the Mishnah, the Tosefta, and the (Babylonian) Talmud, it became the norm to engage official reciters (*Tannaim*) to "publish" and propogate other texts as these became known and current in the Babylonian academies, during the seventh to tenth centuries.

In its essence, this procedure differs little from the earlier activity of the Palestinian academies, which—during the second to fifth centuries—were active in studying and propagating their traditional "texts." This may help explain and provide a model for the development of the early tradition-units—of Mishnah, toseftan *baraitot,* and midrashim, which were transmitted and redacted in Palestine during this time—and their subsequent redaction into the literature of the classical rabbinic period. It may be suggested that, as these units became redacted into a lengthy, fixed text, which was recorded and transmitted as a written copy, they also re-entered the study hall, where their presentation continued to evolve through an oral transmission process. This continued until they were again reset, in different constellations, as a new "work," which, in turn, continued the process of written and oral transmissions. In this way, each codification became a "bottle-neck" through which the texts entered and were retransmitted, with the passages constrained and modified by the already existing, codified texts. The different works of the rabbinic corpus thus provide what I might call "snapshots" or "fossils" of the passages as learned in the academies." And while halakhic material demanded a more vigorous preservation of the original language and were thus subject to less variation, aggadic passages may have lent themselves to further artistic and literary development on the part of the new reciters, as we have seen above.[51]

These two cultures of transmission, the oral and the written, existed side by side, and influenced each other, precisely during the period of transition from the earlier culture of oral transmission to the later manuscript culture. As long as the study-circles retained a continuity with the past modes of learning, as they did in Palestine in the early Byzantine period, and in Babylonia until the end of the geonic era, the particular texts recited by them continued to "live" and "evolve." This process continued effectively until the extinction of the older ways of learning and transmission, around the ninth–tenth centuries, but was abandoned even earlier when texts had to be carried from one culture to another, to the newer Jewish centers of the West, in Byzantium, Italy, North Africa and Spain. From then on, manuscript transmission took over, bringing with it a wealth of new procedures and problems.

While this study pertains to a particular case of textual transmission, it can also provide an example and a model for the combined influences of orality and literacy in the general transmission of literary texts during transitionary periods. It emphasizes the importance of the study of modes of learning as they impinge upon and influence the content of that learning, of the study of textual traditions within a wider social and cultural web, and of the mutual influence of scholarly societies living in close proximity.

NOTES

1. S. Reif, "Aspects of Mediaeval Jewish Literacy," in *The Uses of Literacy in Early Mediaeval Europe*, ed. R. McKitterick (Cambridge, 1990), 138 (and n. 9),

146; M. Beit-Arié, *Hebrew Manuscripts of East and West: Towards a Comparative Codicology* (London 1992), 11.

2. B. Gerhardsson, *Memory and Manuscript: Oral Tradition and Written Transmission in Rabbinic Judaism and Early Christianity* (Uppsala, 1961), 93ff., 122ff., 128ff.; D. Zlotnick, *The Iron Pillar—Mishnah* (Jerusalem, 1988); and cf. J. Neusner, *The Memorized Torah: The Mnemonic System of the Mishnah,* (Chico, Calif., 1985), 112f.

3. S. Lieberman, "The Publication of the Mishnah," in *Hellenism in Jewish Palestine* (New York, 1962), 83–99.

4. Ibid; and J.N. Epstein, *Mavo le-Nusaḥ ha-Mishnah,* (Jerusalem, 1963–64), 688–702; Gerhardsson, *Memory and Manuscript,* loc. cit.

5. See Y. Sussman, "Ve-shuv le-Yerushalmi Neziqin," *Meḥqerei Talmud* ed. Y. Sussman and D. Rosenthal (Jerusalem, 1990), 1:106–111 and the notes there; also 90–92, and notes 155–160.

6. See J. Heinemann, *Agadot ve-Toledoteihen* (Jerusalem, 1974).

7. See discussion on "*megilat setarim*" in Lieberman, 87f.; Gerhardsson, 160ff.; and in Epstein. See also below, note 37.

8. I include in this term the early amoraic (aggadic) midrashim, Genesis Rabbah, Leviticus Rabbah and Pesiqta de-Rav Kahana, as well as the bulk of the midrashim included in the so-called Midrash Rabbah to the five scrolls (*megillot*), although some parts of these latter midrashim were included in the works in later times.

9. The edition printed in Constantinople is now recognized to be the *editio princeps,* and not the Pesaro, 1519 version; see M.B. Lerner, "Ha-Defus ha-Rishon shel 'Midrash Ḥamesh Megillot,'" in *Yad le-Heiman, The A.M. Haberman Memorial Volume,* ed. Z. Malachi (Lod, 1983), 289–311.

10. *Midrasch Echah Rabbati,* ed. S. Buber (Vilna, 1899).

11. A. Marx, "Review of Midrasch Echah Rabbati, S. Buber, ed.," *Orientalistische Literaturzeitung* 5, 7 (July 1902), 293–296.

12. P. Mandel, "Midrash Lamentations Rabbati: Prolegomenon, and a Critical Edition to the Third Parasha" (Hebrew), Ph.D. dissertation, Hebrew University, 1997.

13. The connections between Babylonia and the centers in Spain, North Africa and Yemen are well-known; see S. Asaf, *Tekufat ha-Geonim ve-Sifruta* (Jerusalem, 1956), 104f. On the connections between the early Ashkenazic culture in (Southern) Italy and the Byzantine culture, especially that of Palestine, see R. Bonfil, "Bein Erets-Yisrael le-Vein Bavel: Qavim le-Ḥeqer Toledot ha-Tarbut shel ha-

Yehudim be-Italia ha-Deromit uve-Europa ha-Notserit bi-Yemei ha-Beinayim ha-Muqdamim," *Shalem* 5 (1987), 1–30; E. Fleischer, *Shirat ha-Qodesh ha-Ivrit bi-Yemei ha-Beinayim,* (Jerusalem, 1975), 425; and Y. Sussman, "Kitvei-yad u-Mesorot Nusaḥ shel ha-Mishnah," in *Proceedings of the Seventh World Congress of Jewish Studies* (Jerusalem, 1981), 3: 234–236.

14. Ch. Milikowsky, "The *Status Quaestionis* of Research in Rabbinic Literature" *Journal of Jewish Studies* 39 (1988), 203, n. 7.

15. Heinemann, op. cit. (note 6 above), 31.

16. See, however, evidence of a more critical approach to scribal copying of Hebrew texts in the medieval period: M. Beit-Arié, "Transmission of Texts by Scribes and Copyists: Unconscious and Critical Interferences" *Bulletin of the John Rylands University Library of Manchester* 75, 3 (1993), 33–51. (And see as well his paper in the present volume, chapter 6.) It remains to be seen whether this is a relatively isolated phenomenon, or whether a similar tradition of critical editing might be attested in earlier times.

17. A. Shinan, "Sifrut ha-Aggadah: Bein Higud al Peh u-Mesoret Ketuvah" *Jerusalem Studies in Jewish Folklore* 1 (1981), 52ff.

18. P. Schäfer, "Research into Rabbinic Literature: An Attempt to Define the *Status Quaestionis,*" *Journal of Jewish Studies* 37 (1986), 146.

19. Ibid., 151; see Ch. Milikowsky's response, "The *Status Quaestionis* of Research in Rabbinic Literature" (note 14 above).

20. In this and future translations, I have filled out the natural elliptic nature of the original; the inclusions are placed in square brackets.

21. In this example, as in the following examples, the presented text of each version of LR is based on an examination of all textual witnesses to the respective textual families. See my dissertation, cited above, and my "The Story in Midrash Echah: Text and Style" (Hebrew), M.A. thesis, Hebrew University, 1983.

22. Palestinian Talmud, Ma'aser Sheni 4, 9 (Venice edition, folio 55b—text corrected in accordance with MSS); Genesis Rabbah, *parasha* 68, *siman* 12, ed. Theodor-Albeck, pp. 784–785. The story appears in slightly different form in the Babylonian Talmud, Berakhot 56b. See Mandel, "The Story in Midrash Echah," 152–156.

23. It should be noted that the two versions use similar sounding, yet etymologically different words for "beams": In the Palestinian Talmud the word is "*shraiin*" (from the root שרי), while the Genesis Rabbah text uses the loan-word "*keshorin*" (from כשור, related to the Akkadian *gusuru*). Nonetheless, it would seem that the etymological explanation given at the conclusion of the story in the

Palestinian Talmud is corrupt; it interprets the second half of the name as the Aramaic *de-qoraia* = of beams. The meaning, however, is the same.

24. The word used here in this text, "shoraya" (שוריא), can only be read as "rows" (plural determinate form of שורה; see M. Sokoloff, *A Dictionary of Jewish Palestinian Aramaic of the Byzantine Period* [Ramat Gan, 1990], 542, s.v. שורה, and cf. 566, s.v. שרי); see below.

25. The phrase "from the top to the bottom, etc." employs the Babylonian Aramaic terminology מלעילא לתתא ומתתא לעילא. Similarly, the interrogative article מי introduces R. Yose's question: מי סליק ליה לאבוך . . . לקפודקיא; usage is unattested in Palestinian Aramaic, and is a typical Babylonian locution.

26. See S. Krauss, *Talmudische Archaeologie* (Leipzig, 1910), 1: 23–26 (and see there notes 305 [pp. 310f.] and 331f [pp. 316f.]). Compare the reading in Version B: The word attested there, "*shorin*" (שורין), may be read as the plural "rows," or (with the *vav* indicating the mobile *sheva*) as the plural "beams."

27. Ed. Theodor-Albeck, 600.

28. *parperet* (plural: *parpara'ot*) is a side dish served before or during a meal.

29. These words, which are both found frequently in rabbinic sources, denote a piece of cloth or napkin, used for various purposes.

30. This line, attested in all text witnesses to Version A, was corrupted in later versions (including the *editio princeps* and all subsequent printed editions) to "*parsaot*" (Persian miles), and then to "*pesi'ot*" (paces).

31. It may be that this text was known to the reciter of Version A as it appears in the Palestinian Talmud (Berakhot 6.6 [Venice edition, 10d]): ואין רשות לאורח ליכנס אחר שלש פרפראות—which is even closer to that of Version A than the Tosefta text.

32. On the tannaim as official reciters of the Mishnah, see the references in note 4 above. On the role of the tannaim in reciting orally the text of the Tosefta (in geonic Babylonia), see S. Lieberman, *Tosefet Rishonim* (Jerusalem, 1937–1939), 2: introduction, 7, 12; Lieberman, *Tosefta ki-Feshuta* (New York, 1955), 1: introduction, 14; Y. Elman, *Authority and Tradition: Toseftan Baraitot in Talmudic Babylonia* (New York, 1994), 71–74. See Elman concerning the hypothesis that the toseftan baraitot, while possibly committed to writing at an early date, "were transmitted in Babylonian Amoraic circles in primarily oral form" (73); and see pp. 275–281.

33. J.N. Epstein, *Mevo'ot le-Sifrut ha-Amoraim,* ed. E.Z. Melamed (Jerusalem, 1962), 140–141; Y. Brody, "Safrut ha-Geonim veha-Tekst ha-Talmudi," in *Meḥqarei Talmud,* 1. 241–242; E.S. Rosenthal, *Talmud Bavli Massekhet Pesahim:*

MS Sassoon-Lunzer u-Mekomo be-Mesorat Ha-Nusaḥ (London, 1985); E.S. Rosenthal, "Toledot ha-Nusah u-Va'ayot 'Arikha be-Ḥeqer ha-Talmud ha-Bavli," *Tarbiẓ* 57 (1988), 1–36. See also the paper by Elman and Ephrat in the present volume, chapter 3; and see below.

34. See Lamentations Rabbati to Lamentations 1:7, ed. Buber, 71; and to Lam 3:42, ed. Buber, 137; and see his notes there.

35. See Lamentations Rabbati to Lam 1:5 (ed. Buber, 65); 1:16 (pp. 80, 83); 3:5 (p. 124), 3:10 (p. 126); and 4:19 (p. 152), and compare the text of the printed editions. In all these places, the text of Version B (including the Buber MS) reads "*Tragianus*" (טרגינוס, טרגיאנוס, טריגינוס), while Version A reads "*Trachianus*" (טרכינוס). The former is attested in the rest of the Palestinian rabbinic literature (in the Babylonian Talmud the name appears without a medial consonant—"*Traianus*" [טרינוס or טורינוס]); the latter is attested nowhere else! On the intervocalic *gamma,* see: D. Sperber, *Dictionary of Greek and Latin Words in Rabbinic Literature* (Ramat-Gan, 1984), 23, notes 10 and 12; P.S. Costas, *An Outline of the History of the Greek Language* (Chicago, 1936), 61.

36. See above, notes 32 and 33.

37. Indeed, Milikowsky has argued against such a possibility; see "The *Status Quaestionis* etc.," 209. There is evidence for the existence of *sifrei de-aggadeta,* "books of *aggadah*" already in Talmudic times; see L. Zunz-Ch. Albeck, *Ha-Derashot be-Yisrael ve-Hishtalshelutan ha-Historit* (Jerusalem, 1947), 336, nn. 23–24. It is unclear, however, whether these "books" were in any way similar to our *aggadic* midrashim.

38. On the *rawi,* see *Encyclopaedia of Islam,* new edition (Leiden, 1995), 8: 466ff, s.v. "Rawi." See also M. Zwettler, *The Oral Character of Classical Arabic Poetry* (Columbus, 1978); and cf. the critique of G. Schoeler, "Die Anwendung der oral-poetry-Theorie auf die arabische Literatur" *Der Islam* 58 (1981), 205–236. See the discussions of I. Goldziher, *Muslim Studies* II, chapter 7: "The Writing Down of the Hadith," 181–188; G.H.A. Juynboll, "On the Origins of Arabic Prose: Reflections on Authenticity," in *Studies on the First Century of Islamic Society,* ed. G.H.A. Juynboll (Carbondale, Ill., 1982), 161ff.; and G. Schoeler, "Die Frage der schriftlichen oder mündlichen Überlieferung der Wissenschaften im frühen Islam" *Der Islam* 62 (1985), 201ff.

39. See also, on the Arabic "*adab*" literature, S. Leder, "Authorship and Transmission in Unauthored Literature," *Oriens* 31 (1988), 67–81; Leder, "The Literary Use of the *Khabar:* A Basic Form of Historical Writing," in *The Byzantine and Early Islamic Near East, I: Problems in the Literary Source Material,* ed. A. Cameron and L.I. Conrad (Princeton, 1991), 277–316. And see below.

40. J. Pederson, *The Arabic Book* (1949), trans. from Danish by G. French (Princeton, 1984), Chapter 3: "Composition and Transmission of Books," 20–36; G. Makdisi, *The Rise of Colleges* (Edinburgh, 1981), 99ff.; G. Schoeler, "Die Anwendung"; and Schoeler, "Weiteres zur Frage der schriftlichen oder mündlichen Überlieferung der Wissenschaften im Islam," *Der Islam* 66 (1989), 38–67.

41. Pederson, 31–36; Makdisi, 140ff.; and cf. the different view of F. Rosenthal, *The Technique and Approach of Muslim Scholarship* (Rome, 1947), 26–27.

42. See, similarly, S. Gandz, "The Dawn of Literature," *Osiris* 7 (1939), 440–463—although his discussion is flawed on several counts; and G. Schoeler, "Mündliche Thora und Hadit: Überlieferung, Schreiverbot, Redaktion," *Der Islam* 66 (1989), 213–251; Schoeler, "Schreiben und Veröffentlichen: Zu Verwendung und Funktion der Schrift in den ersten islamischen Jahrhunderten," *Der Islam* 69 (1992), 1–43. For a similar solution to the problem of variants in the Babylonian Talmud, see S. Morag, "Le-Inyan Ha'avarato Be-'al Peh Shel ha-Talmud ha-Bavli," in *Meḥqerei Talmud* (Jerusalem, 1993), 2: 346–348; and cf. Milikowsky, 211; and see Reif (note 1 above), 146.

43. G. Buckler, "Byzantine Education," in *Byzantium,* ed. N.H. Baynes and H.L.B. Moss (Oxford, 1948), 212.

44. Ibid.

45. See the papers in the volume *Byzantine Books and Bookmen* (Washington, D.C., 1975).

46. C. Mango, "The Availability of Books in the Byzantine Empire, A.D. 750–850," in *Byzantine Books and Bookmen,* 30f.

47. A. Cameron, *Christianity and the Rhetoric of Empire: The Development of Christian Discourse* (Oxford, 1991), 109.

48. See C.H. Roberts and T.C. Skeat, *The Birth of the Codex* (London, 1987). On the relatively low role of orality in Byzantine culture, see H.G. Beck, "Der Lesekreis der byzantinischen 'Volksliteratur' im Licht der handschriftlichen Überlieferung" in *Byzantine Books and Bookmen,* 49; cf. H. Hunger, *Schreiben und Lesen in Byzanz: Die byzantinische Buchkultur* (Munich, 1989).

49. See Brody and E.S. Rosenthal; and cf. the oft-quoted citation of the tenth-century Gaon, Aaron Ha-Kohen Sargado, who states: ". . . our entire *metiva* (= yeshiva), of which it is known that its [textual] version is from the mouths of the great ones, and most of whom do not know what a book is" (*Otsar ha-Geonim* to Yevamot, par. 170, cited by Brody, 241).

50. See the appellation of the works *Heikhalot Rabbati* and *Heikhalot Zutrati* as *mishnayot she-ha-tannaim shonim 'otan* = "*mishnayot* that the tannaim recite" (*Otsar ha-Geonim,* Ḥagigah, 14); and the "midrash" known as *Pereq Ḥaserot*

ve-Yeterot cited as a *mishna ḥitsonit* = "an external mishnah" (*Otsar ha-Geonim,* Megilah, 48)—both by Rav Hai Gaon of the eleventh century. Cf. *Otsar ha-Geonim,* Ta'anit, no. 7, p. 8. Similarly, the midrash known to us as *Midrash 'Aseret ha-Dibrot* (= sections 21 through 24 of *Pesiqta Rabbati*) is referred to using the same phrase: *ve-anu shonim be-mishnah ḥitsonit* = "and we recite in an external mishnah." J. Miller, *Teshuvot Geonei Mizraḥ u-Ma'arav* (Berlin, 1888), no. 132, p. 30b, and no. 17, p. 42a. The well-known Midrash Rabbah to Ecclesiastes (*Qoheleth*) is referred to in one early medieval manuscript as *midrash Qohelet shelatannaim* = "midrash Qoheleth of the tannaim"—a reference, I believe, to the text of that midrash as written down from the mouths of the tannaim, who recited it by heart!

51. Cf. the similar model posited by Milikowsky, 208–211 (but see remarks by P. Schäfer, "Once Again the *Status Quaestionis* of Research in Rabbinic Literature: An Answer to Chaim Milikowsky," *JJS* 40 [1989], 90ff.); see also Elman, *Authority and Tradition,* 278–281.

THREE

Orality and the Institutionalization of Tradition: The Growth of the Geonic Yeshiva and the Islamic Madrasa

DAPHNA EPHRAT AND YAAKOV ELMAN

Shlomo Dov Goitein rightly characterized the Jewish and Islamic components of a "Mediterranean society," which extended far beyond the Mediterranean littoral, as "book cultures," though important places were reserved for an oral component in both. The purpose of the following analysis, which is the product of a collaboration between an Islamicist and a Judaic scholar, is to determine more exactly the role that orality played within the elite educational institutions which coexisted in tenth-century Baghdad, the geonic yeshiva and the Islamic madrasa.

The close cultural, geographical and temporal proximity of these two institutions, one of which was in decline and the other newly founded, would seem to make a comparative approach potentially fruitful. Indeed, A.S. Tritton suggested that Jewish institutions served as a model for the Muslim, though S.D. Goitein expressed doubt as to their comparability. "The yeshiva was pre-Islamic, and, even during the heyday of Islam, differed completely from its Islamic counterpart, the madrasa (as far as it could be compared with the yeshiva at all)."[1] Despite Goitein's skepticism, however, our hope is that such an approach will yield insights important to an understanding of both institutions, even if it is only to point out their differences and the differences in the two societies which nurtured them.

George Makdisi's characterization of Islam could equally well be applied to rabbinic Judaism, of which geonic Judaism is an early exemplar.

> Islam is, first and foremost, a nomocracy. The highest expression of its genius is to be found in its law; and its law is the source of legitimacy for other expressions of its genius.[2]

Despite this basic similarity, however, Goitein's skepticism was well-founded. The madrasa was in its formative stages, and was, as we shall see, in many respects still a gloried *ḥalqa,* or study-circle. It remained, as we shall see, of marginal influence during the eleventh century. The geonic yeshivot had long since developed well beyond the study-circles of earlier times, and the two major yeshivot played a much more central role in the life of the Jewish community than did any two madrasas, even one the size of the "glorious" Nizamiya. Another contrast relates to textuality. While conservative tendencies on both sides resisted the process of shifting over to purely scribal transmission of legal traditions, at least to some extent, it would seem that the geonic yeshivot were far more successful in this resistance, at least in regard to the primarily Oral Torah, the Talmud.

Thus, though the parallels to be adduced are sometimes quite suggestive, only ancillary use will be made of the comparative method to fill in the gaps which exist on the Jewish side. It is for that reason that we begin with the Jewish side of the question. If in the end we conclude that both geonic Judaism and Islam follow a similar paradigm of institutionalization, our conclusion will be based purely on data available from Jewish sources, and not because of the tempting parallels. The pattern discerned in the Islamic sources have not been used to fill the gaps in the Jewish record. Due regard for divergences will be made. In particular, it should always be borne in mind that the madrasa was supported both politically and economically by the dominant culture, while the yeshiva served a tolerated minority, and had to fend for itself.

Our discussion will center around three poles: (1) the state of legal discussion and its canonization; (2) the place of orality in the transmission of secondary scripture and in the transmission and development of legal discussion; and (3) the nature of the institutions in which oral/written legal discussion had its place. Before we begin, we should emphasize that orality in this context refers to oral transmission and not merely an emphasis on memorization. Both cultures valued prodigious memories. As Makdisi points out, "persons [possessing such memories] were referred to in the biographical works as 'oceans' (*bahr*) of learning, 'receptacles' (*wi'a'*, pl. *au'iya*) of knowledge."[3] On the rabbinic side we may point to the famous description of the disciples of Rabban Yoḥanan ben Zakkai, one of whom is described as a "cemented cistern which does not lose a drop."[4] For our period note R. Aaron Sargado's proud boast that most of his yeshiva did not know what a book was, a passage to which we will have occasion to return in the course of this discussion. In eleventh-century Baghdad the two traditions differ not in this but in their attitude to the process of transmission.

Islamic law had certainly developed a strong book tradition by the time of the organization of the madrasas; in contrast, the geonic yeshivot struggled to maintain a privileged position for orality while yielding to the demands of the book culture within which it found itself.

The Amoraim and their successors, rabbinic authorities of the third through the sixth centuries, and the anonymous redactors created what would become an "oral scripture," whose text did not become absolutely fixed until well into modern times. Moreover, the earliest datable fragments of talmudic codices now available do not precede the eleventh century, though earlier, undatable fragments do exist. A consensus has emerged which fixes the middle of the eighth century as the first reduction of the Babylonian Talmud in writing.[5] Indeed, the mid-eighth century crops up over and over as the beginning of the reduction to writing of many genres in Babylonian Jewish literary history.[6]

Both the geonic yeshiva and the Islamic madrasa developed *after* their essential secondary scriptures resembled their classic forms. That is, the amoraic traditions were collected in the Babylonian Talmud before the rise of the large geonic yeshivot, and the compilation of Prophetic traditions, the *ḥadith*s, in six canonical collections, had been completed in the century before the founding of the first great madrasa, the Nizamiya, in 1067. However, while the Talmud itself incorporated a huge amount of legal debate and dialectic, the talmudic *shaqla va-tarya,* Islamic legal reasoning, *diraya,* was, in large measure, a creation of the madrasa. And though the Talmud was to an extent still open to geonic legal reasoning, as later medieval traditions report, it had in nearly all important essentials been closed before the transformation of the amoraic study circles to the geonic yeshivot.[7]

The fullest description of a geonic academy in Iraq dates from the tenth century, in the account of R. Nathan ha-Bavli, an account which, in Menahem Ben-Sasson's analysis, was intended to encourage the communities of North Africa to continue their support of these institutions.[8]

> The author of this composition wished to make clear to his readers that it is in Babylonia . . . that the central Jewish institutions of leadership exist, and that they [still] function[ed] as in ages past. The crises which passed over them at that time [= close to the middle of the tenth century] [were] merely transient phenomena. . . .[9]

The crises referred to here are clearly the power struggles of the first half of the tenth century; Ben-Sasson notes that evidence for monetary contributions and religious inquiries ceases from the beginning of the ninth century to the thirties of the tenth, though contacts are renewed from the 980s to the end of the first third of the eleventh century. The portrait R. Nathan paints of the geonic yeshivot dates from period of crisis: the last Gaon he mentions is R. Aaron Sargado, head of the Pumbeditha yeshiva from 943–960, and one of R. Saadia Gaon's antagonists. Even if the picture that R. Nathan provides errs on the side of stability and grandeur, we may gain some indication of the size, organization and functioning of the geonic yeshivot in the eleventh century from this account of the situation in the previous century. Unfortunately, for information on curriculum we must turn to other, more indirect sources.

Aside from the Gaon and his immediate associates, some seventy scholars sat facing him, arrayed in seven rows. These constituted the geonic Sanhedrin, the high court. The first row of ten was made up of seven *reshei kalla,* who were "heads of the rows," and three *ḥaverim,* colleagues. Each of the seventy had his individual rank, determined entirely by descent, as, indeed, was the Gaonate itself, dominated as it was by four or five families. That is, even if the heir was young, and not as advanced in learning as his father had been, or, for that matter, as those of the seventy who sat "below" him, he would still inherit the position, with one exception, to be discussed below. Generally speaking, ability was recognized by an increase in stipend, not in rank, and, of course, no *ḥaver* could aspire to the Gaonate unless he was a member of the requisite family, in which case he might already be Head of the Court, and sitting, in the case of the Suran academy, to the Gaon's right. Those outside these "seeded players," to borrow a term from tennis, numbering some four hundred, were not assigned specific ranks or places, and stood in back of the lecture hall.

Most historians who have written on the period have rightly emphasized the rigidity of the hierarchical system just described.[10] Ben-Sasson, on the basis of Geniza fragments of the Arabic original which he published, has modified this picture slightly. In the case of a vacancy among the seventy leading scholars, a suitable junior candidate, that is one from a requisite family, would be promoted immediately from the ranks of the four hundred to the ranks of the seventy.

As Ben-Sasson notes, in that case it is most likely that those who had been lower in rank would advance one place, thus opening up a place. How often this occurred is of course impossible to say, but it is hardly likely that it was a common occurrence. However, since R. Nathan's intent here is to depict the yeshivot as open to newcomers and outsiders and therefore worthy of the support of those who were geographically distant, it may be supposed that this description represents the greatest opportunity for outsiders that the author could find to include in his description. In sum, the yeshivot were hierarchal, all-but-closed institutions.

So too in the matter of curriculum. The curriculum of the geonic yeshivot was almost entirely restricted to the Babylonian Talmud. While there was some study of its associated compilations, those of historical interest, such as the Mishnah, Midrash and Tosefta, as R. Natronai Gaon (853–857) reports, this interest was peripheral.[11] In R. Natronai's account, after morning prayers, the yeshiva divided into two groups, those whose primary concern was Talmud, and those who were primarily "memorizers" (*Tannaim*), who then occupied themselves with Mishnah, Midrash and Tosefta.

It was thus only those whose professional role was to present texts orally who were involved with nontalmudic texts on a steady basis. Indeed, the responsum essentially deals with one of the concluding morning prayers, *Uva' le-Tsion,* which serves as a symbolic fulfillment of the talmudic injunction to devote one third of one's time to study of Bible, Mishnah, and Talmud, respectively. The particular study session described really served as an extended end to morning prayers, and extended only to the fourth hour of the day, that is, to the latest allowable time for morning prayers. Thus, this responsum, which serves as an important source for our knowledge of the geonic curriculum, serves also to underscore the overwhelming importance of Talmud study as against any other subject.

Talmud study alone consumed the intellectual energy of the scholars and disciples of the yeshivot. Other texts were analyzed only when relevant to this central one. As R. Natronai ruefully admits, even the requisite Bible study that the Talmud mandates was neglected because of "poverty."

It is true that book lists and fragments recovered from the Geniza attest to a lively, even consuming interest in the Bible, with many translations and commentaries, as well as biblical books (often subdivided into sections, two for the Pentateuch and five for Psalms).[12] Indeed, Goitein suggested that the popularity of biblical studies was due to the difficulty in concentrating on more demanding studies in the heat of the Egyptian day, and that talmudic studies were pursued at night![13] However, he also notes the comparative paucity of talmudic commentaries, and that of those few which have been found in the Geniza, some private annotations betray a lack of familiarity with Aramaic. It may be that the popularity of biblical texts reflects the taste of the *bourgeoisie,* whose records are so well represented in the Geniza. While knowledge of the Bible could well have been expected of a rabbinic scholar (as in the case of Maimonides' contemporary, R. Yosef Rosh Haseder b. Jacob b. Eli, who mandates its study, but only in the most basic way—to ensure expert ritual reading of the text),[14] he could not be seen to fall short of the general population in this respect. In addition, the popularity of biblical study in twelfth-century Egypt may reflect a response to the Karaite challenge—the popular analogue of R. Saadia Gaon's biblical commentaries in the tenth century[15] and R. Samuel b. Hofni Gaon's in the eleventh. It was not a subject which was necessarily well represented in the curricula of the geonic yeshivot in Baghdad, though it was certainly reflected in the curricula of the lower schools.

Goitein's distinction between halakhic compendia and talmudic text and commentary, while useful in some respects, does not apply to the geonic yeshivot. There, halakha was clearly the essential part of Talmud study; the two were intimately connected, and so the paucity of running commentaries to talmudic passages was more than made up by the geonic responsa, which frequently dealt with problematic talmudic passages, and their more general halakhic works, including compendia and responsa both. Indeed, Goitein may be correct in seeing the genesis of the compendia as halakhic lectures in the halls of the yeshivot,[16] but they would have been considered as part of the talmudic course of study.

Finally, as Goitein himself realizes, the geonic yeshivot, or at least the Suran academy, judging from R. Nathan's description, functioned more as sanhedrins (high courts) than as educational institutions.[17]

It is clear from R. Natronai's description that nontalmudic texts were recited, though it is not clear whether written copies existed. As far as the text of the Talmud itself is concerned, however, a fair amount of evidence for its basically oral nature in geonic times exists. One of the most important of these pieces of evidence in this regard comes from the hand of the aforementioned R. Aaron Sargado. Before we examine this geonic responsum, however, it would be well to place the question of orality within some historical perspective, especially since it has recently been questioned.

The amoraic period was certainly one of a pervasive orality, when Scripture itself was often quoted from memory, despite strictures to the contrary,[18] when amoraic masters hardly ever had recourse to written texts with which they were not already intimately familiar,[19] and when the semi-graphic "signatures" of prominent rabbinic figures[20] correspond to what may be expected of a society in which literacy is not to be taken for granted, when variant versions both of legal traditions and of tradents can almost always be attributed to the problematics of oral transmission. We hardly ever find the Babylonian sages depicted as writing; scribes produced legal documents. It is noteworthy that, in contrast to the situation in tannaitic Palestine, where, for example, many stories of R. Meir's scribal abilities and practices are preserved, we do not find such stories told of Babylonian amoraim. Oral transmission in such a context was thus axiomatic, almost unconscious. Whether because of cultural and religious conservatism, the cost of writing materials, or a combination of these and other factors, it is clear that the period was one in which written transmission was not a conscious choice.

In the geonic period, however, oral transmission of the Babylonian Talmud was a conscious choice, given the prevalence of book culture. Moreover, for the Talmud, at least, oral transmission was privileged; the Geonim themselves seem to have authorized the making of written copies only in extenuating circumstances.[21] The Talmud continued to be transmitted orally as late at the tenth century, and in all probability, this situation continued to the close of the geonic yeshivot in the next century. Neither one of these matters is in doubt, but their nexus requires explanation, and here the Islamic parallels may be of help, if only by contrast.

It is one thing to maintain the coherence and accuracy of one's oral tradition within a small, select circle of disciples and memorizers, as was the case in amoraic times.[22] It is quite another to do so within a large academy. Eidetic memory and incisive analytic abilities do not often occur in tandem; hence the earlier, amoraic institution of the *Tanna,* the "living book," whose function it was to recite authoritative texts which others then analyzed.

In one of his responsa, the tenth-century Gaon of Pumbeditha, R. Aaron Sargado, argued in support of his yeshiva's reading of an amoraic statement in bYev 39b as a question (*be-tmiha'*) rather than as a declarative statement. Before proceeding to defend his interpretation contextually, he notes that regarding "our whole yeshiva, of which it is known that its version [of the Talmud] is from the mouths of the great ones, . . . most of them [i.e. the members of the yeshiva] do not know anything of a book." For this reason, its recital, that is, its enunciation of the statement as a question, must be accepted. As Yerachmiel Brody points out, R. Aaron here argues for the superiority of his school's version of the talmudic text on the basis of its unbroken tradition which reaches back to the Amoraim, and because of the oral nature of that tradition, which, in that cultural context, would have been considered more reliable.[23] Beyond that, however, is the nature of the issue, which is inextricably associated with the orality of the tradition. The point at issue is the way the statement was enunciated, namely, as a question rather than as a declarative sentence. If the fact of orality were not beyond dispute, the argument would lose much of its force.[24]

Now, it may be assumed that not all of the members of the yeshiva had actually memorized the entire Talmud. We may presume, as Brody has suggested,[25] that most knew only parts of it; we may even assume that those tractates dealing with civil law were most widely known, since this area of law was more assiduously cultivated than others, as Goitein has observed.[26] We have many more geonic monographs on various aspects of this subject than on matters of liturgy and ritual, for example. But the geonic devotion to oral transmission goes beyond its mere fact, as R. Aaron's statement demonstrates. Oral transmission was not only the proper way of doing things; it was also considered more reliable than written transmission, and it is to orally transmitted texts that the Geonim turn when questions arise regarding the proper reading of a particular passage, as Y. N. Epstein and Y. Brody have shown.[27]

This devotion to oral transmission of a large, complex and difficult text raises two questions which are actually two aspects of one issue. First, why did the Geonim maintain this difficult system of memorization of large bodies of text in an era when, unlike the earlier periods, orality was giving way to textuality, when legal and liturgical handbooks were being composed in written form,[28] and when, as Reif points out, "the spread of the codex is not therefore to be explained as a reflection of an intellectual and literary development which might just as well have produced an oral response, but of evidence of a concern for authorisation and institutionalisation"?[29] Indeed, according to S. Asaf, though the great geonic halakhic compendia date from the middle of the eighth century, the earliest geonic responsa date to before 689.[30] Second, why was this concern for institutionalization through the fixing of written texts not extended to the Talmud, which was after all the authoritative text *par excellence*?

Before an answer to these questions is suggested, let us proceed to examine the solution to this problem provided within the context of the Islamic madrasa. "Whomever God intends to benefit, He grants right understanding of religion . . . knowledge is maintained only through teaching."[31] So goes a tradition ascribed to the Prophet of Islam. Many traditions sing the praises of knowledge—knowledge which comes from spiritual insight and is grounded in the Qur'an—and extol the power of learning. Admittedly, Islamic religion does not acknowledge privileged classes within the community of believers; all believers are equal citizens in the kingdom of Allah with the same basic rights and duties. Nevertheless, those who have been granted knowledge, the *'ulama'*, are placed at the pinnacle of society, above all other believers, even above kings. With knowledge and the consequent strengthening of faith comes the extra responsibilities of leadership. It is the duty of the *'ulama'* to disseminate Islamic teachings as widely as they can through instruction and the example they set.

But, like all other Islamic traditions, the traditions relating to the prerogatives and duties of the *'ulama'* were subject to different interpretations in different historical settings. Thus, in the eleventh century—a period which witnessed rigorous debates over proper creed and behavior, debates which posed a threat to the stability of Sunni, orthodox, Islam—the *'ulama'* were seemingly more determined than their predecessors to delimit the boundaries of legitimate knowledge and transmit that knowledge to later generations of Muslim scholars. How, even without formal and stable institutions, could the *'ulama'* of that period guarantee their exclusive authority to transmit Islamic learning and assure the perpetuation of their group? This paper, in trying to answer this question, focuses on the *'ulama'* of eleventh-century Baghdad, the scene of the consolidation of Sunni Islam and the elaboration of its forms of organization.

In the first four centuries of Islam, and just after, the transmission of Islamic learning took place in a variety of informal frameworks, especially in mosques, where teachers, or *shaykh*s, would sit in teaching circles (*ḥalqas*) with their students. From at least the late eleventh century, however, following the systematization of Islamic law, there grew up a kind of institution devoted largely to legal learning, the madrasa.

Indeed, the madrasas may be seen, at least at first glance, as something new: schools founded on substantial pious endowments, known as *awqaf*, for the teaching of a fairly uniform curriculum under the supervision of paid teachers. Education in the madrasa consisted of textbooks—the legal treatises written by the "founding fathers" of each of the four "orthodox" legal traditions in Sunni Islam—and commentaries upon their works written and compiled by Muslim scholars over the centuries. In Baghdad, the cradle of the institution in its "mature" form, the madrasa was a sort of combination of a mosque, at which study was restricted to one of the orthodox legal schools, and the adjacent inn (*khan*), where students lived; all this was given economic support to a degree unprecedented in the history of Islamic education.[32] The importance of the madrasa to contemporaries may be seen from the testimony of the poet Abu Ja'far al-Biyad; when he saw the first madrasa erected in 1067 for the Hanafi school in Baghdad, the poet cried out in wonder at the beauty of the building and the considerable equipment placed at its disposal: "Education was on its way to vanishing, until the revelation of the mystical person who gathered it together at the sacred tomb of Abu Hanifa. This country, too, was declining until Abu Sa'ad [the treasurer of the Seljuk state] appeared and brought it back to life."[33]

The madrasa very quickly became part of urban Muslim life, just like the mosques and the rulers' palaces. The pious endowments dedicated by the rulers to the establishment and maintenance of the madrasa and its teachers and students increased its attractiveness, and eventually enabled it to develop as the principal forum of study in the Muslim Near East, similar to the university in the present-day West.[34] But for all the establishment of endowed and structured institutions of learning, it was not around madrasas that scholarly groups clustered and constructed their useful identities. Nor were madrasas institutions of higher education in the expected sense of the term. Rather, the explanation of the process of consolidation and institutionalization, I would like to suggest, lies in cultural and social practices beyond the organizational framework of Islamic education.

As early as the second Islamic century there developed definite procedures for preserving and transmitting of religious learning. The rapid growth of the corpus of traditions of the Prophet, *ḥadith,* collected, and extraneous material that made their way into *ḥadith* literature, stimulated Muslim scholars to set forth principles for the determination of the validity of the sources and for proper transmission. The science of source criticism they developed to deal with forgeries reflects the highly personal character of early Muslim scholarship. Did any transmitter know his predecessor in the chain of transmitters personally, the critics asked, and can the list of the transmitters, the *isnad,* be traced back to the Prophet? It was this sense of obligation to secure the trustworthiness of each link in the chains of authorities that gave rise to the regularization of the transmission of Islamic learning by an *ijaza,* a certificate to the effect that the student had studied a book with a teacher: the student had heard the teacher dictating the book (*sami'a minhu*) and had transcribed what he had heard, or he had himself read his transcription to the teacher (*qara'a 'alayhi*), who corrected any mistakes in the student's recitation and copy. At a higher level, the student could ask for an *ijaza* of a different kind, certifying that he was competent to teach a certain book or subject, or to issue legal opinions (*fatwas*) as *mufti*. An *ijaza* could be an elaborate document, mentioning a whole chain of transmission from teacher to student over the generations, and so inserting the recipient into a long chain of intellectual ancestors.[35]

In addition to collecting *ijazas,* Muslim scholars developed the practice of composing *mashyakhs* (also called *ma'jam, farhasa,* and *barnamaj*); book-length lists of those with whom they studied and on whose authority they dictated *ḥadiths.*[36] These *ma'jams* vary somewhat in form and in the amount of detail they record about an individual's education. However, organized around the names of particular teachers with a note of the works studied under their direction, they all convey the idea that only individuals could impart and grant authority carried into the very texts transmitted from one generation of scholars to the next. The important element was thus of personal contact, of hearing the text directly from the *shaykh,* and entering through him an unbroken chain of authority. In order to establish his scholarly credentials, the student would go from one teacher to another, in one city after another, and ask for *ijazas* from all those whose courses he attended. Summing up the accomplishments of Abu Hafs al-Muwaddid, one of the celebrated Baghdadi traditionalists (d. 1210), his biographer says of him: "The traditions which he had received by oral transmission were remarkable as coming from the highest authorities, and as he traveled through various countries teaching [them] to others, he became the link which connected the rising generation of traditionalists to the past. He filled the earth with his certificates (*ijazat*) which he gave to those who heard him deliver traditions and with licenses to teach, which he granted to his disciples."[37] Indeed, the image of the '*ulama*' as living links in unbroken chains of oral transmission runs like a thread through their biographies.

To be sure, written texts played an important role in religious education and intellectual activity as a whole during the Middle Ages, during what Franz Rosenthal has called the "manuscript age."[38] Starting in the late third Muslim century, a homogeneous corpus of authoritative texts was in the process of developing, constituting an alternative to the old method of gathering knowledge. Gradually collection of books became available for the use of scholars in mosques and schools; and students, not having the means to purchase the books they needed, undertook the task of transcribing their own copies. But for all the availability of written texts, the old practices and rituals of oral transmission (recitation, dictation, oralized reading) remained the normative practice, as ample examples of the negative attitude toward a student who simply read a text to himself demonstrate. That the codex (be it the manuscript or the printed book) imitated the very form of oral transmission with its *isnad* formula is itself evidence of the persistence of the forms of oral transmission in written culture. The author has "heard from" or "takes from" this or that authority, and now "he is handing it down from him" (*rawa ʿanhu*); that is, the book represents a continuing and unbroken oral communication, which is transmitted further by the author.[39]

True knowledge derives only from a learned person, insisted Badr al-Din Ibn Jamaʿa, the early fourteenth-century scholar and jurist, and not from books; those who attempted to rest their education on the written word were guilty of "one of the most scandalous of acts," for "taking books [alone] leads to spelling errors and mispronunciation."[40] But the insistence on the necessity of learning from individuals and not from books alone had reasons other than the securing of accurate reading and transmission of the texts. The process of writing and the physical, written book as a means of transmitting knowledge might have posed a challenge to the *ʿulama*ʾ as the ones who could impart true knowledge and grant authority carried over into the very texts transmitted from one generation of scholars to the next. Added to this challenge was the threat that private, or silent, reading may lead to misinterpretation or even introduce innovations.

Developed in the earlier decades of the accumulation and transmission of Islamic learning to ensure an accurate understanding of the Islamic religious law, the *shariʿa* was fully transmitted from one generation to another. In the eleventh century, institutionalized oral transmission of legal materials easily served the *'ulama'* as a means to assure their control over the preservation and dissemination of religious lore. It is therefore no wonder that the close association between orality and authority persisted as a model.

As the core element in the culture of the learned and their image of institutionalization, the construction of the links in the chains of transmitters determined the character of relationship between the *shaykh* and his disciple. The authors of biographical dictionaries frequently make use of the term *suhba*—"friendship" or "apprenticeship"—to describe this relationship. The term described a pattern of personal relationship which permeated medieval Muslim societies: between a scholar and a ruler who became his patron, between a rich merchant and his apprentice, or between a senior official and a junior official under him. In the context of education, *suhba* implied an extremely close personal and intellectual relationship between teacher and student, one fostered over the course of many years.[41]

The emphasis on personal relationships between the *shaykh* and his disciple, and the use of the term *suhba* to describe them, should not appear surprising. The idea that the tighter the relationship between a master and his disciple, the more the student would be considered a reliable source for future generations lay at the heart of the transmitting process from the time of the Prophet of Islam and his companions, or *sahaba*. In Shi'i Islam, this association between intimate acquaintance and authority bore a special meaning; the Shi'i traditions relating how Muhammad dictated to 'Ali every Koranic verse immediately upon its revelation, portraying 'Ali as his closest most trustful companion—were all meant to legitimate the claim that 'Ali, and the Shi'i *imamas* after him, possessed divine authority, equal to that of Muhammad.[42] The Sunni *'ulama'* are, of course, mere interpreters of the Sunna of the Prophet, his sayings and doings that were eventually established as legally binding precedents. But their claim to be the only ones to possess perfect knowledge of the Koran and the Sunna, and hence the "heirs of the Prophets," rested on the existence of an unbroken chain of his sayings from teacher to teacher across the generations.

By hearing Islamic teaching directly from his *shaykh* and obtaining *ijaza* from him, the disciple could enter into a chain of transmitters, but in order to assure the perpetuation of the master's teaching, as well as of the entire chain, that teaching had to be put into writing. As most teachers tended to hide their voices, either because they considered their own opinions as less important than the inclusion of their names in the chain, or because they did not dare to make their opinions public, they normally had their close disciples carry out the task of writing.

The teacher would read the text aloud so that the student could check his version against his and thereby make the necessary corrections. The student would write his master's commentaries on a given text, in its margins, between the lines, or even between the words, and later produce the lecture course with the commentaries. To assure the accuracy of the produced text, the student would then read it aloud to the teacher, and thereby make the necessary corrections. If the teacher was the author of the book, he would normally publish it through dictation (*imla'*), given either from a written copy or from memory. To this was added the transcriptions, the abridgements, and continuations of the master's works, activities through which devoted students expressed their respect for their master's achievements and commitment to spread his teaching. This system allowed a constant dialogue with the text and between the transmitters themselves; leaving enough room for disputation, even for originality and creativity, controlling variations and innovations at the same time.

The idea of hearing Islamic teaching directly from the teacher, reading to him and clinging to him, remained alive long after the appearance of the madrasa in Baghdad. Remarkable testimony with regard to the effect of the traditional patterns of transmission is reflected in the preservation of the seating arrangement in the madrasa study group, or *ḥalqa*: the students sitting in a semicircle, with the teacher at the remote end and his closest disciple, or *sahib*, next to him.

The preference shown for the teacher as against the institution, and the great degree of authority given to the former, are clearly reflected in the description of events on the inaugural day of the *al-Madrasa al-Nizamiya,* the most glorious institution of its kind in Baghdad. Appointed to the post of teacher of religious law in the madrasa was Abu Ishaq al-Shirazi, one of the greatest scholars of religious law in Baghdad and a leader of the Shafi'i school in the city. On his way from his home to the madrasa, al-Shirazi was informed that the land which had been set aside for the building of the madrasa had been illegally expropriated from its owners, and he therefore refused to take up his position there. Only after much pleading on the part of his students and a formal declaration by the *vezir* that only for his sake had the madrasa been established did he agree to accept the appointment. When al-Shirazi died, the gates of the madrasa were closed and his students went into mourning for their great master. For an entire year, the madrasa remained closed by order of the *vezir*; when its gates opened again and a new teacher of religious law was appointed, al-Shirazi's disciples did not permit him to assume the post which had belonged to their master.[43]

The centrality of the teacher had other expressions. Wherever the *ḥalqa* was convened, be it in a mosque, or the teacher's private home, or in the madrasa, it was always the teacher who was the one responsible for determining the acceptance (or non-acceptance) of students and the order of the sitting within the group, the frequency of its assembly, as well as the texts studied, and the sequence of all instruction. In addition, he was the one who ordained his students, by granting them the *ijaza*. The *ijaza,* of course, retained its traditional character: a personal certificate conferred by one teacher at a time to teach a certain text only, and never developed into an established university degree, such as the *licentia dicendi,* which was granted by European universities with the consent of the Church authorities.[44]

Naturally, to have studied in some capacity with an especially prominent scholar and obtain the *ijaza* from him, rather than to study in a certain educational institution, was the goal of seekers of knowledge. Such, for example, was the objective of the travels in search of knowledge (*rihla fi talab al-'ilm*) of the young Abu Sa'd al-Isfahani (d. 1145). After he had heard traditions in his home town, he set on a long journey to Baghdad to study under Abu Nasr al-Zainabi, a member of the famous Hanafi scholarly family. While still on his way, the news of Abu Nasr's death reached him. Filled with despair, he started to cry lamenting his death and wondering whom he will have as a master.[45] Whether fact or fiction, such stories could have reasserted and nourished the traditional patterns of transmission.

The biographies also yielded illustrations of the persistence of the old character of admission into the study circle, one decided solely by the *shaykh* according to the educational qualifications and performance of those who gathered around him. Al-Mutawalli, who became the teacher of law in the famous Nizamiya madrasa, related to his students the following anecdote going back to his days as a student: "I came from beyond the Oxus, and entered [the mosque where] Abu al-Harith b. Abi al-Fadl as-Sarakhsi was lecturing in garments much used and not much as are worn by men of learning. I attended the class of as-Sarakashi, and sat among his disciples who were seated at the end of his class. A question was brought up for disputation, and I spoke and raised objections. When my turn was over, Abu al-Harith ordered me to move up closer, and so I did. And when my turn had come up again for disputation, he brought me closer still and continued to do so until my seat was next to him. Thereafter, he saw to all my needs and took me as one of his followers.[46] Mutawalli considered his experience with Sarakhsi as one of the most pleasant incidents in his academic career. Not only was he allowed to attend Sarakhsi's study-circle, despite his being a new scholar in town and the shabby clothes he wore, but was invited by the professor to sit next to him, a privilege reserved for the master's most competent and closest disciples.

In any event, as the teacher taught his students only the "knowledge" inherent in the text which he himself had written, or which had been passed down to his own teacher as the latest link in an unbroken chain of transmitters leading back to the original author, this transmission of knowledge, imprinted with the teacher's legal method and religious outlook, could have taken place just as successfully anywhere that a study group could have met. Even scholars who taught or studied in the madrasas of Baghdad continued to meet in improvised study groups and circles which were led by the *shaykhs* in mosques and private homes. Thus, for example, it is told of Abu al-Barakat al-Anbari that, during his course of study in the Nizamiya madrasa, he lived in the home of his *shaykh,* as his private pupil.[47]

The centrality and authority of the teacher, and the fact that the madrasa is barely mentioned in literature of the period, as against the many testimonies to study groups outside the institution, may all attest to the marginality of madrasa, indeed of any form of organization, in the culture and society of the learned. Teachers came to the madrasa in order to obtain an official post and its accompanying salary; students, in order to receive stipends and living quarters. This is not to say that the madrasas of Baghdad were not centers for the instruction of the Islamic legal and religious sciences; with the most renowned *shaykhs* of the city holding teaching positions in them, they seem to have attracted many seekers of higher education. However, the study itself took place, both within and outside the madrasa, according to the traditional patterns of the transmission of Islamic learning and tradition. Created as a means of safeguarding "true religion" and to guarantee financial support to the religiously learned, the madrasa was, in other words, but a new, more institutionalized form of organization, into which the essential cultural and social practices were poured.

But while far from transforming Islamic education, the growth of madrasas in Baghdad, and probably in other Muslim cities, eventually brought a change in the character of the '*ulama*' group. Not only did the new schools provide for a more prosperous cultural elite, but by attracting scholars of different intellectual traditions and geographical origins, they enhanced the consolidation of a local and more coherent group of '*ulama*' in eleventh-century Baghdad. At the same time, a new meaning of the term '*alim* was created: a legal expert usually employed to carry on his scholarly and professional activities. How the '*ulama*' of that period in Baghdad and elsewhere in Islamic cities exploited the new schools to become a group more well defined in membership and structure is an issue which requires further study.

We now return to our geonic academies. Was it sheer conservatism which kept oral transmission of the Talmud privileged, or was it also the usefulness of orality in maintaining the status of the institution within whose precincts—and only within those precincts—prospective students of the Oral Torah could master their discipline? Or was it the need to maintain control of the talmudic text, which was after all the foundation of all halakha, just as the oral recitation of texts leading to the *ijaza* served to maintain the '*ulama*''s control?

Sheer conservatism alone cannot account for this phenomenon, since in other areas—the fixing of the liturgy and the composition of legal treatises, especially—writing was widely used. Even more remarkably, we have reports of two occasions on which the Babylonian Talmud itself was written down and made available to those outside the Babylonian yeshivot.[48] However, these are exceptions which prove the rule, for these reports refer to the dissemation of the Talmud to the far-flung reaches of the exile in Spain. In

North Africa, likewise, large libraries of basic texts were collected.[49] Clearly, the Geonim recognized that for those communities beyond Iraq, where their jurisdiction did not extend and where the insistence on oral transmission was impractical, the only way to reach out and maintain contact with those communities was by creating or fostering a shared rabbinic culture. In these cases, written exemplars of the Talmud had to be provided, just as halakhic and liturgical compendia were sent to North Africa from time to time.

The latter was, as we have seen, the be-all and end-all of the yeshivot themselves, dominating the curriculum beyond all measure, and serving to maintain the role of yeshivot as custodians of what had emerged as the central text of rabbinic Judaism. Note that, unlike the curricula of the madrasas, the ongoing compilation and composition of new geonic texts seem not to have affected the yeshiva curriculum. The continuing publication of halakhic compendia, biblical commentaries and philosophical works did not enter that curriculum. It should be remembered that, as noted earlier, the Sura yeshiva, for which we have R. Nathan ha-Bavli's description, functioned more as a high court than an educational institution, as Goitein recognized.

The madrasa did not have this character, since Islam did not develop an intricate system of courts; indeed, in stark contrast to the rabbinic practice, courts consisted of just one judge. Thus, the madrasa, as a purely educational institution, was more open to new texts and new students. Moreover, the tradition of oral transmission weighed less heavily on these schools. Perhaps their more stable financial base served to allow for a greater openness as well. This greater openness extended not only to texts, but to faculty and student-body as well.

In the closed, hierarchical world of the geonic yeshivot, such a text could not be yielded to the profligate accessibility which the manuscript culture made possible. Brody notes that such insistence on memorization would have limited the circle of scholars, but, he observes that, in any case, "other considerations make it likely that these circles were not overly large," citing R. Nathan ha-Bavli's estimate of 400 students.[50] Indeed, given the rigid, hierarchal and exclusivist nature of the yeshivot, it is likely that a larger number was not desired. If we add the aforementioned 400 to the seventy ranked members of the yeshiva, and double that number to include Sura's sister institution, which may well have been smaller, we have a class of less than a thousand scholars in all of Babylon, since the two yeshivot seem to have jealously guarded their position as elite institutions. It is also possible, of course, that their student body had dwindled in R. Nathan's time, due to the unsettled conditions attendant upon the coming of the Buwaihids.[51] However, since, as Ben-Sasson has demonstrated, R. Nathan was concerned to point out that the yeshivot functioned in much the same way as they ever had, his estimate of their size was presumably in line with the conditions at the beginning of the tenth century or earlier.

Actually, we may assume that even when texts were made available, local transmission was done orally, as well, as Goitein notes. "Learning by rote the exact wording and cantillation of an ancient text was regarded as a prerequisite for its proper interpretation in higher studies, as it was in the elementary school."[52] This was altogether feasible when we consider that "only the select few, those who prepared themselves for the posts of judge and spiritual leader, made extensive studies of the Talmud and the literature that accrued around it."[53]

If that is the case, however, it would seem that memorization was the rule for both the periphery *and* the center. To carry this logic a step further, then, it would seem that our written texts exist *only* because of the need to maintain contact with the periphery, as Brody has suggested.[54] Within each community, oral transmission would have been the case. This would help explain the absence of the geonic halakhic compendia from the curriculum, since they are in large measure merely compilations of talmudic passages.

Thus, different policies were pursued in regard to these essential areas of geonic concern, the liturgical, the halakhic, and the talmudic text. In the case of the first, we may assume that rabbinic Jewry as a whole knew how to pray rabbinically, though not necessarily in the Babylonian mode. Jews of each locality had memorized the local order of prayer. However, note that the first "order of prayer," that attributed to R. Amram Gaon in the middle of the eighth century, was more a guide than a text. Thus, the promulgation of an authoritative *siddur* or *seder* was intended, as Lawrence Hoffman has put it, to "canonize" the order of prayer, but not necessarily the prayer book. The Babylonian order of prayer, or, more precisely, that of the yeshivot, would prevail over Palestinian or Karaite challenges, just as Babylonian halakha and customs would prevail over the Palestinian.

In the case of halakhic codifications, the intended audience must be assumed to have been much smaller, and was made up of local authorities outside of Babylonia. Here we have the essential assertion and exercise of geonic authority. It may be assumed that the recipients of geonic responsa and of their halakhic compilations were themselves scholars, and had mastered the talmudic text, at least in regard to certain areas of legal expertise. Thus, among the geonic responsa we find questions sent in regard to the proper reading or interpretation of particular talmudic passages.

However, having come this far, we must now downplay the role the oral transmission played in maintaining Iraq's role of the center as opposed to the periphery. And, indeed, the talmudic text had reached beyond the bounds of Babylonia centuries earlier.[55] Oral transmission and memorization, and not necessarily from a written text, both at the center and on the periphery, were the standard, traditional, accepted modes of doing things, as noted above. On the other hand, we cannot connect the insistence on oral transmission with the need to preserve the position and financial stability of the yeshivot, since these were not always at issue.

We return to the statement of R. Aaron Sargado, which was quoted above, regarding "our whole yeshiva, of which it is known that its version [of the Talmud] is from the mouths of the great ones, and most of them [i.e., the members of the yeshiva] do not know anything of a book." His claim is not primarily one of oral transmission—everyone did that—but of *direct* transmission from "the mouths of the great ones." That is, the talmudic texts of the yeshivot were more reliable than the competing texts that may have been available to his interlocutors, for three reasons: their amoraic *origin*, and the fact that they were *directly* and *orally* transmitted from their source. The factor of origin insures that the text is authoritative, and its direct oral transmission insures its textual reliability. The true Torah—the accurate text of the Talmud—comes ultimately from Pumbeditha, as R. Aaron would have it. We may now understand why the geonic concern for institutionalization through the fixing of written texts did not extend to the Talmud; as far as they were concerned, it *was* fixed, but orally.

Thus, unlike the *siddur,* which could be made available *as a whole,* the true and accurate Talmud could only be consulted in Babylonia. Whether or not a geonic system comparable to that of the Islamic *ijaza* existed to preserve the inviolable transmission of the talmudic text cannot be stated with any certainty. But whatever the system was, the origin of the text in the Babylonian yeshivot was itself its own *ijaza,* so to speak. In the exclusive world of the geonic yeshiva, the Gaon, together perhaps with the *reshei kallah,* was the guarantor of accuracy of transmission, as is indicated by the many geonic responsa dealing with variant readings.

The interface between orality and literacy in the Islamic madrasa is sufficiently different from that of the geonic yeshiva to preclude any easy comparisons. Transmission in the madrasa is direct, and from the "mouths of the great ones," but it is not primarily oral, nor is orality privileged in that it is held to produce a more accurate text. Indeed, the lesson of *ijaza* is just the reverse; neither oral nor written transmission *alone* is to be trusted. Now, the Geonim were certainly aware of the pitfalls of entrusting important matters to the vagaries of human memory, and, as Brody points out, alternative variants are frequently cited in geonic discussions, especially in the latter half of the period.[56] As noted earlier, the geonic yeshivot must have employed some system which served the same function as *ijaza,* but orality was itself of greater importance within the geonic context. Transmission in the yeshivot was primarily oral; in the madrasa it was primarily written.

Several other distinctions must be emphasized as well. The madrasa in the eleventh century was still in many respects a glorified study-circle, with students dependent on one master, as formulated above: "wherever the *ḥalqa* was convened, be it in a mosque, or the teacher's private home, or in the madrasa, it was always the teacher who was the one responsible for determining the acceptance (or non-acceptance) of students and the order of the sitting within the group, the frequency of its assembly, as well as the texts studied, and the sequence of all instruction." Note that "when al-Shirazi died, the gates of the madrasa were closed and his students went into mourning for their great master. For an entire year, the madrasa remained closed by order of the *vezir.*"[57] Again, "to have studied in some capacity with an especially prominent scholar and obtain *ijaza* from him, rather than to study in a certain educational institution, was the goal of seekers of knowledge."[58] When the young Abu Sa'd al-Isfahani set out to study under Abu Nasr al-Zainabi, and news of Abu Nasr's death reached him, he lamented his death and wondered to whom he could now turn for instruction.

The primacy of the individual master is reminiscent of a conversation reported of Rava and his disciples, which, incidentally, was reported only because it relates to the legal question of whether a teacher is considered to be in the service of his charges. "Master," said the scholars to Rava, "you are loaned to us." He took umbrage at this. "Do you wish to deprive me of my property? On the contrary, you are loaned to me, for I can switch you from one tractate to another, while you cannot [do the same to me]."[59] In this respect, the madrasa was much closer to the amoraic *metivta* than it was to the geonic yeshivot, with their faculty and institutional character.

Again, the madrasa was a vehicle for transmitting its *madhab*; it was not its creator. The geonic yeshivot claimed, with some reason, to be the heirs of the very creators of the Babylonian Talmud. Note R. Sherira's casual mention of his ancestor, the amora Rabba b. Abbuha, "who went to Shekhneziv and to Shili and to Mahoza."[60] The newly founded madrasas could make no such claim and thus could claim no monopoly.

Moreover, there is an interesting difference in the character of the literature studied, a difference which is perhaps all the more important to emphasize, given the many other parallels and similarities between the two traditions. While the process of collection of *hadith*s is clearly reminiscent of the redaction of the Mishnah and the compilation of *baraitot,* the redaction of the Bavli, which gave it its overwhelming dialectical character, is parallel to the Islamic *diraya,* which ultimately was equated with *fiqh,* "law." Those who could engage in *diraya* looked down on those who were restricted to *riwaya,* or memorization of traditions, much as the amoraim looked down on their *tannaim,* those "living books" of the amoraic era.[61] Despite all these similarities, there is one great difference. The Talmud is an amalgam of *riwaya* and *diraya,* as are the halakhic compendia; in Islam they were kept separate, both in terms of the compilations in which they were enshrined, and in terms of the need for *ijaza*. Makdisi cites an interesting dispute which highlights this distinction:

> Ibn al-Jauzi defended Ibn al-Madhhab [for claiming *ijaza* for parts of the *Musnad* for which he had not received *ijaza* from Ibn al-Qati'i] on the basis that only common, ordinary muhaddithun . . . insist that the master should sign the authorization. In other words, this principle is not required by hadith-experts who are learned in the law. Ibn al-Jauzi then said: "This does not call for censure; since once it is known for certain that he learned [heard] the book, it becomes permissible for him to write his certificate of audition [*sama*'] in his own hand, in order to enhance the importance [probative value] of books. It is a cause for surprise to see how these hadith-experts allow one to say, orally, 'So-and-so informed me . . .' [in reference to an authority from whom a hadith is received orally] but refuse him to write his certificate of audition in his own hand. . . ." In other words, if the transmitter of a hadith was allowed, himself, to attest to the authenticity of his authority to transmit the hadith, then the transmitter of a book should also himself be allowed to do the same with the book.[62]

Al-Jawzi here takes the measure of the inconsistent approach to written and oral transmission, an approach which privileged the oral over the written. Al-Jawzi died in 1257, and thus was opposing a perspective which would have been prevalent in the centuries before—the time of the geonic yeshivot. But this merely underscores the difference between the two traditions. The Islamic madrasa was, in its early days, still closely tied to the *ḥalqa,* and still privileged oral transmission. But as the *ḥalqa* gave way to the madrasa, orality gave way. The geonic yeshivot, despite their size and central position within the Jewish community, still retained the old preference for oral transmission.

It was its combined economic, political and religious might which made the madrasa so successful. But if the madrasa was, at least in the eleventh century, essentially marginal to the study of Islamic sources, that may be due in no small measure to its lack of monopoly on the texts upon which all depended. One who had *ijaza* could go out and teach, and his text was written, not oral. Even if he guarded it jealously, and transmitted it by recitation, the text still existed in written form. No *ḥaver* could go out and establish a new geonic yeshiva; the story of R. Aha of Shabha, the purported author of the earliest geonic compilation, the *She'iltot,* which attributes the compilation to R. Aha's loss of the Gaonate and his subsequent move to Palestine, demonstrates this assumption. The contrast between the continued and restricted oral transmission in the heartland of Babylonian Jewry and the openness of Islamic society in this regard is striking. In the very same city, Baghdad, the Islamic oral traditions were made available in written form, with suitable mechanisms to insure accurate transmission, while, presumably with similar mechanisms to insure accuracy, Babylonian Jewry restricted access to this most basic of all Jewish legal texts.

Without the political and economic power of the regime behind them, it appears that the geonic yeshivot, like the Jewish community as a whole, had to fend for themselves. Despite the geographical proximity, the two situations that the two institutions faced were fundamentally dissimilar. Babylonian Jews were a tolerated minority, a minority which was, especially in the tenth and eleventh centuries, hard put to maintain its central institutions even with help from abroad, while Islam had comparatively endless resources at its disposal. Islam could afford to invest in what was for a time a marginal institution. The geonic authorities hardly felt able to do so. Indeed, the very size and exclusivity of the geonic yeshivot underscores this point. As noted above, the Suran academy, as glorious as it was, supported some four hundred disciples and seventy scholars.[63] While this is larger than any madrasa, it is small in the aggregate. While the closed, hierarchal nature of geonic society certainly played a large role in this, economic factors must have as well. Could more have been afforded?

Thus, a Gaon might argue, if accessibility to higher rabbinic education had to be limited, why not set the standard so as to maintain the old tradition of oral transmission? True, the Gaonate itself remained in the hands of a few families, jealously guarded from generation to generation. But in essence and in general the requirements were intellectual, and, to the geonic mind, the requirement of orality helped maintain those standards.

NOTES

1. A.S. Tritton, *Materials on Muslim Education in the Middle Ages* (London, 1957), 35; see S.D. Goitein, *A Mediterranean Society: The Jewish Communities of*

the Arab World as Portrayed in the Documents of the Cairo Geniza (Berkeley, 1967–1988), 2:198, but compare his remarks on p. 403: "The yeshiva was pre-Islamic, and, even during the heyday of Islam, differed completely from its Islamic counterpart, the madrasa (as far as it could be compared with the yeshiva at all)."

2. George Makdisi, *The Rise of Colleges: Institutions of Learning in Islam and the West* (Edinburgh, 1981), 8.

3. Ibid., 99.

4. mAvot 2:8.

5. See M. Beit-Arié, "Perek Shirah," Ph.D. diss., Hebrew University, 1967, 154; and Beit-Arié, *Hebrew Codicology* (Paris, 1976), 9–10; see also the literature cited in Avigdor Shinan, "Sifrut ha-Aggadah: Bein Higgud al Peh u-Masoret Ketuvah" *Jerusalem Studies in Jewish Folklore* 1 (1981): 45, n. 2; Martin S. Jaffee, "Writing and Rabbinic Oral Tradition: On Mishnaic Narrative, Lists and Mnemonics," *Journal of Jewish Thought and Philosophy* 4 (1994) 123–146; D. Rosenthal, "Mishnah Avodah Zara: Mahadurah Biqortit u-Mavo," Ph.D. diss., Hebrew University, 1980, 96–106. See our discussion of Stefan C. Reif, *Judaism and Hebrew Prayer: New Perspectives on Jewish Liturgical History* (Cambridge, 1993) below, and see the important analysis of M. Ben-Sasson, "Ha-Mivneh, ha-Magamot veha-Tokhen shel Ḥibbur Rav Natan ha-Bavli" in *Tarbut ve-Ḥevrah be-Toledot Yisrael bi-Yemei ha-Beinayim: Qovetz Ma'amarim le-Zikhro shel Ḥayyim Hillel Ben-Sasson*, ed. R. Bonfil et al. (Jerusalem, 1989), 152 and the article cited in n. 36.

6. This does not mean that rabbinic texts were not written down before that time, though many scholars would agree with that statement, but that the entire Talmud was still orally transmitted; see Avigdor Shinan, "Sifrut ha-Aggadah," 44–45. Shinan suggests that we must allow for the possibility that both written texts and oral traditions circulated contemporaneously. While texts in Middle Hebrew I must have been written down before the end of the fourth century (see Y. Elman, "Babylonian Baraitot in Tosefta and the 'Dialectology' of Middle Hebrew," *Association for Jewish Studies Review* 16 [1991], 1–29), this does not necessarily mean that they were easily available, or that they would be resorted to even if they were; see Elman, *Authority and Tradition: Toseftan Baraitot in Talmudic Babylonia* (New York, 1994), 278–281.

Despite Shinan's reservations, and the literature he cites in n. 1, amazingly little unequivocal evidence for the circulation of written legal texts in the amoraic and post-amoraic periods exist. In the end we may have to distinguish, as indeed Shinan does, between the situation in regard to aggadic texts, which could circulate in writing, as witness the *sefer aggadata*, and halakhic texts, which could not. See N. Danzig, *Mavo le-Sefer Halakhot Pesuqot im Tashlum Halakhot Pesuqot,*

(New York, 1993), 5 n. 13, and Y. Elman, "Orality and the Redaction of the Babylonian Talmud," *Oral Tradition* 14 (forthcoming).

7. See Yaakov S. Spiegel, "Leshonot Perush ve-Hosafot Me'uḥarot ba-Talmud ha-Bavli," *Te'udah* 3 (1983) 91–112. The one important legal element which may be post-redactional is the attempt to fix the determination of amoraic disputes, the *hilkhata* comments, which were interpolated into the text of the Talmud.

Concerning the question of the size and nature of the amoraic yeshivot, for a final statement of the debate between David Goodblatt and Isaiah Gafni, see Gafni's remarks at the end of his "He'arot le-Ma'amaro shel D. Goodblatt," *Zion* 46 (1981) 55–56, where he emphasizes the importance of examining the talmudic material; see also his more recent revisit of the issue in his *Yehudei Bavel bi-Tequfat ha-Talmud: Ḥayyei ha-Ḥevra veha-Ruaḥ* (Jerusalem, 1990), 177–236. However, while he notes that "I am not far from several (*kamah*) of Goodblatt's conclusions, in particular in regard to the appearance [of the terms] *kalah* and *pirqa* [as late]," (55), he maintains his position on the use of the terms *yeshiva* and *metivta* as having undergone a certain development during the amoraic period, to the point where at the end of that period the stage was set for the geonic use. Even if Gafni's philological observation is valid, his assumption that this change in terminology reflects an essential change in the institution itself remains in doubt. For our purposes here, however, it is sufficient to note that Gafni seems in the end to agree with Goodblatt as far as the early amoraic period is concerned; see also his passing comment in *Yehudei Bavel,* 186.

8. A. Neubauer, *Medieval Jewish Chronicles* (Oxford, 1895), 2:77–78, and see Ben-Sasson, esp. the new text on pp. 194–195.

9. Ben-Sasson, 157. See also p. 159.

10. See Ben-Sasson, 174, n. 89 and the literature cited in nn. 1, 92, and 97; in general, see his discussion of the issue on 173–178.

11. *Teshuvot ha-Geonim: Sha'arei Teshuvah,* ed. Z.W. Leiter (New York, 1946), no. 55.

12. See S.D. Goitein, *Sidrei Ḥinnukh bi-Yemei ha-Geonim u-Veit ha-Rambam: Meqorot Ḥadashim min ha-Genizah* (Jerusalem, 1962), 151–153.

13. Ibid., 164.

14. Ibid., 148–149.

15. See Eliezer Schlossberg, "Magamotav ha-Ḥevratiyot shel Ḥibburei R. Saadia Gaon," *Asufot* 6 (1992) 71–85.

16. Goitein, *Sidrei Ḥinukh,* 154.

17. Ibid., 145.

18. This was already noted by the medieval commentators, the Tosafists, who

thus explained the existence of conflated and spurious verses in the Talmud; see Elman, *Authority and Tradition,* 47–48. For the strictures against quoting Scripture from memory, see bGit 60a.

19. Birger Gerhardsson, in his classic study on oral transmission, *Memory and Manuscript: Oral Tradition and Written Transmission in Rabbinic Judaism and Early Christianity* (Uppsala, 1961), suggests that "teachers and pupils, practised in the art of writing, were naturally unable to avoid enlisting the help of the pen in their efforts to master the rapidly expanding oral doctrinal material which was so important to them" (160). He views the writing tablets (*pinqasayot*) and "scrolls of secrets" (*megillot setarim*) as such. However, his references, few as they are, are mostly either Palestinian or referring to Palestinian sages, and not to amoraic Babylonia. Presumably the Sasanian world differed from the Greco-Roman. See yMa'as 2:4, which is Palestinian, bMen 70a, which refers to the Palestinian amora Ilfa, and bShab 156a, which refers to the Palestinian R. Yehoshua b. Levi, or the *megillat setarim* which Rav found in R. Hiyya's house (note that his references bShab 6b, 96b, bBM 92a are really one, since the very same quotation appears in three places).

The case of the "book of the aggadah" may be different. There was one in the *be rav* (bSanh 57a); R. Nahman had one (bBer 23b) — though he himself hardly ever proffers an aggadic comment! There was one named after R. Hisda and Rabbah b. R. Huna (bShab 89a), though whether they had owned it or whether it was a collection of their own aggadic comments is unclear. R. Hisda directed R. Tahlifa b. Avina to record something in his *aggadata* (bḤul 60b). See n. 6 above.

20. See bBB 161a.

21. Yerahmiel [Robert] Brody, "Sifrut ha-Geonim ve-ha-Tekst ha-Talmudi," *Meḥqerei Talmud,* vol. 1, ed. Yaakov Sussman and David Rosenthal (Jerusalem, 1990), 237–304; see his remarks on p. 281. Brody has now published a wide-ranging survey of geonic (textual and literary) culture, in which he summarizes his findings, *The Geonim of Babylonia and the Shaping of Medieval Jewish Culture* (New Haven, 1998); on this issue, see 156–160.

22. See Gafni's remarks above at n. 7.

23. Brody, "Sifrut ha-Geonim," 241–243.

24. Ibid., 241–243.

25. Ibid., 241, n. 20.

26. Goitein, *A Mediterranean Society,* 2: 208.

27. See Brody, "Sifrut ha-Geonim," 243–244, and Y. N. Epstein, *Mevo'ot le-Sifrut ha-Amoraim* (Jerusalem, 1962), 140–141, 143. However, Epstein also cites a responsum of R. Hai Gaon, one of the last of the Geonim, in which it is stated

that the amoraic stricture against writing halakhot ("those who write halakhot are equivalent to those who burn the Torah") applied only to earlier times, "but now when hearts have become constricted and people (*'alma*) need to look into a text (*nosaḥ*), those who write halakhot do well." It would seem that here R. Hai refers specifically to the writing of halakhic compendia, and not to the Talmud itself.

28. See Reif, *Judaism and Hebrew Prayer*, 122–128 in conjunction with 146–152.

29. Ibid., 149.

30. S. Asaf, *Tequfat ha-Geonim ve-Sifrutah: Hartsa'ot ve-She'urim* (Jerusalem, 1976), 133.

31. Bukhari, *Book of Knowledge* (*Kitab al-'ilm*), 10.

32. The most important and comprehensive study on the *madrasa*, its roots, nature and educational structure is that by George Makdisi, who has published several articles on the subject, as well as a book, *The Rise of Colleges* (see n. 2 above).

33. As quoted by the chronicler Ibn al-Jawzi, in his book *al-Muntazam fi Ta'rikh al-Muluk wa-'l-'Uman* (Hyderabad, 1940), 8: 245.

34. On the spread of the madrasa throughout the Fertile Crescent and in Egypt during the later Middle Ages, see especially: Dominique Sourdel, "Reflexions sur la diffusion de la madrasa en orient du xie au xiiie siècle" *Revue des études islamiques,* 44 (1976) 165–184; Jamine Sourdel-Thomine, "Locaux d'enseignements et madrasas dans l'islam medieval," in ibid., 185–197.

35. The origin and concept of *ijaza* has been discussed in length. See especially Ignaz Goldziher, *Muslim Studies,* trans. C.R. Barber and S. M. Stern (London, 1971), 175–180; Tritton, *Materials,* 40ff; As-Salih, *'Ulum al-ḥadith* (Beirut, 1965), 95ff; Makdisi, *The Rise of Colleges,* 140–152; Bukhsh Khuda, "The Educational System of the Muslims in the Middle Ages," *Islamic Culture* 1 (1927), 455–457. George Vajda, "De la transmission orale du savoir dans l'Islam traditionnel," in *La transmission du savoir en Islam,* ed. Nicole Cottard (London, 1983), 4–6, gives examples of several different types of *ijazas.* For a complete bibliography, see *EI*², s.v. "Idjaza."

36. The most important work on this genre of Muslim literature is that of George Vajda, many of whose articles were gathered together in *La transmission.* As-Sakhawi, in his *al-I 'lan bi'l-tawdikh li-man dhamma ahl al-tawarikh* (translated in Franz Rosenthal, *A History of Muslim Historiography,* [Leiden, 1952], 376–378) listed the *mashayakhs,* the earliest of which date from the fourth Muslim century. For a complete bibliography on this genre, see *EI*², s.v. "Fahrasa" and "Idjaza."

37. Ibn Khallikan, *Wafayat al-a'ayan wa-anba' al-zaman* [The Book of Deaths of Distinguished Persons] (Beirut, 1908), 3: 453.

38. Franz Rosenthal, *The Technique and Approach of Muslim Scholarship* (Rome, 1947), esp. 6–7.

39. See the remarks of Johannes Pederson on composition and transmission in *The Arabic Book,* trans. G. French (Princeton, 1984), 22–23, and also Jonathan Berkey, *The Transmission of Knowledge in Medieval Cairo: A Social History of Islamic Education* (Princeton, 1992), 21–43. On the survival of oral rituals and practices into the twentieth century see Dale Eickelman, "The Art of Memory: Islamic Education and its Social Reproduction," *Comparative Studies in Society and History* 20 (1978), 501.

40. Cited in Berkey, 26.

41. On the *suhba* in the context of Islamic education see George Makdisi, "Suhba et riyasa dans l'enseignement medievale," *Recherches d'islamologie: Recueil d'articles offert á Georges C. Anawati et Louis Gardet par leurs collégues et amis.* (Louvain, 1977), 207–222; idem, *Colleges,* 128–129. On the significance of *suhba* in other social contexts see Goitein, *A Mediterranean Society,* 2: 275–277.

42. On the transmission of the *imam*'s superior knowledge see Etan Kohlberg, "Imam and Community in the Pre-Ghayba Period," in Daid Arjomand, ed. *Authority and Political Culture in Shi'ism* (Albany, 1988), 25–30.

43. The events of that year are recorded by the chronicler Sibt Ibn al-Jawzi in his book, *Mira'at al-zaman* [Mirror of the Age] (Ankara, 1968), 135.

44. Historically, all degrees are teaching certificates. The earliest form of the academic degree involved an examination in a certain branch of learning such as arts, and medicine. This examination was designed to guard against favoritism and monopoly in the determination of the admission into the guild of masters which first appeared in northern Europe in the twelfth century, and formed the nucleus of the university. On the development of the academic degree see especially C.H. Haskins, *The Renaissance of the Twelfth Century* (Cambridge, Mass., 1982), 370–371.

45. Al-Suyuti, *Tabaqat al-huffaz* [The Biographies of the Reciters of the Koran and the Hadith] (Cairo, 1973), 467.

46. Ibn Khallikan, 2:91.

47. Ibid., 95; Al-Isnawi, *Tabaqat ash-Shafi'iya* [The Biographies of Shafi'i Scholars] (Baghdad, 1970), 1: 121.

48. See Brody, "Sifrut ha-Geonim," 242.

49. See S. Reif, *Judaism and Hebrew Prayer,* 150, *apud* M. Ben-Sasson.

50. Brody, "Sifrut ha-Geonim," 241, n. 20.

51. See Menahem Ben-Sasson, "Shivrei Iggerot meha-Genizah: le-Toledot Ḥiddush ha-Qesharim shel Yeshivot Bavel im ha-Magreb," *Tarbiẓ* 56 (1987), 171–173 and the literature cited there.

52. Goitein, *A Mediterranean Society,* 2: 209.

53. Ibid., 208.

54. Brody, "Sifrut ha-Geonim," 242; see also the illuminating remarks in Ben Sasson, 160. See now Avraham Grossman, *Ḥakhmei Tsorfat ha-Rishonim: Qoroteihem, Darkam be-Hanhagat ha-Tsibbur, Yetsiram ha-Ruḥanit* (Jerusalem, 1995), 422–236, which became available to us after this essay was written.

55. Brody, "Sifrut ha-Geonim," 288.

56. Ibid., 239, n. 11, and attendant text.

57. Above, p. 122.

58. Ibid.

59. bBM 98a.

60. *Iggeret,* ed. Lewin, 82.

61. Makdisi, *The Rise of Colleges,* 144.

62. Ibid., 145.

63. See Brody, "Sifrut ha-Geonim," 241, n. 20.

FOUR

Transmission in Thirteenth-Century Kabbalah

MOSHE IDEL

THE TRAIN OF TRANSMISSION

The study of the transmission of elements of culture, and their role in intellectual, religious, and other cultural change, may be carried out from various angles. Two in particular provide a salutary contrast to students of culture. On the one hand, there is *translatio studii,* the translation of the subject from one cultural sphere to another, one school of thought to another. In the case of religious change, elements are transferred from one religion to another and cause change so great as to generate the recognition that another religion has been produced or, in cases of lesser change, generate syncretistic phenomena. In any case, transmission is viewed abstractly, in a gross way; systems impinge on one another, interact and become transmuted.

On the other hand, cultural transmission and change may be viewed on the individual level, from the point of view of personal contacts, studying two adjoining links in the chain of transmission. Only later on, perhaps much later on, does the work of a few individuals yield massive transformations, immense cultural alterations. For example, the appropriation of Muslim neo-Aristotelianism by medieval Jewish philosophy was primarily the work of Maimonides; in Renaissance Europe, the whole corpus of Platonic, Neoplatonic and Hermetic writings was made available—translated, annotated and published—by virtually one person, Marsilio Ficino.

These great cultural changes are rarely a matter of the transmission of esoteric oral lore, or initiation in ancient theological or mystical doctrines; more often, they are effected by translation and general teaching of written material. The role of personal contact is rarely so crucial as in the transmission of kabbalistic lore.

In this case, we may designate contacts as "micro-chains," in contrast to the "macro-chains" of large-scale cultural change. The latter often involves massive ruptures, abandonment of what had prevailed in the recent past, and consigning eternal verities to the proverbial "dustbin of history"—often in an amazingly short space of time. In the case of the former, transmission involves more than trading information, translation of texts, and the appropriation of new ideas. As a precondition of all the above, and as the basis for what was to come, a certain type of new understanding of the significance of one's religious life had to be inculcated. Indeed, the crucial role of the master-adept relationship has stood at the center of a whole series of studies of the social context of mystical knowledge.[1]

In the following, I will restrict my analysis of this phenomenon to one century and one cultural orbit, namely, thirteenth-century Spain. In this way I hope to be able to draw some preliminary distinctions in an area which is still a *terra incognita* in the study of Jewish mysticism: the concept of esotericism, and the manner in which esoteric concepts have been transmitted, or have been conceived to have been transmitted.

My primary concern is to examine the importance of one type of transmission, that is, oral transmission, during the first generation of Spanish kabbalists. Kabbalah, the major form of medieval Jewish mysticism, emerged in the thirteenth century and produced a large variety of voluminous documents that can be studied in some detail.[2] In these documents the direct transmission of esoteric lore is mentioned time and again. But my concern here is not to prove the existence of earlier esoteric concepts or techniques, transmitted orally before being reduced to written form in the thirteenth century, important as such a subject may be for the history and prehistory of Kabbalah.

Here I am primarily concerned with how the kabbalists themselves viewed the importance of such transmission, and not, at least at this point, with the actual rituals of transmission, on the one hand, or the question of to what extent these ideas mirrored the reality of transmission.[3] In short, my concern is more with the rhetoric of transmission, the image of an esoteric tradition, than its actual praxis. I shall thus ignore the question of the actual transmission of esoterica in early kabbalistic circles,[4] and concentrate my attention on the meaning of such transmission in various kabbalistic schools of the thirteenth century.

In order to highlight the unique character of this transmission, I will briefly compare some aspects of it to what transpires in modern scientific endeavor. Though these two areas of knowledge are radically different in terms of both the object of research and the methodologies adopted to carry forth that study, they are structurally similar in ways vital to both, and a comparative approach similar to that proposed by Henri Atlan, may be of real benefit.[5]

Transmission of both religious and scientific knowledge involves a learned Informant, the Content of the information, the process of Transmission itself, and last but not least, the Recipient.[6] First, a kabbalist instructs his disciple, an act which at times has the character of an initiation rite. Likewise, a scholar may inform his graduate students, or assistants, or colleagues, of his recent findings. This takes place in a special environment, a symposium or a conference, involving highly ritualized forms of discourse.

Despite these surface correspondences, the differences between the two realms are profound. The kabbalist or religious teacher wishes to impart sacred knowledge, with a clear realization of the transformative effect of such knowledge on the psyche of his student or colleague. In some kabbalistic circles the imparting of the sacred, esoteric tradition establishes a boundary between initiates and outsiders; in some cases this involves the line between Jews and gentiles as well.[7]

Thus, while scientific information is, at least in theory, intended to be universally available, kabbalistic traditions are frequently intended to be secret, restricted to a few initiates or *illuminati*. Secret religious doctrine becoming available to the masses is deplorable; on the other hand, scientific knowledge which is restricted to a few practitioners signifies a defect in its dissemination. Closely tied to this concern is the matter of misinterpretation. Scientific misunderstanding does not incur the dangers attributed to kabbalistic misapprehensions: heresy, disintegration of the receiver's personality, madness. Kabbalistic secrets are after all "secrets of the Torah." The nature of God, of reality, of the soul, or even of history, as in eschatological matters—all of these matters affect the initiate's understanding of sacred Scripture.

In short, science attempts to confer structure to inchoate reality; tradition, however, confers meaning to lore or praxis that has already been fraught with meaning. Transmission, or the imaginary construction of such transmission, is a major means by which Jewish thinkers have linked the external face of Judaism, chiefly, its ritualistic side, to its more inward aspects.

The importance of the concept of oral transmission and oral tradition has a long and vital history in rabbinic Judaism. Its importance in kabbalistic writings and thought merely carries on and perhaps intensifies that importance. It may be worthwhile to delineate, briefly, some of the precedents which influenced the early kabbalists in their regard for the importance of oral tradition.

a. From its beginning, rabbinic Judaism held to primacy of its oral tradition, the "Oral Torah." Its formative compilations, the Mishnah, the Talmuds and various midrashic collections had their genesis in the work of small study-circles whose traditions were passed on orally. The restricted orality of these groups is reflected in the group study of the early kabbalists.
b. Oral transmission was thus both reliable and authoritative. Since religious traditions cannot be empirically verified, or duplicated for testing purposes, the identity of the Informant is almost as important as the content of tradition. While experiential kabbalistic lore, as described below, depends more on repetition and praxis than on explanation, religious esotericism is much more fideistic and experimental than other religious knowledge.

c. Last but not least, the view that some religious knowledge, especially theological knowledge, must only be transmitted orally is already explicit in earlier rabbinic texts; indeed, this view inspired some of the kabbalists as well as Maimonides, as in his *Guide of the Perplexed.*[8]

CONCEPTUAL TRANSMISSION

In this section I will attempt to uncover the differences between the transmission of religious concepts, on the one hand, and that of modes of behavior and esoteric techniques, which are often transmitted mimetically.[9] In the latter case, a great deal of emphasis is put on the identity and psychological makeup of the Recipient, as well as the identity and authority of the Informant. In this context, the mode of Transmission serves, along with the authority of the Informant, to ensure the religious validity of the Content of the tradition. While some aspects of these pertain to scientific discourse as well, the essential concern there is with the correctness of the information transmitted; the identity of the Informant and Recipient are of secondary importance. But beyond its informational value, religious traditions have another dimension, which scientific data do not; religious doctrines so transmitted must be congruent with the general outlook of the particular religion concerned, and/or the worldview of the Informant. Moreover, it must be perceived as religiously significant to the Recipient.

There is yet another aspect of the transmission of esoterica which does not occur in other realms, even non-esoteric religious ones. At some level, an esoteric tradition must partake of the recalling of a certain aspect of the primordial revelation, a fragment of knowledge which reverberates in the very soul of the Recipient. Antiquity, which is not only irrelevant to scientific exchange, but positively deleterious to the status of the information imparted, enhances the tradition's authority in a religious context. Indeed, novelty rather than antiquity is desired; the *antiqui* have long since lost out to the *moderni*.

The authority of the Informant is derived from that of the founder of the religion, tradition, sect, or school; in the case of kabbalah, however, there are a number of candidates for this position: Adam, Abraham, and, last but not least, Moses. It is the latter who is portrayed as the prototype of both Recipient and Informant of secret lore. Thus, kabbalistic teachings are often depicted as stemming from "the mouth of Moses."

In conceptual transmission, as defined above, primordial knowledge has its own importance, quite independent of the importance of the current Informant; it must be accepted as authoritative, and must be perpetuated, because of the identity of its original Informant—the initiator of the human chain, behind whom stands divine authority. The current Informant is more a vessel for transmission than a creator of esoteric lore.

On the other hand, in those types of esotericism or mysticism which are more experiential, and consist more of the knowledge of techniques for inducing mystical experiences, the authority of the Informant, original or current, is reduced, indeed, often drastically diminished, since the Recipient may reproduce the experience.

Let me exemplify these two types of transmission by means of two quotes from a kabbalistic text composed by a thirteenth-century kabbalist, the Castilian R. Isaac b. Jacob ha-Kohen. One deals with the reliability of an experiential issue, the efficacy of magic; the other with esoteric lore *per se.*

> According to the Kabbalah that was transmitted to the masters of this wisdom from the mouths of the ancient sages: We have known that indeed R. Sherira and R. Hai,[10] blessed be their memory, were competent in and received this science[11] as a tradition transmitted in their hands, master from the mouth of master, and sage (*zaqen*) from the mouth of sage, a gaon from the mouth of a gaon,[12] and all of them have used the magical practices of *Hekhalot Zutartei,* namely, the *Shimmusha de-Shedei,* in order to climb the ladder of prophecies and powers by means of it.[13]

Elsewhere in the same treatise it is said that a certain esoteric topic

> is transmitted in the name of the ancient sages who made magical use of *Shimmusha de-Hekhalei Zutartei* and *Shimmusha de-Shedei,* and it is ladder by which they attained degrees of prophecy and its powers.[14]

It should be emphasized that these quotes both assume that the ancient masters indeed practiced both magical and mystical—here designated as "prophetical"—kabbalah. But—and this is crucial for the point I wish to make—despite R. Isaac's insistence on the importance of the chain of tradition he cites, the text has little if at all to do with the actual practice of a thirteenth-century kabbalist, at least in the way described. In other words, the grandeur of the ancients, their unquestioned religious authority, is made to confer an aura of holiness on the kabbalah as sublime lore; kabbalistic texts which promote this image are less concerned with the actual kabbalistic praxis as such, at least as far as the kabbalist depicts himself in his own writings. The reliance on the achievements of the ancients as mystics and magicians was essential in order to foster the status of nascent medieval kabbalah. It is this search for authority, more than anything else, including its specific contents, that counts in these contexts.

Let me adduce another text to illustrate my point, this one from one of the paragons of medieval Judaism, as well as one of the earliest promoters of mystical lore, R. Moshe b. Naḥman, Naḥmanides. In his introduction, he warns the reader of his *Commentary on the Torah* of the futility of attempting to understand this mystical lore, unless he has first been initiated into it by a master.

> I adjure all who look into this book not to reason or entertain any thought concerning any of the mystical hints which I record regarding the hidden matters of the Torah, for I do hereby firmly make known to him that my words will not be comprehended nor understood at all by any means of reasoning or contemplation, unless [the one seeking to understand such lore has received it] from the mouth of a discerning kabbalist [speaking] into the ear of an understanding recipient. Reasoning about [such doctrines] is foolish; any irrelevant thought can cause much damage, without any [corresponding] benefit.[15]

Naḥmanides stresses the need to receive the interpretation of his kabbalistic hints from an expert master;[16] otherwise, speculation as to their meaning will be damaging. Though different from the claims of R. Isaac ha-Kohen, who enlisted the titles of ancient books and extreme practices, such as magic and prophecy, in order to enhance the knowledge he was to impart, Naḥmanides' argument is nevertheless based upon the same affirmation of antiquity, without, at the same time, providing detailed information about the concepts or praxis of this allegedly ancient kabbalistic lore. Though Naḥmanides does not mention ancient books to underscore the antiquity of his kabbalistic knowledge, he does describe Moses as the single source for authoritative esoteric lore.

It must be emphasized that although oral transmission is a prerequisite for understanding kabbalistic doctrine, this is not Naḥmanides' sole requirement. Clearly, not everything which is transmitted orally constitutes part of kabbalistic teaching and esoteric discipline. At least one other aspect of the transmitted lore is essential: it must be related to hints concerning topics inherent in the Torah. In other words, the oral tradition must address issues explicit or implicit in canonical writings. This is apparent from another of Naḥmanides' assertions.

> Indeed, this matter contains a great secret of the secrets of the Torah, which cannot be comprehended by the understanding of a thinker, but [only] by a man who acquires it, learning [it] from the mouth of a teacher,[17] going back to our master Moses, [who received it] from the mouth of the Lord, blessed be He.[18]

It should be noted that here, unlike in the previous text, the emphasis is on the Informant, while the qualities of the Recipient are not mentioned at all. In yet another text, his *Sermon on Ecclesiastes,* Naḥmanides declares that

> These issues[19] and others like them cannot be understood properly in any essential way from one's own reason[20] but by means of kabbalah. This issue is explained in the Torah to whomever has heard the meaning of the commandment by kabbalah, as is proper—a receiver [*meqabbel*] from the mouth of [another] receiver,[21] [going back] to our master Moses, [who received it] from the mouth of the Lord.[22]

We may infer that, according to Naḥmanides' rhetorical strategy,[23] and in my opinion, so too in his practice, esoteric issues included under the rubric of "kabbalah" must be transmitted orally.[24] However, it is important to note that at times Naḥmanides alludes to some theosophical doctrines, including his explicit naming of the sefirot, without alluding to the fact that he is revealing some esoteric lore.[25] In other words, it may be that the theosophical content which serves modern scholarship as the principal criterion for the definition of this kind of mystical lore did not serve Naḥmanides in the same way—it did not necessarily serve to demarcate the realm of kabbalah. It should also be noted that Naḥmanides has no other option than to declare Moses as the original human Informant; he alone is mentioned in the quotes presented above. Moreover, his role is the one implied in another important discussion, namely, Naḥmanides' disquisition, such as it is, of the location of the supernal palaces, the *heikhalot,* or *Ma'aseh Merkavah.* He asserts that, despite the fact that he does not know it, he assumes that "there was an oral tradition which [extends to the time] when Ezekiel and Isaiah came and linked it [to the biblical text]."[26]

This emphasis on the central role of orality for the transmission of kabbalistic information seems to be the result of two different considerations. One is the actual practice in the circle of Naḥmanides;[27] the other is the conscious attempt of the main halakhic elite of Catalonia—the primary elite in thirteenth-century kabbalah—to keep to itself the "secrets of the law."[28] It is noteworthy that Naḥmanides does not mention a term found in Jewish esoteric, and even talmudic, texts: *roshei peraqim,* "chapter headings," namely, general hints, or perhaps some principles concerning esoteric issues.[29] His reluctance to employ, or his decision to marginalize, such an important term in this context reflects Naḥmanides' view that kabbalistic lore should be transmitted or, more precisely, reproduced, in a faithful manner and without elaboration.[30]

TRANSMISSION OR EXEGESIS

The last third of the thirteenth century saw the emergence of highly elaborate kabbalistic systems. Some fourfold exegetical systems, such as those of Isaac ibn Latif, Joseph Gikatilla, Moses de Leon, the Zohar and the Tiqqunei Zohar, and that of Bahiya ibn Bahya, on the one hand,[31] and that of Abraham Abulafia, on the other, is evidence for the period's deep interest in hermeneutics, a much deeper and broader interest than before. Other writers on Kabbalah—R. Joseph of Hamadan, late in the century, and R. Isaac ben Samuel of Acre, at the beginning of the next—show a strong interest in exegetical methods, though not in all aspects of the hermeneutic enterprise, nor as systematic an interest.[32]

In contrast to Naḥmanides, however, all of these kabbalists are representatives of a distinct type: none of them, as far as I know, was an important halakhic authority, and none of them played a leading, or even important, role in the internal affairs of their respective communities. Moreover, despite their achievements as kabbalists, it is far from clear whether they ever produced, or were capable of producing, in-depth or wide-ranging legalistic studies.[33] They mark the appearance of a distinct, new type: the kabbalist.

These innovative kabbalists[34] may well be described as members of a "secondary elite," namely, educated individuals who were uncomfortable with the more "mainstream" intellectual stance into which they had been educated, and were in more or less continuous search of new types of thought. Maimonidean philosophy most often constituted their starting points; less common was an involvement with the views of Naḥmanides.

The restless intellectual search which marked them stands in sharp contrast to the role played by their contemporaries and seniors, the "primary elite" of Catalonia and Castile, who managed to combine the roles of authoritative halakhic authority and kabbalist. Naḥmanides in Gerona, R. Shelomo ben Abraham ibn Adret (Rashba) in Barcelona,[35] R. Moses ben Simeon of Burgos, and R. Todros ben Joseph ha-Levi Abulafia in Toledo were all accomplished kabbalists who were also active either as social leaders or halakhic authorities; in all these cases there is no evidence of an interest in systematic kabbalistic hermeneutics.

In my opinion, this distinction between the two groups is highly significant for a proper understanding of kabbalistic conceptions of the nature and role of hermeneutics. On the one hand, we have a secondary elite strongly interested in the presentation of hermeneutic systems, and on the other, a primary elite which is not. The interests of the secondary elite mark the manner in which these kabbalists define their subject. Abraham Abulafia, for example, enumerates the three principles of Kabbalah as follows:

> . . . letters, combinations [of letters] and vowels. . . .[36] Their acronym is 'AZN, which can be permutated as Tzo'N. . . . The permutation controls the letters, the vowels control the permutation, and the spirit of man, given by God, controls the vowels until they cause the emergence and illumination of the concept proper[37] [for any] intelligent kabbalist.[38]

According to other kabbalists in Abulafia's circle, Kabbalah is defined not by specific doctrines but by its linguistic methods. Among these were *gematria, notarikon, temurot,* that is, the permutation of Hebrew letters; their acronym, GiNaT, "the Garden of [the Nut],"[39] often serves as a metaphor for mystical speculations.[40] Both Abulafia's emphasis on language and the various mechanical permutations of its elements, and his acquaintances' emphasis on the more formal aspects of textual manipulation, involve facile manipulation of texts more than the interplay of esoteric concepts, which in the past constituted and would later constitute the inner religious core of canonic kabbalistic writings. Though Abulafia was insistent, as were other kabbalists, on the importance of maintaining the esotericism of mystical knowledge, he is also aware of his own tendency to reveal it rather than to withhold it. Thus, he declares, in a rare example of conscious kabbalistic exotericism:

> Though I know that there are many kabbalists who are not perfect [in their knowledge], and think that withholding a secret doctrine [testifies] to their perfection [in this science], I care neither about their thought nor of their condemning me for disclosing [these secrets], since my view on this matter is very different from, and even in direct contrast to, their own.[41]

Immediately after this declaration, Abulafia discloses his view that *Ma'aseh Merkavah,* the Account of the Chariot—one of the most important esoteric topics in Jewish mysticism, and one which has strong rabbinic support for its esoteric nature—should be understood neither as a visionary experience, nor as an allegory for metaphysics, as in Maimonides, but as a matter of letter permutations of divine names. It is thus not a doctrine, but an interpretative technique, and perhaps also a mystical technique.[42]

In sum, the various hermeneutic systems devised by late thirteenth-century kabbalists were deemed to extract new kabbalistic doctrines, or to elaborate upon existing doctrines, from Scripture. This type of Kabbalah, with its emphasis on innovation, constituted a considerable departure from the dominant perception of Kabbalah as an ancient, precious fund of esoteric lore, which consisted of certain concepts or explanations of certain aspects of Scripture, and which must be transmitted and preserved without change.

The emergence of the fourfold exegetical system, at the end of the thirteenth century, is an essential ingredient of the nascent innovative Kabbalah. Historically considered, this connection is of vital importance.[43] Transmission has been reduced to handing down certain methods, exegetical or technical, much more than instruction into doctrine or theory. It is for this reason that the contents of Naḥmanides' mystical tradition could continue to constitute a distinct kabbalistic school which was perpetuated orally and in secret for at least three generations after his demise. This cannot be said of any of the systems of innovative Kabbalah of his juniors and those of the next generation.

TRANSMISSION OF METHODS AND EXPERIENCE

Speaking abstractly, it may seem that tradition and experience stand at loggerheads, as competing methods of acquiring esoteric knowledge. Given the veneration with which tradition was endowed by the kabbalists themselves, the mystical insights achieved by experiential methods could easily be overcome by traditional doctrines, even obliterating such knowledge. Indeed, the question of the extent to which mystical experiences themselves are shaped and determined by tradition, or alternately, have a status independent of it, is part of an ongoing controversy in some academic circles.[44] However, since tradition as construed in that debate has a more general sense than that which forms the essential center of this paper—the matter of oral transmission, I will not advert to that general debate. Rather, I shall focus my short discussion on the question of the status of experientially derived esoteric knowledge in the view of a few thirteenth-century kabbalists. According to a treatise belonging to the realm of ecstatic Kabbalah:

> The essence of this issue cannot be conceptualized, *ex definitio,* nor discussed orally, and even less in written form; for this reason it forms part of what is called Kabbalah, or "chapter headings,"[45] namely, the principles [of this knowledge].[46] [This is because] the meaning [of these chapter headings] depends upon the [ability] of the recipient to [understand it] in detail and [thus] divest [his soul from corporeality]

> and [then] delight. The Kabbalah is transmitted only [by means of] "chapter headings."[47]

Thus, the impossibility of transmitting the *content* of the Kabbalah in detail, and the consequent transmission of only the general principles, tends to devalue the importance of detailed kabbalistic doctrine, since the details will be shaped by each and every recipient according to his own understanding. The experiential methods of acquiring such knowledge thus become primary. The issue of delight and sweetness recurs several times in this treatise, and the author's assumption is that such knowledge is acquired experientially, and not dialectically. The emphasis is thus not on ratiocination but on practical techniques for obtaining such lore. The anonymous kabbalist confesses that after his rather modest philosophical studies he has encountered:

> a divine man, a kabbalist, who taught me the path of Kabbalah by "chapter headings." Despite my little knowledge of natural science, it [=the path of Kabbalah] seemed to me invalid [from a philosophic point of view], [but] my master said to me: "My son, why do you reject an issue you have not experienced? Indeed, it would be worthwhile to experience it."[48]

This emphasis on experiment and experience is not unique to this kabbalist. R. Abraham Abulafia, who may be none other than the "divine man" mentioned in the passage just cited, notes in one of his writings that the study of mystical texts on his part did not induce mystical experiences in him; rather, it was only when he received a revelation that his approach to mystical texts, among them the two most important mystical sources for Abulafia, *Sefer Yetsirah* and Maimonides' *Guide of the Perplexed,* become more experiential.[49]

In a passage from his *Sefer ha-Ḥesheq,* Abulafia classifies orally transmitted kabbalistic traditions as the *lowest* form of Kabbalah.

> In order to understand my intention regarding [the meaning of] the *qolot* [voices], I shall hand down to you the well-known *qabbalot,* some of them [which have been] received from mouth to mouth from the sages of [our] generation, and others that I have received from the

> books called *sifrei Qabbalah,* composed by the ancient sages, the kabbalists, blessed be their memory, concerning the[se] wondrous matters,[50] [together] with other [traditions] bestowed on me by God, blessed be He, which came to me from ThY[51] in the form of the "daughter of the voice,"[52] these being the higher *qabbalot* [*qabbalot elyonot*].[53]

This is one of the few instances in which Abulafia explicitly mentions his reception of oral traditions from some masters. Only in one other case, when speaking of the esoteric traditions concerning the secrets contained in Maimonides' *Guide,* that Abulafia again mentions an oral tradition.[54] As we have seen, he attributes a relatively low status to such orally transmitted lore. This is again demonstrated, though indirectly, in an earlier work of his, where he defines the *mevin,* "the one who understands," as being higher than the *ḥakham,* who receives his knowledge from books.

> If he obtains it from the Kabbalah, that is, from one who has himself obtained it from the contemplation of the Divine Names or from another kabbalist,[55] he is called a *mevin.*[56]

Higher still is the *da'atan,* the "one who knows," who received the content of esoteric knowledge from his own understanding. And still higher is the *rav,* "the master," who has received his knowledge as a revelation from the divine intellect. Thus, for an ecstatic kabbalist, orally received traditions are far lower in rank than those received from the "mouth of the Agent Intellect."

Indeed, the very resort to the metaphor of the "mouth" for the relation of the human to the cosmic intellect is very significant, because it transposes the image of transmission here below, viz., the horizontal, to a vertical, namely, the mystic's connection with the divine world by means of the intellect.[57] Moreover, Abulafia's use of this metaphor may indicate that the Agent Intellect was conceived of as a master, or even the master *par excellence,* in the manner in which Hindu mystics conceived of the *guru* as a cosmic power.[58] This emphasis on the supernal spiritual source of the Kabbalah, in lieu of the more concrete flesh and blood teacher in Naḥmanides, is just one of the differences between the conservative Kabbalah of the

Geronese master and the innovative Kabbalah as envisaged by Abulafia. Revelation is not only the prerogative of the ancient masters, especially Moses, as Naḥmanides and his school would maintain, but also of the medieval mystics, whose contemporaneous revelations may be assigned to an even higher plane than that of the ancient masters.[59]

The passage quoted above is based upon two distinct approaches: the ancient Jewish one, found in the Talmud, whereby esoteric lore is transmitted only to one who is wise, *ḥakham,* and understanding, *mevin,* and further, whose understanding is *mi-da'ato,* on his own, by his own mind.[60] However, Abulafia has broken what are two talmudic phrases, *ḥakham,* and *mevin mi-da'ato,* "one who understands on his own," into three, and further attributed different meanings to each of the three, as though they signify three distinct activities. These activities are further connected to the well-known distinction between acts performed in writing, those done orally, and purely mental endeavor, a division which is crucial for the proper carrying out of Abulafia's mystical techniques.[61] Now, just as the *mevin* is greater than the *ḥakham,* and the *da'atan* greater than both, so too are oral recitations of the Divine Names and the written permutations of the letters inferior to their inner, mental pronunciations.[62]

Abulafia also mentions, as in the second passage quoted above, that he has received traditions orally from "the mouths of the sages of his generation."[63] Thus, though such traditions do play a role in Abulafia's Kabbalah, it has only a limited one, and is of lower degree than Abulafia's own discoveries, or revelations. Oral teachings provide him with the techniques for attaining mystical experiences, and not, as in Naḥmanides, the passing along of substantive esoteric lore. The master, who plays an important role in Abulafia's system, serves primarily as an external catalyst, a fairly limited function.[64]

Elsewhere, Abulafia describes Kabbalah as follows:

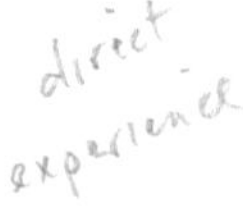

> The purpose intended by the ways of the Kabbalah[65] is the reception of the prophetic, divine and intellectual influx from God, blessed be He, by means of the Agent Intellect, and causing the descent of blessing, and providing, by means of the [Divine] Name, for the individual and the community.[66]

While the image that Naḥmanides wishes to project is that of a reliable transmitter of esoteric traditions, as in the texts from his writings quoted above, Abulafia would have been pleased to have been viewed as a recipient of kabbalistic lore by means of divine revelation. Naḥmanides' perception of Kabbalah returns to the founding experience of Moses in the glorious past, with Kabbalah constituting the essential reverberation in the present of this formative experience. For Abulafia, however, this humanly transmitted lore is a lower form of knowledge, which can and should be transcended by resort to higher forms of revelations in the glorious present, directly from the source of all knowledge, the Agent Intellect, and thus ultimately from God. This latter form of revelation presents the recipient with detailed knowledge of esoterica, while that which comes by tradition involves only the "chapter headings." Abulafia wished to short-circuit the chain of human transmission by establishing direct contact with the spiritual source. For him, the past is significant only insofar as it provides techniques which shorten the way to the divine, rather than certain fixed doctrines to be passively accepted and then transmitted. His concern is with the present and immediate future.

In sum, the role of the authoritative master who is expert in certain esoteric concepts, and was esteemed most highly by the primary elite—as was Naḥmanides—becomes of much less moment within the value system of the secondary elite. Members of that elite are concerned with the examination and preparation of future recipients, and the fostering of mystical techniques which open the way to new revelations.

With the emphasis transferred to the future and future practitioners of the kabbalistic arts, it is no wonder that we know so very little about the masters of the secondary elite, kabbalists such as Isaac ibn Latif, Joseph Gikatilla, Moses de Leon, Joseph of Hamadan, and Abraham Abulafia; indeed, in most cases their very names are unknown to modern scholarship—only their treatises remain, their authors anonymous. In the case of the conceptual Kabbalah, where the Informants, the masters, were all-important, we know much more; we can trace their identities. R. Yehudah ben Yaqar, Naḥmanides, R. Shlomo ibn Adret, R. Shem Tov ibn Gaon, R. Meir ibn Avi Sahulah, and R. Yom Tov Ishbili share the more conservative form of Kabbalah, which has been handed down from master to disciple for approximately a century and a half. While this conceptual Kabbalah is concerned with reconstructing the vestiges of those primordial experiences, by studying and preserving the remnants of the secret tradition transmitted by God to Moses, the exemplary recipient of revelation, the kabbalists of the innovative, secondary elite, were more concerned with their own mystical experiences, or the avenues open to the realization of such experiences, namely, mystical techniques.

In sum, while Naḥmanides and his school primarily functioned as curators of esoteric lore, Abulafia, like some of the other innovative kabbalists such as Gikatilla and de Leon, should be envisaged as "artists" of Kabbalah, who transformed it into an art rather than a store of traditional teachings.

PARTICULAR VERSUS UNIVERSAL TRANSMISSION

The shift from conceptual to technical transmission caused an important change in the very nature of the kabbalist's relation to Scripture. The more conservative conceptual transmission was deeply related to the text, that is, it exploited many of the idiosyncratic qualities of the Hebrew text, and was closely concerned with its eschatological and ritual content.

Technical transmission, on the other hand, was much freer in its handling of the text, since its reductionistic use of letter-permutations allowed the same methods of interpretation to be employed in any passage, no matter what the ostensible content might be. A gifted kabbalist may manipulate the text, employing the more general hermeneutic either for exegetical purposes, or to attain mystical experiences.

Of course, as noted above, the emphasis on method over detail revolutionized the very concept of Kabbalah. Let us examine two more passages dealing with the importance of "chapter headings" from the works of ecstatic kabbalists, one from a follower of Abulafia, and one from the master himself. Let us begin with an excerpt from *Sefer ha-Tseruf,* by an anonymous disciple.

> Whatever is transmitted concerning this lore [merely constitutes] "chapter headings," and requires intellect [to understand]. [That is why] it is called "intellectual Kabbalah,"[67] and is unlike other sciences, that is, the propadeutic ones, which are transmitted alone. . . . But this

> lore, known as Kabbalah, is impossible to transmit *in toto* orally, nor even in written form, even for thousands of years. And no matter how great the kabbalist's interpretive effort, everything [remains but] a hint and "chapter heading."[68]

The emphasis upon the application of intellectual understanding in order to understand kabbalistic lore is a unique feature of this text, which on the other hand criticizes philosophy as being too scholastic, and transmitting knowledge without advancing it by an innovative approach. In a Platonic vein, Kabbalah is conceived of as an invitation to decode, elaborate, and expand—rather than merely reproduce and repeat. The very resort to "chapter headings," namely, the principles that are, by definition, themselves starting points rather than final statements, is quite representative of ecstatic Kabbalah. The recourse to philosophic methods, despite the ecstatic kabbalists' critique of it, may be understood as the synthesis of the individual strand of the linguistic Kabbalah, which apparently preceded it, and neo-Aristotelian philosophy, especially that devised by Maimonides, which is part of the more general Jewish intellectual tradition imbibed by these kabbalists. This is Abraham Abulafia's major contribution, as an ardent student, teacher and commentator of Maimonides' *Guide*, but one who was also profoundly influenced by the traditions associated with the linguistic techniques of *Sefer Yetsirah* and the Ashkenazi Hasidim.

Let us return to the "chapter headings" themselves; Abulafia himself writes in one of his epistles that

> Despite the fact that Kabbalah is transmitted to all the *illuminati* in general, not every listener and receiver is able to actualize it. [This is] because what is transmitted from it are but "chapter headings" [and intended only for] those who are wise, understanding and "from their own knowledge."[69]

Kabbalah thus became, in many circles, a much more open-ended theory, whose contents may vary, become enriched and also reflect, to a certain extent, the personality and concerns of the kabbalist, as much as the nature of the religious tradition from within which it had emerged. The introduction in this context of the Aristotelian epistemological concept of "actualization" is particularly significant, and is crucial for understanding of the relationship between philosophy and Kabbalah in Abulafia's thought: Kabbalah is a type of information *in potentia,* which is intended to be actualized by the recipient. Given the medieval valuation of matters *in actu* over those merely *in potentia,* there can be no doubt that Abulafia considered his elaborations of the traditional "chapter headings" to have been of higher standing. We can easily understand why Abulafia considered these elaborations inevitable. The ecstatic kabbalist would receive the proper interpretive methods by oral transmission, and then employ them to achieve either a state of heightened consciousness or kabbalistic interpretation of scriptural texts.

Let me adduce one more quote that emphasizes the great importance given the preparation of the recipient:

> The secrets of the Torah, the secrets of reality and the foundations of the commandments, are only transmitted orally, face to face, from a perfect person to someone who merits receiving perfection, [but only] after testing and trial [regarding his] intention, that is, [that of] the recipient: if he is meritorious, it is right to transmit [them] to him, or not.[70]

It should be noted that the many quotes from Abulafia's *Sefer Shomer Mitsvah* adduced here in the context of our discussion of matters of transmission are not accidental; they are not the result of my decision to disinter this forgotten treatise. In my opinion, the question of the proper methods of transmission was central to the subject of this work, because it is dedicated to one of Abulafia's own students, R. Shlomo ben Moshe ha-Kohen, who left Sicily, apparently in order to return to his native Galilee. The occasion of Abulafia's composition of this treatise may explain his emphasis on the lower status of written, as opposed to oral, transmission. In other cases, where it is Abulafia who left his students, and dedicated works to them, we do not find this emphasis.

GRADUAL TRANSMISSION

Both conceptual and technical transmission take into consideration the spiritual development of the recipient. Despite their differences, both agree that esoteric traditions must be transmitted only gradually. In the case of the Naḥmanides' school, some secret topics are not to be revealed before the recipient reaches the age of forty, and even then, as we might have expected, they are to be transmitted orally, so as to maintain their secrecy,[71] a policy not only reasonable in itself, but one which has strong support in rabbinic tradition, to the effect that some issues should not be revealed until late in the program of studies.[72] This is made explicit in Abulafia's *Sefer Shomer Mitsvah:*

> The kabbalist may not reveal [kabbalistic secrets] and explain them in writing, but he should disclose one handsbreadth while covering two. But when [the kabbalist encounters] a person who is prepared and worthy of having [these secrets] revealed to him orally, he should first reveal two handsbreadth while covering one. And if [the recipient] will receive it, and really desire to complete what he has begun, some topics may be revealed, in accordance with [the recipient's] capacity to receive them; these [topics] should not be hidden from him, though they are, by nature, hidden and occult and essentially concealed.[73]

Elsewhere in the same treatise we learn that:

> Despite the fact that wondrous secrets[74] emerge out of their numbers [*gematriot*], these secrets[75] should be taught only orally, and only after much labor concerning the essence of the paths of Kabbalah, so that the knowledge of truth should not be given to the recipient in a random manner. But it is necessary that at the beginning he should put forth great efforts to [follow] the ways and paths of Kabbalah, which are the ways which open to gates of the heart, in order to understand the truth. Whoever wishes to enter the depths[76] of truth, according to the Kabbalah, must at the beginning lay the foundations of wisdom and understanding within his heart.[77]

The disclosure of the seventh and most advanced hermeneutical method is conditioned by Abulafia on the prior oral reception of the knowledge of the Divine Names of 42 and 72 letters, together with the transmission of "some traditions, even 'chapter headings.'"[78] Moreover, the emphasis on the importance of systematic study, including, it would seem, oral instruction and technical exercises, which are mentioned in some of Abulafia's writings and those of his followers, assumes that these are more pertinent than more conventional religious behavior to the attainment of an understanding of kabbalistic secrets. Again, the end of this statement may imply the necessity of philosophical study as an important step in the drive to attain such understanding. Abulafia believed that philosophy—in particular that of Maimonides—can help in purifying some central theological concepts which are generally misunderstood by some readers of the Bible. His kabbalistic approach therefore emphasizes a gradual intellectual and spiritual development, culminating in a deeper penetration of the secrets of the Torah rather than in cultivating the development of an elite into which the student will aspire to assimilate himself in terms of ethos and behavior.

LATER REPERCUSSIONS

The duality of conservative/conceptual and experiential/innovative types of Kabbalah is a crucial feature of this lore during the latter part of the thirteenth century. Without a commonly held point of view, kabbalistic works would diverge, and the project which began in the late twelfth century, to offer kabbalistic teachings as an attractive alternative to philosophical speculation, would soon dissipate. However, with the decline of ecstatic Kabbalah, and the consequent neglect of its emphasis on hermeneutic methods and experiential techniques, the Kabbalah would soon after its emergence lose its inertia and yield only fragmentary systems, combining different proportions of the two trends, varied according to place and circumstance. Nevertheless, with its variegated hues, the kabbalistic systems which survived and/or developed became more popular, moving from the elite to somewhat larger audiences, and also from the periphery to a more central position.

A somewhat more universalistic cast in innovative Kabbalah facilitated its acceptance by later Jewish kabbalists, who studied its texts independently of a master and a guiding tradition, and then by Christian kabbalists, especially insofar as the hermeneutical facets of Kabbalah are concerned.

With the movement of Spanish Kabbalah to Italy at the end of the thirteenth century, mainly by means of written documents—as evident from the writings of R. Menahem Recanati, and at the end of the fifteenth century, as can be seen from the writings of R. Yoḥanan Alemanno — the esoteric features of Spanish Kabbalah have been dramatically reduced. In the case of the latter, this attenuation is not only a consequence of his study of kabbalistic texts without a teacher, but also of his sustained effort to offer a philosophical interpretation of this lore, which generally encourages a more universalistic approach. Indeed, this approach is evident as late as the beginning of the seventeenth century.[79]

The ascent of a rhetoric of transmission is evident in the views of R. Isaac Luria, at least as represented by R. Ḥayyim Vital, and represents a much more exclusivistic view of such transmission.[80] On the other hand, the Christian kabbalists, who were inclined to accept claims of an ancient pedigree for the object of their interest, were also more inclined to accept the authenticity of rather innovative kabbalistic texts.[81] This is true also of R. Abraham Cohen Herrera, an early seventeenth-century Amsterdam kabbalist; he repeatedly emphasizes the importance of oral tradition from master to disciple, but at the same time he offers strongly philosophical interpretations, which were inspired by scholastic and Renaissance types, as well as by a variety of Jewish philosophic works.[82] The absorption by the developing Kabbalah of philosophical concepts, as well as the full-fledged philosophical interpretations of Kabbalah, are palpable examples of an attenuation of the role of transmission and of the influence of individual masters; these forms of Kabbalah represent a plug-in to the macro-chains of cultural transmission.

NOTES

1. See, e.g., *Abba, Guides to Wholeness and Holiness East and West*, ed. John R. Sommerfeld (Kalamazoo, Mich., 1982); *Le Maitre Spirituel selon les traditions d'Occident et d'Orient = Hermes*, Nouvelle serie, no. 3 (1983), *Direction spirituelle et psychologie* (Les Etudes Carmelitaines, 1951); Jacques Vigne, *Le maitre et le therapeute* (Paris, 1991).

2. On the concept of transmission in Ashkenazi esoteric literature see Daniel Abrams, "The Literary Emergence of Esotericism in German Pietism," *Shofar* 12 (1994), 72–73; Elliot R. Wolfson, *Through a Shining Light*, (Princeton, 1994), 234–247.

3. See Joseph Dan, *The Esoteric Theology of the Ashkenazi Hasidism* (Jerusalem, 1968), 74–75 [Hebrew]; M. Idel, "Defining Kabbalah: The Kabbalah of the Divine Names," in *Mystics of the Book: Themes, Topics, & Typology,* ed. R. A. Herrera (New York, 1993), 100–102, as well as Wolfson, ibid. For more on esotericism in a fourteenth-century Kabbalistic text written in central Europe, see M. Idel, "An Anonymous Kabbalistic Commentary on *Shir ha-Yiḥud*" (forthcoming)

4. See, e.g., the texts quoted by Gershom Scholem, *Origins of the Kabbalah,* tr. A. Arkush, ed. R.J. Zwi Werblowsky (Princeton, 1987), 40–41, 226; on the Ḥasidei Ashkenaz genealogies of transmission see Dan, *The Esoteric Theology,* 14–20, and Ivan G. Marcus, *Piety and Society, The Jewish Pietists of Medieval Germany* (Leiden, 1980), 122 and 85.

5. Henry Altan, *A tort et a raison* (Paris, 1986).

6. Moreover, the whole process should be viewed in the broader perspective of the culture, which may encourage, foster, or discourage oral transmission. In fact, different types of cultures would host in different ways, if at all, the transmission phenomena.

7. The more particularistic approach of Spanish Kabbalah was sometimes attenuated or even obliterated in Italian Kabbalah. Abraham Abulafia taught this lore to Christians, and was prepared even to discuss it with the Pope. About this dichotomy between the two forms of Kabbalah, see M. Idel, "Particularism and Universalism in Kabbalah, 1480–1650" in *Essential Papers on Jewish Culture in Renaissance and Baroque Italy* ed. D. Ruderman (New York, 1992) pp. 324–344. See also Marcus, *Piety and Society,* 85.

8. See bḤag 13a; Gershom Scholem, *Jewish Gnosticism, Mekavah Mysticism and Talmudic Tradition* (New York, 1960), 58; G.A. Wewers, *Geheimnis und Geheimhaltung in rabbinischen Judentum* (Berlin, 1975); and Morton Smith, *Clement of Alexandria and a Secret Gospel of Mark* (Cambridge, Mass., 1973), s.v. secret, secrecy; Alexander Altmann, "A Note on the Rabbinic Doctrine of Creation," *JJS* 6–7 (1955–1956): 195–206, M. Idel, "Secrecy, Binah and Derishah", in *Secrecy and Concealment* ed. H. Kippenberg and G. Stroumsa (Leiden, 1995). On medieval views of oral transmission see Isadore Twersky, "The Contribution of Italian Sages to Rabbinic Literature" *Italia Judaica, Atti del I Convegno internazionale — Barri, 18–22 maggio, 1981* (Rome, 1983), 386–387.

9. The existence of the famous rabbinic concept and praxis of *shimmush talmidei ḥakhamim,* namely a life in the presence of the great sages, attending them and learning thereby how to behave as well as having the student's personality impressed by that of the master, is relevant for our discussion.

10. This seems to be part of the *imaginaire* of the thirteenth-century Kabbalists, who attributed to these sages a knowledge of Kabbalah. Indeed, some texts found in Ashkenazi writings also attribute to this figure mystical topics. See Dan, *The Esoteric Theology,* 11, 124–128; Scholem, *Origins,* 322.

11. *Ḥokhmah,* a term that can be translated here as lore.

12. This term designates a medieval religious leader in the early medieval Middle East.

13. *Sullam ha-nevu'ot ve-kohoteiah.* R. Isaac ben Jacob ha-Kohen, *Ma'amar ha-'Atsilut ha-Smalit,* ed. G. Scholem, *Mada'ei ha-Yahadut* (Jerusalem, 1927), 2:90.

14. Ibid., 98. compare also 82, 92, 98, 107, 110. The term *Kabbalah mesura* occurs several times in his treatises; see pp. 93, 103, 111. Gershom Scholem, *Major Trends in Jewish Mysticism* (New York, 1967), 120.

15. Ch. D. Chavel, tr., *Commentary on the Torah* (New York, 1971), 15–17. For more on Naḥmanides' esotericism see M. Idel, "We Have No Kabbalistic Tradition on This," in *Rabbi Moses Nahmanides (Ramban): Explorations in His Religious and Literary Virtuosity,* ed. I. Twersky (Cambridge, Mass. 1983), 51–73.

16. Compare the text quoted from a responsum of R. Hai Gaon and analysed in Idel, "Defining Kabbalah," 101–102.

17. See also above in the passage quoted from the preface to the *Commentary on the Pentateuch.*

18. *The Commentary on Job,* in *Kitvei ha-Ramban,* ed. Ch. D. Chavel (Jerusalem, 1964), 1:23.

19. Traditions related to the cosmic cycles, *shemittah* and *yovel.*

20. *mi-da'at 'atsmo.*

21. Compare the responsum of R. Hai Gaon, discussed in more detail in Idel, "Defining Kabbalah," 101–102.

22. *Kitvei ha-Ramban,* 1:190.

23. See Elliot R. Wolfson, "By Way of Truth: Aspects of Nahmanides' Kabbalistic Hermeneutic" *AJS Review* 14 (1989), 103–178.

24. This assumption has some antecedents in earlier period in the Rabbinic texts. See Wewers, *Geheimnis und Geheimhaltung*; Smith, *Clement of Alexandria*; Gershom Scholem, *Jewish Gnosticism, Merkabah Mysticism and Talmudic Tradition* (New York, 1960) 58.

25. I assume that it would be better not to automatically identify any recourse to theosophical terminology with the esoteric Kabbalah Naḥmanides claimed that he does not reveal. This is an issue that is worthy of a detailed treatment in itself.

26. *Kitvei ha-Ramban,* 1:163.

27. See M. Idel, "On the History of the Interdiction against the Study of Kabbalah before the Age of Forty," *AJS Review* 5 (1980): Hebrew Section, 6–9.

28. See M. Idel, "Kabbalah and Elites in Thirteenth-Century Spain," *Mediterranean Historical Review* 9 (1994), 5–19.

29. See bḤag 13a.

30. For a different view of Naḥmanides, which assumes that he indeed was much more of an interpreter than his rhetoric would allow,see the abovementioned study of Wolfson (note 23 above).

31. Idel, *Kabbalah: New Perspectives* (New Haven, 1988), 210–218; idem, "PaRDeS: Some Reflections on Kabbalistic Hermeneutics," in *Ioan Culianu Memorial Volume,* ed. J. Collins and M. Fishbane (Albany, 1995), 245–264; Daniel Matt, "The Old-New Words: The Aura of Secrecy in the Zohar," in *Gershom Scholem's Major Trends in Jewish Mysticism, 50 Years After,* ed. P. Schäfer and J. Dan (Tübingen, 1993), 181–208.

32. See M. Idel, "Prometheus in a Hebrew Garb," *Eshkolot,* New Series, 5–6 (1981), 119–123 [Hebrew].

33. See Idel, "Kabbalah and Elites."

34. On this kabbalistic type, in opposition to the conservative Kabbalah, see Idel, "We Have No Kabbalistic Tradition on This"; and *Kabbalah: New Perspectives,* 212–213, and the study mentioned in the following footnote.

35. See Moshe Idel, "Naḥmanides: Kabbalah, Halakhah and Spiritual Leadership" (forthcoming); idem, "Kabbalah and Elites" (note 28 above).

36. See also *Shomer Mitsvah,* MS Paris BN 853, fol. 78b.

37. *Tsiyyur*; on this medieval concept see H.A. Wolfson, "The Terms *Tasawwur* and *Tasdiq* in Arabic Philosophy and Their Greek, Latin and Hebrew Equivalents" *The Moslem World* (April, 1943), 1–15.

38. *Sefer Ḥayyei ha-'Olam ha-Ba',* MS Oxford 1582, fol. 45b. See also M. Idel, *Language, Torah, and Hermeneutics in Abraham Abulafia* (Albany, 1989), 3–11. On the influence of this quote on R. Mordekhai Dato's description of R. Moses Cordovero's kabbalistic activity see Idel, *Studies in Ecstatic Kabbalah* (Albany, 1989), 137.

39. That is, *ginat egoz*

40. See the discussions of this acronym in R. Barukh Togarmi and Joseph Gikatilla's early *Sefer Ginnat 'Egoz.*

41. *Sefer 'Otsar 'Eden Ganuz* MS Oxford 1580, fol. 55a.

42. More on this issue see Idel, "*Ma 'aseh Merkavah*"

43. On the last quarter of the thirteenth century as one of the most creative period of Kabbalah see Idel, *Kabbalah: New Perspectives,* 211–212.

44. See the three volumes of studies edited by Steven T. Katz, *Mysticism and Religious Traditions* (Oxford, 1983), *Mysticism and Philosophical Analysis* (Oxford, 1978) and *Mysticism and Language* (Oxford, 1992) as well as the opposite stand as presented in the studies edited by Robert K.C. Forman, *The Problem of Pure Consciousness, Mysticism and Philosophy* (Oxford, 1990).

45. *Rashei peraqim.* This term will occur again in a passage from this book to be quoted here below.

46. *Ha-kelalim.* See the view of Rav Hai Gaon, *Otsar ha-Geonim,* ed. B. Levin, Ḥagigah, p. 12; Scholem, *Jewish Gnosticism,* 58.

47. *Sefer Sha'are Tsedeq,* ed. Y.E. Porush (Jerusalem, 1989), 9.

48. *Sha'arei Tsedeq,* 23. For another view of Jewish esotericism in terms of an experiential event, the union with God, see the view of the mid-eighteenth-century Hasidic master Rabbi Menahem Mendel of Premiszlany, quoted and discussed in Idel, *Kabbalah: New Perspectives,* 58.

49. *Sheva' Netivot ha-Torah,* in Adolphe Jellinek, *Philosophie und Kabbala* (Leipzig, 1854), 21.

50. A list of ancient mystical books appears in a similar context in his epistle *Sheva' Netivot ha-Torah,* 21.

51. In the manuscript: *MHTY*; it is possible that this is one of the many errors of the copyist of this manuscript that is, unfortunately, a unique one. If so, we should read the sentence as follows: "which came to me in the form of *Bat Qol.*" However, it is possible that Abulafia alluded to the Greek form *THY,* namely God, and then *MTHY* would mean "from God." Abulafia uses the form *THYV* in order to point to God already in his earlier *Sefer Get ha-Shemot;* see Idel, *Language, Torah, and Hermeneutics,* 24.

52. *Bat Qol.* See above at the beginning of this text the mentioning of the *Qolot,* voices. It is also possible that the similarity between the sounds and written forms of *Qolot* and *Qabbalot* is also implied in the idea that traditions coming from above are voices.

53. Compare to his epistle *Sheva' Netivot ha-Torah* 21, where he counts the revelation from the Agent Intellect as higher than the secrets he learned from various esoteric books. Cf. M. Idel, "Maimonides and Kabbalah," in *Studies in Maimonides,* ed. I. Twersky (Cambridge, Mass., 1990), 57–58.

54. See Idel, ibid., 58–59 and 69 n.90. On the superiority of oral transmission to written documents, see Abraham Abulafia's view discussed in Idel, *Language,*

Torah and Hermeneutics, 46–55. For the Renaissance misunderstanding of the identity of Abulafia's master as Maimonides himself see Chaim Wirszubski, *Pico della Mirandola's Encounter with Jewish Mysticism* (Cambridge, Mass., 1988), 87–88, 91–98.

55. Later on he mentions "a genuine Kabbalist" as the necessary source, in the vein of Nahmanides' first passage quoted above.

56. According to the translation of Scholem, *Major Trends,* 137. The Hebrew original has been printed there on p. 376 note 75.

57. See also *The Mystical Experience in Abraham Abulafia,* (Albany, 1987), 180–184.

58. Scholem, *Major Trends,* 140.

59. *Studies in Ecstatic Kabbalah,* 50–51.

60. See bḤag 12a. On the various varia and analyses of this text see David Halperin, *The Merkabah in Rabbinic Literature* (New Haven, 1980), 11–12.

61. See Idel, *The Mystical Experience,* 24–37.

62. Ibid., 20–21.

63. See Idel, "Maimonides and Kabbalah, 69 n. 128.

64. See Scholem, *Major Trends,* 137.

65. Described previously as transmitted themselves orally. See below.

66. *Shomer Mitsvah,* MS Paris BN 853, fol. 48b. On this view of Kabbalah, which assumes both mystical and magical aspects, see my discussion of the mystico-magical model, as exposed in *Hasidism: Between Ecstasy and Magic* (Albany, 1995).

67. *Qabbalah sikhlit.* This view, characteristic of some of the innovative Kabbalists, has been reiterated by several Kabbalists, especially in the period of the Renaissance and later on. See also below n. 78.

68. MS Paris BN 770, fol. 175b.

69. *Sheva' Netivot ha-Torah* 12.

70. *Shomer Mitsvah,* fol. 74ab.

71. See Idel, "On the History," 6–9.

72. yAZ 2.8

73. *Shomer Mitsvah,* fol. 48b.

74. *sodot nifla'ot.*

75. *sitreihem.*

76. On this term in relation to secrecy see Idel, "Secrecy, *Binah* and *Derishah.*"

77. *Shomer Mitsvah,* fol. 78a.

78. *Sheva' Netivot ha-Torah,* 20.

79. M. Idel, "The Magical and Neoplatonic Interpretations of Kabbalah in the

Renaissance" in *Jewish Thought in the Sixteenth Century,* ed. B.D. Cooperman (Cambridge, Mass., 1983), 186–242, "Major Currents," 345–368; "Kabbalah, Platonism and Prisca Theologia: The Case of Menasseh ben Israel" in *Menasseh ben Israel and his World,* ed. Y. Kaplan, H. Meshoulan, and R. Popkin (Leiden, 1989) 207–219.

80. See his introduction to *Sefer Ets Ḥayyim,* where he declares that the reliable Kabbalah was transmitted only until Naḥmanides; cf. *Shevah Ḥokhmat ha-Kabbalah,* printed in *Sha'ar ha-Gilgulim* (Premiszlany, 1975), fol. 26cd.

81. See Wirszubsky, *Pico della Mirandola,* 198–200, 262–263.

82. Cf. Alexander Altmann, "Lurianic Kabbalah in a Platonic Key: Abraham Cohen Herrera's Puerta del Cielo" *HUCA* 53 (1982), 321–324. Nissim Yosha, *Myth and Metaphor* (Hebrew) (Jerusalem, 1994).

FIVE

Beyond the Spoken Word: Oral Tradition and Written Transmission in Medieval Jewish Mysticism

ELLIOT R. WOLFSON

TRANSMISSION OF SECRETS AND FORMATION OF A FAITH COMMUNITY

A salient feature of the proliferation of Jewish mysticism in the High Middle Ages is the apparent clash between the novel and unprecedented forms of Jewish spirituality, on the one hand, and the recurring claims that these forms are the authentic and ancient traditions of Judaism, on the other. The key to assessing the complex issues that arise from the affirmation of these ostensibly opposing views is an exploration of the cultural forms of transmission of knowledge and practice in the relevant mystical fraternities.

In this study, I will examine the mechanism by which the Provençal and Spanish kabbalists of the twelfth and thirteenth centuries were instructed in the traditions and practices considered to be unique to their respective groups. The particular perspective from which I will investigate this issue is the interplay between oral transmission of esoteric wisdom and the production of written texts of either an exegetical or revelatory nature. Participation of individuals in these circles was based principally on their receiving proper instruction in mystical matters pertaining to both true beliefs and right actions. To understand the social constitution of these groups, it is necessary to consider the means by which these traditions and practices were disseminated. Furthermore, the relative exclusivity or inclusivity of a given group was determined by these pedagogical concerns. The more esoteric the means of transmission or the more recondite the content of the doctrine, the more restrictive the group.

In the twelfth and thirteenth centuries, Jewish mysticism was clearly an elitist enterprise far removed from what scholars today would call popular religious culture. There is little historical evidence that large numbers of people in any geographical area were influenced by mystical beliefs and practices. Furthermore, the extant historical documents provide us with relatively sparse biographical information about the Jewish mystics themselves. In fact, we have a significant number of textual compositions (especially from Castile in the later part of the thirteenth century) either without any attribution or falsely ascribed to ancient authors. The fainthearted individual, intimidated by anonymity or pseudepigraphy, has no business entering the palace of medieval Jewish mystical speculation. Nevertheless, from the literary style and substance of the relevant texts, it is reasonable to conclude that the kabbalists, for the most part, were practicing rabbinic leaders or had been trained in the talmudic academies and were thus well-versed in classical Jewish learning. From a sociological point of view, one must presume, moreover, that in practical matters Jewish mystics availed themselves of the religious institutions that served the rest of their extended communities. In that respect, it is doubtful that the kabbalists were separated from the society at large, as one might find, for example, in a Christian monastic order, even though there is good reason to assume that they belonged to small fraternities made up exclusively of fellow practioners. One must suppose that to some degree these circles functioned autonomously, laying claim to a secretive knowledge that explained the essence of Judaism but that was not readily available to all Jews in an equal manner.

The issue of education, therefore, is not a tangential one. On the contrary, it goes right to the heart of the matter of identity formation on both the individual and the communal levels. Naturally, one must be careful not to make a judgment about the formation of medieval Jewish faith communities in general based on the evidence culled from the writings of the kabbalists. That evidence must be viewed as idiosyncratic, or at the very least highly selective. On the other hand, the kabbalists were part of the larger world of rabbinic culture, which had a major role in shaping the identity of Jews in the Middle Ages as a unique community of belief vis-à-vis other religious traditions, principally Islam and Christianity. Even though the teachings and practices of the kabbalists were presumed to be esoteric, the overriding belief espoused by them was that the secret gnosis represented the truest and innermost dimension of Judaism. The kabbalists believed that their doctrines were at the core of Judaism and, as such, were relevant for the education and formation of Jewish society at large. At the current stage of scholarly research, however, it cannot be determined with precision how the educational process unfolded with respect to the transmission of esoteric knowledge. Indeed, at the moment only the questions seem clear: Were there clandestine meetings in which the master communicated the secrets orally to the disciples? Or were there study groups in which older esoteric documents (*megillot setarim*) were analyzed, interpreted, and expanded into more elaborate theosophical systems and/or mystical ideologies?[1] Or did the exposition of secrets emerge in the context of explicating traditional literary sources that were part and parcel of the medieval rabbinic library, for example, talmudic legends, midrashic anthologies, and liturgical works? If there were in fact study groups dedicated to the exegesis of mystical secrets, within what educational framework did they convene?

JEWISH MYSTICISM AND THE HERMENEUTICS OF ESOTERICISM

Whatever the mystical components of the various trends of speculation that scholars refer to by the generic title Jewish mysticism, a more appropriate term to characterize this body of lore is esotericism, *ḥokhmat ha-nistar,* a set of doctrines that are deemed secretive and that must therefore be transmitted only to a small circle of initiates.[2] In his essay "Das Verhältnis Maimunis zur jüdischen Mystik," published in 1936, Alexander Altmann noted that the "esoteric nature of mystical teachings in Judaism is expressed by the terms *sod* ('secret'), *sithrey Torah* ('mysteries of the Law'), and their equivalents. Obscure though the historical origins of Jewish mysticism are, and especially its connections with the various schools of prophecy, apocalyptic literature, and Gnosis, a definite esoteric posture, setting down a precise form of transmission, had evolved as early as the tannaitic period."[3] Altmann went so far as to suggest that the exclusive transmission of mystical knowledge from master to disciple attested in rabbinic sources may be due to the influence of Hellenistic mystery religions. Be that as it may, it is noteworthy that Altmann discerned that in Jewish mysticism, beginning in its early stages, the notion of secret is essential. Indeed, Altmann's remarks suggest that in his opinion the mystical phenomenon must be circumscribed within the framework of esotericism.

Gershom Scholem, for his part, distinguished sharply between mysticism and esotericism. The former, he maintained, "means a kind of knowledge which is by its very nature incommunicable," insofar as the object of mystical experience is inexpressible in human language, whereas the latter involves "a kind of knowledge that may be communicable and might be communicated, but whose communication is forbidden."[4] Despite the clear presence of mystical elements in the Jewish sources, there seems to me little doubt that the issue of esotericism in the way delineated by Scholem is much more critical in assessing the nature of what we will call Jewish mystical speculation in its different varieties or trends. Indeed, the experiential aspects of Jewish mysticism are contextualized within a hermeneutical framework predicated on some form of esotericism. To borrow the formulation of Antoine Faivre, "active esotericism is the privileged form of hermeneutics."[5] Elaborating on this point in another context, Faivre writes: "The etymology of 'esotericism' clarifies the idea of secret by suggesting that we can access understanding of a symbol, myth, or reality only by a personal effort of progressive elucidation through several successive levels, i.e., by a form of hermeneutics."[6] The word "esotericism" is thus meant to convey the notion that there is an inner tradition that cannot be conveyed except to select individuals who ascertain or gain access to the secret through hermeneutical means. This point has also been expressed by Moshe Idel: "Kabbalah is by definition an esoteric body of speculation; whether in its theosophical-theurgical explanation of the rationales for the commandments, or in the ecstatic trend dealing with techniques of using divine names, esotericism is deeply built into this lore."[7] Nothing is more important for understanding the mentality of the kabbalist than the emphasis on esotericism. The possession of secret gnosis (related to both ideas and rituals) empowers the kabbalist, for he alone has the keys to unlock the hidden mysteries of the tradition.

ORALITY AND ESOTERICISM

Esotericism has informed Jewish spirituality from ancient times. One thinks immediately of the apocalyptic notion of *raz,* which referred to a secret transmitted to select individuals of extraordinary caliber or pedigree.[8] The secret could relate to history, cosmology, or eschatology. The influence of the apocalyptic notion of secret is evident in Qumran texts and the New Testament.[9] Jewish esotericism of the late Second Temple period, preserved in oral traditions and written documents, also provides the matrix for the significant emphasis on mysteries in Gnosticism and Jewish Christianity[10] as well as the ancient Jewish mystical-magical speculation preserved in Hekhalot literature.[11] On occasion these secrets are portrayed as being recorded in books of limited circulation (sometimes the secrets are said to be inscribed on the heavenly tablets) that can be revealed again to the particular visionary.[12] The topos of celestial or hidden books, whose primary aim is to establish a credible chain of tradition as a source of esoteric knowledge, continued to influence Jewish mysticism and magic through the generations.[13] Thus we find, for example, various references to such works in the *Zohar.*[14] The Spanish halakhic authority and kabbalist, Solomon ben Abraham ibn Adret, refers in one of his responsa, presumably directed against Abraham Abulafia,[15] to one who is a prophet or one with whom an angel communicates and for whom he writes a book.[16] Another striking example of this phenomenon is found in the following line of succession generated by the *'Iyyun* circle and incorporated by the fourteenth-century kabbalist, Joseph ben Shalom Ashkenazi, in his commentary on *Sefer Yetsirah:* "The teacher of the first Adam was Raziel, and that of Shem Yofiel, and that of Moses Metatron, and that of Elijah Maltiel. Each and every one of these angels would transmit the tradition (*qabbalah*) to his student by means of a book or orally."[17] The receiving of esoteric knowledge from a text is combined here with the emphasis on oral reception, a hermeneutical strategy that will be discussed more fully below. The notion of angelic disclosure of secret knowledge underlies the phenomenon of maggidism that became prevalent in sixteenth-century kabbalistic circles,[18] but which has an earlier source in Jewish mysticism.[19]

Equally important, however, is the fact that in the formative period of classical Judaism, the rabbis viewed select issues as arcane and therefore improper for public discussion or exposition.[20] There is, in first instance, the well-known mishnah in Ḥagigah 2:1 in which three subjects, illicit sexual relations, the account of creation, and the account of the chariot, are signaled out as sections of Scripture that cannot be studied openly.[21] In addition, in several places in rabbinic literature mention is made of *sitrei torah,* the "mysteries of Torah."[22] The oral nature of the transmission of the mysteries of Torah and the high level accorded the individual who is worthy to receive them is affirmed in the following anonymous interpretation of the verse, *'al ken 'alamot 'aheivukha,* "Therefore do maidens love you" (Song of Songs 1:3):

> If a man reads [Written Torah] but he does not study [Oral Torah], he is still standing outside.[23] If he studies [Oral Torah] but he does not read [Written Torah], he is still standing outside. If he reads [Written Torah] and studies [Oral Torah] but he does not serve the scholars (*shimmesh talmidei ḥakhamim*), he is like one from whom the mysteries of Torah are hidden, as it says, "Now that I have turned back, I am filled with remorse; [Now that I am made aware, I strike my thigh. I am ashamed and humiliated, for I bear the disgrace of my youth]" (Jer 31:19). However, if the man reads the Torah, Prophets, and Writings, and he studies Mishnah, the exegetical works on halakhah and aggadah (*midrash halakhot we-'aggadot*), and he serves the scholars, even if he dies or is murdered for His sake, he is eternally happy. Thus it says, "Therefore do maidens love you." (Song 1:3)[24]

Implicit in the exegesis of the verse from Song of Songs is the play on words of *'alamot,* "maidens," and *ha'alamah,* "concealment." The anonymous rabbinic sage discerns a reference in this verse to the *sitrei torah,* the mysteries that are concealed from most people. In order to receive these mysteries, which are transmitted orally from master to disciple, one must not only read the Written Torah and study the Oral Torah, but one must also minister to the scholars in a personal way. The point here seems to be that only one who has immediate access to the sage will be in a position to receive the secrets through a direct, oral transmission, from mouth to mouth. The one to whom the secrets are revealed truly loves God and merits eternal felicity for he is prepared to sacrifice his life on behalf of the divine. The scholar who receives the mysteries from the master is feminized through the hermeneutical lens of the rabbinic reader of the biblical text.

An interesting comment regarding the need to conceal these secrets, which are thought to be derived exegetically from Scripture, from those who are not ready to receive them occurs in Song of Songs Rabbah 1.2: "R. Simeon ben Ḥalafta and R. Ḥaggai said in the name of R. Samuel ben Nahman: 'The lambs (*kevasim*) will provide you with clothing' (Prov 27:26). It is written *kevasim,* for when your students are small you should conceal (*mekhabesh*) from them words of Torah, but when they grow you should reveal to them the secrets of Torah (*sitrei torah*)." A similar passage that relates more specifically to the secrets of the chariot is found in bḤag 13a: "[R. Joseph] said to them [those who asked him to expound the account of the chariot]: It has been taught, 'Honey and milk are under your tongue' (Song 4:11) — matters that are sweeter than honey and milk should be under your tongue. R. Abbahu said [it] is derived from here: 'The lambs will provide you with clothing' [*kevasim li-levushekha*] (Prov 27:26) — matters that are the mysteries of the world [*kivshono shel 'olam*] should be under your garment." Implicit here is the midrashic technique "do not read X but Y," which is employed in this context to articulate the rabbinic idea that certain issues must remain secret and thus hidden under one's garments. Indeed, this interpretation is supported by a variant manuscript reading of the text as well as by a citation preserved in the commentary on *Sefer Yetsirah* by Judah ben Barzillai and in Jacob ibn Habib's *Ein Ya'aqov:* "R. Abbahu said [this] is derived from here: 'The lambs will provide you with clothing.' Do not read *kevasim* but rather *kevushim,* that is, matters that are the mysteries of the world should be under your garment."[25]

Mention should also be made of the expression *sodah shel torah,* the "secret of Torah," employed in Song of Songs Rabbah 1.8, where it refers to the figurative or non-literal sense of Scripture derived through an apparently non-mystical, exoteric method of exegesis. On the other hand, the term *sitrei torah,* referring in a technical sense to esoteric secrets, is employed by the anonymous redactor(s) in bPes 119a in interpreting the words *we-limekhaseh 'atiq* in Isa 23:18: "this refers to the one who conceals the matters that the Ancient of Days (*'atiq yomin*) concealed. And what are they? The secrets of Torah." A related exegetical turn is taken in a passage in Genesis Rabbah 1.5 interpreting the verse "that speak haughtingly (*'ataq*) against the righteous (*tsaddiq*)" (Ps 31:19): "[this refers to] the Righteous One, Life of the Worlds [i.e., God] who hid (lit., removed, *he'etiq*) things from His creatures." The sense of an esoteric meaning of Torah is also implied in the following interpretation in bḤag 14a of the words, "were shriveled" (*'asher qummetu*) in the verse, "How they were shriveled up before their time and their foundation poured out like a river" (Job 22:16): "These are the scholars who bend (*meqammetin*) themselves over words of Torah in this world; the Holy One, blessed be He, reveals to them the secret (*sod*) in the world-to-come, as it says, 'their foundation (*yesodam*) poured out like a river.'" Although not stated explicitly, I assume that the secret here has an exegetical reference, i.e., God discloses the secret of Torah in the world-to-come to the scholars who have dedicated their lives to study in this world. Finally, in mAvot 6.1, in a statement attributed to R. Meir, the one who studies Torah for its own sake merits various things, including the disclosure of secrets of Torah, *megallin lo razei torah.* I will provide one more example of the rabbinic concern with esotericism from the midrashic compilation, Genesis Rabbah 1.3.[26] According to this text, Simeon ben Yehosadaq asked Samuel ben Nahman, identified as a *ba'al haggadah,* "master of folklore," whence the first light of creation was created. Samuel responded that God wrapped himself in light as in a garment and its splendor shone from one end of the world to the other. The reader is told, moreover, that Samuel revealed this information in a whisper, which led Simeon to ask him, since the point is made explicitly the verse, "wrapped in a robe of light You spread the heavens like a tent cloth" (Ps 104:2), why did he transmit it in a whisper? To this query, Samuel responded: "Just as I heard it in a whisper so I said it to you in a whisper."

Presented here is a code for the transmission of esoteric doctrine: even if the specific idea can be deduced from an explicit scriptural passage, still it must be revealed "in a whisper," i.e., not in a public manner, if it has been so received.[27] The oral nature of the transmission of this motif is underscored by variant readings of this text and parallel versions in other midrashic compilations where the expressions *qibbalti,* "I received,"[28] *qibbaltiha,*[29] "I received it," or *'amruha li,* "they it said to me,"[30] are used in place of *shama'ti,* "I heard" or *shema'tiha,* "I heard it." The general connotation of the word *shama'ti* in rabbinic texts is a literal repetition or memorization of a teaching that is considered to be an authoritative tradition. The point is made by Birger Gerhardsson: "The formula 'I have heard' (*shama'ti*) shows that we are not here dealing with statements which the rabbi has found in some written text; he has heard them as tradition from his teachers."[31] However, Gerhardsson qualifies this claim with an important observation: "The possibility that what is comprised under this quotation formula may exist partly in private note-books is naturally not excluded."[32] The connotation of *shama'ti* need not necessarily be an aural reception, but it may simply mean "I have deduced," "I have understood," or "I have learnt." This meaning of the locution *shama'ti* will resurface in a later discussion of medieval sources. With regard to the text from *Genesis Rabbah,* however, it seems that the hearing of the esoteric doctrine is actual. Nevertheless, it is still not clear if the secret that has been orally transmitted is from a verbal or a written source. There is an explicit acknowledgement in the passage that the secret could have been deduced from Scripture. Samuel's response that he must transmit it in a whisper because he received it in such a way does not directly challenge the point that the secret is encoded in the biblical text and it is conceivable that what he received in a whisper was an oral exposition of this very verse. Another example that may be adduced as confirmation of the idea that esoteric matters are to be divulged through oral transmission is found in the interpretation of the word "enchanter" (*laḥash*) in Isa 3:3 given in bḤag 14a: "the one to whom it is worthy to transmit words of Torah that are given in a whisper (*be-laḥash*)." In this case it seems fairly obvious that the issue is the elucidation of esoteric doctrines from the text of Scripture. We can well imagine that the explication is of an oral nature, but it is nonetheless exegesis of a written text.

Esotericism on the part of the rabbis, therefore, was intended to prevent the composition of texts rather than the dissemination of secrets preserved in oral or written form. The thematic link between orality and secrecy is epitomized in the midrashic text wherein the Mishnah is called the *mistorin* (or *mistirin,* from the Greek *mysterion*) of God.[33] The particular context in which this occurs reflects an obvious polemic against those who wanted to commit the Oral Torah to writing.[34] Although in this case there is nothing especially esoteric or mystical about that which should be left oral, reflected in the passage is a correlation between that which is hidden and that which is transmitted orally. This correlation clarifies the use of *mistorin* to refer to the Mishnah, i.e., the Oral Torah can be called God's mystery because it should not have been formalized in a written document.

In the case of medieval Jewish mysticism, esotericism—a chord that strikes very deep in the religious mentality of Jewish mystics to this very day[35]—is strongly linked to an emphasis on orality as the vehicle of transmission. An interesting example from a prekabbalistic work, the commentary on *Sefer Yetsirah* by Judah ben Barzillai al-Barceloni, is worthy of citation. According to the system that he develops, the first of the entities created by God is the Holy Spirit (*ruaḥ ha-qodesh*), also identified as the glory (*kavod*), Presence (*shekhinah*), and the first of the ten *sefirot* enumerated in *Sefer Yetsirah.*[36] In response to the question why the rabbis never spoke of such a critical idea as the Holy Spirit, Judah writes: "The sages did not speak of this explicitly so that people would not come to contemplate what is above . . . Therefore they would transmit this matter to their students and sages in a whisper and privately, through an [oral] tradition (*qabbalah*)."[37] Although the issue of orality is related to esotericism already in the rabbinic sources, as I have noted, it is in the mystical traditions that the oral nature of the transmission of esoteric doctrines is underscored to an extent unprecedented in the earlier literature.

In the writings of medieval Jewish mystics, esotericism is strongly linked to an emphasis on orality as the vehicle of transmission. Although these issues are related already in classical rabbinic sources, as I have noted, in the mystical texts the oral nature of the transmission of esoteric doctrines is underscored in an unprecedented way. Indeed, the most common term used by Jewish mystics of this period to refer to their teaching is *qabbalah,* derived etymologically from the word *qibbel,* i.e., to receive, and the masters of the esoteric knowledge are called *ba'alei qabbalah* or *mequbbalim*. In this context, the term *qabbalah* connotes reception of an occult lore or practice that has been transmitted orally. The connection between esotericism and orality is affirmed in one of the most important documents for the study of early theosophic kabbalah, the letter written in the mid-1230s by Isaac the Blind, the Provençal master considered to be the source of the theosophic ideas and contemplative practices that influenced the major circle of Catalonian kabbalah.[38] In the letter, Isaac reports that he has learnt a lesson from the behavior of his "ancestors," i.e., his maternal grandfather, Abraham ben Isaac of Narbonne, and his father, Abraham ben David of Posquiéres, who never allowed a word dealing with esoteric matters "to escape their lips and they conducted themselves with them [with those not initiated into the secret doctrine] like men who were not versed in the [mystical] wisdom."[39] The intent of the letter was to express Isaac's anger at the dissemination of kabbalistic doctrines in northern Spain on the part of his own students, presumably Ezra and Azriel of Gerona. Isaac criticized the composition of such treatises for, as he puts it, "that which is written has no case," *ha-davar ha-nikhtav 'ein lo 'aron,*[40] i.e., the author cannot control the fate of a document's distribution after it has been composed. Isaac, therefore, presents himself in this epistle as one who is very reluctant to disclose matters publically, especially through the medium of a written text. Hence, he insists on two separate occasions in the letter that he cannot elaborate a particular doctrinal point in writing.

Many textual examples could be cited to demonstrate the reluctance on the part of kabbalists in this early period to write an explanation that was considered by them to have been passed on through a continuous chain of oral tradition. Indeed, mystics representing the three dominant trends of Spanish kabbalah in the thirteenth century—linguistic mysticism (those kabbalists whose principal interest consisted of speculating on the nature of the Hebrew alphabet), theosophic kabbalah (the system based on the doctrine of ten dynamic powers that comprise the pleroma of divine energies, most frequently referred to as the *sefirot*), and prophetic kabbalah (the system whose main focus is the attainment of a state of mystical ecstasy, characterized as *unio mystica,* through various meditative techniques including letter combinations and permutations of the divine names) — all profess that their respective teaching is a *qabbalah,* an orally received doctrine. Moreover, in the various circles of kabbalists, oral teaching was upheld as one of the main media for transmission of esoteric ideas and practices. In spite of the fact that thirteenth-century esotericism should be characterized as a transition from an oral to a written culture, a process that culminates in the composition and dissemination of the *Zohar* in the 1280s and 90s, there is ample evidence that kabbalists adhered to a code of esotericism that prohibited the complete exposure of sensitive theological issues of a theoretical or practical nature in writing.[41] Even Moses de León, who expounded freely on esoteric matters in his Hebrew writings and in the *Zohar,* occasionally adopts a more conservative approach and insists on the need to conceal a matter or to withhold its full disclosure.[42] The typological distinction between conservatism and innovation is problematic if pushed too far to the extreme.[43] A subtler approach is necessary, one that takes into account the possibility that within one thinker there may be a clash between the two approaches.

It is likely that the kabbalists were influenced in part by the formulation of Maimonides who likewise emphasized that the "secrets of Torah," consisting of the account of the chariot and the account of creation, which represented for him metaphysics and physics respectively, had to be explained orally. Maimonides goes so far as to say that "this knowledge was only transmitted from one chief to another and has never been set down in writing."[44] In a slightly different manner, Maimonides argues that this knowledge is hidden in parables in both scriptural and rabbinic texts, though they have never been set down in any systematic way.[45] In spite of the many differences in approach between Maimonides and the kabbalists, there is a basic similarity in terms of the formal acceptance of esotericism that is linked with orality.[46] Maimonides assumes that the oral tradition consisted of philosophic doctrines that were cultivated by Jews but never committed to writing in a comprehensive or systematic manner. By contrast, Jewish mystics make a claim for specific ideas that are, to a great degree, unique to the respective mystical systems and are thus not traceable to any one source. Clearly, for this reason the vexing (and, in my opinion, methodologically flawed) search for the "origins" of the kabbalah has no analogue in the study of medieval Jewish philosophy.

The impact of Maimonides is particularly evident in one of the earliest systematic characterizations of kabbalah found in Ezra of Gerona's commentary on Song of Songs. The treatise cannot be dated with any precision, though it may be surmised that it was composed sometime in the late 1220s or early 1230s.[47] In the introduction to the work, Ezra traces the chain of transmission of the knowledge of God's name from biblical antiquity (beginning with Abraham) to his own time. I pick up the description after the Sinaitic revelation: "From that time until now there has not been in Israel any generation that has not received the tradition of wisdom, which is knowledge of the name (*yedi'at ha-shem*), through the order of the tradition (*qabbalah*), the Oral Torah."[48] In a somewhat contradictory manner, Ezra asserts in another passage that since the destruction of the Temple "this wisdom has ceased in Israel." In the second context he also concludes, following the approach of Maimonides, that it is only due to the efforts of the sages who scattered references to the kabbalistic truths in the midrashim and the talmudic aggadot that remnants of the tradition were preserved for posterity.[49] As he puts it in another passage: "The words of the sages, blessed be their memories, are absolutely complete and perfect . . . all their words were said through the holy spirit by allusion in order to arouse the hearts of the enlightened ones, the kabbalists (*ha-maskilim ha-mequbbalim*)."[50] This latter point is central to Ezra's hermeneutical effort (though in this regard he is by no means unique) to recast biblical texts in light of kabbalistic theosophy insofar as he reads the former through the lenses of the rabbis whose words have also been theosophically transformed.

I cannot enter into all the details of Ezra's thought, but two points are especially noteworthy. First, Ezra perceived his own time as a propitious one for the reconstruction of kabbalistic truths that ultimately go back through an oral chain to the beginnings of Judaism as recorded in biblical history. It is likely that Ezra's justification for explicating kabbalistic secrets in his own work is related to his own advancing age and to the approaching of the sixth millenium in the year 1240, which was linked to much messianic speculation in eschatological works written in the twelfth and thirteenth centuries.[51] The implicit messianic rationale for the disclosure of esoteric wisdom, in my opinion, explains Ezra's choice of an exegetical work on Song of Songs as the vehicle to communicate his ideas, for this scriptural book was understood from the rabbinic period as a messianic allegory. In Ezra's own words:

> For many years I have seen this and that [secret tradition] and I have kept quiet, and my hand has clapped my mouth,[52] until I entered the fifth grade[53] as it says, one [year] from the years of life.[54] I see that the day has declined before me and old age is quickly approaching; therefore I have undertaken to explain one of the twenty-four books that comprises delights, and speaks of glorious mysteries and secrets . . . and this is the book of the Song of Songs. I will explain it according to my strength as I have received from my teachers, and I will attend to the rationales for the commandments, and illustrate the secrets of the account of creation.[55]

Approaching the end of his life, Ezra felt compelled to commit to writing the kabbalistic secrets that he received from his teachers. As his genre he chose an exegetical work, a commentary on the Song of Songs, in which he included a discussion on the mystical reasons for the commandments and the secrets of cosmology, two topics that he obviously considered essential to kabbalah. The choice of this particular biblical text by Ezra can be properly appreciated only if one bears in mind that one finds in his commentary an underlying emphasis on the imminent redemption set to occur in the sixth millenium according to the doctrine of cosmic cycles (*shemittot*) that he accepted.[56] The point is alluded to, for instance, in the following passage in the commentary: "'For now the winter is past' (Song 2:11), this symbolizes the completion of the end and the departure of the exile; 'the blossoms have appeared in the land' (Song 2:12), this refers to the approaching days of repose and the coming of the inheritance and rest."[57] To be sure, in contrast to other kabbalists, including his younger colleague Naḥmanides,[58] Ezra does not advocate the calculation of a specific date of the redemption. On the contrary, in the introduction to the commentary he cautions the reader: "Know that there are figures of speech (*meshalim*) in this book whose details cannot be explained in any manner, like 'the blossoms have appeared in the land, the time of singing has come, the song of the turtledove is heard in the land,' concerning these [images] and others like them we cannot examine them in detail but only explain that this is a symbol for the greatness of the coming days of rest, and the winter for the passing days of exile."[59] Despite his reluctance to specify the date of redemption, it is nevertheless a sensitivity to the impending end of exile and beginning of the redemption that, no doubt, was behind Ezra's decision to write a commentary on Song of Songs and to contextualize kabbalistic secrets in such a setting. This must be explained in terms of the long-standing exegetical tradition, attested in the Targum to this book as well as in isolated midrashic comments collected in various works such as Song of Songs Rabbah, which read the song as a recounting of Israel's *Heilsgeschichte,* from the exodus from Egypt to the future redemption, a point that Ezra makes explicitly.[60] Given the eschatological and messianic allusions in this text according to older forms of midrashic exegesis, it is understandable why Ezra would have viewed the work as the perfect hook upon which to hang kabbalistic doctrines that should be disclosed at the moment of history when the redemption is imminent. What book could have served better than the Song of Songs as the medium to express the message of redemption as the sacred union of the masculine and feminine aspects of the divine? The erotic drama of lover and beloved is transferred by Ezra to the dynamic between these attributes. In that sense the kabbalistic reading of Song of Songs is concomitantly a messianic reading; indeed it is not possible to separate the mystical and the messianic for the historical process of Israel's exile and return to the land dramatized in the dialogue of the lover and beloved is at the same time a reflection of the rupture and reunification of the masculine and feminine aspects of the divine.[61]

The second point is that the essence of the kabbalistic tradition has to do with knowledge of the divine name, a notion found as well in the fragments attributed to the kabbalists of Provence, Abraham ben David, Jacob ha-Nazir, and Isaac the Blind.[62] Such a characterization of kabbalah is also found in one of Ezra's epistles[63] and recurs in the writings of Azriel;[64] it is also the basis of Asher ben David's treatise *Perush Shem ha-Meforash,* which begins with the statement, "we have received a tradition in our hands from our ancestors" concerning the theosophic meaning of the Tetragrammaton.[65] The identification of the name as one of the secrets of Torah or as part of the mystical praxis of ascending to the chariot is found in other writings from the medieval period, for example, in the northern French exegetes, Solomon ben Isaac of Troyes and his grandson Samuel ben Meir.[66] Traditions concerning the name are preserved as well by the German Pietists of the twelfth and thirteenth centuries[67] and by Abraham Abulafia and his followers in the thirteenth and fourteenth centuries.[68] That kabbalah was construed in this way is critical for it indicates a common heritage of Jewish esotericism (which, indeed, may be traced back to earlier sources)[69] shared by these different groups.

An important corollary to the claim that *qabbalah* refers to esoteric truths that have been transmitted orally is the view that these truths cannot be deduced by the power of reason or supposition (*sevara'*), a position that, *prima facie,* is at odds with Maimonides who states explicitly that he deduced knowledge of the secrets of Torah on the basis of conjecture and supposition rather than divine revelation or oral transmission from a teacher.[70] The position is stated explicitly by Naḥmanides who writes near the conclusion of the introduction to his commentary on the Torah that one will not understand the allusions he has made to the secrets of Torah by means of the intellect or understanding, but only through an oral reception, "from the mouth of a kabbalistic sage to an ear that receives" (*mipi mequbbal hakham le-'ozen meqabbel*).[71] The rejection of reason as a means to comprehend or ascertain esoteric wisdom is affirmed by a host of kabbalists through the generations, in many instances relying on or paraphrasing the formulation of Naḥmanides, as we find, for example, in Abraham ben Eliezer ha-Levi of the fifteenth century and Ḥayyim Vital of the sixteenth century.[72] The ostensible opposition of reason and tradition is stated boldly in the second principle of an anonymous text that enumerates several introductory principles for the study of kabbalah: "The one who enters this wisdom must know that it is called *qabbalah* for one must receive it orally and it cannot be comprehended by the intellect for it is above the intellect, even above the first intelligible."[73] I will mention here one other text wherein such a position is affirmed for it sheds much light on the correlation of orality and esotericism. The text is also significant for it allows one to view the inner struggle in the mind of a kabbalist between the radical denial of the efficacy of human reason as a means to apprehend secrets, on the one hand, and the basic tendency to affirm the cognitive faculty as the distinctive mark of humanity, on the other.

The relevant passage is found in an extraordinary collection of kabbalistic secrets (written in all probability in the first decades of the fourteenth century) transmitted in the name of an anonymous elder (*zaqen*):[74] "This matter is very deep to comprehend until it is received from the mouth of the one who hears with his ears from what has been received from the mouth of the elder. You should take this principle in your hand: all the allusions hinted at in this book did not come about accidentally but only after examination, and it has already been alluded to in known places that reason (*sevara'*) in these contexts is very harmful and it does not help, until [the matter] is received orally (*sheyequbbal peh 'el peh*)."[75] The point is reiterated in a second passage from this anthology, which reflects the language of Naḥmanides:[76] "As I indicate these awesome matters to you, remember the great principle that I brought to your attention when you first entered the chamber and that is that you should not trouble your reason to comprehend these allusions, for with regard to them reason is of no avail but only a tradition."[77]

The primacy of orality in the transmission of kabbalistic teaching is emphasized in the following passage from this work: "Had you received this secret mouth to mouth, then you would have known who are the ones that enter the chambers of the king."[78] In another passage, after explicating the "secret of Abraham and Sarah," which involves more generally the mystical significance of masculinity and femininity, the author writes that "the elder did not want to elaborate this matter, and he warned us not to write that which we had received."[79] A strict code of esotericism is upheld in yet another passage, which is an elaborate exposition of the rabbinic idea that the building of the tabernacle reflects the creation of the world: "I have received in this matter that he whispered in the ear of one of his students what you see alluded to here, and if you comprehend one thing from another, 'they will be yours alone, others having no part with you' (Prov 5:17)."[80] The initial transmission of the secret is oral, by means of a whisper,[81] but this knowledge is imparted in a secondary sense to someone who has the power to deduce it on his own, to understand one thing from another.[82] In accord with the view of Maimonides, this anonymous kabbalist assumes that the mysteries of Torah are communicated either orally by someone else or discovered exegetically by one with the requisite intellectual capabilities.[83] According to another passage, when the elder wished to convey the secrets related to Amalek, he "chose two of his greatest [students] and brought them to a room within a room, and he transmitted to them the chapter headings."[84] The most dramatic example occurs in another passage wherein the elder scolds his disciple for asking him why Elijah did not experience physical death:

> He took hold of the hand of one of his students and brought him into the room within a room. He said to him, "Have I not rebuked you several times not to ask me this question before your comrades?"[85] The student trembled, and the master said to him, "Place your head between your knees,[86] and I will whisper in your ears what I have received in the matter of Elijah." The student covered his face in his cloak, placed his head between his knees, and the master whispered in his ear.[87]

The claim to orality professed by this anonymous kabbalist is linked to the view (also expressed by Maimonides)[88] that the writing down of the doctrine would prove to be potentially dangerous insofar as it may lead to the misunderstanding of a sensitive theological issue on the part of an individual not sufficiently trained in esoteric lore. Nevertheless, the threat of forgetfulness is so strong that transgressing the oral nature of transmission is inevitable, although the manner in which the secret is disclosed preserves the esoteric quality by being deliberately allusive (again the model seems to have been Maimonides who advocates a form of esoteric writing to convey secrets).[89] Reflecting on the task of writing the angelic names, the author comments: "I considered writing the matter in a greatly concealed allusion out of fear of forgetfulness."[90] In a second passage, the author states that the small amount that is written of the mystical doctrines is for the sake of memory.[91] In a third passage, the author instructs the reader: "You must know that these chapters require an expansion of language and a complete tradition, but the little that has been mentioned is out of fear of forgetting the intention of the verses to which there have been allusions."[92] The point is elaborated in a fourth passage in more detail as a general hermeneutical principle:

> What the disciple receives from his master he writes down on account of forgetfulness. We have received this wondrous and great secret, in which are contained all wisdoms, from the great and known sage. Every enlightened person will understand from his words to the point where his intellect and expansive wisdom reaches. The sage said, "Come and I will show you great principles in these few words, and these words to which I allude are like grains of wheat in relation to all the results, labors, and benefits that derive from them."[93]

Ideally, esoteric matters are to be transmitted orally because their ultimate grounding is in the oral tradition. Due to the weakness of human memory, however, had these matters not been committed to writing, forgetfulness and the eventual obliteration of the mystical secrets would have prevailed. The frank admission of this author, which again resonates with a position taken by Maimonides,[94] provides a key for understanding the motivation of many mystics at this time who wrote down the doctrines that they considered to be part of the oral heritage of Judaism. Thus, we find a similar justification for writing down esoteric matters given by Abraham Abulafia in his *Or ha-Sekhel* as a preface to his exposition of the secret concerning the motif of the image of Jacob engraved on the throne of glory:[95] "Verily, at this time that which was hidden has been revealed because forgetfulness has reached its limit, and the end of forgetfulness is the beginning of remembrance."[96] Generalizing beyond the specific context, we can assume that Abulafia believed that cultural amnesia was a rationale for disclosing hidden secrets in an esoteric manner. It is likely, moreover, that this concern with guarding against forgetfulness is part of Abulafia's larger messianic agenda.

In spite of his prolific literary activity, Abulafia maintained that the kabbalistic tradition in its essence, which involved knowledge of the divine name,[97] should not be conveyed in writing. Notwithstanding a concerted effort to reveal the concealed depths of the Jewish tradition, Abulafia occasionally adopted the view that what is truly esoteric cannot be written. Thus, in the context of explicating traditions regarding Enoch-Metatron in *Sitrei Torah,* one of his commentaries on Maimonides' *Guide of the Per-*

plexed, Abulafia reminds the reader, "All these matters, and others that are similar to them, are from the words of the sages of kabbalah; they possess wondrous secrets that are inappropriate to be written."[98] Similarly, he emphasizes in a number of his works that the esoteric reasons for the commandments, in contrast to their literal explanation, must be transmitted orally.[99] Abulafia claims, moreover, that the ecstatic techniques that he reports, principally the various permutations of the divine names, have been transmitted orally through the generations. Here I will mention several key texts, though many more could have been adduced to prove the point. In one of his many treatises still buried in manuscript, *Sefer Mafteaḥ ha-Ḥokhmot,* Abulafia distinguishes three levels of meaning in the text that correspond to three levels of religious perfection: the simple or contextual meaning (*peshat*) corresponding to the class of the righteous (*tsaddiq*), the secrets of Torah known through the way of philosophy or science (*sitrei torah ʿal derekh ḥakhmei ha-meḥqar*), i.e., the allegorical meaning, corresponding to the pious (*ḥasidim*), and the comprehension of the text as an amalgam of divine names corresponding to the prophets (*nevi'im*).[100] The way of reading associated with the attainment of prophecy is presented as the "true tradition" that has been transmitted orally. In Abulafia's own words: "If you want to reach the level of Torah where you will be prophets, you must follow the way of prophets, for their way was to combine all of the [letters of] Torah, and to grasp it from beginning to end as the way of the holy names, as the true tradition (*ha-qabbalah ha-'amitit*) has come to us that the entire Torah is the names of the Holy One, blessed be He, from the *bet* of *bere'shit* (Gen 1:1) to the *lamed* in *leʿeinei kol yisra'el* (Deut 33:12)."[101] In *Sitrei Torah* he distinguishes three types of sages: the prophets (*nevi'im*) who are forced by the divine influx to speak or to write, the wise of heart (*ḥakhmei lev*) who speak through the holy spirit and who write books on the divine wisdom according to what they have received orally from the prophets or indirectly from their compositions, and the philosophers (*ḥoqrei madaʿ*) who attempt to understand the hidden matters through their own understanding and reason.[102] Despite the obvious influence of Maimonides on Abulafia,[103] the notion of kabbalah that he proffers is such that the mystical truth is based on an oral, prophetic tradition (unique to the Jewish people) that transcends the bounds of human reason.[104] Not only is it the case that the prophetic kabbalah exceeds the rational bounds of philosophy, but the latter can contradict the former. As Abulafia states in *Sitrei Torah,* "It is known by the kabbalists from amongst our colleagues, who received from the prophets who spoke with God and God spoke with them, that the philosophers erred in their minds with respect to many matters of faith."[105]

The true tradition of which Abulafia speaks—that the Torah in its entirety is composed of the names of God—is known from other contemporary sources, including the German Pietists,[106] theosophic kabbalists,[107] and other rabbinic figures such as Sedeqiah ben Abraham, author of the halakhic compedium, *Shibbolei ha-Leqet.*[108] The most important source for Abulafia's formulation, however, is Naḥmanides who likewise refers to the conception of the Torah in its entirety being composed of the names of God as a true tradition (*qabbalah shel 'emet*).[109] (Abulafia on many occasions explicitly cites or paraphrases Naḥmanides.)[110] According to Abulafia, the exegetical decoding of the scriptural text as an aggregation of divine names is the true Oral Torah that cannot be committed to writing.[111] Thus, in the epistle in which he delineates the seven hermeneutical paths, *Sheva' Netivot ha-Torah,* Abulafia describes the seventh path as the "truth and essence of prophecy, which consists of the matter of the knowledge of the comprehension of the essence of the unique name. . . . It is not appropriate to write in a book the substance of this path, which is called holy and sanctified, and it is impossible to transmit any traditions, even the chapter headings, except if the one who desires it has at first orally received knowledge of the forty-two-letter name and the seventy-two-letter name."[112]

At best, written texts contain allusions, or in the traditional idiom "chapter headings," that the enlightened will understand through the exercise of his own understanding. In a second passage from *Sheva' Netivot ha-Torah,* Abulafia describes the requisite combination of oral reception and hermeneutical creativity: "The kabbalah brings forth the hidden from these matters, from potentiality to actuality, and it reveals the mysteries in them to each recipient (*mequbbal*). And the recipient, in accordance with his capacity, his receptivity, and his effort, brings forth what is in potentiality into actuality, for even though the kabbalah is transmitted to every enlightened person in general, not every one who hears it and receives it can bring it into actuality."[113] In the continuation of that passage, Abulafia cites the relevant rabbinic sources (as well as Maimonides' use of them) that enumerate the specifications required for an individual to receive esoteric knowledge. Indeed, the only esoteric writing that is justified is one in which the secrets are alluded to in such a way that he who has received the oral tradition will be able to interpret and expand the written allusions. In *Sitrei Torah,* Abulafia elaborates on this point, closely following the Maimonidean hermeneutic:

> There is no doubt that the enlightened can comprehend one thing from another. Therefore, the one who composes a book on a matter as deep as this can rely on the knowledge of those who understand, for the book cannot adequately reveal the mysteries. . . . The rational faculty is obligated to speak of it and to assist him in comprehending what he has heard. . . . The intention is to reveal the hidden matter according to its need, to arouse the intellect to draw forth until it comprehends it with an enduring comprehension that will not be forgotten or obliterated.[114]

The approach adopted by Abulafia is summed up in his description of Maimonides' orientation in the beginning of *Ḥayyei ha-Nefesh,* another one of his commentaries on the *Guide.* Reflecting on Maimonides' programmatic discussion in the introduction to the third part of the *Guide,*[115] Abulafia notes that Maimonides revealed what he had to reveal so that the enlightened reader would understand, but at the same time he concealed matters so that the unworthy would not understand. The two extremes of revealing what must be concealed and concealing what is appropriate to reveal must be avoided. The recommended middle path involves "making allusions that are proximate to one's knowledge."[116] The Maimonidean resolution to the tension between the mandate to conceal secrets, on the one hand, and the need to reveal them, on the other, was widely adopted by kabbalists of the various schools in the thirteenth century. With respect to this critical issue, therefore, it would be prudent on the part of intellectual historians of this period to recognize the shared assumptions of the philosophical and the mystical traditions. Maimonides was not simply a negative catalyst in the evolution of Jewish mysticism in thirteenth-century Spain.

Let me conclude this section by noting that the appeal to an oral transmission (*qabbalah*) appears in many anonymous tracts that deal principally with the mysticism of divine names or letters of the Hebrew alphabet, a mysticism that is virtually indistinguishable from magical praxis and that is rooted in much older trends of Jewish esotericism. The first example that I will provide is from the introduction to a text on the divine names extant in various manuscripts and printed in *Sefer Razi'el,* an anthology of mystical and magical texts printed for the first time in Amsterdam, 1701. The text has been attributed to the circle of *Sefer ha-Temunah.*[117] Whether or not we accept this attribution, it is clear that the work originated in a group of Spanish mystics whose central concern was speculation on the letters of the Hebrew alphabet. This text represents a stage of Castilian kabbalah preceding the generation of the kabbalists referred to by Scholem as the "gnostic circle," which included Jacob and Isaac ha-Kohen, and their disciples, Moses ben Simeon of Burgos and Todros ben Joseph Abulafia. Some of their own writings, including, most importantly, *Sefer ha-'Orah* of Jacob, reflect this concern with the mystical nature of the alphabet and the names of God.[118] Additionally, in this circle we find compositions dedicated to the mystical nature of letters, vowel-points, and cantillation signs. The orientation exemplified in these texts has a parallel in the linguistic mysticism of Joseph Gikatilla, most fully expressed in his *Ginnat Egoz,* as well as in the circle to which Moses ben Shem Tov de León apparently belonged in the early stage of his career.[119] It is likely that this linguistic mysticism, whose roots extend into the soil of ancient merkavah speculation, was probably cultivated in Germany whence it passed into Castile.

I cite the relevant text in accordance with the superior reading found in manuscript: "The one who has received the [visual] form (*tsiyyur*) of the alphabet will then understand this great and awesome secret [concerning the name of God], for the ancient Geonim put a ban on the disclosure of this secret, which is the essential name, as it is written, 'A fountain locked, a sealed-up spring' (Song 4:12)."[120] The text ends with a chain of tradition, obviously based on the beginning of mAvot: "This is the tradition (*qabbalah*) received by Moses from the mouth of God at Sinai and he transmitted it to Joshua, and Joshua to the elders, and the elders to the prophets, and the prophets transmitted it to the members of the Great Assembly, for they were masters of wisdom (*ba'alei ḥokhmah*), masters of tradition (*ba'alei qabbalah*), masters of fear (*ba'alei yir'ah*), masters of honor (*ba'alei kavod*), concerning whom it is written, 'the secret of the Lord is with those who fear Him' (Ps 25:14). And they hid it within the secrets of the Talmud (*sodot ha-talmud*), for it is all a tradition [given] to Moses at Sinai (*qabbalah le-mosheh mi-sinai*)."[121] The last claim is not substantially different from that of Ezra examined above, which is, moreover, very typical for theosophic kabbalists.

The second example is taken from one of the most enigmatic kabbalistic works, *Berit Menuḥah,* which was probably composed in the mid-fourteenth century in Spain. The text begins with the assertion that the "secret of the great name" (*sod ha-shem ha-gadol*), which here has an explicit theurgical application, was transmitted by the sages "from chamber to chamber, in great secrecy and with perfect intention, mouth to mouth."[122] The anonymous author of this text proceeds to trace a chain of transmission of the secret of the name that extends from Adam to the Geonim. Interestingly enough, after the chain is completed, mention is made of the fact that three angels, Sham'uel (or Shemu'iel), Metatron, and Yahoel, "reveal the secrets of this name to [human] beings in order to make known His splendor and the glory of His strength."[123] One may presume that the angelic revelation of the secret of the name takes the place of the oral transmission, which apparently has ceased in the geonic period.

PROPHETIC REVELATION AND THE ORAL CHAIN OF TRADITION

Having established the correlation of esotericism and orality in thirteenth-century kabbalistic literature, it is necessary to assess more critically the existing claims to orality in the relevant texts. After completing that task, we will be in a position to suggest a model that will highlight the interface of orality and textuality as it emerges from the Jewish mystical sources of this period.

The intricate relation of oral tradition and written transmission in Jewish mysticism can be clarified only on the basis of a comprehensive study of orality in classical Jewish sources. While such a project clearly lies outside the purview of this study, as a working hypothesis the following may be suggested: the role of orality in rabbinic culture is not to exhibit a conservative mindset but the very opposite, i.e., to mask novelty and innovation, which in effect serves as an impetus or catalyst for more creativity. The correlation of orality and conservativism in nonliterate societies has become a commonplace in cultural anthropology. A typical formulation of this position is given by Walter Ong: "Since in a primary oral culture conceptualized knowledge that is not repeated aloud soon vanishes, oral societies must invest great energy in saying over and over again what has been learned arduously over the ages. This need establishes a highly traditionalist or conservative set of mind that with good reason inhibits intellectual experimentation."[124] In the case of the few scholars who have more recently paid attention to the question of orality in the kabbalistic sources, there has been a tendency to adopt the correlation of oral culture and conservatism. The problem that I have with this strategy is that the paradigm upon which it is based is not applicable to the kabbalistic circles in particular or to the larger elitist rabbinic culture in general. That is, within the highly literate atmosphere of the rabbinic academies of late antiquity and the Middle Ages, and in geographical regions as distinct as Palestine, Babylonia, North Africa, and Central Europe, the role of orality has never been to inhibit intellectual experimentation. On the contrary, oral tradition has functioned as a means of fostering new ideas or interpretations of traditional texts as well as instituting new rituals. The claim to orality, therefore, is a means to legitimate and contextualize innovations as authoritative tradition. Even if we accept at face value the assertion of Jewish mystics that esoteric traditions were transmitted orally, we need not posit that the exponents of these traditions were conservative in their orientation. The presumption that creative innovation is operative in the oral stage is supported both by an understanding of the specific role of orality in rabbinic culture as well as from a more general consideration of medieval European society, especially in the twelfth and thirteenth centuries when new ideas were typically presented as the old traditions. Medieval Jewish mystics should not be isolated from their Jewish heritage or from their immediate intellectual and social environment.

It is important to recall the chain of tradition (*shalshelet ha-qabbalah*) that appears in late thirteenth- and early fourteenth-century kabbalistic material. The obvious purpose of this chain is to explain the historical evolution of the kabbalah. According to one version of the *shalshelet ha-qabbalah,* the originator of the chain is the prophet Elijah who revealed the secrets to Abraham ben Isaac, who then revealed them to his son-in-law, Abraham ben David, who in turn revealed them to his son, Isaac the Blind.[125] According to another version, Elijah revealed the secret gnosis to Jacob the Nazirite, who transmitted it to Abraham ben David, who in turn passed it on to his son, Isaac the Blind.[126] In yet another version of the chain, Elijah revealed the secrets to David, the father of Abraham ben David, who revealed them to his son, and Abraham passed them on to his son, Isaac the Blind, who disseminated them to Ezra and Azriel of Gerona, and to Naḥmanides.[127] Finally, another version of the chain reports the following sequence: Elijah, Isaac ben Abraham of Narbonne, Jacob the Nazirite, Abraham ben David, and Isaac the Blind.[128] That the chain begins in every case with Elijah attests to a remarkable self-awareness on the part of later kabbalists that something new has appeared on the scene in twelfth-century Provence. The point was made by Scholem who noted that the tradition of a revelation of Elijah may be regarded "as testimony that in this circle something really new had burst forth from the depths."[129] This is strengthened in Scholem's view by the fact that the claim for this revelation is associated in most of the documents with the innovative Provençal doctrine of mystical intention in prayer. In another context, Scholem makes a similar point by noting that through the notion of the revelation of Elijah the kabbalists "wished to communicate something which obviously had not come to them through the traditional and generally accepted channels."[130] On the other hand, as Scholem also astutely observed, the choice of Elijah as the one who reveals these truths helps to guarantee the traditional and authoritative status of the content of the revelation, given Elijah's standing in the normative rabbinic tradition. I would add, moreover, that the function of revelatory experience within traditional societies is often a means to corroborate accepted views. Indeed, from an epistemological perspective, it can be argued that the content and form of an individual's experience is shaped by the traditional assumptions of the given society to which that individual belongs.[131] It is thus unwarranted to distinguish too sharply between tradition, revelation, and interpretation.

It must be noted that these chains of tradition are relatively late and there is no clear indication in the earlier sources themselves that the Provençal or, for that matter, the Geronese kabbalists attributed kabbalistic teachings to Elijah.[132] We cannot be certain, therefore, that the first kabbalists were aware of the problem that this notion seeks to address, i.e., the problem of a seemingly innovative doctrine that is to be presented as tradition. On the contrary, the stated position of Ezra of Gerona or that of Naḥmanides is a direct challenge to the claim made by the later kabbalists (although, ironically, it appears that this chain was first articulated by the students of Naḥmanides' students): in the case of both Ezra and Naḥmanides it is emphasized that the kabbalah is an ancient Jewish lore, indeed part of the oral tradition par excellence, *torah shebe'al peh,* going back to Abraham according to the former or Moses according to the latter. There is, then, no need for a revelation of Elijah to transmit esoteric knowledge that should have been transmitted in a continuous manner. One could suggest, of course, that the function of the revelation of Elijah is to make one aware of the traditions that were forgotten temporarily. But this is not explicitly (or implicitly) stated in any of the relevant reports. The revelation of Elijah is related to an awareness of a novel religious experience that later kabbalists mask in this particular traditional guise.

It may be concluded, therefore, that while it is true that the early masters are depicted as preservers of a received tradition, the source of this tradition lies with Elijah. This factor has to be considered in any discussion on the problem of orality and oral transmission in early kabbalah. The effort to link the issues of orality and conservatism, on the one hand, and written composition and innovation, on the other, should be reassessed in light of the kabbalists' own admission that the chain of tradition begins with a revelation of Elijah. In effect, the conserving tendency is predicated on a prior innovative stage. That is, the claim for linear reception, and thus the forging of an authoritative chain, is meant to legitimate that which is revealed spontaneously by the prophet to the first link in the chain. The conservative trend, therefore, must be seen in dialectic relation to the innovative. Consistent with early forms of Jewish creativity, claims to oral tradition are often the means to cloak creativity.

ORALITY AS EXPOSITION OF TEXTS

In this final section of this paper I would like to explore another crucial dimension of the problem of orality within the Jewish mystical tradition. To state at the outset my hypothesis: there is no orality that does not presuppose textuality.[133] One should avoid the spectrum of an oral-written dichotomy with a pure oral tradition on one end and the written page of text on the other.[134] We must focus our attention rather on the intermediate combination or interface[135] of oral and written. After all, as I have noted above, when discussing medieval Jewish mystics we are not talking about preliterate cultures for which we can assume a "primary oral"[136] phenomenon totally divorced from written literary traditions. On the contrary, we are speaking of groups within medieval Jewish society that demonstrated a high degree of literacy.[137] The circles of kabbalists in Catalonia and Castile are, in Brian Stock's terminology, "textual communities," for they demonstrate a "parallel use of texts, both to structure the internal behaviour of the groups' members and to provide solidarity against the outside world."[138] It would be wise to consider the cultural context in which kabbalah flourished as being simultaneously oral and written. The role of orality as may be gathered from the existing kabbalistic materials is, again to borrow the formulation of Stock, "to function in a reference system based on texts."[139] The center of gravity for the medieval kabbalists shifts from the oral to the written despite their claims to the contrary. If there were older oral traditions, in the medieval European milieu these traditions were contextualized in written texts, and in the process they were themselves transformed so that there was a close interdependence between the spoken and the written. This is not to deny the possibility of oral discourse as a means by which knowledge was transmitted. One must avoid the postmodernist temptation to view orality *sub specie litterae,* which one scholar has aptly referred to as the "textualization of orality."[140] I accept the probability that kabbalists imparted esoteric doctrines and practices through oral performance. My point is, however, that for these medieval Jewish mystics, orality consisted primarily of exposition of written texts. The oral tradition, *qabbalah,* is thus mainly textual, or text-related, and in that respect we do well to speak of orality intersecting with textuality.

Before elaborating on this let me make a philological observation that has not been sufficiently noted in the scholarly literature. An examination of the use of the very terms *qabbalah,* "tradition," or *qibbalti,* "I have received," in the relevant literature indicates that we are not in every case talking about an oral transmission that precludes any written evidence. Let us first turn our attention to what is generally considered the first document of the medieval kabbalistic tradition, the *Sefer ha-Bahir.* The mode of presentation of the *Bahir* is midrashic, i.e., views are presented as exegesis on select verses and placed into the mouths of rabbinic personalities.[141] There are no overt claims to the antiquity of the doctrines expounded, although this is implied by the literary presumption of the text, nor are any of the ideas legitimized through a continuous chain of oral transmission. This text is classified as a kabbalistic work for we impute to it what we know from other documents that employ this term or related terms to name the transmission of an esoteric doctrine regarding the dynamic gradations (*sefirot*) of the divine.[142] In the *Bahir,* however, there are competing theosophies, reflecting the composite and highly redacted nature of the text, and in only one stratum is there a sustained reflection on the ten powers of the divine realm. For the purposes of this study, I am focusing on the use of the root *qbl* in the bahiric text, and thus I will not enter into the complicated question of protokabbalistic sources, oral or written, that may prove to be the foundation of the *Bahir.* In one instance the word *qibbalti,* "I received," is used in connection with a theosophic reading of Ex 20:11 according to which the six days of creation are transformed into symbols for six divine emanations.[143] In this case, then, the *qabbalah* is an esoteric recasting of a biblical text in light of certain theosophical assumptions. In a second passage we read: "R. Rehumai said, 'Thus I received (*qibbalti*) that when Moses wanted to know the knowledge of the awesome and glorious name, he said, 'Show me Your glory' (Ex 33:18). He wanted to know why one righteous person experiences goodness and another evil, and why one wicked person experiences goodness and another evil."[144] It is instructive that the problem of theodicy is here treated under the rubric of knowledge of the name of God and this is further associated with a reception of a tradition on the part of R. Rehumai. What is most revealing, however, is the fact that the passage is based on the interpretation of Ex 33:18 in bBer 7a. The force of the locution "I received," therefore, must be "I received an interpretation of the traditional source." We may conclude, therefore, that on philological grounds the word *qibbel* in the *Bahir* denotes reception of an exegetical tradition.

Let me here mention two other striking examples of this phenomenon. The first is from Moses ben Simeon of Burgos, a Castilian kabbalist active in the second half of the thirteenth century. Moses begins his commentary on the forty-two-letter name of God as follows: "We have a complete tradition from R. Hai, blessed be his memory, who received from the Geonim who preceded him, and from the sages who preceded the Geonim going back to R. Akiva and R. Ishmael the High Priest, may peace be upon them."[145] Scholem accurately described this composition as an anthology arranged from different sources.[146] Whether Moses of Burgos himself is responsible for these traditions or not, he reports them as a something he has received. Now, it is evident that in this context the force of the terms *qabbalah* and *masoret,* which I have rendered with the one English word "tradition," cannot be a direct oral transmission insofar as Hai Gaon lived two centuries before Moses of Burgos. Hence, these terms signify that Moses of Burgos received through a textual channel an authoritative teaching that is attributed to Hai Gaon. The textual connotation of the word *qabbalah* is implied in a second passage from the same work: "After we have informed you that we have mentioned the sayings of those who speak by means of the Holy Spirit and the sages, blessed be their memory, regarding the status of the greatness of the aforementioned name [of forty-two letters], we will write the essence of the names in their vocalization as we have received and the variant readings that we have found in the writings of the Geonim, blessed be their memory."[147] One may be tempted to argue that in this case the expression "we have received" (*qibbalnu*) contrasts with "we have found" (*matsa'nu*), the former denoting an oral reception and the latter a discovery in a written text. However, a circumspect reading of the text in context indicates that the two expressions are not in opposition at all. The term *qibbalnu* signifies the act of orally receiving a tradition as authoritative, but the source of that tradition is a literary document. Thus, immediately after presenting the vocalizations of the forty-two-letter name, the author writes: "Now we shall begin to explain the meaning of the words and letters by way of proper tradition (*'al derekh qabbalah nekhonah*) from the learned of the world, the kabbalists (*ge' onei 'olam mequbbalim*), from the secrets of their exalted and inner intentions that edify wondrous matters." The complex explanations offered by Moses of Burgos on the forty-two-letter name of God are drawn from existing texts that he may well have received from his teachers.

Another example of the confluence of orality and textuality can be found in the following passage from an anonymous text extant in manuscript: "This is the novel explanation that I received (*qibbalti*) from the sage, R. Joseph Gikatilla, may God watch over and redeem him, concerning the secret of the vocalization of the unique name (*sod niqqud ha-shem ha-meyuḥad*), which is known to every kabbalist, for it is the root and principle of everything."[148] *Prima facie,* it would seem that this provides a perfect example of the recording of a tradition that someone received orally and directly from Gikatilla. However, upon closer examination it becomes apparent that the author is citing a text of Gikatilla that he has referred to as the *ḥiddush* that he received from him. Hence the opening statement, "this is the novel explanation that I received from the sage, R. Joseph Gikatilla," must be construed in one of two ways: either the person actually received this text from Gikatilla or he received the text and considered it to be an authentic work of Gikatilla. The second explanation seems to me more likely. We may conclude, then, that in at least some relevant cases, the word *qabbalah* signifies the transmission of an authoritative tradition that may have been preserved in a written document.

Along similar lines, it should be noted that the expression *shama'ti,* "I have heard," does not always connote an aural reception. On the contrary, in medieval mystical texts, as in rabbinic sources,[149] the expression *shama'ti* can refer to a "hearing from books,"[150] i.e. comprehension of a written artifact or acceptance of the latter as authoritative. I will provide in this context one illustration of this usage of a term that the unreflective ear might simply assume signals a direct oral reception. In a fragment of a letter addressed to Naḥmanides on matters pertaining to prayer, an anonymous inquirer explains his reason for turning to the rabbi for guidance: "Even though I have found other sages of the kabbalah saying similar things, I have not heard [anything] from the holy mouth (*lo shama'ti ken mi-pi qadosh*) concerning the matter of prayer."[151] The writer of the letter is seeking to receive a response from Naḥmanides concerning the mystical intention of prayer. What is critical for this analysis is the fact that the locution "to hear from the mouth" does not denote oral reception in a literal sense, but means rather to receive a teaching from a certain authority even if it be in written form.[152]

I do not mean to challenge entirely the reliability of a mystic's assertion that he has received such and such a tradition from a particular sage. We, indeed, find in many instances that the formulations *qibbalti mipi,* "I received from the mouth," and *shama'ti mipi,* "I have heard from the mouth," indicate the reception of that which has been transmitted orally. My point is, however, that even in many of these cases what has been transmitted is a tradition that has been recorded in written form that the master passes on to his disciples in an oral way, i.e., in the context of teaching them by reading the recorded traditions and expounding upon them. Frequently, these oral expositions of written traditions themselves become texts at the hands of the disciples, which, in turn, facilitate later oral and written exposition. In this way the material that served as the core curriculum for the different circles of mystics was built up. An interesting example of this is found at the end of a codex of kabbalistic sources from the thirteenth century (the manuscript is written in a beautiful Spanish script and is to be dated to the fourteenth or fifteenth century; it is assumed that this codex was used by Johann Reuchlin as is attested by his *De Arte Cabalistica*).[153] The anonymous hand who assembled together the different material writes: "I have written this book in which there are kabbalistic explanations so that I will remember what I have received from the great and elderly sages, men of understanding, blessed be their memory. And I adjure all my descendants to guard this book[154] so as not to show it to empty people who would destroy their souls by thinking thoughts they did not understand."[155] I do not think this comment was added by the particular scribe who copied this codex, but it is rather the remark of the anonymous kabbalist who created a text by stringing together all these other literary compositions.

It follows, then, that the oral traditions were not by definition nontextual. Moreover, once one appreciates the complex interplay of orality and textuality, one may conclude that the oral nature of esotericism is not necessarily marked by a conservative orientation. On the contrary, the function of oral transmission for the kabbalists was not to conserve ancient doctrines or practices in a rigid way, but to provide a context for innovative interpretation, expansion, and application. We can well imagine that disciples sat and learnt from masters who taught orally the esoteric gnosis and the techniques for mystical experience, but these masters were, first and foremost, expositors of texts that may have preserved older traditions in some recorded form. The kabbalah, whether theosophic or ecstatic, is unequivocally related to textual explication.

Claims to orality in thirteenth-century Spanish kabbalah should be viewed as a link in the ongoing chain of textual exposition, a process that by nature generates rather than restricts novel interpretations and creative exegesis. Like other interpreters operating within the framework of traditional hermeneutics, the kabbalists preserve something of older traditions even as they are transformed or recast in a new light. The strict adherence to esotericism on the part of the kabbalists in the twelfth and thirteenth centuries, expressed in their unwillingness to commit to writing the secret traditions, does not in and of itself prove the unqualified and uniform authenticity or antiquity of the traditions that they cultivated. On the contrary, one could construct an equally, if not more, plausible argument to the effect that the role of oral transmission is to allow for the expression of new ideas that were perceived as ancient by the mystics. The potential tension between older texts, whether midrashic or even mystical, and the insights of the incipient kabbalah is mitigated by the incorporation of these ideas as part of the oral tradition. This is the only way to account rationally for the fact that so many different groups in this period are claiming for their respective mystical systems the status of an ancient doctrine that has been passed on in a continuous manner through the generations. If the critical scholar is to accept the veracity of this claim for one author or his school, then he must be prepared on logical grounds to accept it for all authors or their schools. One can see immediately the absurd conclusions to which this position would lead.

In support of my argument, let me note that the earliest reports about an oral tradition received from a teacher almost invariably involve the exposition of some text, either biblical, liturgical, or aggadic in nature. Due to the limitations of space, I can only provide a few striking illustrations of the phenomenon that I described. Let us consider, for example, the oft-cited remark of Ezra of Gerona reporting the tradition of Isaac the Blind: "Our teacher, the pious one, blessed be his memory, said: The essence of worship of the enlightened and those who meditate on His name is 'cleave to Him' (Deut 13:5), and this is the great principle in the Torah concerning prayer and blessings, to harmonize his thought and his faith as if he were cleaving above, to unite the name in its letters and to comprise within it the ten *sefirot* like a flame that is bound to the coal."[156] Here the master gives general instruction about the mystical and theurgical significance of liturgical worship, but it is expressed in a distinctively midrashic manner. The kabbalah, in short, is presented as an exegetical reflection on the verse from Scripture.

Let us turn our attention to the nature of the kabbalah of Isaac the Blind reported by another Geronese kabbalist, Jacob ben Sheshet, in a passage from his *Sefer ha-Emunah veha-Bittaḥon.* Reflecting on the Aramaic translation of Onkelos on Lev 13:18, Jacob writes: "This is comparable to the explanation, 'He looked into the Torah,' He saw the essences (*ḥawwayot*) with Himself, for they were the essences from Wisdom, and from those essences, which were the essences of Wisdom, He discerned that they would be manifest in the future. Thus I heard this discourse in the name of the pious one, R. Isaac the son of R. Abraham, blessed be his memory."[157] The oral tradition in this case is an explanation of the aggadic motif found in the very beginning of the midrashic collection, *Bere'shit Rabbah,* regarding God's looking into the Torah as the vehicle of creation. Given the theosophic identification of God and the Torah, Isaac the Blind interprets the rabbinic comment as an articulation of the idea that God gazes into his own image and contemplates the inner essences of Wisdom. The kabbalistic tradition, therefore, is essentially an exposition of the midrashic text. Interestingly enough, in the continuation of the passage, Jacob ben Sheshet states that the kabbalistic interpretation of Isaac the Blind accords with the philosophical view expressed by Maimonides concerning God's knowledge of particular existents through self-contemplation. Even though the substance of the philosophic and kabbalistic sources may be identical, in an epistemological sense the two are distinguishable, for the former is a matter of knowledge (*yedi'ah*) and the latter a matter of faith (*emunah*).

To cite one more example from this work of Jacob ben Sheshet: "Thus have I received from the mouth of (*qibbalti mipi*) the sage, R. Isaac the

Frenchman, may his memory be for a blessing."[158] In this case, Jacob ben Sheshet is reporting a direct oral transmission of a tradition. But what is the content of the tradition? It is an explanation of the aggadic motif of the wine reserved for the righteous in the world to come, *yayin ha-meshummar ba'anavav*.[159] In particular, the oral tradition recorded in the name of Isaac is that this eschatological wine is the very opposite of the wine that Eve reportedly gave to Adam in the Garden of Eden, for which she was punished with the blood of menstruation.[160] The nature of the kabbalah, it will be readily admitted, is an exposition of a rabbinic text. Similarly, in another one of his treatises, *Meshiv Devarim Nekhoḥim,* Jacob ben Sheshet reports that he has heard an explanation on the expression *giborei khoaḥ,* "mighty creatures" (Ps 103:20), from "the sage, R. Barzillai."[161] The tradition received by Jacob is an esoteric reading of the scriptural verse.[162] In a second passage from this work, Jacob reports that he has received a kabbalistic interpretation of Ps 24:7, which is compared to the explanation of this verse attributed to "the sage, R. Ezra," i.e., Ezra of Gerona.[163] Further support for my thesis is found in an anthology of doctrines reported as kabbalah in a relatively early codex of kabbalistic traditions, apparently originating in the school of Solomon ibn Adret, the leading disciple of Naḥmanides in Barcelona. After having examined the manuscript carefully, I have come to the conclusion that in most instances the kabbalah is an explanation of some authoritative text, whether liturgical,[164] biblical,[165] or rabbinic.[166] Hence, the claims *qibbalti,* "I received," and *shama'ti,* "I heard," signify the reception of an exegetical teaching as authoritative.[167] Interestingly enough, in his supercommentary on the esoteric allusions in Naḥmanides' Torah commentary, Shem Tov ibn Gaon mentions secrets that he received orally from his teachers, Solomon ibn Adret and Isaac ben Todros.[168] The nature of these secrets, however, is very much related to textual exegesis, as we find, for example, in the mysteries of impregnation (*sod ha-'ibbur*),[169] levirate marriage (*sod ha-yibbum*),[170] sacrifices,[171] and Ezekiel's chariot.[172] In a similar vein, Isaac of Acre states that the disciples of Naḥmanides reported that they received from his mouth that each occurrence of the Tetragrammaton in Scripture refers to the supreme divine being, the Cause of Causes (*'illat ha-'illot*).[173] What is most significant for my analysis is the fact that the oral tradition is an interpretative strategy of reading the biblical text.

One other example is instructive as it illustrates a change in status from one generation to the next. In his commentary on the aggadah in bBer 7a concerning Ishmael ben Elisha's vision of Akatriel in the Holy of Holies, Ezra of Gerona notes that "we have received (*qibbalnu*) that he is called the guardian of Israel."[174] The force of Ezra's having received this as an oral exposition of a text is highlighted if one compares his words to the following comment of the Castilian kabbalist, Todros Abulafia, writing sometime in the 1270s: "I have received (*qibbalti*) that this is [Akatriel's] name, and thus I have seen it written in the words of some of the kabbalists, which are hidden, concealed, and closed, that [Akatriel] is the guardian of Israel."[175] Writing at a later stage, Todros Abulafia has no problem reporting this interpretation as a literary quotation, whereas for Ezra the same tradition is an oral report. The fact that Ezra did receive this orally (presumably from Isaac the Blind) does not necessitate the assessment that it represents a conservative orientation. I do not envision the recasting of talmudic aggadot, or the commentaries on the prayers, as a secondary process in the formulation of kabbalistic doctrine, functioning therefore as a kind of *asmakhta'* in traditional rabbinic literature, i.e., textual support for an autonomous doctrine. On the contrary, I suggest that we look at the process of formation of these ideas as a result of an inner hermeneutic whereby there is a gnostification of aggadic and liturgical texts. Here I am deliberately using Scholem's terminology. However, I do not suggest that the gnostification occurs from the outside, i.e., through the imposition of an extrinsic system on Jewish material, but rather from the inside.[176] It is possible that in the kabbalah one finds the elaboration of ancient Jewish mythologoumena that may be reflected in the doctrines of Gnosticism, Mandeanism, or Judeo-Christianity,[177] but it is also possible that the parallels between these forms of gnosis and kabbalah can be explained by similar hermeneutical developments occurring independently at two periods of history.[178] Perhaps we may see the development of mythical theosophies, inherently connected in the Jewish tradition with an esotericism resulting from a hermeneutical process, that may, at different historical junctures, presumably under similar socio-economic, political, and cultural conditions, repeat themselves and produce corresponding phenomenological results without any evident historical or textual link. With such a model in mind, we must seek the roots for the mythos and theosophy alike in the hermeneutical patterns of the different Jewish textual communities responding to the shared base text of Scripture in all its fluidity and complexity.

The thesis that I have presented, that there is no orality that does not presusppose textuality, lends support to the claim that at the oral stage itself there is innovation, specifically as exposition of texts. To reiterate the statement of Faivre that I mentioned at the outset: "active esotericism is the privileged form of hermeneutics." Although from a quantitative standpoint the proliferation of written texts does harbor creativity and new interpretations, from the perspective of hermeneutical method there is no discernible difference between the oral and the written stages of transmission. Let us consider once more the figure of Naḥmanides who explicitly describes kabbalah in the most conservative terms as a corpus of limited secrets passed through the generations in a continuous chain of oral tradition.[179] I have argued that, in spite of Naḥmanides' declarations, he expands the range of kabbalistic secrets through a consistent and innovative hermeneutical posture vis-à-vis Scripture as read often through the lenses of rabbinic aggadah. I further suggested that a major source for Naḥmanides' kabbalistic explanations is the *Sefer ha-Bahir*, which was received by him as a literary document and read as part of the traditional aggadah.[180] I find little evidence that Naḥmanides ever relies on a purely oral tradition in the manner that he suggests in his more general definitions of kabbalah. In my view, kabbalistic secrets emerge from an exegetical effort to fathom the text. This is particularly relevant in the many cases in Naḥmanides' commentary where he insists that the literal sense converges with the esoteric or kabbalistic, a phenomenon that has been noted by several scholars.[181] If there were in fact received traditions, then they did not necessarily inhibit or restrict the exegetical process. Indeed, in a second study on Naḥmanides, I suggested that a particular esoteric truth, the secret of the garment (*sod ha-malbush*), which Naḥmanides considers to be too recondite to elaborate upon in writing and thus proclaims after alluding to it, "but I cannot explain" (*we-lo 'ukhal lefaresh*), is in fact a theosophic recasting of an aggadic source in *Bere'shit Rabbah,* which itself is a mythic, if not theosophic, reading of the biblical text.[182] The deep secret, whatever its phenomenological affinity to ideas expressed in earlier documents, is derived in the manner that I have just outlined. The esoteric truth thus arises from and within the hermeneutical relation of the reader before the text.

As I have argued elsewhere, the key exegetical term employed by Naḥmanides to bridge the gap between text and interpretation is *remez,* which signifies an allusion or hint encoded in Scripture.[183] The belief (affirmed by Naḥmanides) that all wisdom, including esoteric wisdom (*ma'aseh merkavah,* the account of the chariot, and *ma'aseh bere'shit,* the account of creation) and exoteric science about the natural world, is contained in the Torah necessitates the further belief that the biblical text either explicitly or implicitly discloses the different types of wisdom. Thus, after making the point in the introduction to his commentary on the Pentateuch that all wisdom is contained in the Torah, Naḥmanides states in his typically laconic formulation, "everything is written in the Torah either explicitly or implicitly," *ha-kol nikhtav ba-torah be-ferush 'o be-remez.*[184] Naḥmanides goes to great length to argue that this is the case, even with respect to the account of the chariot, which is not discussed in the Torah, for if all wisdom could not be extracted from the Torah, that would imply that the Torah was deficient. Particularly significant is Naḥmanides' reflection on this issue in his sermon, *Torat ha-Shem Temimah.* He writes:

> I am perplexed for I see that the Torah speaks of the account of creation (*ma'aseh bere'shit*) and cosmology (*ḥokhmat ha-yetsirah*), but I do not know where it alludes to the account of the chariot (*ma'aseh merkavah*). The supernal chariot (*merkavah ha-'elyonah*), which is the knowledge of the Creator, is written in the Torah, but I do not know where there is an allusion (*remez*) in the Torah to the chariot of the palaces (*merkavah shel hekhalot*). Perhaps it was an oral tradition until Ezekiel and Isaiah came and gave it textual support.[185]

In this passage, Naḥmanides entertains the possibility that there was an oral tradition regarding the lower chariot not written in the Torah. Interestingly, in the case of the vision of the enthroned glory beheld by Isaiah and Ezekiel the oral tradition itself functions as the text that legitimates the revelatory experience.[186] Moreover, even in this context Naḥmanides maintains that the upper chariot, which is the gnosis about God, is written in the Torah. To the extent that Naḥmanides affirms the view that the lower chariot is structurally parallel to the upper chariot,[187] one may conclude that, since knowledge of the latter is deduced from Torah, there is some measure of knowledge about the former as well.

With respect to secretive matters, then, one might say that, according to Naḥmanides, the Torah, much like Apollo as described by Heraclitus, "neither declares not conceals, but gives a sign."[188] The master of esoteric knowledge is one who can read or decode those signs. I submit that such reading is a form of extracting the secret from the text. To be sure, from one perspective, the tradition (*qabbalah*) is independent of the scriptural text, and precisely on account of that tradition is the text interpreted in a particular way. On the other hand, it cannot be said that the secret does not emerge from the text for that would imply a source of truth extraneous to the Torah. The point is made clear in Naḥmanides' statement that "the account of creation is a deep mystery that cannot be understood from scriptural verses, and it is not clearly understood except through the kabbalah going back to Moses, our master, [who received it] from God. Those who know it are obligated to conceal it."[189] In a similar vein, he remarks on another occasion that the notion of the upper and lower waters "is from the matter of the account of creation, and you should not expect me to write anything about it, for it is one of the mysteries of the Torah, and the verses do not require this explanation, for Scripture does not elaborate on this matter and the explanation is forbidden for those who know it, how much more for us."[190] On the surface it appears that Naḥmanides blatantly denies the possibility of extracting the esoteric gnosis (related specifically to the account of creation) by exegetical means from the text of Scripture.[191] The rhetorical flourishes of Naḥmanides, however, do not match his own exegetical practice. Time and again, esoteric matters are teased from the text on the basis of allusions that are decoded in light of a hermeneutics of recovery. Naḥmanides' insistence that Scripture cannot yield secrets except to one who has received the tradition is equivalent to his claim that with respect to these matters reason is of no avail. In truth, Naḥmanides utilized both reason and exegetical principles to elicit the mysteries encoded in Scripture. The intentional concealment of these secrets is not an indication that in his mind they could not be derived from the Torah. The contrary seems to be the case, and only that possibility makes the act of concealment necessary. My interpretation is confirmed by Naḥmanides' celebrated remark concerning the prohibition of illicit sexual relations: "We do not possess in our hands any tradition (*davar mequbbal*) about this, but according to supposition (*sevara'*) there is in this matter a secret of the secrets of creation (*sodot ha-yetsirah*), which is conjoined to the soul, and it is in the category of the secret of impregnation (*sod ha-'ibbur*) to which we have already alluded."[192] Naḥmanides acknowledges that he is not the recipient of an authoritative tradition to explain these biblical verses, but he surmises on the basis of reason that the matter is related to the secrets of creation. One cannot fail to note the irony here: The very same Naḥmanides who insists on a rigorous dichotomy between oral tradition (*qabbalah*) and ratiocination (*sevara'*) in this context employs the latter to ascertain the nature of the former. Naḥmanides' refusal to elaborate on the esoteric matter is not based on his disclaimer that he has no received tradition. The hint that he does offer indicates that he knew perfectly well the secret of illicit sexual relations and precisely for that reason he concealed more than he revealed.

Solomon ibn Adret succinctly formulated the twofold nature of his teacher's hermeneutic: "In everything for which there is a tradition . . . at times the matter is alluded to in Scripture. It is not that this allusion is necessitated [by the text] but only that the tradition necessitates it. And the matter is verified by [both] Scripture and the tradition."[193] The dialectical interplay of creative hermeneutics and conservative tradition may be adduced as well from the following remark of ibn Adret's disciple, Shem Tov ibn Gaon. Commenting on the verse, "The cherubim shall their wings spread out above" (Ex 25:20), Shem Tov initially remarks that he cannot explain this matter, but he then immediately mentions the explanation of his teacher, Isaac ben Todros, in his kabbalistic commentary on the *maḥzor.* This explanation is followed by a telling remark regarding Shem Tov's perception of Naḥmanides' role in the disclosure of secrets: "When you perceive this matter from a kabbalist, you will understand this, but not prior to it. The rabbi, blessed be his memory, revealed much to the enlightened (*maskil*), one man from the mouth of another, going back to Moses, our master, peace be upon him. I, too, will reveal more to you if you will comprehend."[194]

When we get beyond the spoken word implanted in our ears by the kabbalists' own language, we realize that oral tradition and written transmission are two stages of a dialectical and hermeneutical process rather than representing conflicting moments in the evolution of Jewish mysticism. There is no reason to posit a rigid dichotomy between the oral and the written, the conservative and the innovative. The education and formation of the medieval kabbalists was such that esoteric traditions, transmitted either orally or in written documents, were conservatively received and innovatively expanded. In the final analysis, the kabbalist of this period was first and foremost a biblical exegete. When we bear this simple fact in mind, it becomes clear that the Catalonian and Castilian mystical fraternities in the most exact sense were textual communities.

NOTES

The final version of this paper benefited from the comments and suggestions that I received from Yaakov Elman, for which I express my sincere gratitude.

1. The presumption that there were older esoteric documents that circulated within elitist circles lies at the basis of Gershom Scholem's historical reconstruction of the origins of kabbalah, which privileges written texts over oral traditions as the primary conduit through which knowledge is transmitted. See D. Biale, *Gershom Scholem: Kabbalah and Counter-History* (Cambridge, Mass., 1979), 133–134. Biale perceptively compares Scholem's view to Nachman Krochmal's description of "how the sefirot theosophy was first developed in Babylonia and was carried westward via Italy to Spain in various 'scrolls and small pamphlets'" (134). Biale also suggests that Scholem's discussion of the influence of Gnosticism on kabbalah reflects Krochmal's theory; see 28, 134, 138, 198.

2. The extreme form of secrecy affirmed by Jewish mystics when compared to other religious traditions has been noted by W. Stace, *Mysticism and Philosophy* (London, 1960), 57. Two helpful surveys on the nature of esotericism may be found in A. Faivre, "Ancient and Medieval Sources of Modern Esoteric Movements," in *Modern Esoteric Spirituality,* eds. A. Faivre and J. Needleman (New York, 1992), 1–70; and Faivre, *Access to Western Esotericism* (Albany, 1994), 3–110.

3. A. Altmann, "Maimonides' Attitude Toward Jewish Mysticism," in *Studies in Jewish Thought,* ed. A. Jospe (Detroit, 1981), 201–202.

4. G. Scholem, "Jewish Mysticism in the Middle Ages," *The 1964 Allan Bronf-*

man Lecture (New York, 1964), 3–4. See Scholem, *Kabbalah* (Jerusalem, 1974), 4. Cf. the characterization of A. Faivre, in *The Encyclopedia of Religion,* ed. M. Eliade (New York, 1987), 5: 158, s.v., Esotericism: "Strictly speaking, gnosis should be distinguished from mysticism, even though they are usually found together. Mysticism, which is more 'feminine,' more nocturnal, voluntarily cultivates renunciation, although this does not exclude a taste for symbolism. Gnosis, more 'masculine,' more solar, cultivates detachment and is more attentive to structures."

5. Faivre, ibid.

6. *Access to Western Esotericism,* 5.

7. M. Idel, *Kabbalah: New Perspectives* (New Haven, 1988), 253. Aspects of Jewish esotericism related particularly to preoccupation with exegetical devices have been studied more recently by Idel in his article "Secrecy, Binah and Derishah," in *Secrecy and Concealment: Studies in the History of Mediterranean and Near Eastern Religions,* eds. H. G. Kippenberg and G. G. Stroumsa (Leiden, 1995), 310–343.

8. See D. S. Russell, *The Method and Message of Jewish Apocalyptic* (Philadelphia, 1964), 107–118; M. Stone, "List of Revealed Things in the Apocalyptic Literature," *Magnalia Dei: The Mighty Acts of God,* ed. F. M. Cross (New York, 1976), 414–452; I. Gruenwald, "Two Types of Jewish Esoteric Literature in the Time of the Mishnah and Talmud," in *From Apocalypticism to Gnosticism* (Frankfurt am Main, 1988), 53–64.

9. See E. Vogt, "'Mysteria' in textibus Qumrân," *Biblica* 37 (1956), 247–257; B. Rigaux, "Révélation des mystères et perfection à Qumran et dans le Nouveau Testament," *New Testament Studies* 4 (1957–58), 237–262; G. Scholem, *Jewish Gnosticism, Merkabah Mysticism, and Talmudic Tradition* (New York, 1965), 3 n. 3; R. Brown, *The Semitic Background of the Pauline Mysterion* (Philadelphia, 1966); M. N. A. Bockmuehl, *Revelation and Mystery in Ancient Judaism and Pauline Christianity* (Tübingen, 1990). See the study of Stroumsa cited below, n. 33.

10. See G. G. Stroumsa, "Moses' Riddles: Esoteric Trends in Patristic Hermeneutics," in *Interpretation in Religion,* eds. S. Biderman and B.-A. Scharfstein (Leiden, 1992), 241–242.

11. On the use of the word *raz* in the Hekhalot literature, see R. Elior, "The Concept of God in Hekhalot Mysticism," in *Binah: Studies in Jewish History, Thought, and Culture,* ed. J. Dan (New York, 1989), 2: 101, 111–112; P. Schäfer, *The Hidden and Manifest God: Some Major Themes in Early Jewish Mysticism* (Albany, 1992), 107–109.

12. See D. Patte, *Early Jewish Hermeneutic in Palestine* (Missoula, 1975), 150–151; for other references to this motif, see E. R. Wolfson, *Circle in the Square: Studies in the Use of Gender in Kabbalistic Symbolism* (Albany, 1995), 156 n. 6.

13. See M. D. Swartz, "Book and Tradition in Hekhalot and Magical Literatures," *Journal of Jewish Thought and Philosophy* 2 (1994), 189–229.

14. See Scholem, *Major Trends,* 174. Scholem considered all citations to such works in the *Zohar* as "fictitious quotations" and "bogus references to imaginary writings." Despite Scholem's understandable scepticism, a careful study of these references remains a desideratum.

15. See M. Idel, *The Mystical Experience in Abraham Abulafia* (Albany, 1988), 1.

16. *She'elot u-Teshuvot le-Rashba,* pt. 1., no. 548, 71d.

17. MS New York, Jewish Theological Seminary of America Mic. 1878, fol. 38a; and cf. Joseph ben Shalom Ashkenazi's commentary on *Sefer Yetsirah* published under the name of the Rabad in the standard editions of that work (Jerusalem, 1962), 10a (with slight variation). The depiction of Adam as the first link in the chain of tradition is affirmed in a number of kabbalistic sources from the thirteenth century. See *Zohar* 1:52a; 2:55a; *R. Moses de León's Sefer Sheqel ha-Qodesh,* edited and introduced by C. Mopsik (Los Angeles, 1996), 17; and the works of Abraham Abulafia and his disciples cited by M. Idel, *Language, Torah, and Hermeneutics in Abraham Abulafia* (Albany, 1989), 17, 151–152 n. 89.

18. On the phenomenon of maggidism in the sixteenth century, see R. J. Zwi Werblowsky, *Joseph Karo: Lawyer and Mystic* (Oxford, 1962), 9–23, 75–83, 103–121, 159–165, 257–286; L. Fine, "Maggidic Revelation in the Teachings of Isaac Luira," in *Mystics, Philosophers, and Politicians: Essays in Jewish Intellectual History in Honor of Alexander Altmann,* ed. J. Reinharz and D. Swetschiniski (Durham, 1982), 141–157.

19. See S. Pines, "Le *Sefer ha-Tamar* et les *Maggidim* des Kabbalists," *Hommage à Georges Vajda,* eds. G. Nahon and C. Touati (Louvain, 1980), 333–363; M. Idel, "Inquiries into the Doctrine of *Sefer ha-Meshiv*" (Hebrew), *Sefunot* 17 (1983), 185–266.

20. Consider, for example, the expression *sod ha-'ibbur,* "secret of intercalation," in bKet 112a, bRH 20b, and bSuk 54b.

21. See D. J. Halperin, *The Merkabah in Rabbinic Literature* (New Haven, 1980), 19–39.

22. yKet 5.4 (ed. Venice, 29d); tKet 5.1; Sifre Numbers 117; and bQid 10b (in that context the reading is *hadrei torah,* "chambers of Torah," rather than *sitrei torah,* "secrets of Torah"); bḤag 13a.

23. "Standing on the outside" is one of the idiomatic expressions found in rabbinic literature to refer to one who is less than perfect or complete. In some contexts it can also refer to a problematic, if not blatantly heretical, view. Cf. bḤag 15a.

24. *Midrash Wayyikra Rabbah,* ed. M. Margulies (New York, 1993), 3.7, p. 74. My interpretation of this text follows the suggestive comments of the editor on p. 74 n. 3.

25. See M. Fishbane, *The Garments of Torah: Essays in Biblical Hermeneutics* (Bloomington, 1989), 23, and references given on 137 nn. 8–9.

26. *Midrash Bereshit Rabba,* eds. J. Theodor and Ch. Albeck (Jerusalem, 1965), 19–20, and the many parallel sources mentioned on 19 n. 10. This midrashic passage has been discussed by a number of scholars. See, in particular, A. Altmann, "A Note on the Rabbinic Doctrine of Creation," *Journal of Jewish Studies* 8 (1956), 195–206, reprinted in *Studies in Religious Philosophy and Mysticism* (Ithaca, 1969), 128–139; and the study of Scholem cited in the following note.

27. See Scholem, *Jewish Gnosticism,* 58. See the interesting comment on this tamudic passage in Nathan ben Yehiel, *Aruch Completum,* ed. A. Kohut, 5:34, s.v. *laḥash:* "The Torah was given in secrecy because of Satan." In emulation of the Sinaitic event, words of Torah must be given in a whisper.

28. This is the reading of MS Paris, Bibliothèque Nationale héb. 149, cited in the register of variant readings in *Midrash Bereshit Rabba,* p. 20, line 3. See also *Midrash Tehillim,* ed. S. Buber (Vilna, 1891), 104:4, p. 440; *Midrash Tanhuma,* ed. S. Buber (Vilna, 1885), Bereshit, 10, p. 6.

29. This reading from MS Munich, Bayerische Staatsbibliothek 117 is cited in the register of variant readings in *Midrash Wayyikra Rabbah,* 31:7, p. 726, line 2.

30. This is the reading in *Midrash Wayyikra Rabbah,* 31:7, p. 726. Cf. *Pesikta de Rav Kahana,* ed. B. Mandelbaum (New York, 1962), 21:5, p. 324: *she'amru li,* "they said to me."

31. *Memory and Manuscript: Oral Tradition and Written Transmission in Rabbinic Judaism and Early Christianity* (Copenhagen, 1964), 133.

32. Ibid., 133 n. 4.

33. Midrash Tanḥuma, Wayyera, 5; *Pesiqta Rabbati,* ed. M. Friedmann (Vienna, 1880), 5, 14b. The expression "mystery of circumcision" (*mistorin shel milah*) revealed by God to Abraham occurs in Midrash Tanḥuma, Lekh Lekha 19. On the notion of the "mystery of God," cf. Midrash Bereshit Rabbah, 50:9, 68:23. An enumeration of the different connotations of the word *misturin* in rabbinic sources is given by Altmann, "Maimonides' Attitude Toward Jewish Mysticism," 215–216 n. 15. It is possible that some of these rabbinic sources reflect the use of

the technical term *mysterion* in early Christian literature. For a recent discussion of this term, see G. G. Stroumsa, "From Esotericism to Mysticism in Early Christianity," in *Secrecy and Concealment,* 289–309.

34. The interplay of orality and textuality in the composition and/or redaction of the Mishnah is a complicated matter that falls outside the scope of this inquiry. For recent discussion of this topic, see Y. Elman, *Authority and Tradition: Toseftan Baraitot in Talmudic Babylonia* (Hoboken, 1994), 71–86; M. Jaffee, "How Much 'Orality' in Oral Torah? New Perspectives on the Composition and Transmission of Early Rabbinic Tradition," *Shofar* 10 (1992): 53–72; Jaffee, "Writing and Rabbinic Oral Tradition: On Mishnaic Narrative, Lists and Mnemonics," *Journal of Jewish Thought and Philosophy* 4 (1994), 123–146, and references to other relevant scholarly literature given on 123–124 n. 3.

35. At present there is a vigorous movement towards wider dissemination of kabbalistic doctrines and an abundance of literary documentation. Hence, in the contemporary context, the emphasis on the secretive nature of the kabbalah implies the inherent incomprehensibility of the ideas rather than the necessity to receive the knowledge directly from an authoritative chain.

36. For discussion of Judah ben Barzillai's views regarding these matters, see E. R. Wolfson, *Through a Speculum That Shines: Vision and Imagination in Medieval Jewish Mysticism* (Princeton, 1994), 148–160.

37. *Commentar zum Sepher Jezira von R. Jehuda b. Barsilai aus Barcelona,* ed. S. J. Halberstam (Berlin, 1885), 189, cited by G. Scholem, *Kabbalah* (Jerusalem, 1974), 6.

38. G. Scholem, "A New Document on the Beginnings of Kabbalah" (Hebrew), in *Sefer Bialik* (Tel-Aviv, 1934), 144. In *Origins of the Kabbalah,* trans. A. Arkush and ed. R. J. Zwi Werblowsky (Princeton, 1987), 254, Scholem dates the letter to 1235.

39. "New Document," 143. For a different rendering see *Origins,* 200.

40. Scholem, "New Document," 143.

41. See Idel, *Kabbalah: New Perspectives,* 20–22.

42. See Y. Liebes, *Studies in the Zohar,* trans. A. Schwartz, S. Nakache, and P. Peli (Albany, 1993), 26–34; E. R. Wolfson, *Circle in Square: Studies in the Use of Gender in Kabbalistic Symbolism* (Albany, 1995), 150 n. 61. See the comment of Idel referred to in the following note.

43. See M. Idel, "We Have No Kabalistic Tradition on This," in *Rabbi Moses Naḥmanides (Ramban): Explorations in His Literary and Religious Virtuosity,* ed. I. Twersky (Cambridge, Mass., 1983), 51–73 (on 71 n. 73, Idel acknowledges that in the zoharic text there are allusions to secrets that must be hidden, but he con-

cludes that much more is revealed than is concealed); idem, *Kabbalah: New Perspectives,* 210–218.

44. *Guide of the Perplexed,* trans. S. Pines (Chicago, 1963), 3.Introduction, p. 415.

45. Ibid., 1.Introduction, p. 7; 1.33, p. 71; 3.Introduction, p. 416.

46. See Altmann, "Maimonides' Attitude Towards Jewish Mysticism," 200–219. The problem of secrecy and esotericism in Maimonides has been dealt with by a number of scholars from various methodological perspectives. The following list of representative studies is very selective: L. Strauss, "The Literary Character of the *Guide of the Perplexed,*" in *Essays on Maimonides,* ed. S. W. Baron (New York, 1941), 37–91, reprinted in *Persecution and the Art of Writing* (Glencoe, Ill., 1952), 38–94, and Strauss, "How To Begin To Study The Guide of the Perplexed," in *The Guide of the Perplexed,* trans. S. Pines, xi–lvi; Strauss, *Philosophy and Law: Contributions to the Understanding of Maimonides and His Predecessors,* trans. E. Adler (Albany, 1995), 95–96, 102–103 (regarding the approach of Strauss to Maimonides' esotericism, see K. H. Green, *Jew and Philosopher: The Return to Maimonides in the Jewish Thought of Leo Strauss* [Albany, 1993], 111–134); H. A. Davidson, "Maimonides' Secret Position on Creation," in *Studies in Medieval Jewish History and Literature* I, ed. I. Twersky (Cambridge, Mass., 1979), 16–40; A. Ravitsky, "Samuel ibn Tibbon and the Esoteric Character of the *Guide of the Perplexed,*" *AJS Review* 6 (1981), 87–123; idem, "The Secrets of the *Guide of the Perplexed:* Between the Thirteenth and the Twentieth Centuries" (Hebrew), *Jerusalem Studies in Jewish Thought* 5 (1986): 23–69, English version in *Studies in Maimonides,* ed. I. Twersky (Cambridge, Mass., 1990), 159–207; Z. Levy, "Hermeneutik und Esoterik bei Maimonides und Spinoza," *Internationaler Schleiermacher Kongress, Berlin 1984,* ed. K.-V. Selge (Berlin, 1985), 541–560; M. Idel, "*Sitre 'Arayot* in Maimonides' Thought," in *Maimonides and Philosophy: Papers Presented at the Sixth Jerusalem Philosophical Encounter, May 1985,* eds. S. Pines and Y. Yovel (Dordrecht, 1986), 79–91; M. Fox, *Interpreting Maimonides: Studies in Methodology, Metaphysics, and Moral Philosophy* (Chicago, 1990), 47–90; S. Klein-Braslavy, *King Solomon and Philosophical Esotericism in the Thought of Maimonides* (Jerusalem, 1996; in Hebrew).

47. See "New Document," 145; *Origins,* 374.

48. *Kitvei Ramban,* 2:478.

49. Ibid., 479.

50. Ibid., 498.

51. The significance of 1240 must be related to a conflation of the passage in bSan 97a to the effect that the world endures for 6,000 years divided into three cycles of

2,000 years, the last one being the days of messiah, and a conception that Jewish authors, beginning with Abraham bar Ḥiyya, apparently borrowed from Christian sources, particularly evident in Joachim of Fiore but going back to the Augustinian theme of seven *aetates mundi* from creation to consummation. The Christian apocalyptic idea involved the typological parallelism between the *hexämeron,* the six days of the week, and six ages of human history followed by the Sabbath corresponding to the seventh age of eternity. Appropriating this worldview the medieval Jewish authors identified each cosmic day with a period of 1,000 years, given the additional rabbinic teaching (based on the metaphor in Ps 90:4) that each day of the Lord extends to a period of 1,000 years. Hence, the six days of creation are the six millennia of history to be followed by a period of rest, which was construed either as total annihilation, the relative cessation of life, or the time of cosmic judgement. The acceptance of this parallel between cosmos and history resulted in the following symmetrical relation: just as Adam was created on the sixth day so the sixth millennium was the appointed time of the messianic redemption when the original perfection of cosmos and humanity would be restored. Such a scheme of human history was adopted and transformed by a number of kabbalists in Northern Spain in the thirteenth century. See the comments of J. Guttmann in his introduction to *Sefer Megillat ha-Megalleh,* ed. A. Poznanski (Berlin, 1924), xiii–xiv; S. Heller-Wilensky, "Isaac ibn Latif: Philosopher or Kabbalist?" in *Jewish Medieval and Renaissance Studies,* ed. A. Altmann (Cambridge, Mass., 1967), 218; idem, "Messianism, Eschatology and Utopianism in the Philosophical-Mystical Trend of Kabbalah in the 13th Century" (Hebrew), in *Messianism and Eschatology: A Collection of Essays,* ed. Z. Baras (Jerusalem, 1983), 221–237; A. Funkenstein, "Naḥmanides' Symbolical Reading of History," in *Studies in Jewish Mysticism,* ed. J. Dan and F. Talmage (Cambridge, Mass., 1982), 139–141.

52. Cf. Job. 40:4.

53. In the first edition of this work published in Altona, 1764, a scribal note suggests that the reference is to the time of death based on bBer 10a where the fifth world of David is connected with the day of death. See also Chavel's edition, p. 479. According to another reading, mentioned parenthetically in the first edition, the text here states that the author was 51 years old. See G. Vajda, *Le commentaire d'Ezra de Gérone sur le cantique des cantiques* (Paris, 1969), 44; I. Tishby, *Studies in Kabbalah and Its Branches* (Hebrew) (Jerusalem, 1982), 1:12 n. 11.

54. A note in the first edition (cited by Chavel) suggests that this may mean one year beyond the life expectancy of seventy years. If that interpretation is correct, then Ezra apparently was 71 when he composed this treatise. See A. Jellinek, *Beiträge zur Geschichte der Kabbala* (Leipzig, 1852), 2:33 n. 4.

55. *Kitvei Ramban,* 2: 479–480.

56. See, e.g., *Kitvei Ramban,* 2:480, 499, 500–502.

57. *Kitvei Ramban,* 2:491. See H. Pedaya, "The Spiritual vs. the Concrete Land of Israel in the Geronese School of Kabbalah" (Hebrew), in *The Land of Israel in Medieval Jewish Thought,* ed. M. Hallamish and A. Ravitzky (Jerusalem, 1991), 250–251.

58. On Naḥmanides' messianic posture in light of the aggressive Christian missionizing in thirteenth-century Spain, see R. Chazan, *Barcelona and Beyond: The Disputation of 1263 and Its Aftermath* (Berkeley, 1992), 172–194.

59. *Kitvei Ramban,* 2:480–481.

60. Ibid., 2:480.

61. See Pedaya, "The Spiritual vs. the Concrete Land of Israel," 249.

62. See G. Scholem, *Reshit ha-Qabbalah* (Tel-Aviv, 1948), 73–74 n. 2. The centrality of the name in the kabbalistic thought of Isaac has been explored in detail by H. Pedaya, "'Flaw' and 'Correction' in the Concept of the Godhead in the Teachings of Rabbi Isaac the Blind" (Hebrew), *Jerusalem Studies in Jewish Thought* 6 (1987), 157–285.

63. "New Document," 155. In MS New York, JTSA Mic. 1878, fols. 12a–b, a passage dealing with the containment of the ten *sefirot* in the Tetragrammaton is transmitted in the name of Ezra. This idea is briefly alluded to by Isaac the Blind. Inasmuch as the study of the *sefirot* is the distinguishing feature of theosophic kabbalah, and the *sefirot* are comprised within the name, it follows that kabbalah can be viewed as an esoteric tradition regarding the divine name.

64. See, e.g., the text published by Scholem, *Madda'ei ha-Yahadut* 2 (1927): 231–232.

65. Text printed in J. Dan, *The Kabbalah of R. Asher ben David* (Hebrew) (Jerusalem, 1980), 13.

66. See Pedaya, "'Flaw and 'Correction,'" 157 n. 2.

67. See J. Dan, *The Esoteric Theology of the Ashkenazi Hasidism* (Hebrew) (Jerusalem, 1968), 74–75.

68. See M. Idel, *The Mystical Experience in Abraham Abulafia* (Albany, 1988), 14–24; *Kabbalah: New Perspectives,* 97–103.

69. See M. Idel, "Defining Kabbalah: The Kabbalah of the Divine Names," in *Mystics of the Book: Topics, Themes, and Typologies,* ed. R. A. Herrera (New York, 1993), 97–122.

70. *Guide of the Perplexed,* 3.Introduction, p. 416. A striking affirmation of the power of reason in the pursuit of mystical gnosis is found in *Zohar Hadash,* ed. R. Margaliot (Jerusalem, 1978), 25c (*Midrash ha-Ne'elam*). R. Haggai is told

that he can join R. Dostai in his excursion to visit R. Eleazar ben Arakh if he is capable of comprehending what he hears. To this challenge R. Haggai responds, "I have heard the matter of the supernal secret, I have contemplated it, and I have proposed an interpretation." The word that I have translated as "interpretation" is *sevara'*, which has the connotation of logical supposition. The point of the passage, then, is that one must be able to discern the meaning of an esoteric matter through the exercise of one's own reason.

71. *Perush ha-Ramban al ha-Torah,* 2 vols., ed. C. Chavel (Jerusalem, 1984), 1:7.

72. See E. R. Wolfson, "'By Way of Truth': Aspects of Naḥmanides' Kabbalistic Hermeneutic," *AJS Review* 14 (1989), 105 n. 6.

73. MS New York, JTSA Mic. 1990, fol. 102a.

74. A brief description of this text is given by Scholem, *Kabbalah,* 61. The text is referred to by Moses Cordovero, *Or Ne'erav* (Tel-Aviv, 1965), 23: *we-hakhi mukhah be-sodot ha-zaqen u-she'arav,* "Thus it has been proven in the secrets of the elder and his gates." In the manuscript that I examined, however, I did not find a source for the custom that Cordovero attributes to this text, which involves sitting on the floor when kabbalah is studied.

75. MS Oxford, Bodleian Library 2396, fol. 6b.

76. That Naḥmanides is the source for this text is enhanced by the fact that this section begins with a citation of his commentary to Gen. 1:8. Naḥmanides is referred to as "the rabbi, may his memory be for a blessing." Cf. MS Oxford, Bodleian Library 2396, fol. 34b. Several times in this collection Naḥmanides is designated *ha-rav ha-naḥmani.* Cf. fols. 6b, 29b, 36b, 38a, 48b, 50b, 52b, 57a.

77. Ibid., fol. 35a. On the necessity to explain esoteric matters orally, cf. fols. 4b, 29a, 33a, 44b, 45b, 53a, 53b, 55a, 61b. Cf. fol. 6a, where it is emphasized that even the very wise students cannot comprehend kabbalistic matters because "it is the way of kabbalists to speak in a concealed language." On the intention to conceal the secrets, cf. fol. 43a. On the distinction between oral tradition (*qabbalat peh 'el peh*) and the exercise of one's intellect (*da'at*) as the means to ascertain wisdom, cf. ibid., fols. 3b–4a. The elder reports what he received from his teacher on a number of occasions. Cf. fols. 33b, 35a, 50a, and 54a (in that context an allusion is made to the ascent, *aliyah,* of the master and his disciple, which serves as the experiential precondition for the disclosure of the secrets). The Mosaic origin of the chain of oral tradition is affirmed a number of times in this text; cf. fols. 3b, 38a, 39a. Cf. fol. 14a where Moses is said to have received the secrets of Torah by means of the combination of letters (*tseruf ha-'otiyyot*). On fol. 39a the elder is said to have seen a *tsefer ha-tseruf,* apparently a treatise on letter permutations. A lengthy discussion on *sod ha-tseruf,* the "secret of permutation," occurs on fols. 53a–b.

78. Ibid., fol. 2b. The following oral tradition is reported on fols. 13a–b: "The eyes of the one who tastes the wine from that blessed cup will be illuminated, and he will see the supernal and lower beings. The pious of Israel (*ḥasidei yisra'el*) have the custom of placing on their eyes a drop of wine from the cup for the sanctification of Sabbath (*kos qiddush shel shabbat*) so that they will merit that blessed cup prepared for the righteous in the Garden of Eden. All this we received from the great rabbi, the pious one, master of secrets." Cf. fol. 14b where the custom to declare a holiday when the study of a book or a tractate was completed is cited in the name of the "midrash of our teacher, the elderly master."

79. Ibid., fol. 4a. The admonition not to write esoteric matters is repeated on fol. 50b.

80. Ibid., fol. 36b.

81. The transmission of secrets by means of a whisper reflects the rabbinic idea of the manner in which an esoteric matter is handed over by a master to a disciple. Cf. bḤag 14a; *Bereshit Rabbah* 1:3, eds. J. Theodor and C. Albeck (Jerusalem, 1965), 19–20, and the many parallel sources mentioned on p. 19 n. 10. The latter passage has been discussed by a number of scholars. See, in particular, A. Altmann, *Studies in Religious Philosophy and Mysticism* (Ithaca, 1969), 128–139; and G. Scholem, *Jewish Gnosticism, Merkabah Mysticism, and Talmudic Tradition* (New York, 1965), 58.

82. On the criterion of understanding one thing from another, cf. bḤag 11b, 13a. The complex relationship of oral reception, innovative exegesis, and revelatory experience is affirmed in a brief comment of Hai Gaon explaining the talmudic dictum that esoteric knowledge must be transmitted in a whisper, in *Otsar ha-Geonim: Thesaurus of the Gaonic Responsa and Commentaries,* ed. B. M. Lewin (Jerusalem, 1931), 4:12, cited by Scholem, *Jewish Gnosticism,* 58 n. 10: "They whisper to him in whispers, give him the principles, he understands them, and from heaven they show him the mysteries of his heart." According to this text, esoteric knowledge is imparted by way of an oral transmission from the master to the disciple, but that knowledge must be interpreted by the receiver of the tradition by applying the general principles that have been disclosed, and this results in a heavenly revelation of the secrets that are lodged in the heart of the initiate.

83. *Guide of the Perplexed,* 1.33, pp. 71–72.

84. MS Oxford, Bodleian Library 2396, fol. 40a. The image of entering into one room after another in order to receive instruction regarding mystical secrets is employed on fol. 11b. See also fols. 46a and 61b.

85. The precise language of rebuke is used in another context; cf. fols. 54a–b.

86. This posture is associated with inducing mystical trances or ecstatic states of

consciousness. See P. Fenton, "La 'Tête Entre Les Genoux': contribution à l'étude d'une posture méditative dans la mystique juive et islamique," *Revue d'Histoire et de Philosophie Religieuses* 72 (1992), 413–426.

87. MS Oxford, Bodleian Library 2396, fol. 30b.

88. *Guide of the Perplexed,* 1.Introduction, p. 6; 1.33, p. 71.

89. Ibid., 1.Introduction, pp. 7–8; 1.33, p. 80; 3.Introduction, p. 416.

90. MS, Oxford, Bodleian Library 2396, fol. 7a. In the continuation of this passage the author proclaims that he can commit to writing angelic names because they will not be comprehensible to anyone except through an oral tradition.

91. Ibid., fol. 51b. On the transmission of chapter headings, cf. fol. 24b.

92. Ibid., fol. 62b.

93. Ibid., fols. 51b–52a.

94. *Guide of the Perplexed,* 3.Introduction, p. 415.

95. Regarding this motif in Abulafia's writings, see E. R. Wolfson, *Along the Path: Studies in Kabbalistic Hermeneutics, Myth, and Symbolism* (Albany, 1995), 20–22 and 135–136 nn. 150–158. In that context, I neglected to mention the pertinent discussion in *Ḥayyei ha-Nefesh,* MS Munich, Bayerische Staatsbibliothek 408, fols. 69b–70a.

96. MS Vatican, Biblioteca Apostolica ebr. 233, fol. 97b.

97. See Scholem, *Major Trends,* 119–155, and the work of Idel cited in n. 38.

98. MS Paris, Bibliothèque Nationale héb. 774, fol. 130a.

99. Cf. *'Imrei Shefer,* MS Munich, Bayerische Staatsbibliothek 40, fol. 224b; *Sitrei Torah,* MS Paris, Bibliothèque Nationale héb. 774, fols. 169a–b; *Ḥayyei ha-Nefesh,* MS Munich, Bayerische Staatsbibliothek 408, fol. 10b. I have discussed these and other relevant passages in "Mystical Rationalization of the Commandments in the Prophetic Kabbalah of Abraham Abulafia," in *Perspectives on Jewish Thought and Mysticism,* edited by A. L. Ivry, E. R. Wolfson, and A. Arkush (Amsterdam, 1998), 311–360. See also M. Idel, *Language, Torah, and Hermeneutics in Abraham Abulafia* (Albany, 1989), 64.

100. See Idel, *Language, Torah, and Hermeneutics,* 109–111.

101. MS New York, JTSA Mic. 1686, fol. 96a.

102. MS Paris, Bibliothèque Nationale héb. 774, fol. 143a.

103. A variety of scholars have discussed the influence of Maimonides on Abulafia. See the study of Altmann cited above, n. 46; Scholem, *Major Trends,* 126, 138–139, and 383 n. 76; Scholem, *The Kabbalah of Sefer ha-Temunah and Abraham Abulafia* (Hebrew), ed. J. Ben-Shlomo (Jerusalem, 1965), 107, 127–129, 151–152; *Kabbalah,* 54; Idel, *Mystical Experience in Abraham Abulafia,* 32, 73–74, 89, 138–139, 179–182, 187; Idel, *Studies in the Ecstatic Kabbalah* (Albany,

1988), 13–14, 16–17, 21 n. 8, 38, 52; Idel, *Language, Torah, and Hermeneutics,* 16–17, 30–31, 42, 45, 106, 120, 167–168 n. 69, 177 n. 134, 189 n. 13, 191 n. 46; Idel, "Maimonides and Kabbalah," in *Studies in Maimonides,* ed. I. Twersky (Cambridge, Mass., 1990), 54–79.

104. Cf. the description of kabbalah as knowledge of the name in *Sheva' Netivot ha-Torah,* in A. Jellinek, *Philosophie und Kabbala* (Leipzig, 1854), 9. The influence of Abulafia is discernible in Joseph Gikatilla, *Ginnat Egoz* (Jerusalem, 1989), 343–344. Gikatilla identifies the "wisdom of Torah" as the "inner wisdom," which is compared to the nucleus of the circle apprehended only by Israel. The Torah is identified further as the twenty-two letters, which are comprised in AHW''Y, the letters of the divine name that add up to twenty-two.

105. MS Paris, Bibliothèque Nationale héb. 774, fol. 140b.

106. Dan, *Esoteric Theology,* 124 n. 45; M. Idel, "The Concept of Torah in the Hekhalot and Its Evolution in the Kabbalah" (Hebrew), *Jerusalem Studies in Jewish Thought* 1 (1981), 47–48; Idel, "We Have No Kabbalistic Tradition on This," 54 n. 10; E. R. Wolfson, "The Mystical Significance of Torah-Study in German Pietism," in *Jewish Quarterly Review* 84 (1993), 43–78.

107. G. Scholem, *On the Kabbalah and Its Symbolism,* trans. R. Manheim (New York, 1965), 37–39; Scholem, "The Name of God and the Linguistic Theory of the Kabbala," *Diogenes* 79 (1972), 76–77; Idel, "Concept of Torah," 23–49.

108. Idel, "Concept of Torah," 54 n. 10.

109. Scholem, *On the Kabbalah,* 38; Idel, "Concept of Torah," 52–55.

110. See Idel, *Language, Torah, Hermeneutics,* 46–47, 66, 171 n. 88; Wolfson, "'By Way of Truth,'" 117 n. 44.

111. See Idel, *Language, Torah, and Hermeneutics,* 48–49.

112. *Philosophie und Kabbala,* 4–5.

113. Ibid., 12. Idel, *Kabbalah: New Perspectives,* 254, remarks that despite the innovative hermeneutical approach adopted by Abulafia, which resulted his prolific literary activity, he still remained faithful to the view that what is truly esoteric cannot be written.

114. MS Paris, Bibliothèque Nationale héb. 774, fol. 121a.

115. For Abulafia's extended discussion of this part of the *Guide,* cf. *Ḥayyei ha-Nefesh,* MS Munich, Bayerische Staatsbibliothek 408, fols. 69a–73a.

116. Ibid., fols. 4a–b.

117. G. Scholem, "The Secret of the Tree of Emanation by R. Isaac: A Treatise from the Kabbalistic Tradition of *Sefer ha-Temunah*" (Hebrew), *Qovets al Yad* 5 (1951), 67 n. 2.

118. D. Abrams, "'The Book of Illumination' of R. Jacob ben Jacob haKohen: A

Synoptic Edition From Various Manuscripts," Ph.D. dissertation, New York University, 1993.

119. See A. Farber, "On the Sources of Rabbi Moses de León's Early Kabbalistic System" (Hebrew), in *Studies in Jewish Mysticism Philosophy and Ethical Literature presented to Isaiah Tishby on his Seventy-fifth Birthday* (Jerusalem, 1986), 67–96.

120. MS Oxford, Bodleian Library 1953, fol. 24b.

121. Ibid., fol. 28a.

122. *Berit Menuḥah* (Amsterdam, 1648), 2a.

123. Ibid., 2b. On the notion that Adam is the first link in the chain of tradition, see above, n. 17.

124. W. J. Ong, *Orality and Literacy: The Technologizing of the Word* (London, 1982), 41. See B. Stock, *The Implications of Literacy: Written Language and Models of Interpretation in the Eleventh and Twelfth Centuries* (Princeton, 1983), 15–16.

125. Shem Tov ibn Gaon, *Badde ha-Aron u-Migdal Hananel,* facsimile edition based on MS 840 in the National Library, Paris, ed. D. S. Loewinger (Jerusalem, 1977), 29; cf. idem, *Keter Shem Tov,* in *Ma'or wa-Shemesh,* ed. J. Koriat (Livorno, 1839), 35b; Shem Tov ibn Shem Tov, *Sefer ha-Emunot* (Ferrara, 1560), 35b.

126. Isaac ben Samuel of Acre, *Sefer Me'irat Einayim by R. Isaac of Acre: A Critical Edition,* ed. A. Goldreich (Jerusalem, 1981), 84.

127. Menahem Recanati, *Perush ha-Torah* (Jerusalem, 1961), 73d. A similar chain of tradition is cited in the name of the "sages of truth" (*ḥakhmei ha-emet*) by Meir ibn Gabbai, *Avodat ha-Qodesh* (Jerusalem, 1992), 2.13, p. 102, and from there it is cited by Elijah Delmedigo, *Matsref la-Ḥokhmah* (Basel, 1629), 15a.

128. According to the manuscript evidence cited by Scholem, *Origins,* 37 n. 61.

129. *Origins,* 245. On the role of Elijah in Jewish mysticism, see also A. Wiener, *The Prophet Elijah in the Development of Judaism: A Depth-Psychological Study* (London, 1978), 78–11.

130. *On the Kabbalah,* 19.

131. This position has been referred to as the contextualist approach. For references to some representative studies, see Wolfson, *Through a Speculum That Shines,* 52 n. 2.

132. Scholem, *Origins,* 36, was of the opinion that even though the traditions relating to the appearance of the prophet Elijah to the earliest kabbalists first appear around the year 1300, everything indicates that they are drawn from traditional material going back to the first Spanish kabbalists. By contrast, I. Twersky,

Rabad of Posquières: A Twelfth-Century Talmudist (Cambridge, Mass., 1962), 287, concluded that the claim for Abraham ben David's acquisition of knowledge through the medium of revelation "seems to be a later accretion."

133. A similar position regarding the interaction of orality and literary traditions in classical rabbinic culture has been affirmed by a number of scholars. See the studies of Jaffee cited above n. 34. For a recently published study that deals with this topic in the biblical sources, see S. Niditch, *Oral World and Written Word: Ancient Israelite Literature* (Louisville, 1996).

134. A number of scholars of late have challenged a rigid dichotomization of orality and textuality in the Middle Ages and have opted for a symbiotic model whereby the two epistemic modes interact and interpenetrate. See F. H. Bäuml, "Medieval Texts and the Two Theories of Oral-Formulaic Composition: A Proposal for a Third Theory," *New Literary History* 16 (1984–85), 41–54; J. M. Gellrich, *The Idea of the Book in the Middle Ages: Language Theory, Mythology, and Fiction* (Ithaca, 1985); J. M. Foley, *The Theory of Oral Composition: History and Methodology* (Bloomington, 1988); Foley, "Orality, Textuality, and Interpretation," in *Vox intexta: Orality and Textuality in the Middle Ages,* ed. A. N. Donne and C. B. Pasternack (Madison, 1991), 34–45; idem, "Word-Power, Performance and Tradition," *Journal of American Folklore* 105 (1992), 275–301; M. Calinescu, "Orality and Literacy: Some Historical Paradoxes of Reading," *Yale Journal of Criticism* 6 (1993), 175–190. See also the works of Stock cited in nn. 107–108.

135. I have borrowed this expression from J. Goody, *The Interface Between the Written and the Oral* (Cambridge, 1987).

136. W. A. Graham, *Beyond the Written Word: Oral Aspects of Scripture in the History of Religion* (Cambridge, 1987), 157.

137. The history of Jewish literacy in the Middle Ages has not been written. For a preliminary study, see S. C. Reif, "Aspects of Medieval Jewish Literacy," in *The Uses of Literacy in Early Mediaeval Europe,* ed. R. McKitterick (Cambridge, 1990), 134–155. Although Reif's study is limited to eastern Jewish communities living under the rule of Islam from the sixth to the eleventh centuries, many of his insights regarding Jewish literacy would equally apply to Jews in Christian Europe.

138. Stock, *Implications of Literacy,* 90. According to Stock, from the beginning of the eleventh century, a new kind of interdependence arose between the oral and the written: "oral discourse effectively began to function within a universe of communications governed by texts" (3). To my mind, this is a satisfactory model for the rabbinic conception of oral tradition in the medieval European centers,

although it would apply equally to a much earlier historical period and different geographical locality.

139. B. Stock, *Listening for the Text: On the Uses of the Past* (Baltimore, 1990), 20.

140. W. Parks, "The Textualization of Orality in Literary Criticism," in *Vox intexta,* 46–61. See also Graham, *Beyond the Written Word,* 19–44.

141. Scholem, *Origins,* 39–44, 49–53; J. Dan, "Midrash and the Dawn of Kabbalah," in *Midrash and Literature,* ed. G. Hartman and S. Budick (New Haven, 1986), 127–139.

142. See Scholem, *Origins,* 49–198; M. Idel, "The Problem of the Sources of the *Bahir*" (Hebrew), *Jerusalem Studies in Jewish Thought* 6:3–4 (1987), 55–72; H. Pedaya, "The Provençal Stratum in the Redaction of *Sefer ha-Bahir*" (Hebrew), *Jerusalem Studies in Jewish Thought* 9 (1990), 139–164; E. R. Wolfson, "The Tree That Is All: Jewish-Christian Roots of a Kabbalistic Symbol in *Sefer ha-Bahir,*" *Journal of Jewish Thought and Philosophy* 3 (1993), 31–76, revised version in *Along the Path,* 63–88 and notes on 187–223.

143. *Sefer ha-Bahir,* ed. R. Margaliot (Jerusalem, 1978), par. 57.

144. Ibid., par. 194.

145. MS Oxford, Bodleian Library 1565, fol. 93b.

146. *Le-Ḥeqer Qabbalat R. Yitshaq ben Ya'aqov ha-Kohen* (Jerusalem, 1934), 122–127.

147. MS Oxford, Bodleian Library 1565, fol. 95b.

148. MS Cambridge, University Library Heb. Add. 645, fol. 20b; MS New York, JTSA Mic. 1878, fol. 26b.

149. See reference to Gerhardsson above, n. 31.

150. I have borrowed this expression from U. Schafer, "Hearing from Books: The Rise of Fictionality in Old English Poetry," in *Vox intexta,* 117–136. The intersection of orality and textuality may also relate to the fact that the dominant mode of reading within the social setting of religious institutions in the Middle Ages was acoustical, i.e., one read with one's ears rather than with one's eyes. On the aural nature of reading in the medieval monastic setting, see Stock, *Implications of Literacy,* 408–409; I. Illich, *In the Vineyard of the Text: A Commentary to Hugh's Didascalicon* (Chicago, 1993), 51–65.

151. MS Parma, Biblioteca Palatina 68, fol. 76a.

152. To take one other illustration from a comparatively later text, the seventeenth-century compendium of halakhic and kabbalistic sources, *Shenei Luḥot ha-Berit* of Isaiah Horowitz (Amsterdam, 1698), 355b: "I have heard with regard to this a wonderful matter in a manuscript." Here we have clear evidence

that the locution "I have heard" functions in a literary context. That is, the author "hears" or comprehends a tradition that he has found in manuscript.

153. See Scholem, *Origins,* 424.

154. The manuscript here reads *shem,* i.e., "name," but I have taken the liberty to assume that the correct reading is *sefer,* which has been rendered as "book."

155. MS New York, JTSA Mic. 1887, fol. 76a.

156. *Kitve Ramban,* 2:522.

157. Ibid., 2:409.

158. Ibid., 2:380. Cf. p. 411, where Jacob ben Sheshet records a reading of a passage from *Sefer Yetsirah* that he heard in the name of "the sage, R. Isaac the Frenchman."

159. bBer 34b; bSan 99a; Targum, Eccles. 9:7; Bemidbar Rabbah 13:2; see L. Ginzberg, *The Legends of the Jews,* 6 vols. (Philadelphia, 1968), 5:29 n. 79, 284 n. 93.

160. For references to this aggadic motif, see Ginzberg, *Legends of the Jews,* 5:101 n. 85. See ibid., 5:98 n. 70, where Ginzberg surmises that the "passage concerning the wine preserved for the pious is probably related to the view that the fruit which brought sin into the world will probably become 'a healing' in the world to come." In support of his explanation, Ginzberg mentions *Wayyikra Rabbah* 12:5, ed. M. Margulies (New York, 1993), 268: "In this world the wine was an obstacle to the world, but in the future the Holy One, blessed be He, makes of it something joyous."

161. *Sefer Meshiv Nekhohim,* ed. G. Vajda (Jerusalem, 1968), 86.

162. Cf. ibid., 81, where Jacob ben Sheshet reports a magical technique that he has heard from a "wise magician," *menaḥesh ḥakham.*

163. Ibid., 96. For a list of the citations in the name of Ezra of Gerona found in Jacob ben Sheshet's writings, see I. Tishby, *Commentary on Talmudic Aggadoth by Rabbi Azriel of Gerona* (Jerusalem, 1945), Introduction, 31–33.

164. MS New York, JTSA Mic. 1878, fol. 4b.

165. Ibid., fols. 6b, 7a, 17a.

166. Ibid., fol. 7b.

167. There are, of course, reports of oral traditions regarding the sefirotic potencies and/or the divine names that are not necessarily linked to specific texts. Cf. Shem Tov ibn Gaon, *Keter Shem Tov,* 36b, 47b. To take another example, the anonymous author of *Ma'arekhet ha-'Elohut* (Mantua, 1558), 66b, remarks that Solomon ibn Adret reported that he received from Naḥmanides that the word *tsiyyon* is one of the technical names for the ninth emanation. The textual nature of the oral tradition is underscored in a second passage from this work where the

author relates having heard that the repetition of the word *mayim* in the legend about Akiva's warning to the other rabbis (according to the version in bḤag 14b) has symbolic significance.

168. In one place, *Keter Shem Tov,* 34a, Shem Tov records a numerological explanation of the word *hit'azzar* in Ps 93:1, which he heard from his teacher who had heard it from R. Shlomo ha-Qatan. The oral tradition is linked specifically to an expostion of a biblical text.

169. Ibid., 29a.

170. Ibid., 31b.

171. Ibid., 32b, 41a–42a.

172. Ibid., 39a.

173. *Sefer Me'irat Einayim,* 219. Cf. *Keter Shem Tov,* 40b.

174. MS Vatican, Biblioteca Apostolica ebr. 185, fol. 3a; see Tishby, *Commentary on Talmudic Aggadoth,* 10.

175. Cf. *Otsar ha-Kavod ha-Shalem* (Warsaw, 1879), 4d.

176. See *Origins,* 66–67. Scholem's views regarding Gnosticism and its relationship to Judaism are complex. See discussion in Idel, *Kabbalah: New Perspectives,* 30–31, and the critique by I. Tishby, "Upheaval in the Research of Kabbalah (On: M. Idel, *Kabbalah: New Perspectives*)" (Hebrew), *Zion* 54 (1989), 210–213. For more recent reviews of the question, see N. Deutsch, *The Gnostic Imagination: Gnosticism, Mandaeism, and Merkabah Mysticism* (Leiden, 1995), 1–17, and J. Dan, "Jewish Gnosticism?," *Jewish Studies Quarterly* 2 (1995), 309–328.

177. See Idel, *Kabbalah: New Perspectives,* 31–32.

178. I. Tishby, "Gnostic Doctrines in Sixteenth-Century Jewish Mysticism," *Journal of Jewish Studies* 6 (1955), 146, articulates a similar position to the one that I am advocating, although he does not place the same emphasis on the hermeneutical dimension.

179. This aspect of Naḥmanides' kabbalah has been championed by Idel, "We Have No Kabbalistic Tradition," and *Kabbalah: New Perspectives,* 20, 212, 253–254. In a more recent publication, "Secrecy, Binah and Derishah," 331, Idel asserts that, according to Naḥmanides, understanding is a tool for the reception of secrets, but not for the extracting of secrets from the text. See also his "R. Moshe ben Naḥman—Kabbalah, Halakhah, and Spiritual Leadership" (Hebrew), *Tarbiẓ* 64 (1995), 535–580, esp. 550–556.

180. "By Way of Truth," 153–178. M. Idel, in his introduction to *The Book Bahir: An Edition Based on the Earliest Manuscripts,* ed. D. Abrams (Los Angeles, 1994), 4 n. 24, expresses doubt regarding my claim that the *Bahir* was the main

kabbalistic source for Naḥmanides with respect to at least two topics, the doctrine of the *sefirot* and the secret of impregnation (*sod ha-'ibbur*). See, however, "By Way of Truth," 177–178 n. 237, where I myself mentioned that Naḥmanides' essentialist interpretation of the *sefirot* did not parallel the view expressed in the *Bahir*. More importantly, the main thrust of my argument concerned support for kabbalistic ideas. When the issue is framed in that way, I still think it is correct to conclude that, for Naḥmanides, the *Bahir* is the critical text, for he often relies on that source to validate his kabbalistic exegesis.

181. D. Berger, "Miracles and the Natural Order in Naḥmanides," in *Rabbi Moses Naḥmanides,* 112 n. 19; B. Septimus, "'Open Rebuke and Concealed Love': Naḥmanides and the Andalusian Tradition," in *Rabbi Moses Naḥmanides,* 21 n. 37; Wolfson, "By Way of Truth," 129–153.

182. E. R. Wolfson, "The Secret of the Garment in Naḥmanides" *Da'at* 24 (1990), 25–49 (English section).

183. "By Way of Truth," 164–165.

184. *Perush ha-Ramban 'al ha-Torah,* 1:3. Naḥmanides' position bears a striking resemblance to the orientation of the German Pietists who likewise emphasize that all wisdom, including the secrets, are contained in the Torah. See H. Soloveitchik, "Three Themes in the *Sefer Hasidim,*" *AJS Review* 1 (1976), 314 n. 7. One text not mentioned by Soloveitchik, but which is very close to the position of Naḥmanides, is Eleazar of Worms, *Perush ha-Rav Ele'azar Mi-Germaiza' al Sefer Yetsirah* (Przemysl, 1883), 1b: "The Torah begins with the *bet* of *bere'shit* and ends with the *lamed* of *le-'eine kol yisra'el* [the numerical value of *bet* and *lamed* is thirty-two, the number of the paths of wisdom] to teach you that everything is alluded to in the Torah (*ramuz ba-torah*) . . . but it is hidden from people, and the secrets of Torah were only given to those who fear him, 'the secret of the Lord is with those who fear Him' (Ps 25:14)." Cf. idem, *Sefer ha-Shem,* MS London, British Museum 737, fols. 205b–206a. Eleazar acknowledges that through the interpretative method, which he refers to by the technical term *talmud,* one can greatly multiply the production of books that make explicit that which is inherent in the scriptural text—a point all the more remarkable in light of the explicit claim in *Sefer Hasidim* (ed. J. Wistinetzki and J. Freimann [Frankfurt am Main, 1924], par. 986) that the production of novel interpretations (*ledabber ḥidushim*) is one of the major temptations that the pietist must overcome. See, in particular, the text of Eleazar published by J. Dan, *Studies in Ashkenazi-Hasidic Literature* (Ramat-Gan, 1975), 46–47 (in Hebrew), and the analysis in I. G. Marcus, *Piety and Society: The Jewish Pietists of Medieval Germany* (Leiden, 1981), 69–70. Regarding the influence of

the Ashkenazi Pietists on Naḥmanides, see also E. Kanarfogel, "On the Assessment of R. Moses ben Naḥman (Naḥmanides) and His Literary Oeuvre," *Jewish Book Annual* 51 (1993–94), 170–172.

185. *Kitvei Ramban,* 1:161.

186. I owe this insight to Yaakov Elman.

187. See "By Way of Truth," 146–148.

188. C. H. Kahn, *The Art and Thought of Heraclitus: An Edition of the Fragments With Translation and Commentary* (Cambridge, 1979), 42–43.

189. *Perush ha-Ramban al ha-Torah,* 1:9 (at Gen 1:1).

190. Ibid., 1:18 (at Gen 1:6). As Elman pointed out to me, implicit in the formulation of Naḥmanides is an argument from proportion. See his "'It is No Empty Thing': Nahmanides and the Search for Omnisignificance," *Torah u-Madda Journal* 5 (1994), 1–83.

191. See Idel, "R. Moshe ben Naḥman," 550–551.

192. *Perush ha-Ramban al ha-Torah,* 2:101 (at Lev. 18:6).

193. Text and translation in Wolfson, "By Way of Truth," 164 n. 186.

194. *Keter Shem Tov,* 39a. Cf. ibid., 37b, where Shem Tov reports that he asked his teacher for an explanation of the different rituals related to the *havdalah* service at the conclusion of Sabbath, and the teacher responded by saying that he could comprehend matters from contemplating the mystical significance of the rabbinic motif of the extra soul (*neshamah yeterah*) on Sabbath. Another interesting example of kabbalah as oral exposition of a text is found in the tradition of Ezra of Gerona cited by Recanati, *Perush ha-Torah,* 65d (a version of the text is found in Azriel, *Commentary on Talmudic Aggadoth,* 46). Ezra reports an interpretation of a passage from bTa'an 25b that R. Jacob the Pious received from R. Nehorai in Jerusalem. The nature of the kabbalah is significant for it is an explanation of a talmudic text, which also provides an explanation for the ritual of water libation in the Temple during the festival of Sukkot.

SIX

Publication and Reproduction of Literary Texts in Medieval Jewish Civilization: Jewish Scribality and Its Impact on the Texts Transmitted

MALACHI BEIT-ARIÉ

In dealing with the scribal transmission of texts written in Hebrew script in the High Middle Ages we should first bear in mind two essential circumstances relating to the composition of medieval texts and their reproduction and dissemination which had an immense impact on the nature of the written transmission and the surviving texts. The first factor concerns the creation of written texts and medieval authorship, and relates to the way in which medieval authors viewed their ownership of their written works. The second one involves the individual nature of Jewish book production, and concerns the scribal re-creation of the copied texts.

In referring to Hebrew manuscripts I mean Jewish medieval handwritten books written in Hebrew characters, without regard to their language. Medieval Jews adhered to their own Semitic script, an offshoot of the Aramaic script, despite the adoption of the spoken languages of the accommodating societies, using this script for texts written in not only the Hebrew language, but also other, borrowed, languages, particularly Arabic and, to a lesser extent, the Romance languages and Judeo-German, in transcription.[1]

PUBLICATION AND DISSEMINATION OF PROGRESSIVE TEXTS

Publication of texts in the chirographic era, to use the phrase coined by Walter J. Ong, differed considerably from publication in the typographic era, and one of the gravest dangers facing the modern editor is to ignore the special circumstances under which texts were published in the Middle Ages and to attribute, unconsciously, the procedure of printed publication to the process of scribal publishing.

The dynamic state of creating a text and its transformational character comes to an end in the typographic era once it is published in print. Notwithstanding the striking evidences provided by analytical bibliographers regarding the changeable and variable nature of printed editions and the modifications and misreadings committed by editors and printers,[2] the printed publication guarantees to a large extent the standardization of the disseminated text at a certain stage. If an author continues to reshape his work, modify and update it, a second edition will standardize the new version, and the two versions will not be confused. But when texts were transmitted by manual copying, works may have been copied at different stages of their creation and consequently disseminated in various original versions, while the author had no control over his text.[3] Copies representing different stages of the text were in circulation. Some of these have survived and are at our disposal; they present a confusing variety of irreconcilable original readings, in addition to variants caused by the physiological and psychological mechanics of copying and the deliberate, critical interference of scribes.

Moreover, we have explicit evidence that important texts were copied and circulated as each section was finished, *before* the completion of the entire work. Shraga Abramson presents many quotations from medieval authors who, in later parts of their works, propose modifications to earlier passages of the same work, a phenomenon which cannot be understood unless those passages were copied and circulated before the completion of the entire work.[4] Illuminating evidence concerning this process of publication is explicitly provided by Jonah ibn Janaḥ (Spain, first half of the eleventh century) in his lexical *Kitab al-'uṣul* (*Sefer ha-shorashim*). In a note to one of the entries the author, writing in Judeo-Arabic, apologizes for misplacing a certain proximate root. He explains that it was impossible to insert it in the preceding proper entry since that part of the dictionary had already been carried out by the riders and disseminated.[5]

Even when a work was completed and released by its author for circulation, he could still revise it. Maimonides, for example, was constantly revising his commentary on the Mishnah, from its initiation until the end of his life. This is evident not only from the drafts preserved in the Geniza and from the many cancellations, alterations and additions in his own fair copy of the work,[6] but also from the fact that he himself explicitly corrected and changed in his responsa his own already circulated text.[7] Maimonides was indeed aware of the problem of authorized versions, as is attested by his inscription and signature at the end of a copy of part of his *Mishneh Torah* copied in his lifetime, and now preserved in the Bodleian Library.[8] Maimonides confirms that the manuscript was corrected according to his own personal copy. This is the only surviving example in a Hebrew manuscript of the practice known in Arabic transmission as *ijaza,* the validation by the author of a final version, which was then recopied by later scribes.[9]

It cannot be denied that there were authors who, aware of the difficulty of updating texts disseminated by copying, endeavored to publish a new authoritative version or versions of their work and to distinguish clearly between the different versions.[10] It seems, however, that the usual way of publishing works in the Middle Ages was to grant free access to the author's copy and let it be copied during its various progressive stages, even without the author being informed about the copies being made. I know of no better illustration of the problems caused by disseminating texts still in the process of being written and of the helplessness of authors in controlling their works than Levi ben Abraham's colophon to his philosophical book *Livyat ḥen,* completed in Arles in 1295. In his colophon he writes that in the course of the creation of his work he made textual and structural changes, and from time to time corrected it and added new material. He has been informed, however, that while this process was still going on, people copied most of the work, and he therefore pleads with those who have copies of one of the earlier versions to correct the text according to the latest version, or replace it with the final version.[11]

Another illuminating source which testifies directly to the peculiar realities of medieval text dissemination is found two centuries later, in the early printing era. It is a manuscript of a commentary on the *Sefer Mitswot ha-Gadol* by Isaac Stein, compiled and copied by his son in Germany in 1506. Having copied twenty-three folios, the scribe remarks that he has found only that part of his father's work actually edited. However, he discovered in his father's copy of the work many interpolated notes which contained, in effect, his commentary on each paragraph of the *SeMaG,* which he endeavored to edit and incorporate into a coherent commentary. Furthermore, the son tells us that there were people who had copied his father's notes many years before his father edited his commentary, while the notes were not yet revised but presented only as drafts to be used during his teaching in the yeshiva and changed following discussions with the scholars. The son asserts that his father was not aware of the copies made from his interpolated notes, as he "has not hidden his copy of the *SeMaG* from those people."[12]

These special conditions of publishing works, or of letting them be reproduced and circulated, interrupted the linear transmission of many texts and instead imposed multi-linear reproduction. This situation may explain the amazing attitude of medieval authors to their own works. Abramson assembled many examples of authors and translators, starting from Saadia Gaon, who appeal to the users of their works to correct any mistake they may find in them.[13] Their appeals do not relate to linguistic mistakes and omissions only, but also to contents. Some authors even encouraged the users to add material, as did Rav Nathan Av ha-Yeshiva in his introduction to a commentary on the Mishnah.[14]

Besides appealing to the copyists to correct and add relevant material, authors granted them an additional role in the recreation of their texts by leaving it to them to complete citations from other works incorporated in their books. Explicit evidence of this practice has been preserved in the text of *Mea she'arim,* a short treatise by Isaac ben Abba Mari of Marseilles, the twelfth-century Provençal author of *Ha-'ittur.* In this work the author cites the *Rif.* In two cases he does not cite the relevant passages but only begins, and then writes, "the copyist should copy from . . . to. . . ." These instructions, apparently normally followed by the copyists, luckily survived the chain of copying in two cases,[15] adding to our elusive knowledge of the ways texts were created and disseminated during the Middle Ages.

Such encouragement to correct, emend and add to authorial texts may also reflect a medieval concept of intellectual ownership altogether different from the modern one, namely, a concept of collective ownership. This attitude may also explain the editorial freedom exercised by scribes in reproducing texts, which brings us to the second fundamental aspect of the transmission of texts written in Hebrew characters. This essential aspect involves the individual nature of Jewish book production, and the differentiation between scribes and copyists.

THE INDIVIDUAL NATURE OF JEWISH MEDIEVAL BOOK PRODUCTION

Latin texts, until the mid-thirteenth century, were mainly produced in, and disseminated by, institutional copying centers of monastic multi-copyist *scriptoria,* or cathedral schools, then by university stationers employing the *pecia* system, and in the late Middle Ages to a large extent by commercial urban and lay ateliers.[16] In contrast, Hebrew medieval books were not produced by the intellectual establishments, or upon their initiative, whether in religious, academic or secular institutional copying centers, but privately and individually, and similarly they were also consumed and kept. A medieval Jew who wished to obtain or use a copy of a certain book would either purchase it from a private owner or hire a professional or semi-professional scribe to produce a copy for him, or he would copy the book himself.[17] While the institutional and centralized nature of Latin book production involved control and standardization of the texts produced,[18] no authoritative supervision was involved in the transmission of Hebrew texts.

Yet, within this individual mode of Hebrew text reproduction there is a fundamental difference between texts reproduced by professional or hired scribes, and owner-produced texts. Our precise knowledge of the self-production practice, and its extent in Jewish booklore, is drawn from colophons. The systematic recording and analysis of almost all the extant manuscripts with colophons, some 4000 in all,[19] indicate that at least *half* the medieval Hebrew manuscripts were personal, user-produced books, copied by educated persons or scholars for their own use, and only half, or most probably less than half, were produced by hired scribes, whether professional or occasional. Such a high rate of non-professional, personal copying certainly reflects the extent of Jewish literacy and education, but it must also have affected the transmission of written texts and their versions.

The common phenomenon of manuscripts being copied by their owners is indeed a principal and striking characteristic of Hebrew book production prevailing in all the vast territories where Jews lived and reproduced literary texts in the Middle Ages in the West and the East (except for Yemen). The same characteristics, by the way, arising from different circumstances, would later typify the lay compilations of vernacular texts in the Latin script, which were, as Armando Petrucci has shown, user-produced books.[20] On the whole, book production in the Jewish world seems to be more similar to that in the Islamic orbit. Notwithstanding the existence of institutional centers of learning and research, which apparently also employed scribes just as caliphs employed calligraphers, numerous public libraries and the extensive commercialization of books through the *warraqīn,* paper and book dealers,[21] the dominant nature of Arabic book production and consumption seems to have been also private, boosted by the early introduction of the cheaper writing material of paper. Yet, though copies produced by Muslim scholars are known, scholars are advised to avoid copying if a book can be purchased, or a scribe can be hired.[22] It seems, therefore, that the extent and the regularity of self-reproduction of literary texts in medieval Jewish society was distinctive in the book civilizations of the Mediterranean basin.

SCRIBAL RE-CREATION OF COPIED TEXTS: BETWEEN SCRIBES AND COPYISTS

There must have been a fundamental difference between the reproduction of texts by a hired scribe and by a *talmid ḥakham,* a learned man or a scholar, who was copying texts for his own use. I suggest calling the former a scribe, and the latter a copyist. One is entitled to assume that the average hired scribe would have been consciously more loyal to his model, probably would have avoided critical and deliberate intervention in the transmission, yet would have been more fallible and vulnerable to the involuntary changes and mistakes conditioned by the mechanics of copying, while the scholar-copyist might intentionally interfere in the transmission, revise his exemplar, emend and reconstruct the text, add to it and modify it according to his knowledge, memory, conjecture or other exemplars, and indeed regard copying as a critical editing and not merely as duplicating.[23] Moreover, logic suggests that scribes would tend to repeat mistakes in their models, while copyists would correct the corrupted text. Indeed, these assumptions can be substantiated and verified by scribes' and copyists' own statements in their colophons.

To be sure, both scribes and copyists were subject to the unconscious mechanics of copying, which inevitably laid many snares and induced unwitting errors. As is well known, the complicated process of copying puts many pitfalls in the way of exact reproduction and frustrates the best intentions of a scribe to adhere to his model, involving, as it does, repeated movements of the copyist's eyes from model to copy and back, which may cause unnoticed omissions, repetitions and transpositions,[24] the memorization of the visually perceived series of words; the impact of converting a text in one format or layout or type of script to a different one; the significant consequences of the apparent phonetic or oral medium involved in copying, whether it be vocal, by reading aloud the copied text,[25] or silent, as in the phenomenon which Havet calls "internal dictating"[26] and to which A. Dain attributes most copying errors, claiming that the visual aspect of the text and incorrect reading affects copying much less than the oral aspect involved in the process;[27] the undefined psychological factors which produce errors of haplography, dittography and association,[28] and so on.[29]

The presumed impact of the psychosomatic mechanics of copying on transmission can be verified by comparing the readings of those surviving manuscripts which were clearly copied from each other. Incontestable evidence of this situation is provided when a colophon of the model is copied by a scribe who then adds to it his own colophon.[30] But the most rewarding comparison is provided when the same text is copied twice by the same hand from the same model within a short time. Such a comparison demonstrates that deviation from the exemplar is not rigidly conditioned by certain psychological, linguistic and mental structures, or by the copyist's spelling habits, pronunciation and associations, but it is rather flexible and open. Both uncritical and critical scribes show that their copying is subject to unstable determinants which may result in them producing two different versions while copying from the same model!

The discrepancies found in a short duplicated copying of a professional scribe represent not only minor punctuation and spelling changes, but also omission and additions, differences in conjugation and the declension of nouns.[31] But unstable and variable results of transcribing texts, which defy theories of text criticism, do not characterize only non-scholarly, hired scribes, but also learned scribes, as the famous Leiden manuscript of the Jerusalem Talmud clearly demonstrates. This important manuscript,[32] copied in Italy in 1289, was commissioned from Yeḥiel ben Yequti'el ha-Rofe, who was a scholar, and should be identified as the author of the halakhic compendium *Tanya* and other works.[33] As he testifies in his colophons, his copying was a critical one, and he endeavored to emend his corrupted model. For codicological reasons Yeḥiel copied twice the text of one folio, in large format. I. Z. Feintuch, who compared the text of the two parallel leaves and analyzed the differences between them, found at least fifty disagreements in the seventy-six duplicated lines! In addition to discrepancies in spelling, grammar and the use of abbreviations, change of names, omissions and additions, there were differences in wording, and some critical interventions which occur in one copy but not in the other.[34]

We should, therefore, acknowledge the vulnerability of texts transmitted both by medieval scribes and by learned copyists. Not only were they involuntarily affected by many elusive psychosomatic factors and by deliberate critical intervention, but the influence of these factors varied and fluctuated within a short space of time.

Both professional scribes and learned copyists were aware of their fallibility and of the unnoticed mistakes that they must have made while transcribing their models. Noticeably different attitudes, however, can be discerned in the various geo-cultural areas of the Jewish book production. One of the diverse scribal formulas in colophons is that of apologizing for having committed errors and begging God's, or the user's, forgiveness while citing Ps 19:13. However, the employment of such a coined formula, which is first attested by the extant colophoned manuscripts in a biblical copy made in Alexandria in 1122,[35] is almost entirely confined to books copied in the Near East, particularly in Yemen. Some Oriental scribes who employed the scribal formula were more specific. Saadia ben David Adani, a Yemenite scribe, copyist and author, who wrote some fifteen surviving manuscripts in Syria and Palestine between 1463 and 1485, adopted a formula specifying the various types of errors committed in copying, namely, mistakes in transcribing, additions, and omissions,[36] indicating that these errors are imposed unwillingly on the copyist. Having apologized for their mistakes, many of those scribes appeal, as the authors themselves did, to future readers to make corrections, thereby acknowledging the mutable nature of the transmission.

Copyists and scribes in other areas, particularly in Byzantium and Italy, and almost never in Ashkenaz (northern France and Germany), would occasionally apologize for having committed, or not having noticed, errors, but not in a formulaic manner, and usually while specifying the causes which provoked and generated the errors. Some of these statements contribute to our poor knowledge of the medieval transmission of texts. Such reflexive colophons, written by copyists and learned scribes alike, start to appear (according to the surviving known manuscripts) in Europe in the second half of the thirteenth century.[37] The most frequent cause to which scribes attribute their mistakes is their erroneous model. Later, they would sometime excuse themselves by explaining that their model was mixed up, or hardly legible or decipherable, or fragmentary. Most scribes and especially copyists who complain about their mistaken exemplars indicate that they did their best to emend their errors as much as they were able to, or admit that they corrected only a portion of them. However, information about emendation of a corrupted model is usually found in the colophons of owner-produced texts, or copies prepared by scholar-scribes, and only rarely in the colophons of manuscripts written by regular, hired scribes. The latter would sometimes admit their incompetence to correct the copied text. Some scribes and copyists blame lack of time, or speed of copying, for their errors, or for not being able to correct the model's errors. Hired scribes reflect in their colophons their harsh conditions and attribute their errors to their poverty,[38] constant worries, wandering, or detrimental environmental conditions.[39] Perhaps the most striking manifestation of the nature of copying by hired scribes is to be found in an undated colophon of an Ashkenazi Siddur, written in the middle of the fourteenth century: "He who is going to curse me while reading this prayer book, the fault is mine and not mine, since I copied it from an erroneous exemplar. Furthermore, I was forced [to copy it], for I sold this prayer book, and, having been hired, I was not able to pay attention to the essence." What this scribe actually says is that copying by hired scribes cannot be critical, and what he implies is that copying should be a critical transcribing of the text.[40]

On the other hand, the fact that learned hired scribes, or those who copied texts for their own use, did copy critically, is reflected in a number of colophons. These copyists conceived it as their duty to improve their exemplars and to produce a better edition of the copied text. In fact, they regarded themselves as critical editors, sometimes even as redactors, so much so that when a copyist refrained from improving his model, he would apologize. It seems that the usual practice of copyists and learned scribes was not only to correct obvious copying mistakes but to edit their model.

The editorial nature of copying is clearly demonstrated by those late scribes who explicitly indicate in their colophons that they used more than one exemplar in producing their copies. Thus, Yekutiel ben Meshulam, having copied Ibn Ezra's Torah commentary in 1312 in Bevagna, Italy, states that he established the text according to two copies (MS Parma, Biblioteca Palatina 3256). Vidal ben Solomon ben Qatorzi produced in 1445, probably in Provence, a copy of Ibn Ezra's commentary to the Pentateuch while using two glossed copies and selecting from each the version he considered to be superior.[41] The sermons of Joshua ibn Shuaib in MS Paris, Bibliothèque nationale hébr. 238, written in 1461 in Béjar (Spain), were copied by Moses ben Solomon Gabay for himself from "two erroneous books."[42] The text of the *Arukh* in MS Munich, Bayerische Staatsbibliothek Cod. hebr. 428, was copied in Ashkenaz in 1444, partly from a long version and partly from a short one, both of which were, according to the copyist, inaccurate. Reuven Vidal Bonastruc proofread and vocalized a prayer book in Avignon in 1453 while consulting various prayerbooks which presented different textual and vocalizing readings.[43]

One of the best demonstrations of the editorial role of late copyists is provided by the scholar Abraham ben Ephraim ibn Sancho, who copied *Ein ha-qore* by Joseph ibn Shem Tov already in the typographic era (in 1537)[44] for himself, probably in Constantinople. In his colophon the copyist informs us that he established an optimal text after having collated five copies of the work found in his town, all representing different versions. He deliberately corrected the grammatical errors of the author, who, despite his great erudition, lacked, according to the copyist, proficiency in the Hebrew language. Furthermore, he also completed the indexes which the author had started but did not finish.[45]

These and other colophons imply that many late medieval copies, particularly those produced for private use, were actually eclectic editions, in which different versions and readings were intermingled and merged by a critical process which included not only selecting readings but also emending and completing, usually without providing an *apparatus criticus*. Such copies involved, in effect, recreating the text. However, there were a few medieval editor-copyists who did exercise some principles of modern textual criticism in their editions of texts. Joseph ben Eliezer of Spain, who copied, in 1375, a supercommentary to Ibn Ezra's commentary on the Pentateuch in Canea (Crete), on his way to Jerusalem, wrote a colophon which he entitled "the scribe's apology." He tells us that he copied the text from an extremely erroneous exemplar and was able to emend part of the mistakes by conjecture and part by acquired knowledge. In addition there were many cases where the author's explanations seemed to him unreasonable, and there he integrated his own opinion into the text. However, in order that his interpolations should not be regarded as the author's text, he took care to indicate his authorship. His awareness of the vulnerability of the scribal transmission and the changeability of the copied text is demonstrated by his adjuration of all future copyists to follow all his interpolations and not to change them even if they disagree with his comments, though he grants them permission to add their own opinions. He further adjured future copyists to copy his "apology" at the end of the book.[46]

Similarly, in a considerable number of manuscripts we find copyist's interpolations clearly labeled by the scribe himself. Manuscripts which record different readings copied in the margins in the scribe's own hand, under the rubric "other book/books," or "other version/versions," or "it seems to me," or which offer alternative vocalizations in liturgical manuscripts, also reflect a more "modern" critical approach, in which copyists adhered to one model while noting different readings from other exemplars in the margins and indicated the *lemma* by the use of signs such as one would find in a modern *apparatus criticus.*[47] Those marginal or interlinear glosses and collations of different readings were frequently interpolated within the text by successive scribes, causing double readings and contamination by relevant but inauthentic material. This phenomenon was very well known to and already deplored by the Geonim and the *rishonim* in their dealings with talmudic text criticism.[48]

To sum up, owing to the circumstances of medieval publication, texts were disseminated at various stages of their creation and revision, and their authors were usually prevented from controlling what happened to them. Just as there was no scriptural authority over the development of Hebrew scripts, the production of the Hebrew books and the transmission of Jewish texts and their dissemination were not subject to any authoritative initiative or supervision, in sharp contrast to ecclesiastical and political control over the development of scripts,[49] book production and text transmission in the Graeco-Latin world. Reproduction and distribution of texts were never institutionalized in Jewish societies, but were carried out by individual private initiative, to a large extent by learned people or scholars who themselves copied the books they wished to study or use. Encouraged by authors to correct their own mistakes, and being aware of the unavoidable corruption of texts by the unconscious mechanics of copying, later copyists certainly did not view copying as mechanical reproduction, but as a critical editorial operation involving emendation, diagnostic conjecture, collation of different exemplars and even the incorporation of external relevant material and the copyist's own opinion. It seems that the copyist's main goal was to establish what Kantorowicz defines as a "richtige," right, version, as opposed an "echte," authentic, one.[50] Consequently, many of our Hebrew manuscripts, at least those produced since the middle of the thirteenth century, present texts not only corrupted by the accumulation of involuntary copying errors, but also distorted by editorial or even redactional reconstruction, by contamination from different exemplars and versions, and by the deliberate integration of related texts.[51] What medieval copyists performed while copying was indeed what in modern theories of criticism is known as deconstructing the text and then reconstructing it. Therefore, many principles and practices of classical textual criticism, such as the establishing of genetic relationships between manuscripts, stemmatic classification, the reconstructing of archetypes and the restoration of the original, are not applicable to Hebrew manuscripts, not only because many of these represent horizontal rather than vertical transmission and so provide us with open recensions,[52] but also because their texts may have been affected by the intervention of learned copyists. Thus, contrary to common belief, medieval verbal texts were not fixed once they were written down. Chirographic and visual texts were as flexible as oral ones.

What is the implication of this iconoclastic presentation of medieval transmission? Should we abandon the medieval manuscripts, especially the later ones, because they offer inauthentic, unstable texts, and have been corrupted by the free critical editing of learned copyist and the whimsical copying errors of preoccupied poor scribes? Of course not. These are the only sources we have. But we must use them with great caution, suspicion and skepticism, and above all refrain from establishing authentic texts, or even critical editions, and rather resort to the safe procedure of multi-diplomatic, synoptic presentation of the transmitted texts, while proposing our critical analysis and reconstruction in the form of notes.[53]

SCRIBAL VISUAL SHAPING OF TEXTS AND THEIR RECEPTION

I should like to add a short paragraph to this chapter and draw the attention of manuscript users to the special impact of Hebrew scribes on the texts not only through the recreation of their verbal essence, but, also by shaping their forms and forging their visual incarnation. Scribes of all cultures were entrusted with the effective responsibility of rendering discursive substance in visible non-verbal shapes and patterns, which affected the meaning of texts and their reception.[54] However, the role of Hebrew scribes in this structural, figural, interpretative and artistic configuration of texts was much more independent and decisive because of the individual mode of Jewish book production, the high rate of user-produced books, and the lack of a guiding authority over the dissemination of texts. In determining the form of the physical book, its size and proportions, and in designing the layout of the displayed copied text, Jewish scribes and copyists themselves created the semiotic representation of various types of texts and generated different conventions of meaningful forms for different genres and functions of texts and books. They had an immense impact on the interpretation and reception of texts by their introduction of titles, initial words, running headlines, decorations and illustrations, diagrams and tables of contents. By selecting the types and sizes of scripts, paragraphing and subdividing, spacing, underlining certain parts or words, or just by using different colored inks, they determined the hierarchical structure and legibility of the texts copied.

Furthermore, certain Hebrew texts, like prayer-books, were virtually created by scribes. Glossed biblical, talmudic, liturgical and halakhic corpora also emerged as sophisticated scribal enterprises, unguided but responding to the changing needs of studying and scholarship and at the same time generating them.[55]

The impact of scribes on the transmitted written text and its reception may be compared to that of the reciters and performers on the oral text, and these observations on the nature of written transmission of Hebrew medieval texts may contribute further arguments for the removal of the cultural barriers between orality and scribality.[56] Furthermore, some of the characteristics of scribal individual reproduction presented here, such as critical intervention, editorial freedom, eclectic conflation of different models and the visual and figural remaking, may very well be found to fit also early Hebrew typographical mass reduplication of medieval texts.[57] If this assumption is right, as random examples hint, the demarcation between oral, scribal and printed reproduction[58] will have to be "rewritten," and perhaps a unified observation of all the sorts of verbal reproduction would emerge.

NOTES

An earlier version of this paper, which contains citations of Hebrew sources, appeared as "Transmission of Texts by Scribes and Copyists: Unconscious and Critical Interferences," *Bulletin of John Rylands University Library of Manchester*

75, no. 3 (Autumn 1993) = *Artefact and Text: The Re-Creation of Jewish Literature in Medieval Hebrew Manuscripts: Proceedings of a Conference Held in the University of Manchester 28–30 April 1992*, 33–51. For a French version see: "Transmission de textes par scribes et copistes: Interférences inconscientes et critiques" in *Les problèmes posés par l'édition critique des textes anciens et médiévaux,* ed. Jacqueline Hamesse (Louvain, 1992), 173–196. Several modifications of and additions to the earlier version can be found in the present paper, which is partly less detailed, partly more elaborate.

1. Cf. Malachi Beit-Arié, *Hebrew Manuscripts of East and West: Towards a Comparative Codicology* (London, 1993), 2–7.

2. See, for instance, Donald Francis McKenzie, *Bibliography and the Sociology of Texts* (London, 1986); G. Thomas Tanselle, *A Rationale of Textual Criticism* (Philadelphia, 1989).

3. With regard to the Christian world, see the illuminating presentation by Ernest Philip Goldschmidt, *Medieval Texts and their First Appearance in Print* (London, 1943), particularly 89–93.

4. Shraga Abramson, "Mehem u-vahem," in *The Book of Sivan: A Collection of Studies and Essays in Memory of the Late Jerusalem Publisher Shalom Sivan,* ed. A. Even Shoshan et al. (Jerusalem, 1979), 3–21.

5. Ibid., 7–8; *The Book of the Hebrew Roots,* ed. A. Neubauer (Oxford, 1875), col. 266 (the original Arabic version); *Sefer Haschoraschim,* ed. W. Bacher (Berlin, 1896), 182 (in Hebrew translation. The passage is not included in Judah ibn Tibbon's translation, based on the first version, and was translated by Bacher from the Arabic manuscripts; cf. his introduction, xxv); see also Y. Yahalom and A. Saenz-Badillos, *Leshonenu* 48–49 (1983–1984), 254. A similar procedure is stated by Maimonides at the end of his epistle dedicatory (to his pupil Joseph ibn Aknin) in the *Guide for the Perplexed:* "I have divided it into chapters, each of which shall be sent to you as soon as it is completed" (trans. M. Friedländer, 2nd edition [London, 1904], 2; cf. Shlomo Pines' translation, *The Guide of the Perplexed* (Chicago, 1963), 4: "I have set it down in dispersed chapters. All of them that are written down will reach you where you are, one after the other").

6. MSS Oxford, Bodleian Library Poc. 295 and Hunt. 117; Jerusalem, Jewish National and University Library Heb. 4° 5703/1–2. The first two of the four surviving *sedarim,* MSS Hunt. 117 and 4° 5703/1, are written on laid paper with single and even chain lines—reflecting early Occidental Arabic papermaking techniques and implying North African production of either the copies or just the

writing material—while the other two *sedarim* are written on typical Oriental paper which attests that they were produced later (note 44 in my *Hebrew Codicology* [Paris, 1977 and Jerusalem, 1981], 29–30, should be corrected accordingly). On the lasting process of the composing and revising the commentary see Simon Hopkins, "The Textual Tradition of Maimonides' *Commentary on the Mishna*," *Sefunot* 20 [New Series 5] (1991): 114–109 (Hebrew).

7. Cf. idem, "Two New Maimonidean Autographs in the John Rylands University Library," *Bulletin of the John Rylands University Library of Manchester* 67 (1985), 719–720.

8. MS Hunt. 80 (Neubauer Catalogue no. 577).

9. Cf. Johannes Pedersen, *The Arabic Book*, trans. G. French (Princeton, 1984), 20–36. See also Jan Just Witkam, "The Human Element between Text and Reader: The Ijaza in Arabic Manuscripts," in *The Codicology of Islamic Manuscripts: Proceedings of the Second Conference of Al-Furqua-n Islamic Heritage Foundation, 4–5 December 1993*, ed. Y. Dutton (London, 1995), 123–136.

10. Probably the most striking example of this phenomenon is furnished by Isaiah di Trani (Italy, first half of the thirteenth century), who revised and published his *Pesaqim* several times (some tractates appeared in five editions), but who tried to differentiate the versions by numbering them (Cf. Abramson, 12–14, for other examples as well).

11. MS Vatican ebr. 192. Cf. Colette Sirat, "Les différentes versions du Liwyat Hen du Levi ben Abraham," *Revue des Etudes Juives* 122 (1963), 167–168. There have been late medieval authors like Petrarch, who preferred to disseminate his works in his own hand; cf. Armando Petrucci, "Reading and Writing Volgare in Medieval Italy," in his *Writers and Readers in Medieval Italy: Studies in the History of Written Culture*, trans. Ch. R. Radding (New Haven, 1995), 193–194. The Hebrew equivalent may be Abraham Farissol: Having been too familiar, as a professional hired scribe, with the corruption caused to texts in the scribal transmission, he preferred to disseminate his own works in his own copying, as is attested by a few manuscripts.

12. MS Oxford, Bodleian Library Mich. 408 (Neubauer Catalogue no. 872), fol. 23v. MS Oxford was recopied in MS Jerusalem, Hekhal Shelomo G 63, now deposited in the Jewish National and University Library, Heb. 8° 6713 (cf. Yehuda Leib Bialer, *Min ha-genazim* [Jerusalem, 1967], 1:13–15, who cites the entire paragraph, without being aware that the manuscript is a copy of the original Bodleian manuscript). In the early fifteenth century Zalman of St. Goar testified that his book *Minhagei Maharil* was copied before its completion and disseminated despite his objection; cf. Yedidya Alter Dinari, *The Rabbis of Ger-*

many and Austria at the Close of the Middle Ages (Hebrew), (Jerusalem, 1984), 279–280.

13. Abramson, 3–7. An additional example can be found in the colophon of Solomon ben Lavi to his translation of *Emunah Ramah* by Abraham ben David ha-Levi (MS London, Jews' College 291).

14. Ibid., 4. To be sure, not all authors encouraged users to correct and improve their works. In a colophon to one part of *Midrash ha-Ḥokhmah,* the philosopher Judah ben Solomon ha-Kohen of Toledo (first half of the thirteenth century) forbids future copyists to copy only a part of his work, and adjures them to be careful in copying it faithfully letter by letter: see MSS Oxford Mich. 551 (Neubauer Catalogue no. 1321), fol. 124r and Poc. 343 (Neubauer Catalogue no. 1223), fol. 89r.

15. Cf. Mordechai Glatzer, *Ittur soferim (Sefer ha-'ittur) of R. Isaac b. Abba Mari: Introduction* (Jerusalem, 1985), 1:96–97.

16. See the concise presentation by Richard Rouse, "Manuscripts, Production of," in *Dictionary of the Middle Ages* (New York, 1987), 8:100–105. Even A. Petrucci, who challenged the traditional view of Latin book production in early medieval Europe as *entirely* concentrated in monastic or ecclesiastical scriptoria, demanded to correct it only "in some measure"; see "Literacy and Graphic Culture of Early Medieval Scribes," in his *Writers and Readers in Medieval Italy,* 77–102, esp. 101.

17. In a long colophon written in 1327 in an unidentified locality, probably in the Middle East, a Karaite scribe apologizes for copying himself the book, which he has much desired, by explaining that he was too poor to purchase books (the fragmentary MS St. Petersburg, National Library of Russia EBP. I 593).

18. See, for instance, the controlled process of producing books in the scriptorium of Frankenthal presented by A. Cohen-Mushlin, *A Medieval Scriptorium: Sancta Maria Magdalena de Frankendal,* 2 vols. (Wiesbaden, 1990). See also M.-C. Garand, "Manuscrits monastiques et scriptoria aux XIe et XIIe siècles," in *Codicologica: Towards a Science of Handwritten Books,* ed. A. Gruijs and J. P. Gumbert, (Leiden, 1980), 3:9–33.

19. Carried out by the Hebrew Palaeography Project and stored in its SFAR-DATA, a sophisticated quantitative database and retrieval system of a large number of measurable codicological attributes recorded in most of the extant explicitly dated, and in the undated but otherwise "colophoned," or named, Hebrew medieval manuscripts. Sponsored by the Israel Academy of Sciences and Humanities, in collaboration with the Jewish National and University Library in Jerusalem, in cooperation with the Institut de Recherche et d'Histoire des Textes in Paris, the Hebrew Palaeography Project has been engaged since its inception in 1965 in

studying and recording most of the visible and quantifiable codicological features and variables of all the surviving dated Hebrew codices and the undated ones with indications of scribes' names, some 5000 manuscripts kept in collections all over the world. Since the early 1970s many of the attributes recorded in the detailed questionnaires have been coded and electronically stored in Jerusalem. Over the past eight years an elaborate retrieving, sorting and linking system was and is still being developed, allowing endless querying of the data, clustering and statistics. See Malachi Beit-Arié, "The Codicological Data-Base of the Hebrew Paleeography Project: A Tool for Localizaing and Dating Hebrew Medieval Manuscripts," in *Hebrew Studies,* ed. D. Rowland and S. Salinger (London, 1991), 165–197 (=*British Library Occasional Papers* 13); updated in M. Beit-Arié, *The Makings of the Medieval Hebrew Book* (Jerusalem, 1993), 41–73; idem, "SFARDATA: The Henri Schiller Codicological Database of the Hebrew Palaeography Project, Jerusalem," *Gazette du Livre Médiéval* 25 (1994), 24–29.

20. Cf. A. Petrucci, "Il libro manoscritto," in *Letteratura italiana,* vol. 2: *Produzione e consumo,* ed. A. Asor Rosa (Turin, 1983), 512–513, 520–522 (available in English, "Reading and Writing Volgare in Medieval Italy," in his *Writers and Readers in Medieval Italy,* 169–235). On later medieval personal manuscript production of popular Latin theological treatises of devotion and the radical rewriting in owner-copied manuscripts of this kind see Eric H. Reiter, "The Reader as Author of the User-Produced Manuscript: Reading and Rewriting Popular Latin Theology in the late Middle Ages," *Viator* 27 (1996), 151–169.

21. See the references in my *Hebrew Manuscripts of East and West,* 120, nn. 9–11; 121, n. 18.

22. See Franz Rosenthal, *The Technique and Approach of Muslim Scholarship* (Rome, 1947), 9–10; see also 30–31 on authors who continue to elaborate their works after their publication ("author's variant readings"), and on an author who informs on the different versions of his works.

23. On the intervention of scribes in the transmission of the prose *Lancelot* and the freedom they felt to make any alternations that they felt would improve the text, see Elspeth Kennedy, "The Scribes as Editors," in *Mélanges de langue et de littérature du Moyen Age et de la Renaissance offerts à Jean Frappier* (Geneva, 1970), 1:523–531.

24. See Eugene Vinaver, "Principles of Textual Emendation," in *Studies in French Language and Medieval Literature Presented to Prof. M. K. Pope* (Manchester, 1939), 351–369.

25. The practice is attested in the Jewish world in by *Sefer Ḥasidim:* "One who used to copy from the Bible and the commentaries . . . and would first read aloud

anything he was writing"; see *Das Buch der Frommen,* ed. J. Wistinetzki (Berlin, 1891), 187, par. 733 = 420, par. 1363. Wilhelm Wattenbach, *Das Schriftwesen im Mittelalter,* 3rd ed. (Leipzig, 1896), 495–496 cites a colophon formula from an eighth-century Latin manuscript, with elements that appear in many later colophons, which indicates reading aloud as part of the copying practice. However, the common assumption of reading aloud in the Middle Ages was recently revised by Paul Saenger, who argues that the separation of words in Latin manuscripts, starting from the seventh century onwards, enabled silent reading and copying, which were well suited to the monastic conditions. Cf. "Manières de lires médiévales," *Histoire de l'édition française* (Paris, 1982), 1:131–141; "Silent Reading: Its Impact on Late Medieval Script and Society," *Viator* 13 (1983): 367–414; and recently *Space Between Words: The Origin of Silent Reading* (Stanford, 1997). See also Roger Chartier, *Forms and Meanings: Texts, Performances, and Audiences from Codex to Computer* (Philadelphia, 1995), 15–16.

26. Louis Havet, *Manuel de critique verbale appliquée aux textes latins* (Paris, 1911), 44–46. Cf. Henry John Chaytor, *From Script to Print: An Introduction to Medieval Vernacular Literature* (Cambridge, 1945), 5–6, 19, on acoustic and "kinesthetic" or "speech-motor" images of words, and the auditory memory of medieval scribes.

27. Alphonse Dain, *Les manuscrits,* 2nd ed. (Paris, 1964), 40–55.

28. For psychological explanations of copying errors see J. Andrieu, "Pour l'explication psychologique des fautes de copist," *Revue des Etudes Latines* 28 (1950), 279–292; S. Tirnpanaro, *The Freudian Slip: Psychoanalysis and Textual Criticism* (London, 1976).

29. For a useful, more recent survey of the various causes for and classification of changes of texts during copying see Martin L. West, *Textual Criticism and Editorial Technique Applicable to Greek and Latin Texts* (Stuttgart, 1973). See also the chapter on textual criticism in Leighton Durham Reynolds and Nigel Guy Wilson, *Scribes and Scholars: A Guide to the Transmission of Greek and Latin Literature,* 3rd ed. (Oxford, 1974), 186–213, 247–250, and the works listed by Leonard E. Boyle, *Medieval Latin Palaeography: A Bibliographical Introduction* (Toronto, 1984), 286–316. In Jewish studies only one contribution can be singled out, that of Saul Liebermann in his book on the textual criticism of the Jerusalem Talmud, *Al ha-Yerushalmi* (Jerusalem, 1929), in which he devotes the first fifty pages to the classification and demonstration of textual errors in the transmission of the Yerushalmi.

30. See some examples in the earlier version of this paper, "Transmission of Texts by Scribes and Copyists," 41–42.

31. For details see ibid., 42–43.

32. MS Leiden, University Library Or. 4720 (Steinschneider Catalogue, Scal. 3).

33. Israel Zvi Feintuch, *Versions and Traditions in the Talmud* (Hebrew) (Ramat-Gam, 1985), 65–76.

34. Ibid., 51–63 (esp. 55–59). On changes in duplicate copyings by the same scribe (or two scribes working together) in Latin manuscripts, see W. M. Lindsay, "Scribes and Their Ways," *Palaeographia Latina* 2 (1923), 21–22.

35. MS St. Petersburg, National Library of Russia EBP. II C144. This is the earliest extant colophon which reflects scribal awareness of unavoidably unconscious copying mistakes. The earliest dated surviving Hebrew colophon, the Cairo Karaite Synagogue Codex of the Prophets, allegedly produced by the masorete Moshe ben Asher in Tiberias in 894/5, does refer to possible copying errors when its scribe admonishes future users for changing his copied text unless they establish that he committed mistakes in the biblical text, its vocalization and Masora. Though such a warning fits the transmission of the Masoretic biblical text, the lack of similar admonitions in later biblical codices may provide an additional support to the doubts recently raised concerning the genuineness of the date and the scribe's name in the Cairo colophon; see Mordechai Glatzer, "The Aleppo Codex: Codicological and Paleographical Aspect" (Hebrew), *Sefunot* n.s. 19 (1988), 250–259. Indeed, these doubts were recently corroborated by a radiocarbon dating by accelerator mass spectrometry carried out by Oxford University's Research Laboratory for Archaeology and the History of Art in January 1996. The calibrated date range of the manuscript parchment obtained with the highest confidence is 1010–1050, the lowest is 990–1170.

36. This formula can be already traced in a manuscript written in Al-Khasfah (Yemen) in 1460 (MS Sassoon 1053).

37. The first time a copyist bothered to state the reasons for his possible mistakes seems to be MS St. Petersburg, EBP. I 48, a Byzantine copy written apparently in 1266. In an incomplete colophon the copyist refers vaguely to a mental as well as physical burden inflicted on him during the copying.

38. These complaints match documentary evidence. On the astonishing inferior salaries of hired scribes in the Middle East see Shelomo Dov Goitein, *A Mediterranean Society* (Berkeley, 1971), 2: 238; Nehemya Allony, "Books and Their Manufacture in Mediaeval Palestine" (Hebrew), *Shalem* 4 (1984), 15–18. The inferior intellectual status of scribes in the social hierarchy of *Ḥaside Ashkenaz* reflected in *Sefer Ḥasidim;* cf. *Das Buch der Frommen,* ed. J. Wistinetzki, 189 (par. 745), where it is stated that copying is the profession of those who are not capable of studying even the Bible or aggadah.

39. For some details see "Transmission of Texts by Scribes and Copyists," 46–47. From other scribal statements I should like to single out the colophon of a lost Karaite manuscript (published by Abraham Danon, "Documents Relating to the History of the Karaites in European Turkey," *JQR* 17 [1926–1927], 165–166) produced in 1343 by a Byzantine hired scribe (the same scribe copied MS St. Petersburg EBP. 183 in 1351). The scribe pleads with future readers or copyists to condone his copying faults, excusing himself by being overwhelmed by troubles and miseries, and especially by the teaching of boys, which inflicts upon him too much distress.

40. MS Oxford, Bodleian Library Mich. 74, fol. 153r.

41. MS Oxford, Poc. 393 (Neubauer Catalogue no. 217), fol. 179r.

42. Cf. Colette Sirat and Malachi Beit-Arié, *Manuscrits médiévaux en caractères hébraïques portant des indications de date jusqu'à 1540*, vol. 1 (Paris, 1972), no. 118.

43. MS Paris, Bibliothèque nationale hébr. 631.

44. In assessing the editorial role of such late copyists and scribes one has to take into consideration that the era of Hebrew typography started at the earliest ca. 1470. Moreover, the territorial range and scope of production of Hebrew printing, the number of printers and editions have been rather limited at least until 1510. Until roughly that time, or perhaps longer, until 1540, individually produced handwritten books have therefore continued to play the main part in reproducing and consuming texts. For geo-chronological data concerning Hebrew printing see the useful tables in Yeshayahu Vinograd, *Thesaurus of the Hebrew Book* (Jerusalem, 1995), 1:24–36 (Hebrew section).

45. MS London, British Library Or. 10550 (Gaster collection no. 760), fol. 69r. See the Hebrew text in Beit-Arié, *The Makings of the Hebrew Medieval Book,* 14; idem, "Methodological and Descriptive Introduction to the Palaeographical Identification" in *Catalogue of the Hebrew Manuscripts in the Bodleian Library: Supplement of Addenda and Corrigenda to Vol. I (A. Neubauer's Catalogue),* ed. M. Beit-Arié, (Oxford, 1994), xxiv. The same copyist apologizes in the colophon of MS Jerusalem, Jewish National and University Library Heb. 8° 931, fols. 61–79, dated 1530 (cf. Beit-Arié and Sirat, *Manuscrits médiévaux en caractères hébraïques,* vol. 3 [Paris, 1986], no. 86), for not being able to contemplate and emend the text due to lack of time.

46. MS Oxford, Hunt. 293, fol. 62r. The present manuscript is not the original copy of Joseph ben Eliezer, but rather a later copy, which preserved the original colophon and indeed the copyist's "apology." Cf. M. Beit-Arié, "Hebrew Manuscripts Copied in Jerusalem Before the Ottoman Conquest," *Jerusalem in the Middle Ages: Selected Papers* (Jerusalem, 1979), 258, n. 46.

47. It is of course possible that the alternative readings were copied from the model, to which they may have been added by different users in the course of time.

48. Cf. *Teshuvot ha-Geonim,* ed. A. E. Harkavy (Berlin, 1887), par. 272 and the citations referred by Shamma Friedman, "A Critical Study of Yevamot X with a Methodological Introduction," *Texts and Studies: Analecta Judaica* (New York, 1978), 1:283–285. See also Ephraim Elimelech Urbach, *The Tosaphists: Their History, Writings and Methods* (Hebrew), 4th ed. (Jerusalem, 1980), 687.

49. See Stanley Morison, *Politics and Script: Aspects of Authority and Freedom in the Development of Graeco-Latin Script from the Sixth Century B.C. to the Twentieth Century A.D.* (Oxford, 1972).

50. Herman Kantorowicz, *Einführung in die Textkritik: Systematische Darstellung der textkritischen Grundsätze für Philologen und Juristen* (Leipzig, 1921), 5. Similarly, Havet, *Manuel de critique verbale appliquée aux textes latins,* already differentiated between "authentique" and "vrai" versions.

51. On the revisions of halakhic books by their readers and users see Israel M. Ta-Shma, "The 'Open' Book in Medieval Hebrew Literature: The Problem of Authorized Editions," *Bulletin of John Rylands University Library of Manchester* 75, 3 (Autumn 1993), 17–24.

52. According to the terminology of Giorgio Pasquali, *Storia della tradizione e critica del testo,* 2nd ed. (Florence, 1952), referred to by West, *Textual Criticism and Editorial Technique,* 14.

53. There are other approaches which limit critical reconstruction of modern editors while not entirely eliminating the critical aspiration of the genealogical theory, such as the separation of parallel archetypes and their uncontaminated copies, as advocated by Pasquali and implemented (before reading him) by John Matthews Manly and Edith Rickert, *The Text of Canterbury Tales: Studied on the Basis of all Known Manuscripts,* 8 vols. (Chicago, 1940), or that suggested by Hiram Peri, who rejects the genealogical methodology while adhering to the critical approach and proposes a "comparative text"; cf. "Une méthode expérimentale de critique des textes," in *Atti dell'VIIo Congresso Internazionale di Studi Romanzi (Firenze . . . 1956)* (Sansoni, 1960), 2: 721–747. My own edition of *Perek Shira,* which was presented in three parallel versions, is also a kind of compromise between the critical instinct and the rigid "diplomatic" view of Joseph Bédier concerning medieval texts; see M. Beit-Arié, "Perek Shira: Introduction and Critical Edition" (Hebrew), Ph.D. dissertation, Hebrew University, 1967. Today, however, I would present the text in a more elaborate, partly synoptic, form, which I hope to be able to materialize.

54. See references in my *Hebrew Manuscripts of East and West,* 121–122, notes 124–127.

55. Ibid., 85–98.

56. Dealing with the interface between the written and the oral, A. N. Doanne introduced the model of "scribally reperformed texts," referring to scribes who are part of the oral traditional culture and who write or copy oral poetic works. Cf. "Oral Texts, Intertexts, and Intratexts: Editing Old English," in *Influence and Intertextuality in Literary History,* eds. J. Clayton and E. Rothstein (Madison, Wisc., 1991), 80–81, 83–85.

57. As they seem to correspond also to the nature of Western printed reproduction with regard to modifications of the text's visual and formal representation. Cf. D. F. McKenzie's seminal *Bibliography and the Sociology of Texts,* and the first chapter in Roger Chartier, *L'ordre des livres* (Aix-en-Provence, 1992), 13–33; available in English as *The Order of Books: Readers, Authors, and Libraries in Europe Between the Fourteenth and Eighteenth Centuries,* trans. L. G. Cochrane (Stanford, 1994), 1–23.

58. One can easily add also electronic, digital, reproduction and rewriting, which allow readers unlimited editorial, even authorial, autonomy, never granted before.

SEVEN

The Sermon as Oral Performance

MARC SAPERSTEIN

In his inaugural sermon, delivered at the Great Synagogue of Venice on August 14, 1593, the talented prodigy Leone Modena compared the art of public speaking to two of the plastic arts so popular in contemporary Italy: painting and sculpture. The painter who makes a mistake has an opportunity to correct it and touch up his work by painting over the careless stroke, or incorporating it into a new design. Sculpture, by contrast, does not tolerate such error. One false blow with hammer and chisel changes the material permanently, in a way that cannot be undone. Writing is therefore analogous to painting. The author in his study may correct what he has written by crossing out a line and reformulating it. Preaching is analogous to sculpture. An erroneous, or ill-conceived, or poorly worded statement, once uttered, cannot be recalled. It is in the public domain and the speaker may be held accountable.[1]

Modena's comparison between the sermon and the arts seems to me a helpful way of understanding the special qualities of the sermon as oral communication in the context of a written culture. While Modena's point may apply to the act of producing a painting or sculpture, it is less apt for the finished product. Conventionally speaking, the visual arts, including painting, sculpture, and architecture, depend upon space, not upon time. The entire work can be perceived instantaneously. Of course, continued viewing will usually enhance appreciation of the work, through attention paid to details and nuances, through observation from different angles. But it is the viewer, not the artist, who controls this process and determines its chronological unfolding. Except for paintings that depict a narrative, and are therefore dependent upon other art forms, a work of visual art has no beginning, middle or end.[2] It is all there for the viewer at once.

The sermon is therefore in the same category as works of literature, music, dance, and theater that unfold over time, in contrast to the visual arts. Here there is a further crucial distinction. Written literature — the poem, the short story, the novel — is delivered by an author to communities of readers. As in the case of the visual arts, the artist is ordinarily not present at all when the work is being experienced. The implications of this go beyond problems of interpretation and meaning. With rare exceptions, authors intend and expect their works to be read from beginning to end. But once the text is in the reader's hands, the author no longer controls the presentation of material. Readers may turn to the final lines of a poem immediately after the first lines, or they may start in the middle; they may flip to the end of a mystery novel before reading the intermediate chapters. By contrast, oral literature and the performance arts — music, dance, drama — depend upon the physical presence of one or more artists whose role is decisive: it is they, not the audience, who control the presentation at the time of the artistic creation.[3]

I want to argue that the sermon shares this quality of the performance arts, for there is no way for the listener to reach the end of the sermon before the preacher is ready for this to happen. We must conceive the sermon not as the text (that frequently is the only record we have of it) but as an oral communication between preacher and listeners that is scripted or recorded in writing.[4] The text therefore bears a relationship to the actual sermon analogous to the relationship of a script to a drama, or a musical score to a piano sonata, chorale, or symphony. Those who know the conventions of a particular art form can read the script and envision the play, with its sights and sounds; they can analyze the score and "hear" the music. But the performance itself is an artistic entity vastly different from its encoded denotations.[5]

The same is true of the sermon. Even assuming, for the moment, that the written text through which the sermon becomes accessible to us is a verbatim recording of the words that were spoken, which is usually not the case, it contains only one component of the totality. Missing is everything encompassed in the word "delivery": elements such as variations of tempo, pitch, emphasis and intensity, gestures and facial expressions, level of animation, occasionally even interaction between preacher and audience.[6] The text of the sermon therefore corresponds to a dramatic script without any stage directions, or to an orchestral score without indications of tempo or musical dynamics. No conventional system of notation has been devised that corresponds to the marks for forte and piano, crescendo and diminuendo, accent and hold, which might indicate how the preacher intended to deliver the written words, or, after the fact, how the delivery occurred. That is why so many texts of sermons by individuals renowned for their preaching prowess often seem flat and totally unexciting.[7]

In a suggestive exploration of the origins of medieval lyric poetry, Maria Rosa Menocal uses modern rock music to make this point forcefully, presenting the lyrics of "Layla" while describing Eric Clapton's rendition of the song:

> To sit and look and read the lyrics of a song is a baffling enterprise and a distorting one, particularly if we do know, and know well, what the song sounds like and what the lyrics sing like; when we can hear, for example, the desperate passion in Clapton's voice as he sings this song—the tune is in F but in the middle of her name, Layla, there is a shocking transition to the remote key of E flat minor, driving the name right through the heart—and the way that [Duane] Allman's inimitable riffs fill the gaps in between those pained "Layla's." Yet it is precisely this we do, as medievalists, if we study and work with the lyrics of the considerable corpus of songs that we have ended up with, prominent among them the lyrics of the troubadours, on both sides of the Pyrenees.[8]

And it is also precisely this we do, if we study and work with the texts of preachers from the long stretch of history preceding tape recordings or videotapes.

Although the performance of music or drama provides the closest analogy for the sermon,[9] certain elements still require refinement. First, there is the expectation that the sermon be written and delivered by the same person. To be sure, there is evidence both of "ghost-writing"—distinguished rabbis writing a sermon to be given by someone else as if it were his own[10]—and "plagiarism"—delivering the sermon of another without acknowledgment or permission.[11] But the dominant model in the Jewish community throughout the ages is that of preachers publicly communicating their own material. There never developed a differentiation of roles analogous to that of the cantor and composer, the former singing music composed and words written by the latter.[12] A similar specialization developed in the performance arts. Of course, Shakespeare played minor roles in his own dramas, and great composers have often conducted and performed their own music. But this is certainly not necessary, or even expected; it is understood that composition and performance are separate endeavors, and that a differentiation of roles will produce the highest artistic achievement.[13]

With the sermon the assumption was different. Indeed, the personality of the preacher was inseparable from the message being delivered. Congregations felt entitled to assume that the preacher fully understood what he was saying, not merely reading what another had written—an expectation similar to that of an undergraduate audience for their professors' lectures.[14] And if the sermon contained a condemnation of inappropriate, sinful behavior, the reputation of the preacher was crucial in giving the message the best chance of being heeded rather than cynically dismissed.[15]

There is a second distinction between the sermon and the other performing arts. The sermon is generally prepared for delivery to a specific audience at a specific time. To be sure, this may be true of the other categories: a play may be commissioned for performance at a festive event of the royal court; a symphony or opera may be written for a special occasion. However, it is usually expected that the play or the musical work will be performed on subsequent occasions, for different audiences, and that it will retain its power, though perhaps shift its meaning, when the artist who composed it is no longer present, and when the occasion for which it was written has been forgotten by all but historians.[16] This is not true for the sermon. Not only is it assumed that later preachers will not ordinarily deliver the sermons written by their predecessors; it is also assumed that the same preacher will not deliver his own sermon more than once. Again there is a striking contrast with the cantor, who would never be criticized for singing the same rendition of *Kol Nidre* two years in a row. The sermon is understood to be an artistic creation for a single performance—as if Mozart would be permitted to present a new piano concerto only once, and neither he nor any other pianist would ever repeat it!

Needless to say, this created an extremely pressured environment for the preacher, especially in those communities where the rabbi was expected to deliver a sermon every week—as was the case in the communities of the Mediterranean basin (Spain, Italy, the Ottoman Empire) and later in Holland. The liturgical calendar presented a set of severe constraints. At best, six days were available for the composition of a sermon, between the conclusion of the Sabbath and the morning of the following Sabbath. During the period of the holidays of the fall and spring, or when special occasions arose in the community—including deaths requiring a eulogy, sometimes with only several hours notice—the amount of time between preaching opportunities was considerably less than a week. Once the sermon was delivered, it was to be set aside, filed away, and a new deadline would loom. And of course, the rabbi had many responsibilities beyond the preparation and delivery of sermons.

Here too an analogy may be helpful. From 1733 until his death in 1750, J. S. Bach served as cantor of the Thomasschule in Leipzig. At each Sunday service, a cantata was performed, its theme connected with the liturgical and scriptural readings. Bach was often expected to compose a new cantata for the occasion, writing the music, rehearsing the musicians, and conducting the performance—and then proceeding to the next assignment. He created under constant deadlines, pouring his energy into a work that would be performed and then (temporarily) forgotten, knowing that no matter how good the new work had been, the following Sunday people would expect something different. Though working within the confines of a highly structured, conventional form, he managed to produce music that pulsates with vitality. Returning to the same mode time after time, he regularly found something new to express, so that each piece takes on an identity of its own.[17] Much of the same holds true for the best of those called upon to deliver a new sermon every week.

Of course, the conception of the sermon as a unique onetime performance was not always honored. Later preachers did sometimes use the works of their predecessors without proper attribution.[18] And preachers did repeat their own material, sometimes revising and adding new content, sometimes without any significant change.[19] There was one kind of sermon, however, that could not readily be re-used. This was the occasional sermon that responded to a specific situation in the life of the congregation. In it, the preacher uses the traditional forms and structures, the classical texts, the standard ideas, to articulate a reaction to and interpretation of a significant event facing the community. In this context, yet another component of the sermon requires consideration: the audience. A playwright or a composer may or may not compose with a specific audience in mind, although sometimes the displeasure of the audience might actually intrude upon the performance. A sermon is much more clearly an act of direct communication. The audience is present not merely to observe or to listen; it is an integral part of the preacher's function to address, educate, inspire, console, even to challenge those to whom he speaks. Therefore, the prior knowledge, presuppositions, perceived needs, and anticipated reactions of the audience at the time of delivery should be a significant component of what the preacher brings to the process of preparing what will be said.[20]

I propose to concretize and illustrate these generalizations with reference to a specific sermon by Saul Levi Morteira, rabbi of the Portuguese community in Amsterdam from 1619 until his death in 1660. More than any other collection I know, the 550 Hebrew manuscript sermons of Morteira reveal the ongoing work of a preacher for whom the sermon was a major responsibility.[21] These manuscripts are particularly valuable for several reasons. First, at least for the early portion of Morteira's career, he was expected to deliver a sermon each week. In many cases, we can document the sermons delivered week after week, moving through the annual cycle of scriptural lessons. They therefore reveal the kind of work that could be produced regularly, under pressure, within a period of several days.

They also show a continuity of approach over time. There are twenty-one different sermons on the lesson *Shemot* (Ex 1–6:1), twenty on *Va-Yeshev* (Gen 37–40) and *Va-Era* (Ex 6:2–9:35), nineteen on *Yitro* (Ex 18–20). This is a very different kind of preaching activity from that of a visitor who comes to a community to deliver a single sermon.[22] Texts of the same genre produced over so many years reveal a depth of knowledge and a sustained creativity that can only rarely be documented. They also show an intellectual and spiritual leader in a continuing relationship with a fairly stable audience over more than a generation. Under these circumstances, familiarity and trust is established; the congregation becomes a constantly changing yet coherent community of listeners. The preacher can expect a level of knowledge based on previous sermons. Indeed, these texts are often self-referential, with Morteira frequently reminding his listeners of how he treated a certain issue on a previous occasion.[23] Listeners also learn what to expect about the sermon's length, structure, and substance; the preacher will usually fulfill, but occasionally decide to subvert, these expectations. In this kind of relationship, certain criticisms may be expressed that would be highly problematic for a newcomer or a stranger.[24] Allusions not made explicit will be readily understood.

The manuscripts are important for a different reason as well. Most of the books of Jewish sermons from the medieval and early modern periods contain texts written for copying or publication after the sermon was delivered.[25] These texts were written by Morteira *before* they were delivered. They are therefore particularly appropriate for the model suggested above of a script or score for a performance. We should not imagine Morteira reading word for word from the pulpit what he had written. He wrote the texts in Hebrew but delivered the sermons in Portuguese. The dense writing—in small letters, cramped lines, on both sides of the page—could hardly have been intended to be read from the pulpit, and certainly not as the basis for a simultaneous translation. As the actor learns the script then sets it aside, as the pianist (and often the conductor) masters and internalizes the music to the point where the score is no longer necessary, so the preacher no longer depended upon the text he had written by the time he ascended the pulpit.[26] While not a verbatim transcript, the manuscripts provide our best evidence for the performance that the congregation of listeners would have experienced.

Rather than drawing from many scattered examples, I will proceed with a detailed analysis of a single text, a sermon delivered in the winter of 1627, which strikes me as illustrating the rhetorical strategies and performative possibilities of Jewish preaching at its best.[27] As with many of the texts for which there was a specific occasion, Morteira appended a note at the end indicating not only the date but the circumstances: "the sermon I delivered on the lesson *Mishpatim* [Ex 21–24] at the time when written reports arrived concerning the great tribulations that were in Jerusalem, may it speedily be rebuilt, in the year 5387 [1627].[28] This sets the sermon in a specific historical context, about which a great deal is known.

In 1625, Mehmed ibn Farukh was appointed governor of Jerusalem. He immediately imposed a harsh, anti-Jewish policy, extorting huge sums of money and imprisoning leaders of the community, including the revered Rabbi Isaiah Halevi Horowitz, for ransom. The Jews of Jerusalem were compelled to borrow 50,000 aspers from Muslim neighbors at a high rate of interest, a situation leading to the bankruptcy of the community and its economic subjugation to the Muslim population.[29] Under these emergency conditions, the Jerusalem leadership sent out emissaries to gather funds in Italy. Even after ibn Farukh was deposed in December of 1626, following prodigious efforts by Jews to intercede with higher levels of the government in Damascus and Istanbul, the economic crisis remained, and a new round of emissaries and epistles were sent to various Jewish communities of the Diaspora. The purpose was to describe the wretched condition of the Jerusalem community and to appeal for funds. The arrival of such a letter in Amsterdam moved the leadership to action. At a special gathering of the three congregations, following a report in which the calamitous conditions of the Jerusalem community were communicated to the audience (probably through a Portuguese translation of the Hebrew letters), Morteira responded to the devastating news in a sermon.[30] It was not his task to make a direct appeal for funds; his purpose was to interpret and explain what had happened, to address questions raised in the minds of the congregants, and to generate support for a substantial community response.

Under such circumstances, a preacher needs to make some tactical decisions. How much time will actually be devoted to the need for money? How much will be an appeal to the emotions, how much to the intellect? What traditional sources will be used, and how will they be interpreted and applied? How will the connection be established between the oppressed and impoverished Jews of Jerusalem and the community in Amsterdam. Will the mood be uplifting and inspirational or condemnatory and frightening, optimistic or lugubrious? Would he speak on behalf of his audience, attempting to articulate their feelings, or would he confront and rebuke them. Morteira used the occasion to expound his views of recent Jewish history, the special character of the land of Israel, and the distinctiveness of the Amsterdam community within the contemporary Diaspora, alongside some powerful condemnations of Jewish shortcomings, past and present, abroad and at home.

As with all of his sermons, Morteira follows the traditional Sephardic style of beginning with a verse from the scriptural lesson (the *nosei,* or theme verse) and a rabbinic dictum (the *ma'amar*).[31] The Torah verse was dictated by a self-imposed constraint; following his pattern, beginning in 1619, of moving progressively verse by verse through the Scriptural lesson, he used a part of the eighth verse as his theme: *he shall not rule over her to sell her to outsiders* (Ex 21:8). In context, this pertains to the law of the Hebrew slave woman and has no obvious connection to the occasion of the sermon. The rabbinic dictum, however, was chosen to be dramatically relevant, especially in its concluding prooftext: "So the sages said, A person who is covering his house with plaster should leave a small space uncovered. A person who is preparing what is needed for a feast should leave out some small ingredient. A person who is putting on all her ornaments should omit one of them, For it is said, *If I forget you O Jerusalem, let my right hand wither* [Ps 137:5]" (bBB 60a).

The introduction to the sermon begins with a general proposition that is both jarring and reassuring. It often happens, the preacher proclaims, that "because of the weakness of human reason, a person will utter insolent words out of the great anguish of pains he cannot bear, and say things that are not true." The examples he gives from the Bible—Joshua, Jeremiah, and Job's wife—illustrate the point that even respected leaders of the people may be driven temporarily to irresponsible utterance. Then the application is made:

> Because of the distress of hearts hearing these tribulations which occurred to [the inhabitants of?] Jerusalem, may it be speedily rebuilt, they have said, "Surely it is not God's will that our people dwell in the Holy Land, for the oppressor's rod has fallen upon them to remove them from upon it." For God has said, *And you I will scatter among the nations* [Lev 26:33], *And He cast them into another land, as is still this day* [Deut 29:27]. . . . I myself have heard some distinguished men, because of their zeal and their pain, saying such things and expressing this idea, out of the anguish of their hearts.

We sense here that the preacher has set for himself a delicate task. He himself has heard a first level of response to the news that he feels constrained to reject at this important public occasion. It is not a "heretical" response of the kind that he would attack in many other sermons. It accepts the providential view of God as responsible for the events of history; it is grounded in biblical verses. And it has been maintained by respected leaders of the community, some of whom were probably sitting right in front of the preacher. Yet Morteira insists that the conclusion—God does not want Jews to dwell in the land of Israel at present—is the wrong lesson to draw.[32] He therefore provides the highest motive for this mistaken conclusion—anguish because of the suffering of fellow Jews—and puts those who hold this view in exalted biblical company. He then sets out to refute it, promising a full argument at some future occasion, contenting himself at present with one proof each from the Torah, the Prophets, the Writings, and the Sages.

But if the suffering of the Jerusalem community was not God's way of removing a Jewish presence from the land of Israel in pre-messianic times, why did it occur? Here we begin to follow the preacher's message step by step. The structure for the second half of the sermon is derived from a verse in Proverbs, "The land shudders at three things, at four which it cannot bear: a slave who becomes king, a scoundrel sated with food, a loathsome woman who gets married, a slave-girl who supplants her mistress" (Prov. 30:21–23). By informing his listeners that this passage, homiletically interpreted, suggests four causes of the disasters in the land of Israel, the preacher achieves several goals. He provides an alternate explanation to the one he has rejected. He similarly roots the contemporary reality in Scripture, so that while still troubling it is no longer bewildering. He orients the listeners ahead of time about the structure of the material to come. And he arouses an element of curiosity: how do these phrases apply to the suffering of Jews in the Holy Land?

The verse from Proverbs is woven together with other verses in a complex pattern. As in several other sermons, Morteira uses a threat from the lesson *Ha'azinu,* "They incensed Me with no-gods, vexed Me with their futilities; I'll incense them with a non-people, vex them with a scoundrel nation [*am naval*]" (Deut 32:21) to introduce the theme of the people's sinful ingratitude to God, making their suffering a measure for measure punishment, and to convey the humiliation of the Jews' subjugation to a people of no stature or dignity. Elsewhere he applies this to the dominance of Christianity;[33] here it is to Islam and the Arabs. He interprets the lamentation "Mount Zion, which lies desolate; jackals prowl over it" (Lam 5:18) as a reaction to the infamy of Arab rule: "all kingdoms are represented by animals, the 'Egyptians' by jackals.[34] *Jackals prowl over it,* a lowly, scoundrel people, without religion or law, as we see with our own eyes this very day. *Because of this our hearts are sick, . . . Because of Mount Zion, which lies desolate; jackals prowl over it* [Lam. 5:17–18]." Then: "This is one of the things at which *the land* (i.e., the land of Israel) *shudders . . . : a slave who becomes king* [Prov 30:21–22]," reflecting Morteira's contempt for the oppressors of Jerusalem, their base lineage, their inferior legal system and faith. This point leads to a contrast between the inhabitants of Jerusalem and of Amsterdam and a connection between the two communities: the Jews of Amsterdam, who live under a highly respected people, bear responsibility for those Jews who suffer from humiliation as well as persecution: "If so, it is proper for us, whom God has placed in a royal land, of religion and law—even though we are all caught up in sin—to help and aid them, so that in their prosperity we may prosper [cf. Jer 29:7], for whoever says, 'I'll be all right, etc.' [cf. Deut 29:18], *the Eternal will never forgive him* [Deut. 29:19]." Here he is speaking on behalf of his audience, in solidarity with them, sharing their perspective.

The parenthetical clause "even though we are all caught up in sin" provided a hint that the preacher's message would contain a rebuke of the congregation he was addressing. The next section, while not yet speaking specifically about Amsterdam, brings the condemnation much closer to home. The second phrase from Proverbs, "a scoundrel [*naval*] sated with food," picking up a word from the *Ha'azinu* verse, is applied to the paradigmatic "scoundrel": "it is Satan, it is the evil impulse, it is the angel of death, the accuser" (cf. Baba Batra 16a). This archetypal enemy is "sated with food" when it is fed the "food of vipers"—the sins and transgressions of the Jewish people. The following passage must have been a moment of high intensity in the delivery, for Morteira plays with the personification of Satan gorging himself on the sins of the Jews, and he provides the menu in exuberant detail. The cumulative impact of the long list must have been troubling to at least some of the listeners:

> Alas, how sated he is with hatred between Jews! How sated with slanderous speech. How sated with vengeful hearts and nurturing enmities. How sated with robbery and violence. How sated with failure to study Torah. How sated with laxity in performance of the commandments. How sated with those who do them for improper reasons, *a commandment of men, learned by rote* [Isa 29:13]. [How sated with those who swear an oath falsely; with those who utter the Divine Name for no good purpose; with those who make vows they do not fulfill. How sated with those who have sexual relations with Gentile women.][35] How sated with the informers, and the apostates. How sated with the arrogant and the haughty. How sated with those who offer up their sons to Molech. How sated with those who mock God's words, with those who behave defiantly. How sated is this scoundrel! Divine Justice cannot annul his wish.

This is a passage in which the voice of the orator can almost be heard despite the dislocation in time. On the hand-written or printed page, the eighteen repetitions of the Hebrew word *kamah* ("how") in five lines produce clutter and make most readers think of a need for the editor's pencil. Spoken by a skilled orator—pausing just long enough for the effect to sink in but not so long that the continuity will be broken, emphasizing the sins he considered most important, perhaps even glancing at specific individuals to whom the phrases applied,[36] piling up example after example until the listeners themselves must have been sated yet terrified at the thought of Satan's surfeit—the effect of this litany must have been electrifying.

Was this passage intended to be heard as describing the behavior of the Jews in Jerusalem? Or those in Amsterdam? Many of the sins specified are conventional and could apply to any Jewish community. "Informing" was a major problem for the Jerusalem community, while it was not for Amsterdam. Yet other transgressions would have been familiar to the listeners from sermons in which Morteira had been explicitly talking about his own community. Particularly sensitive were the references to sexual relations with Gentile women, a familiar theme in Morteira's rebukes, and to "apostates," those former New Christians who abandoned the Jewish community and tried to gain acceptance once again in the Christian world. It is likely, therefore, that many listeners would have heard Morteira as recounting at uncomfortable length the religious failings of those whom he addressed.

But why then was the Jerusalem community punished? Why was the learned and pious Rabbi Horowitz, esteemed author of *Shenei Luḥot ha-Berit,* imprisoned and humiliated? This is addressed in the continuation of the passage. Once permission is given for Satan to act, he does not distinguish between righteous and sinners. Indeed, he actually begins with the righteous, as biblical verses reveal (citing Ezekiel 21:8 and 9:6), for "they are the heroes, they are the walls, they are the towers for those who would not implore God." The section ends with a summons to repentance, clearly addressed to the listeners: "Be men, take it to heart, prepare and set things right, give help against the enemy, for God will be merciful; be established through righteousness [cf. Isa 54:14], and return to God, for He is gracious and merciful, and He will feel regret about the evil."

At this point, the listeners might have drawn a deep breath and taken stock. The litany of failures to which they had just been subjected may have hit close to home, but there was no explicit warning that they themselves would be punished. Yet they would have known that the preacher had not concluded; there were two more phrases from the Proverbs verse to be applied. Unwilling to continue at the same level of intensity, Morteira returned to the verse. But the listeners, treated to a quick discourse on the deep structure of Jewish historical experience, would not have long to relax.

The third phrase from the Proverbs passage, "a loathsome woman who becomes married," is not explained at first. The preacher begins his discussion by reasserting a traditional national theodicy:

> This is what experience has shown us from the day when God chose us and took us as His people. *So Jeshurun grew fat and unruly, you grew fat and gross and coarse, he forsook the God who made him and spurned his supporting Rock* [Deut 32:15]. But we have not opened our eyes, nor have we learned a lesson from the many times when this was the cause that brought us so much misfortune, for when things were good, we have always turned to evil. To this very day in the long and bitter exile, we have not turned back from this way. Whenever God is generous to us, giving our remnant a respite, instead of this beneficence from God leading us to cling more closely to Him and strengthening us in His service, the beneficence becomes the cause of increasing sin and transgression: conflicts and sins and battles, envy and hatred for each other, until God afflicted us, so that we sought Him in distress, and chastisement brought [us] to anguished whispered prayer [cf. Isa 26:16].

Starting in the distant biblical past, with the establishment of the covenantal relationship between God and the people of Israel, a single verse from *Ha'azinu* is summoned as the paradigm of Jewish experience made more tragic because it has been repeated so many times. The words "we have not opened our eyes" and "to this very day" prepare the listener for something unpleasant that will be applied to the preacher's own community. They may indeed have reminded listeners of a powerful sermon of rebuke entitled "The People's Envy" that he delivered about five years before, bearing an extremely pessimistic message about failing to learn from past mistakes; there the application to contemporary Amsterdam was unmistakable.[37] But for the time being, the offenses remain in the past.

At this point, Morteira applies the Proverbs verse, using the "loathsome woman" to refer to the Jewish people, despised in exile, and her "marriage" having reached a status of success and prosperity through its unique relationship with God, thereby creating an intolerable situation. He then returns to the motif of learning from history with greater specificity and, we may imagine, with increased intensity of voice:

> Whoever is wise would understand this and learn from earlier times: from the greatness and glory, the affluence and wisdom that were long ago in the [Jewish communities of the] kingdoms of Spain and France. Let him see now: all is destroyed and abandoned, nothing remains. He may cry out, "Aha! O Eternal our God, what is this all about? Will You totally destroy the remnant of Your estate?" [cf. Ezek 11:13]. If he had any insight, he would turn his words back against himself. *The judgments of the Eternal are true, they are just in their entirety* [Ps 19:10]. Let him read the matters in the judicial questions and responsa left by these sages: the abundance of violence, the lust, the envy, the conflicts, the informers [about Jews to the government], the most serious sexual offenses, sexual congress with Gentile women, the neglect of Torah, the eager pursuit of money, and similar things that can be found in these books by anyone who would read them.

The passage is remarkable in several ways, not the least of which is Morteira's invocation of the responsa literature not as a repository of legal precedent but as a historical source for material of ethical, homiletical value. There is almost a mockery of traditional Jewish lament, expressed in the rhetorical outcry to God following the destruction of great Jewish communities. The answer is obvious in the literature of past centuries. Here we encounter a powerful ambivalence toward the communities of France and of Spain. On the one hand, "greatness and glory, affluence and wisdom." But Morteira implies that this is not the full truth; there is a darker reality beneath the surface, accessible (to those who read Hebrew) in the dense pages of legal texts. These reveal the lives not just of the spiritual and intellectual leaders but of the entire population of Jews, and the resulting picture, Morteira insists as he reiterates many of the sins from his earlier litany, is dismal indeed.

By this time, listeners would have been quite certain that the preacher was not going to limit himself to a history lesson, that application to the present was certain to come. And he does not disappoint, invoking the recent history both of Amsterdam and of Jerusalem:

> Still, we have not learned! Even today, we are worse than our ancestors. Did we not see during the good days that confronted us in this

> city how many conflicts occurred and how many bans were enacted, until war and loss of money and pestilence came, Heaven protect us! And so in Jerusalem, the holy city, may it be quickly rebuilt: for the past three years there was peace and tranquillity in the land. But we knew the bewildering and chaotic conflicts among the Jews, until the anger of Satan boiled over against them and destroyed them, as our eyes see this very day. Truly, experience teaches the truthfulness of the rabbinic statement, "poverty is fitting for Israel like a red rose upon a white horse" [bḤag 9b]. Even a minor sin committed in that land is much greater than in another place, for it is done in God's presence. We see this in the verse, *The people who provoke My anger continually, in My very presence* [Isa 65:3], and in the verse, *My eyes and My heart will be there always* [1Kgs 9:3]. How much greater is the transgression committed in the king's palace, in the king's very presence, than that committed in one's own house!

The reference to Amsterdam has been fleeting and allusive, yet unmistakable. Few in the audience would not have had strong memories of the conflict surrounding Morteira's friend, the now deceased Dr. David Farar,[38] the bitter split surrounding the formation of a break-away congregation from "Beth Jacob." When his own congregation was vindicated following an appeal to the Dutch authorities, Morteira delivered a celebratory sermon emphasizing reconciliation. Here the mood is quite different, as he points to the conflict as a cause of upheavals in the subsequent years and suggests that the legacy of divisiveness has not yet ended. The "war and loss of money" following in the wake of the conflicts similarly alludes to realities everyone well knew: the termination of the Twelve Years' Truce between Spain and Holland in April 1621, the imposing of new embargoes against Dutch ships and merchandise in all Spanish territories, and the rapid reversal of fortune for the Jewish merchants, from vigorous economic expansion to severe economic slump.[39]

The events in the Jewish community of Jerusalem could not have been nearly as familiar to the audience, which had to accept Morteira's authority on this matter. The early 1620's, following the arrival in Jerusalem of R. Isaiah Halevi Horowitz, were considered to be years of tranquillity, prosperity, and even messianic promise.[40] As for the "bewildering and chaotic conflicts among the Jews," this may refer to the collaboration of Jews as informers to government officials about Jews who settled in Jerusalem without government authorization.[41] The point he is making is that the contrast between external tranquillity and internal strife in Jerusalem created an unstable situation that had to change. As in so much of traditional historiography, the political events involving the Muslim governor ibn Farukh are only the epiphenomena of a deeper reality, the structures of which are encoded in the Bible. It is as if the Muslim authorities were not protagonists at all.

Amsterdam and Jerusalem are thus set up in ambiguous juxtaposition. First a parallel is made: contentious behavior has within the past few years led to loss of prosperity and to suffering in both. Then the distinctiveness of the Holy Land is emphasized. Earlier in the sermon he emphasized one fundamental difference between the two communities: Jerusalem subjugated to "a scoundrel people," Dutch Jewry living in "a royal land, of religion and law." Now a different contrast is drawn: the unique closeness of the divine presence to the land of Israel makes it especially sensitive to the smallest sin, incapable of tolerating even a minor transgression. In other words, the listeners should not conclude that the greater intensity of suffering in Jerusalem proves that its inhabitants must have sinned more than the present company. The juxtaposition of the two cities would have the effect upon the listeners both of dignifying Amsterdam and sounding the jeremiad that more suffering is in store at home unless things improve.

Morteira then turns back to the implications for his own community. "Why then are we irresolute in our actions? Why do we undermine our preparations to accept all God's kindnesses, while we anger Him over the good things He gives us? *I lavished silver on her, and gold, which they used for Baal* [Hos 2:10]. Indeed, how great is the obligation of the leaders of these congregations to bestir themselves to improve our way of serving God, in that He has favored us more than any other Jews in the Diaspora."[42] To concretize this point, the preacher continues with an extremely powerful and interesting passage ranging through the great Jewish communities of the world and succinctly specifying the humiliations and persecutions distinctive of each.

> Where here are the taxes of Venice? The censorship of books that is all over Italy? The seizing of children for forced conversions? The sign of the [Jewish] hat that is there? The Ghettos? The need to receive permission [to remain] every so often? Being shut in at the evil time [Holy Week]? Where is the derision shown toward the Jews of Rome, [forced to] go out naked on their holidays, forced to attend their services, forced to bow down to the Pope? Where are the blood libels of Poland? Where are the humiliations of Germany? Where are the hours when they prevent us from attending the [commercial] fairs? The entrances through which we may not walk, the wells from we may not drink? Where is the harsh oppression of Turkey? The poll tax that is levied there? The cruelty of the Gentiles? The fire thrown into houses? The deadly tortures connected with the manufacturing of their clothes? Where is the degradation of Barbary? Where is the youngster who will strike an old man? Where are the animal carcasses which they compel us to remove from their paths?[43]

Like the earlier litany of sins in Satan's feast, this series of rhetorical questions was clearly intended not for the written page but for the modulations of the preacher's voice, though its power remains palpable in its written form, even without the preacher's voice to enhance it. He begins with his own native city of Venice, which Amsterdam Jews looked upon as a model: older, larger, more established, more cosmopolitan than their own, the city to which they turned for guidance and leadership when problems arose. Yet it could not be denied that the Jews of Venice, and Rome, and the rest of Italy, suffered from disabilities and humiliations that were simply not present in Amsterdam. And if that was true of Italy, how much more was it true for other great Jewish communities of the Diaspora: Poland, Germany, Turkey, North Africa. As in the previous passage of rebuke, timing in delivery is crucial. With each clipped phrase, the preacher must have paused long enough to allow the verbal picture to register in the minds of the listeners.

After piling up his evidence, and suggesting that he could add even more, Morteira reaches his conclusion with the appropriate lesson: "And much more of the like, that our brothers, the entire house of Israel, suffer throughout their dispersion in exile. But God has brought us out from there. Why then are we ungrateful? Why do we not wake up and open our eyes [to see] that just as God has favored us more than all our brothers, so should we surpass them all in our conduct, serving as an example, a model of goodness and decency, especially by helping the Holy City at a time like this?" In addition to the general conclusion of reforming behavior, the practical application to the specific situation has now been made.

The final section of the sermon is introduced by the last phrase in the Proverbs verse, "a slave-girl who supplants her mistress" (Prov 30:23). Citing verses to establish that the "mistress" is Jerusalem and the "slave-girl" any other land, Morteira draws a harsh lesson, shifting the spotlight entirely to the Jews of the Diaspora: the greatest disgrace of all for Jerusalem is that "her children give all its goodness and its glory to her slave-girl. They forget her [the mistress], giving every kind of joy and honor to slave-girls in the land of their enemies, in their exile, in a land not theirs." After having dramatically emphasized the uniqueness of Amsterdam in the Diaspora, the preacher now shifts his ground, placing Amsterdam in the harsh, traditional, undifferentiated category of "exile" and "land of your enemies" (cf. Lev 26:41). Compared with Italy, Poland, and Morocco, the situation in Amsterdam was vastly better, but it was still exile, a "land not theirs."

For the alert listener, the use of the word "they forget her" would have raised the association with the Psalmist's pledge never to forget (Ps 137:5), and perhaps even Morteira's use of this verse in the rabbinic dictum cited at the beginning of the sermon. It is precisely this dictum that he now takes up, to signal the sermon's approaching end, though not that the final words will all be pleasant to hear. The rabbinic statement, which specifies ways for Jews living in the land of Israel following the destruction to remember Jerusalem properly, allows the preacher to draw a contrast with the behavior of his congregants. The three elements of the dictum are used to refer to three examples of conspicuous consumption. "They did not say 'covering his house with paintings,' but 'A person who is covering his house with *plaster,*' yet still a small space should be left as a reminder of the destruction. . . . Why then should the Jews of the Diaspora seek *spacious upper chambers* [Jer 22:14]?"[44] The rabbinic statement continues, "A person who is preparing what is needed for a feast," speaking about what is necessary; even from this, he should leave out something as a reminder of the destruction. They were not even thinking, explains Morteira, of "those banquets that destroy people's savings; of this, the prophet said, *They lie on ivory beds, stretched upon their couches, feasting on lambs from the flock, and on calves from the stall . . . They drink from the wine bowls and anoint themselves with the choicest oils, but they are not concerned about the ruin of Joseph* [Amos 6:4,6]."[45] Here the prophetic verse has specific resonance for those whose lack of response to the community relief effort shows indifference to the sufferings of Jews in the Holy Land. Finally, the rabbis speak of "A person who is puffing on her ornaments," namely:

> those ornaments appropriate to a woman in exile, who would not transgress the words of the prophet who cries out against them when in abundance. "She should omit one of them" as a reminder of the destruction. But they do not act this way; rather, they see how they can outdo the ones who preceded them, so that *a slave-girl supplants her mistress* [Prov 30:23] by acting this way in their exile.

In this section, Morteira gives a succinct reprise of the central theme and the tripartite division in "The People's Envy"—condemnation of expenditures on unnecessarily large and beautiful houses, sumptuous meals, and lavish clothing and jewelry. This time there is no reference to the arousal of envy and hostility in the host population. In accordance with the occasion, the preacher emphasizes the failure to follow the tradition of abnegation in memory of the destruction of the Temple, the failure to remember Jerusalem and its suffering inhabitants.

The rabbinic dictum has been interpreted and applied, and the listeners would know they were nearing the end. At this point the preacher shifts to a climactic peroration, recapitulating the three areas of offensive behavior just outlined, transposing the negatives into positive ideals:

> How good and how fine it would be for every person to take pride and to compete with his neighbor not in the great size of his house but in the greatness of his soul, which is the house of ethical virtues and intellectual attainments. Not in foods but in feeding the poor and abundant charity. Not in clothes, but in a good name and serenity and in imitation of God's ways and in the mystical garment of good deeds.[46] This

> would be the "remembering of Jerusalem," this would be the shortening of our exile. And now that we fail to do this, the plagues of Jerusalem mount. Perhaps we may open our eyes from preoccupation with ourselves to see whether the way we are following is good, so that these afflictions will no longer come upon it. . . . *That is why the members of the Va'ad passed the ordinances they did to help in its redemption,* so that the feet of Israel will not move from upon it.

With this allusion to a decisive act by the lay leadership that everyone in the audience must have known,[47] the preacher has accomplished everything of substance on his agenda. Only the conventional obligations of the genre remain. His insistence upon a continued Jewish presence in the land of Israel—picking up his refutation of the view expressed in the introduction (God does not want our people to dwell in the Holy Land at present)—is now connected with the theme-verse from the scriptural lesson, cited at the beginning of the sermon: "He shall not rule over her to sell her to outsiders" [Exod. 21:8]. It returns, near the very end, as a framing device.[48] In a characteristic homiletical inversion, the phrase is removed from the simple meaning of its original reference—the Hebrew slave woman—and applied to the land that is currently under the power of aliens: "*And which of My creditors was it to whom I sold you off?* [Isa 50:1]. For it is not sold, only given for temporary keeping, and therefore Israel will not lose her presumptive rights, she will forever remain upon it." Not surprisingly, after a long passage of criticism, set on the broad canvas of Jewish history and geography, the preacher ends on a positive course of action linked with the traditional messianic hope.

What would the assembled congregation have remembered from this sermon? They would not have learned much about the details of the persecution in Jerusalem; that was not the preacher's purpose. Perhaps the four-part verse from Proverbs and its interpretation, or the three-part rabbinic dictum as applied by Morteira, would have remained with them. Some listeners may have been impressed by the point about the corruption of the earlier Jewish communities of Europe, as revealed in the responsa literature. Some would perhaps have been moved by Morteira's stress on the link between dissension and rupture in the community and the economic reversals that followed soon after, or the comparison between Amsterdam and Jerusalem, the claim that inner communal tensions led to external calamity in both. But perhaps more than any substantive argument, they would have recalled the rhythms and cadences and modulations of the preacher's voice at the climactic moments in the sermon: the litany of sins evoking a picture of Satan cramming his maw to the point where he can eat no more ("How sated . . . !"), and the globe-hopping tour of world Jewish centers, each community with its distinctive disabilities from which Amsterdam is free ("Where are . . . ?"). These are the kind of high points that remain fixed in the acoustic memory even after the structure of the sermon has been forgotten.[49] The Hebrew text written by Morteira is a rather impressive script for this special occasion. If his abilities as a speaker were comparable to his abilities as an author, the audience may well have experienced an unforgettable performance.[50]

NOTES

1. Leone Modena, *Midbar Yehudah* (Venice, 1602), 8a–9a, translated in Saperstein, *Jewish Preaching 1200–1800* (New Haven, 1989), 408–409, cf. 406. This introduction draws on *topoi* of Jewish pulpit oratory: the difficulty of pleasing everyone, and the claim that it would really be better to remain silent than to speak.

2. The application of the concept of beginning, middle and end to the causal movement in time of literary plot goes back, of course, to Aristotle's *Poetics,* Book 7, 1450b; cf. C. S. Baldwin, *Ancient Rhetoric and Poetic* (Gloucestor, Mass., 1959), 149.

3. On the need for the artist's presence as a defining characteristic of performance art, see RoseLee Goldberg, *Performance Art: From Futurism to the Present* (New York, 1988), 8. The obvious corollary about controlling the presentation in time is, as far as I know, my own. On the fundamental distinction (often not appreciated in classical theory) between theatre and the poem or novel as art forms, see Marvin Carlson, *Performance: A Critical Introduction* (London, 1996), 82.

4. This means that the analysis of the effect of the sermon should be, insofar as possible, in terms of listener response, not reader response. Stanley Fish, after a precise unpacking of thwarted expectations aroused by a single sentence in a sermon by Lancelot Andrewes, concedes that "my analysis of the sentence is more tortuous and torturing than the reader's experience of it" (*Is There A Text in the*

Class [Cambridge, Mass., 1980], 186). No matter how fastidiously that sentence was delivered by Andrewes, it is even more unlikely that a listener would have reacted in the way described by Fish. Later in the essay, he does talk about listener reaction (188).

5. Compare the statement in the foreward to the printed edition of Moliere's *L'Amour médecin* (quoted from the London, 1714 translation of John Ozell): "'Tis generally known that Comedies are only writ to be Acted; and I wou'd have no Body read this but such as have Eyes to discover the Acting in the Reading of it." Cited by Roger Chartier, *Forms and Meanings* (Philadelphia, 1995), 52.

6. For recognition of the importance of this element by Jewish writers, with their recommendations for appropriate use of voice, gesture, and body language, see Judah Messer Leon, *The Book of the Honeycomb's Flow,* trans. and ed. by Isaac Rabinowitz (Ithaca, 1983), 116–131; Henry Sosland, *A Guide for Preachers on Composing and Delivering Sermons: The Or Ha-Darshanim of Jacob Zahalon* (New York, 1987), 138–144. On the importance of delivery (*pronuntiatio* or *actio*) in classical rhetorical theory, see Brian Vickers, *In Defence of Rhetoric* (Oxford, 1988), 65–67. On Christian preachers, see (among many possible examples) the treatments by Th.-M. Charland, *Artes praedicandi,* in *Publications de l'Institute d'Etudes Mediévales d'Ottawa* 7 (1936), 219–226, 332, and Hilary Dansey Smith, *Preaching in the Spanish Golden Age* (Oxford, 1978), 60–69.

7. It was reported that the great seventeenth-century preacher Bossuet, when shown the printed text of his funeral oration for Nicolas Cornet (delivered in 1663, published in Amsterdam by the heirs of the deceased in 1698), said that he did not recognize in it his own work. *Ouevres de Bossuet,* 4 vols. (Paris, 1682), 2:1a. Cf. also Patricia Tracy, *Jonathan Edwards, Pastor* (New York, 1979), 83: "The printed page cannot adequately convey the emotional impact which Edwards's revival sermons had on his flock."

8. Maria Rosa Menocal, *Shards of Love: Exile and the Origins of the Lyric* (Durham, N.C., 1994), 151. She continues, later, to make a general point: "The paradox, then, is that the song lyric is a composition keyed to and written for an aesthetic, that of music, that is dramatically different from the aesthetics of writing which is meant to be read; on the other hand, we often are limited to the discourse and the aesthetics of the written and read text both to convey the essence of the song (as in the setting out of the lyrics of "Layla") and to do anything critical with it" (152–153). The same paradox applies to study of the aesthetics of the sermon. Cf. also the statement of a leading historian of performance art: "The history of performance, like a history of theatre, can only be constructed from scripts, texts,

photographs and descriptions from onlookers. What was once to be seen, or to be heard, must now be reconstructed in the imagination," RoseLee Goldberg: *Performance: Live Art, 1909 to the Present* (New York, 1979), 6.

9. Cf. Smith, *Preaching in the Spanish Golden Age,* 63: "The sermon may, therefore, be considered not only as a conceptual but also as a musical structure. The preacher must be able to perform with the control of an actor, fitting words, tone, expression, and gesture together appropriately, yet without seeming in the least theatrical." For Renaissance application of rhetorical conceptions and terms to music, see Vickers, *In Defense of Rhetoric,* 360–372. The most effective use of the analogy between sermon and dramatic performance I know is by Harry Stout: "To appreciate [George] Whitefield's printed sermons fully, we have to read them less as lectures or treatises than as dramatic scripts, each with a series of verbal cues that released improvised body language and pathos," *The Divine Dramatist* (Grand Rapids, Mich., 1991), 40, and see his full discussion, xix–xxi and 40–43.

10. One of the sermons printed in Leone Modena's book of sermons is labelled, "Sermon for a Bar Mitzvah: I composed it for a youth when he reached the age of 13 . . . that is why it is very short" (*Midbar Yehudah,* [Venice, 1602], 94b; for a second such sermon see 96b). Also preserved in manuscript are sermons he wrote for his eldest son to use on his Bar Mitzvah, and a "Sermon for Sukkot, delivered by my son R. Mordecai of blessed memory in Florence, and later also by Mr. Barukh Luzzato, my student, in Venice, and also by my grandson, Isaac, in 1637. See *Ziqnei Yehudah,* ed. Shlomo Simonsohn (Jerusalem, 1956), 16 n. 36. In the long list of his occupations, he includes "[writing] sermons for others"; see Mark Cohen, ed., *The Autobiography of a Seventeenth-Century Venetian Rabbi: Leon Modena's Life of Judah* (Princeton, 1988), 162.

11. The most blatant example I have encountered involves Moses Edrehi, born in Morocco in 1774, who went to the Sephardic community in London and then to Amsterdam. In 1809, he published in Amsterdam a book entitled *Yad Mosheh,* which contains 14 sermons he had delivered in Morocco, London, and Amsterdam itself (see Abraham Ya'ari, "R. Moshe Edrehi u-Sefarav," *Kiryat Sefer* 33 [1957–58], 521–528). To my knowledge, it has not been noticed that long passages from these sermons were taken almost word for word, and without any acknowledgement, from the Amsterdam, 1645 edition of Saul Levi Morteira's *Giv'at Sha'ul.* To publish under one's own name material from the book of sermons by one of the leading rabbis of the same community—apparently confident that no one would read both books—strikes me as a new height for *chutzpah.* I plan to document the "borrowings" in a different context. Anecdotes about preachers who pretended to

be the Maggid of Dubno or who passed off the Maggid's parables as their own—anecdotes in which the true Maggid vindicates himself—show the continued expectation that the sermon *should* be the preacher's own creation.

12. For a contrast between preachers and cantors regarding originality in the period of late antiquity, see Ezra Fleischer, *Shirat ha-Qodesh ha-Ivrit bi-Ymei ha-Beinayim* (Jerusalem, 1975), 266–267. At first, the cantor who led communal worship actually composed his own innovative poems on the themes of the fixed liturgy (ibid., pp. 49–51), but the separation of function between poet and "performer" became quickly established.

13. Alternative models, in which the differentiation between author/composer and performer is blurred or non-existent, include bards of oral poetry, medieval troubadours and jesters, modern comedians and other improvisational performers. Cf. Carlson, *Performance,* 83. These figures share a characteristic of the preacher that traditional actors or musicians do not.

14. Note the complaints cited in my *Jewish Preaching,* 55 (with n. 31). This expectation tests Walter Ong's generalization that "in all oral performance, the question of originality as a virtue does not even arise. The oral traffics in the already known." (*Rhetoric, Romance, and Technology* [Ithaca, 1971], 37.)

15. For the problematic relationship between preacher and congregation in the sermon of rebuke, see *Jewish Preaching,* 46–50, with illustrative texts 416–424. An English divine, Cornelius Burges, preaching to the House of Commons on a fast day in 1640, complained, "If the Preacher come home to convince the Conscience of particulars that need reformation, (which yet was the old course, and should be so still) the Preacher is either derided as worthy of nothing but contempt, or else censured as indiscrete, rash, factious, and seditious." John Chandos, ed., *In God's Name: Examples of Preaching in England 1534–1662* (Indianapolis, 1971), 349. Chandos, however, condemns the opposite tendency, "the promiscuous amplifying of every common theologaster and loud-mouthed malcontent with a taste for haranguing his equals, or for that matter, his superiors" (xxv).

16. On the shifts of meaning concommitant with a play's transition from its original performance at the court of Louis XIV to an urban audience in Paris, see Chartier, *Forms and Meanings,* 43–82.

17. See *Grove's Dictionary of Music and Musicians,* 10 vols. (New York, 1959–1961), 1:305. Five annual cycles of cantatas, totaling 295, were written, of which 265 were composed between the years 1723 and 1744; see ibid., 310–315. A similarly frenetic schedule of composition and performance under a deadline was sometimes applied to playwrights. In the foreword to *L'Amour médicin* cited

above (n. 2), Moliere wrote that "It was Proposed, Written, Learn'd, and Acted in Five Days" (Chartier, *Forms and Meanings*, 52).

18. In addition to the case of Moses Edrehi, cited above, there is evidence in the manuscript sermons of Saul Levi Morteira that a rabbi in Ancona delivered some of the sermons in the 1760s, some 140 years after they were first written. Presumably, he did not announce that he was presenting an earlier rabbi's work.

19. Here too, Morteira's manuscripts provide abundant evidence, for he regularly noted at the end all subsequent occasions when he used the same sermon, occasionally recording the new material he added. During his 40-year tenure, he may have given the same sermon as many as five times.

20. Here too, performance art theory is helpful. See the recent formulation of Marvin Carlson, *Performance*, 197: "The audience's expected 'role' changes from a passive hermeneutic process of decoding the performer's articulation, embodiment, or challenge of particular cultural material, to become something much more active, entering into a praxis, a context in which meanings are not so much communicated as created, questioned, or negotiated. The 'audience' is invited and expected to operate as a co-creator of whatever meanings and experience the event generates."

21. On the manuscripts, see my "*Your Voice Like a Ram's Horn*" (Cincinnati, 1996), 370, n. 15; 412 n. 3. I am currently preparing a monographic study of these sermons, in which the conclusions to be stated hereafter will be fully documented.

22. For example, the great Christian revivalist preachers, such as Vicente Ferrer in the fifteenth century and George Whitefield in the eighteenth; or the itinerant Jewish *maggidim* of eastern Europe.

23. Virtually every sermon, including those in the printed *Giv'at Sha'ul*, contains at least one reference to a previous sermon. An interesting justification of the need for recapitulation, based on the difference between oral and written communication, can be found in a late sermon (ca. 1645) on Genesis 29:7 from the lesson *Va-Yetse* (MS 2:46r): "If these words [from the theme verse] had been read from a book, there would be no need to review what was already established in the preceding verses, which are linked together with those that follow them. However, since they have been spoken orally, and a year or two passes between one verse and its predecessor, it is absolutely necessary to review briefly what we have already said about them, for they are an introduction to the verse we shall examine today, and it is impossible to understand what is meant without first presenting what came before."

24. There are, however, certain advantages of an outside preacher with an

established reputation. See the formulation by Harry Stout in *The New England Soul: Preaching and Religious Culture in Colonial New England* (Oxford, 1986), 193, about the unique dynamic of Whitefield's career as "itinerant evangelist": "The itinerant speaker—neither employed by nor in authority over a particular congregation—was freed to establish a special rapport with his audience that dramatically altered the flow of authority in public communications."

25. See the discussion in *Jewish Preaching,* 18–24.

26. Note the statement made by Evelyn Simpson about Morteira's London contemporary, John Donne. "He never read his sermons, but neither did he preach extempore. He prepared his sermons very carefully, made voluminous notes, and then committed the whole discourse to memory." *John Donne's Sermons on the Psalms and Gospels* (Berkeley, 1963), 6. A similar statement is made by John Chamberlain, in *Increase and Multiply: Arts-of-Discourse Procedure in the Preaching of Donne* (Chapel Hill, N.C., 1976), 115–116. On Puritan preachers in New England, see *Salvation in New England,* ed. Phyllis Jones and Nicholas Jones (Austin, 1977), 17: "The use of manuscript in the pulpit was strongly discouraged by both Puritan and courtly audiences. . . . Such a formal degree of preparation—writing an exact copy and memorizing it for delivery—was in general reserved for infrequent and important state occasions. . . . Ordinarily, the preacher memorized not a fully written copy of his sermon but a much briefer outline of its major arguments, topics, and texts, which he called notes." Morteira's manuscripts show that what was unusual for the Puritan preachers was his regular pattern.

27. Much of the manuscript's first page is illegible from the microfilm because of ink showing through from the other side, and could not be used when this article was written. I have since deciphered the page from the actual manuscript in Budapest. Nothing in that material affects the following presentation; I hope to publish the Hebrew text of the entire sermon elsewhere.

28. All references to the sermon are to Budapest Rabbinical Seminary Hebrew MS 12, vol. 3, folios 95r–96v, on Exodus 21:8 of *Mishpatim.*

29. The major source for these events is the account in the anonymous *Ḥorvot Yerushalayim,* published at Venice, which had become a center for the gathering of financial aid, in 1631. See the recent edition edited and annotated by Minna Rozen (Tel Aviv, 1981), 50–67, for the editor's review of the events, including a table for all exactions paid by the community and its leaders. See also Avraham Ya'ari, *Sheluḥei Erets Yisra'el* (Jerusalem, 1977), 263–270; idem, *A Goodly Heritage* (Jerusalem, 1958), 11–17; Yitzhak Ben-Tzvi, *Erets Yisra'el ve-Yishuvah bi-Ymei ha-Shilton ha-Ottomanit* (Jerusalem, 1976), 220–225; S. W. Baron, *Social and Religious History of the Jews* (New York, 1983): 18:157.

30. The circumstances of the setting is surmised from internal evidence in the manuscript. That it was a gathering of the three congregations is implied by Morteira's reference to "the leaders of these congregations" (below). That a report had previously been read is suggested by Morteira's reference near the beginning of his sermon to "these tribulations that befell [the inhabitants of?] Jerusalem," without specifying any. A few moments later, he speaks of tailoring his message to the limited time he has available at the present occasion. From external sources, we know that the decision by the representatives of the three congregations was taken on February 7, 1627 (below, n. 47), a Sunday, the beginning of the week in which the lesson *Mishpatim* would have been read. The special gathering could have been held any day of that week, including on the Sabbath, February 13.

31. On the background of this form, see *Jewish Preaching,* 66–69; on Morteira's use of these in his sermons, see "*Your Voice Like a Ram's Horn,*" 107–126.

32. Note that the introduction to *Ḥorvot Yerushalayim* is devoted to a detailed defense of the community leaders' decision to remain in Jerusalem during the period of oppression, against "those who say it would have been better to leave Jerusalem" (78). Minna Rozen, the editor, wrote, "there are grounds to assume that after ibn Farukh was deposed, powerful voices from the Diaspora continued to complain about the continuation of the settlement in Jerusalem," impelling the author to his response (69). Morteira's sermon provides evidence for, and an initial response to, such questions raised in the Diaspora. While most of the arguments in *Ḥorvot Yerushalayim* explain the decision to remain in practical terms, some of them are more ideological (68–70, 79–86).

In the present context, I can only raise an issue that deserves fuller exploration: the relationship between the position attested by Morteira, and his refutation of it, and the little book entitled *Sefat Emet* published at Amsterdam in 1707 by Moses Hagiz. Hagiz sets out to refute very similar views that he has heard in Amsterdam: "These verses teach, in their view, that it is not God's will that the Jewish people dwell in those 'lands of the living' until He gathers in our dispersed," or even more extreme, "Now that God has abandoned that good land, the people that dwell in it are prostrate under the burden of their sins, and God considers their dwelling in that land to be a sin" (*Sefat Emet,* [Jerusalem 1881], 10b, 6b; [Jerusalem, 1987], 30, 22). Hagiz cites additional statements indicating a full ideology of Diaspora living, rejecting any essential difference between the land of Israel and the Diaspora at present, considering any city in which Jews are well treated and allowed to prosper as equivalent to Jerusalem, and rejecting any need for concern over the suffering of Jerusalem. In response, he denounces those who hold such views as ignorant or heretical, claiming their true motivation is to justify a life free from the yoke of Torah. Like Morteira later in his sermon, he not only refutes the biblical argument, but explains why those living in the land of Israel suffer so greatly. Did the views cited by Morteira become radicalized over the following eighty years, or did he decide on this occasion to respond only to the moderate form, and to present them in the most charitable way? For the context of Hagiz's book, see Elisheva Carlebach, *The Pursuit of Heresy* (New York, 1990), 58–63.

33. A sermon delivered on Sabbath of Repentance in 1641 is built upon this verse: MS 3:237r and following. Listeners may have remembered a similar theme from a sermon delivered in 1623 entitled "Despicable and Vile," stating, "it is a severe punishment to be given over into the hands of a person who is vile and despicable" (MS 4:65v). Both of them treat Christianity with the discourse of contempt.

34. For the association between "jackals" (or perhaps "foxes": *shu'alim*) and Egyptians, see Lamentations Rabbah and Rashi on Song 2:15. Morteira applies the rabbinic reference to the Egyptians of antiquity to the contemporary Muslims.

35. The material in brackets was written by the author between the lines as a later addition, though presumably part of what he intended to say.

36. Jacob Zahalon, in his Preacher's Manual, wrote that "if the preacher is reproving the people, he should lower his head, [focusing] his eyes directly at the people themselves" (*A Guide for Preachers,* 144).

37. *Giv'at Sha'ul,* sermon on *Shemot;* see annotated translation and introduction in my *Jewish Preaching,* 270–285.

38. See the review of events with bibliography in "*Your Voice Like a Ram's Horn,*" 373–374.

39. See Jonathan Israel, "The Changing Role of the Dutch Sephardim in International Trade, 1595–1715," in *Dutch Jewish History* 1 (1984), 35–37, summarizing his more detailed earlier studies (see footnotes 6 and 12).

40. See Ya'ari, *Sheluḥei Erets Yisra'el,* 262; cf. *A Goodly Heritage,* 12: "It was reported in all countries that we were dwelling in peace and security."

41. Cf. Baron, *SRHJ,* 18:161–162. Baron twice uses the phrase "chaotic conditions" to describe the circumstances in Jerusalem (162, 163).

42. The reference to "these congregations" probably indicates that all three congregations met together for the special occasion on which this sermon was delivered. The last five Hebrew words of this section translate, "Here this matter should be developed at length;" they were probably written by Morteira when he temporarily left off writing the text of his sermon as a reminder to himself of how he intended to continue. Indeed, the following paragraph, which appears to be

written with a somewhat finer pen point, goes on to specify the uniqueness of Amsterdam.

43. Full annotation for this rich passage cannot be attempted here because of space considerations.

44. The reference to "paintings" alludes to the use of artwork to decorate the homes, a practice about which Morteira seems to have felt some ambivalence. Cf. "*Your Voice Like a Ram's Horn,*" 416, including n. 20.

45. Cf. the use of this verse in the same context in the earlier sermon, "The People's Envy," *Jewish Preaching,* 282.

46. *Ḥaluqa de-rabbanan,* literally: "robe of the sages." This refers to the garment worn by the righteous in the world to come (see Zohar 1:66a). Morteira referred to this kabbalistic term on other occasions in his sermons: cf MS 2:239r bottom.

47. The decision made by fifteen lay leaders on February 7, 1627 was to borrow 1800 florins from the Dowry Fund in order to send a total of 2400 florins to "our brothers dwelling in Jerusalem." Ya'ari, *Sheluḥei Eretz Yisra'el,* 265, citing Brugmans and Frank, *Geschiedenis der Joden in Nederland* (Amsterdam, 1940), 254. Cf. Isaac Emanuel, "Tsiyyuan shel Qehillot ha-Sefaradim be-Amsterdam u-ve-Curaçao la-Arets ha-Qedoshah u-li-Tsefat," *Sefunot* 6 (1962), 413 n. 2, providing the reference in "Libro dos Termos da Ymposta da Naçao," fol. 19b.

48. This recourse to the theme-verse at the very end of the discourse, rather than as a structuring element, seems to be characteristic especially of Morteira's eulogies. See "*Your Voice Like a Ram's Horn,*" 385, 397, 433. The sermon is thus framed through the rhetorical device of *chiasmus:* theme-verse then rabbinic dictum at the beginning, dictum then theme-verse at the end.

49. Cf. the report of a young man's memory of Ezekiel Landau's voice at the beginning of a eulogy, cited in *Jewish Preaching,* 360; or Zalman Shazar's recollection of the Maggid of Minsk in *Morning Stars* (Philadelphia, 1967), 67–68; or Vladimir Jabotinsky's statement that, after many years, he "could still hear [Herzl's] voice ringing in my ears as he took the oath [at the Sixth World Zionist Congress], *im eshkaḥekh Yerushalayim tishkaḥ yemini*" (cited in Shmuel Katz, *Lone Wolf,* 2 vols. [New York, 1996], 53). An analogy from American experience would be the memory of Martin Luther King's "I have a dream" peroration.

50. I am grateful to my colleague Nancy Berg for her careful reading of a draft of this article and for her perceptive suggestions to improve it.

EIGHT

From East to West: Translating Y. L. Perets in Early Twentieth-Century Germany

JEFFREY GROSSMAN

I

Yiddish literature today is available to most of its readers only in translation, and however much one may wish it were otherwise, this is likely to remain the case in the near and more distant future. While there are various ways professional readers of Yiddish literature can respond to this situation, among them nostalgia and denial, one response, recognized by translators of Yiddish literature, at least in their capacity as translators, consists in taking problems of translating Yiddish literature seriously and, consequently, taking seriously the question of how translated Yiddish works function for an audience that cannot read the works in Yiddish.

This essay seeks to respond to the current situation of Yiddish by providing a case study focusing on how the writer Y. L. Perets was translated into German at the beginning of the twentieth century.[1] One could no doubt also consider how Perets (and other Yiddish writers, for that matter) has been translated into other languages — English, Hebrew, French, Russian, etc.—but for various reasons, including the fact that German is my main area of research, the German context will be considered here. Since Y. L. Perets occupied a central position in modern Eastern European Jewish culture, the focus of his work seems appropriate for a case study of this kind.

There are other reasons for considering the early twentieth-century German context. That context, for instance, resembles the current situation in the United States and other parts of the English-speaking world, and much of Europe, insofar as many (not all) readers of Yiddish literature consisted of Jews who, as the descendants of Yiddish-speakers, had become secularized and acculturated to German culture. These readers often bore a complex relationship to the Yiddish-speaking world, which appeared at once related to them on one level and utterly foreign on another. The differences between the German context at the beginning of the twentieth century, when Yiddish literature was still in its early stage, and the present context, marked as it is by the awareness of a once-thriving modern, secular Yiddish literature, which was annihilated in Europe and has declined in the United States from its once vibrant life, are considerable, but those differences only heighten the need for comparative study of other contexts where Yiddish was transmitted to non-Yiddish-speaking readers.

In Germany, from the Enlightenment to the twentieth century, the dominant image of the Yiddish language was a negative one. Moses Mendelssohn's oft-cited remark that "the Yiddish language has contributed not a little to the immorality of the common man; and I expect a very good effect on my brothers from the increasing use of the pure German idiom" was symptomatic of attitudes prevalent in late eighteenth-century Germany and served as a model for Jewish adherents of the Enlightenment.[2] It was an image held, moreover, by a wide range of observers, Jewish and non-Jewish, who otherwise differed considerably in their own notions about the nature of Jews and Jewish life in Germany and Europe overall.[3] In Eastern Europe where, as in Germany, Moses Mendelssohn served as a model for Jewish adherents of the Enlightenment, the early negative image of the Yiddish language ultimately underwent a transformation. Writers like Sholem Abramovitsh (writing under the name of Mendele Moicher Sforim) and Y. L. Perets ultimately recuperated and transformed the Yiddish language by the late nineteenth century, thus transvaluing Yiddish into an aesthetically and intellectually legitimate language of Eastern European Jewish culture.[4] In Germany, though, the language came to signify that which most Jews and non-Jews by the late nineteenth century felt Jews needed to escape—the "backward" culture of the "ghetto" or autonomous society in which the vast majority of European Jews, east and west, had lived until the onset of Jewish emancipation around 1780 in the German-speaking lands. While many German Jews, and especially German Jewish intellectuals and economic elites tended to shun the Yiddish language, antisemites exploited it as a way to reveal the purportedly "culturally inferior" otherness of Jews and, often, to mock the aspirations of German Jews to acquire German culture.[5]

When Perets's translators first began to translate his stories, they found themselves in need of strategies that would do more than introduce a prominent writer from a minor or even obscure literature into one of the dominant cultures of western Europe. They needed, in addition, to overcome the negative valence that attached to Yiddish, which suffered at once from stigmatization and lack of institutional support. Unlike other literatures, large or small, Yiddish lacked a long and established secular literary tradition, a university base like Oxford or the Humboldt University, with its apparatus of chaired professors, research assistants, doctoral candidates and librarians; it lacked a state and the accompanying academies that provide an added institutional framework for supporting the national literature—factors, in other words, that can and do help elevate the status of a culture, or a writer considered "representative," whether at home or abroad or both.[6]

Despite the absence of an established Yiddish literary institution, certain conditions in Germany were conducive to the transmission of a Yiddish writer like Perets at the turn of the century. The influx of East European Jews to Germany as the result of pogroms and economic plight in Eastern Europe beginning in the late nineteenth century raised for German Jews the need to become more familiar with East European Jewish culture. The same period witnessed the arrival in Germany of neo-romantic literary and cultural forms. For all their differences, the George-Kreis, the poetry of Rilke and Hofmannsthal, the essays of Paul de Lagarde and Julius Langbehn's *Rembrandt als Erzieher*, all expressed disenchantment with modern industrialized society and technology, seeking refuge in a cultural realm removed from the constraints of *Gesellschaft* and, often presented in mystical or quasi-mystical terms. The same tendencies, frequently called anti-modern, but indeed symptomatic of one strand of modern literary culture, aided the positive reception of Martin Buber's rewritings of Hasidic tales. It remains to ask whether and to what degree such factors influence the translation and reception of Y. L. Perets's stories.

Perets's German-language translators included two of the more central proponents of Yiddish culture generally, the Yiddish literary critic Isidor Elyashev (1873–1924), better known by the pseudonym Baal Makhshoves,[7] and Nathan Birnbaum (1864–1937), who wrote under the pseudonym Matthias Acher and became one of the principal organizers of the 1908 Czernovitz Conference on Yiddish where Yiddish was declared a national language of the Jewish people.[8] A third translator of Perets was a Jew from Russia named Alexander Eliasberg (1878–1924), a scholar of Russian literature who translated Dostoevsky, Tolstoy, Pushkin, Czechov and Turgenev, among others, into German. Eliasberg's was one of five names to appear on the title page of a journal, *Neue Jüdische Monatshefte* (1916–1919), which served as an organ of the *Komittee für den Osten* (Committee for the East), a German Jewish organization that came into existence during the First World War and sought to form an alliance between German and East European Jewry. The committee and its journal formed an anomaly in that they managed to bring together both moderate Zionists, like Adolf Friedemann and Franz Oppenheimer, and opponents of Zionism like the neo-Kantian Hermann Cohen and Eugen Fuchs, chairman of the *Centralverein deutscher Staatsbürger jüdischen Glaubens.* Like *Ost und West* (1901–1923), a diaspora national Jewish magazine which published the work of Nathan Birnbaum and Baal Makhshoves, *Neue Jüdische Monatshefte* sought to mediate East European Jewish culture, including Yiddish literature, to a German-speaking audience.[9] Unlike *Ost und West,* the magazine accepted a Jewish national definition only for East European Jewry. Many of its articles nonetheless revealed how the confrontation with East European Jewish culture during the war produced for many liberal German Jews a sense of Jewishness that went beyond mere religious affiliation.[10]

II

This essay focuses mainly on the translations published in these journals or produced by these translators, the most prolific and influential translators of Yiddish literature in the early twentieth-century German context. By focusing on several translations of stories by Perets, it seeks to disclose the different strategies Perets's translators employed as they rewrote his work to make it accord with their own ideologies regarding the place of Jews in German and European society, and with their own poetics regarding how the work of a leading Yiddish writer should appear to his German-reading audience.

Rewriting, a term proposed by the late André Lefevere, may consist of translations, anthologies, editor's introductions, literary histories, criticism, reviews and so forth. Rewritings "are designed to adapt works of literature to a given audience and/or to influence the way in which readers read a work of literature."[11] Rewriters tend to adapt literary works in the service of an ideology or poetics or both, or by seeking a compromise between the ideologies and poetics of the source text and the target literary and cultural system.[12] Ideology, here, is defined non-pejoratively and resembles a "system of beliefs," but differs from traditional rational views that such systems are well-articulated, and includes the notion that ideology exhibits "affective, unconscious, mythical or symbolic dimensions" which constitute human beings as subjects and color how one views and interacts with the world.[13] The strategy of translation may result from a sense of ideological necessity, as when the nineteenth-century German writer Karl Gutzkow edited out many passages of Georg Büchner's play *Danton's Tod* (*Danton's Death*) to have it approved by censors.[14] Or, a rewriter may seek to introduce an ideologically charged innovation in the target culture. When, for instance, Jewish translators, under the influence of monotheistic Islamic philosophy in the Middle Ages, began for the first time to translate Greek philosophy into Hebrew, their "extension of Hebrew into entirely new fields of discourse had to offer these subjects a certain aura of legitimacy, in the eyes of their advocates; even as the critics of philosophy had to be distributed by what for them was a profanation of the Holy tongue."[15]

Authors, moreover, whom Maimonides "did not favor . . . either were not translated, or were translated at a relatively late date."[16]

The aspect of poetics most applicable in this essay refers to what can be called the functional aspect, that is, the "concept of what the role of literature is, or should be, in the social system as a whole."[17] German Romantic poets and critics asserted that poetry should express the spiritual unity of the people and thus proceeded to collect chapbooks and folksongs like *Des Knaben Wunderhorn* (1805–08). The English Romantic poets Wordsworth and Coleridge prefaced *Lyrical Ballads* with the claim that it was written, as poetry should be, in the "real language of men in a state of vivid sensation."[18] Socialist Realism, on the other hand, maintained that literature should serve the revolution or, as the case may be, the socialist state, while deconstruction, as practiced by Paul de Man, argued that what counts as literature are texts that "unsay" that which they purport to say.

III

Ost und West promoted Perets's work from the outset, but it also helped rewrite Perets and Yiddish literature, a rewriting suggested by the editors' early programmatic statements. The editors of *Ost und West* claimed to detect the emergence of a "specific Jewish cultural nuance"[19] and sought to integrate Jewish culture with modern tendencies in art and literature as part of a program to develop a pan-Jewish diaspora national culture. In pursuit of this program, they would enlist, or to paraphrase Michel de Certeau, "poach" upon Eastern Jewish literature and culture. Thus, one article proclaimed a central aim of *Ost und West* to be the "building of bridges between the Jewish East and Western Jewry."[20] The same article was framed by the title "The Transformation of Russian Jewry" placed above four pictures depicting four generations of Russian Jews, each increasingly modern and more secular in appearance. The same first year issue of the magazine published a translation, from the Hebrew, of Perets's popular story "Four Testaments," depicting the spiritual and moral decay of four generations of Jews as they become increasingly secularized in the modern period, a contrast producing a complex set of signs, calculated, it would appear, to provoke

Western Jews into simultaneously recognizing the modernity of Russian Jewry and the dangers of assimilation.[21] The publication of this article and story point to the ways that *Ost und West* sought to provide a framework for reading Yiddish literature in Germany.

The different translations of Perets's work attest to the diverse ways in which German-language translators read Perets and, at the same time, reveal the role that ideology played in such translations. Consider how translators rewrote the first line of Perets's "Mekubolim" ("Kabbalists"), an ironic story about the two last remaining mystics of a small town, one of whom is the old head of a once esteemed yeshiva, the other his last pupil. The story describes how the impoverished mystics, reduced to hunger, each compete to be the more pious.[22] The opening line of "Mekubolim" consists of Perets's own rewriting of a popular Yiddish proverb, *Toyre iz di beste skhoyre* ("Torah"—in the broad sense refering to the study of biblical and talmudic teachings—"is the best merchandise"), in a phrase ("in shlekhte tsaytn falt afile toyre—di beste skhoyre—oykh" ["in bad times even Torah— the best merchandise—falls, too"]) that appropriates the proverb as an element of Yiddish folk culture and transforms it into a comment on the contemporary state of East European Jewish society undergoing economic and spiritual decay in its small towns.[23] The kabbalist rabbi of the story himself becomes the central image of this decadence when he seeks to diminish the achievement of his deceased student whose fasting had apparently raised him to the highest level of piety where one hears disembodied music. The rabbi remarks: "only several more days [of fasting] . . . and he would have died under the kiss of God," thus revealing his own envy and rendering ironic the piety of one whose lessons on the highest state of spirituality the student had presumably put into practice.

"Mekubolim" appeared probably for the first time in German in a translation by Albert Katz already in 1895 under a changed title, "David und Jonathan," which obscured somewhat the reference to Kabbalah, a not unsurprising change since the story appeared in the *Allgemeine Zeitung des Judentums,* the central organ of liberal German Jewry, for whom Kabbalah, much like the Yiddish language, had in the nineteenth century frequently represented something of a disinherited tradition.[24] At the same time, the story's ironic, though not hostile, treatment of its subject enabled the *Allge-*

meine Zeitung des Judentums to find a place for a Yiddish writer's work in its pages. In the next quarter of a century, at least four more translations of "Mekubolim" appeared and the five different translations of the first sentence, alone, suggest how different translators sought to rewrite the story according to different cultural and ideological frameworks.

> Die Zeit, in der talmudische Gelehrsamkeit bei den Juden hoch im Kurse stand, ist längst vorüber. (The time when talmudic learning had a high rate of exchange among Jews is long past.)[25]

> In schlechten Zeiten verliert auch die Lehre Gottes—bekanntlich die beste Ware—ihren Wert. (In bad times, even the teachings of God—known to be the best commodity—lose their value.)[26]

> In schlechten Zeiten fällt selbst die Torah, unser höchstes Gut, im Werte. (In bad times, even the Torah, our greatest possession, falls in value.)[27]

> In schlechten Zeiten sinkt sogar die beste Ware—die göttliche Wissenschaft—im Werte. (In bad times, even the best commodity—the divine science—sinks in value.)[28]

> In schlechten Zeiten sinkt sogar der Wert der besten ware, der Thora. (In bad times, even the value of the best commodity, the Torah, sinks.)[29]

The advent of deconstruction and "discovery" in English (through translation) of Mikhail Bakhtin's theories of discourse have prompted professional readers of literature to emphasize the multivalence or polyphony of the poetic text. A brief survey made 70 years ago of how translators translated a single text over a quarter of a century would have had no trouble making a similar point. At least one of the translators, Alexander Eliasberg, was himself aware of the text's multivalence and proceeded, consequently, to rewrite it in different ways for different audiences. When he translated "Mekubolim" for an illustrated volume published by the Verlag für jüdische Kunst und Kultur (Publishing House for Jewish Art and Culture) and thereby targeting a Jewish audience, Eliasberg simply retained the word "Torah." The title of the volume, *Musikalische Novellen,* points, moreover, less to the story's ironic treatment of Hasidism than to the text's emphasis on the spirituality of music. In another version, published in a small, easily affordable volume with a mainstream publisher, Insel Verlag, probably around 1920, Eliasberg translated the word "Torah" as "göttliche Wissenschaft," thereby investing Torah with the secular authority of modern science or scholarship, while simultaneously reading East European Jewish culture and Kabbalah in terms of the German *Wissenschaft des Judentums,* which had tended historically to view its achievement as culturally surpassing, and at times in opposition to, precisely those forms of Jewish exisence that the story depicts, like Kabbalah and traditional Jewish rabbinic authority.[30]

The different translations of this sentence, moreover, provide a key to the different positions the translators take toward the place of Jews in Germany and Europe, while simultaneously revealing how they seek to appropriate Perets's story for their positions.[31] Nathan Birnbaum translates "Toyre" as "die Lehre Gottes," a reading closest to that of Jews, secular or religious, who had a traditional East European Jewish education. Birnbaum proceeds throughout this translation, as in other stories that he translated for the same volume, to retain as frequently as possible the Yiddish term and explain it with a footnote.[32] He retains yeshiva (transliterated: "Jeschiwe"), describing it in a footnote as "Höhere Talmudschule," whereas Albert Katz transliterates the plural form of the same word as "Jeschiboth," an orthography that accepts the norms of transliteration used in nineteenth-century German scholarship, but which fully disregards contemporary Askhenazic pronunciation in Hebrew and Yiddish. He thus diminishes the foreignness of the text, but at the cost of effacing elements of contemporary Jewish culture that could be easily preserved in the German.[33] Katz places the term in quotation marks and immediately provides a translation, *Talmudschule,* in parenthesis, while Zlocisti omits the Hebraic term altogether, writing simply "Talmudlehrhaus." In the Insel Verlag version, Eliasberg includes "Jeschiwe" which he explains in a footnote, but which he leaves unexplained in the version for a Jewish audience.[34]

Again, the different uses translators make of footnotes reveals a different orientation toward the relationship between text and audience. Unlike Eliasberg, who retains some Hebraic and Yiddish terms, particularly if they are of a high and generally religious register, like "Jeschiwe," Birnbaum also includes colloquial expressions of a middle-range register, as when he writes: "Das verarmte Städtchen hatte immer weniger und weniger Essen geschickt, immer weniger 'Täg'[2)] vergeben" ("The impoverished little town had sent less and less food, provided ever fewer 'teg'[2)]"), where the footnote explains the term "Täg," the practice by which community members provide Yeshiva students with meals on various days of the week.[35] Birnbaum virtually Yiddishizes the translation, thereby producing a text suffused with incomprehensible Hebraic terms that, without the abundance of footnotes, would leave the average German reader mystified. In this way, Birnbaum enlists Perets's story in the service of a pedagogical program by which the language and social practices of Eastern Jewry become those *not* of a "foreign" people whose way of life needs to be explained, but of a more *authentic* Jewish world for German Jews to emulate. In his introduction, Birnbaum provides a defense of his translational strategy coupled with instructions on how to read the text:

> [The translator] only grudgingly decides to use footnotes which are, indeed, not really appropriate for a poetic work since they offend the eye, and what is worse, disturb the fluency and ease of poetic perception in the reader. And yet, it cannot be done otherwise, and nothing remains but to ask the reader to use these references methodically and with moderation. They should only be read the first time around and be learned well (*gut eingeprägt*) at that time, but thereafter, the pure text alone should always be enjoyed.[36]

Leaving aside the question whether the word "pure" (*rein*) properly describes Birnbaum's translated texts, or any other for that matter, it soon becomes clear that the translator intends more than to merely instruct his readers in the aesthetic pleasures of the East European Jewish milieu. Birnbaum, who was an active diaspora nationalist, public speaker and prolific journalist, hoped rather to convey what he considered to be the "spirit" of the East European Jewish people, as manifested in the Yiddish language, to Western Jewish readership. The key to Jewish survival, he maintained in another article, consisted in the acquisition of Yiddish, which he considered, without elaborating precisely how or why, to be a language "spiritually familiar" *even* for the non-Yiddish-speaking Jews of Western Europe.[37]

Perets's own neo-romantic interest in Hasidism indeed coincided with similar interests among German Jews (and non-Jews), but "neo-Romanticism" and "Hasidism" can nonetheless mean different things for different readers and (re)writers, as shown by the way Perets's story "Tsvishn tsvey berg" was translated.

IV

Perets's story, "Tsvishn tsvey berg" ("Between Two Mountains") centers on the conflict between an anti-Hasidic Mitnaged or ultraorthodox rabbi, called the Brisker Rov in Yiddish and simply "der Rabbi" in German, and his former prize pupil who flees the Rov's tutelage to become ultimately a revered Hasidic Rebbe, or zaddik, as he is called in the German version. Perets included "Tsvishn tsvey berg" in a collection he published entitled *Khsidish,* and like "Mekubolim," the story continues to occupy a central position in the Perets and Yiddish canon.[38] One of Perets's more important early attempts to represent Hasidism for a modern, non-traditional readership, the Yiddish version of the story focuses on the conflict mentioned above, but the overall thrust of the German translation is to reduce conflict and opposition between the Hasidim and the Mitnagdim, and between the worlds of Eastern and Western Jewry, while inserting numerous allusions meant to encourage identification with the Jewish *Volk.*

Perets's narrative strategy consists in using a first person narrator to convey, through testimony, his experience of the power of Hasidism, a device that enables the narrator to speak subjectively but in a voice familiar to a non-Hasidic Yiddish-speaking audience, thus investing the story with the credibility of the modern witness who employs the same language (or discourse) as his audience to mediate the image of Hasidism.[39] The German translation presents an additional stage in the mediation that seeks to represent Hasidism, but it now seeks to represent Hasidism and the literature of East European Jewry in ways that will make them more acceptable to a German readership. The anonymous translator excises or alters numerous passages that would only confirm the predominantly negative image of East European Jewry—passages, for instance, that refer to practices or events involving money and wealth.

When the German narrator describes the ability of Reb Yekhiel, the wealthy admirer of the zaddik, to find able scholars who would marry his daughters, in German he omits the Yiddish narrator's observation that Reb Yekhiel also provided the groom with "thousands of ducats" to do so.[40] When the Yiddish narrator describes Reb Yekhiel in hyperbolic, pejorative Yiddish as a "wealthy man, a rich man old and [established and] loaded with money (*an oysher, a fartsaytisher ongeshtopter oysher*)," the German text transforms him into a figure of emulation. Reb Yekhiel becomes "honest and upright (*bieder[. . .] und brav[. . .]*)," not to mention very pious, thereby acquiring attributes that appear nowhere in the Yiddish text.[41] Similarly, when the German version describes the "unsparing and merciless" Brisker Rov's persecution of the Hasidim, the Rov may still excommunicate Hasidim, but he becomes, in practice, somewhat less "merciless" and "unsparing" and thus no longer has "the beard of one caught reading a Kabbalistic text shaved off by gentiles," as he does in the Yiddish version, since having gentiles forcibly shave off another Jew's beard transgresses norms of civility that the German Jewish translator would like to show other Jews, and particularly eminent rabbis from Eastern Europe, engaging in.[42] Such acts would, if read in a certain light, only confirm the negative stereotypes of East European Jewish culture as "backward." At a time when the rising tide of East European Jewish immigration in Germany was threatened by xenophobic opponents, the translator appears to have found such passages detrimental to their cause and, particularly, to the task of building bridges between the Jews of East and West.[43]

The translator's tendency to excise passages that fail to conform ideologically to a certain image of East European Jews contributes to one of the German translator's larger strategies: that of collapsing differences between diverse Jewish groups and presenting an image of a unified Jewish *Volk*. Reducing the Rov's inhumanity is one way to achieve this collapse.[44] Another is to describe the Hasidic Rebbe and Mitnagdic Rov in terms that reveal them to have similar qualities, something that the German text achieves where Perets's Yiddish source does not even try. The translation of Hebraic or Aramaic terms (referred to in Yiddish as *loshn koydesh* or "holy language") particularly lends itself to such rewritings. The large component of Yiddish vocabulary, which derives from Middle High German or modern

German is frequently, if not always, cognate with modern German and is employed more commonly in the discourse of more mundane realms of life.[45] The small Hebrew-Aramaic component tends to occupy a higher register and to occur more in the discourse of religious study or intellectual writings specific to Jewish life.[46] Translating such terms thus highlights what has been called the *cultural turn* in translation, that is, the need to translate the *cultural* discourse more than the language of the source into that of the target culture.[47]

As suggested in the previous discussion of Birnbaum's translation, when translating Hebraic or Aramaic terms, the translator may translate the word as literally as possible or seek to replace it with a new term or metaphor that differs linguistically, but has an equivalent function in the target culture. Alternatively, the translator may retain the Hebrew or Aramaic word with or without an explanatory footnote or elaboration in the text. The translator of "Tsvishn tsvey berg" tends to eliminate the Hebrew terms altogether, seeking appropriate German replacements. One result of these changes is an acculturation of the text that integrates it into a German universe of discourse, while simultaneously achieving that collapse of difference among the opposing characters of the text. When, for instance, the Yiddish version seeks to emphasize the Brisker Rov's intellectual abilities while conveying his forceful opposition to Hasidism, we read that the Rov was by nature "noykhem ve-noyter ke-nakhash,"[48] literally "vindictive and vengeful as a serpent," an expression derived from the Talmud where it is claimed that one "who does not avenge himself and retain anger like a serpent, is no [real] scholar" and hence implying critical acumen or a "razor-sharp mind."[49] In the context of the Yiddish story, the reference turns out to be ironic since the Brisker Rov is indeed vindictive in his pursuit of the Hasidim, but ultimately shown to have an understanding of God's way inferior to that of the Rebbe. As a result, the Rov ultimately ceases his persecution of the Hasidim.

The German version omits the allusion, which most German Jewish readers would probably not have recognized, and also omits all reference to the Talmud, thus removing the expression from the discourse of religious commentary. In German, the rabbi behaves not like a serpent, but holds "scharfsinnige, haarspaltende Vorträge" ("sharp-witted, hair-splitting lectures"), while the zaddik, presented in Yiddish as a "talmid muvhak" ("excellent" or "brilliant student"), is now also described as displaying "Scharfsinn." The word *Scharfsinn* appears here probably because it was a convention in German to refer to brilliant talmudic scholars as "scharfsinnig," rather than "genial" or "hervorragend," as does the nineteenth-century Jewish historian Heinrich Graetz in his *Geschichte der Juden*.[50] *Scharfsinn* had become a term that described a peculiarly *Jewish* form of intelligence that could be combined with antisemitic images of Jewish "talmudic" casuistry.[51] The zaddik of the German story thus differs from the rabbi not by the *nature* of his intellect, which in Yiddish is never described in terms identical to that of the rabbi, but by the way he applies it. While the rabbi applies his *Scharfsinn* to observance of the law, the zaddik applies it pietistically toward improving the lot of the common people. The Yiddish text expresses this difference by using terminology that describes the depth of their different human qualities, pointing toward the different discursive rules they adhere to; in German, their intellectual qualities become two different moments within one discourse.

If the translation of Hebraic terms like "noykhem ve-noyter" and "talmid muvhak" moves opposed characters of the story discursively closer, the translation of a term like "kol yisroel" (literally, "all Israel") seeks to move the text closer to the audience by introducing the word *Volk,* which is absent from the Yiddish, and thereby emphasizing in German the importance of viewing the Jews as one people. When, for example, the future zaddik Noah dreams of being led by the Brisker Rov through a cold, inhuman crystal palace, he pleads to the rabbi: "rabbi, firt mich aroys fun danen! Ikh vil nisht zayn aleyn mit aykh! Ikh vil zayn tsuzamen mit kol yisroel!" ("Rabbi, lead me out of here. I don't want to be alone with you. I want to be together with all Israel").[52] In German, we read: "O Rabbi, ich will nicht in diesem glanzvollen Palast allein sein; ich sehne mich nach meinen Volksgenossen" ("O Rabbi, I don't want to be alone in this magnificent palace. I long for my fellow people").[53] By supplanting the Yiddish "vil zayn tsumen mit kol yisroel" ("want to be with all Israel") with "sehne mich nach meinen Volksgenossen" ("long for my people"), the translator de-emphasizes the conflict between the Brisker Rov's devotion to a cold and rational religious law and the future zaddik's desire to serve the people. Instead, it emphasizes service to *one's own* people. The term "Volksgenossen," unlike "Ganz Yisroel," which the translator uses elsewhere in the same story, signals precisely that powerful image of the *Volk,* which George L. Mosse once defined as a "third force" that had the capacity to attract adherents of the Left and the Right, Jews and non-Jews, in early twentieth-century Germany.[54] This insertion of the term "Volk" recurs throughout the translation, thus ultimately signaling an overall discursive and ideological shift in the German version, a shift that moreover integrates the story into one of the more powerful ideological trends in early twentieth-century Germany.

When, for instance, the Yiddish narrator later expresses Reb Yekhiel's attraction to the zaddik, we read: "Ikh bin aykh afile orev, az zayn harts hot getsoygn tsu a rebben vi mit tsvangen" ("I even assure you that his heart was drawn to a rebbe as with pinchers").[55] The German translator rewrites: "sein Herz zog ihn zum Zaddik, bei dem doch jedermann aus dem Volk stets Rat und Belehrung finden konnte" ("his heart drew him to the zaddik, with whom everyone from the people [*Volk*] could always find advice and instruction").[56] When Noah is told by a cart-driver to wander wherever his feet should take him, in Yiddish, he "understands and goes into exile" ("der rebbe hot farshtanen, un hot zikh gelozt in golus arayn").[57] The German narrator, in contrast, interprets the meaning of the remark by inventing a passage nowhere to be found in the Yiddish: "Noa verstand diese Weisung. Er wanderte Jahre lang herum, *das jüdische Volk in den ärmsten und unwissendsten Schichten lieben zu lernen*" (Noah understood this instruction. He roamed for years, *learning to love the Jewish people* [*Volk*] *among the poorest and most ignorant classes*).[58]

Finally, the translator rewrites the conclusion of the story, thereby inscribing the discourse of the *Volk* into the story's narrative framework at the moment of closure. On Simḥat Torah, the Brisker Rov, now indebted to the zaddik for saving his daughter's life, joins his former pupil on his balcony overlooking the shtetl as it comes alive with joy and singing in harmony with nature. The Yiddish text reads: "Un ale zingen—der himl zingt, di galgalim zingen, un di erd fun unten zingt, un di nishome fun der velt zingt . . ." ("And everyone sings—the heavens sing, the wheels [of God's throne] sing, and the earth from below sings, and the soul of the world sings").[59] The Rov imposes the strict rule of religious law, insisting on saying the afternoon prayers and thereby shattering the image. David Roskies has suggested that most readers found in Perets's story of Simḥat Torah a celebration of Judaism's "universal appeal . . . : music, joy, nature, unity."[60] The German translator offers an alternative reading. He rewrites "di nishome fun der velt" to read "die Volkseele."[61] The German Perets story thus presents Hasidic life as the way into the "soul of the *people*" rather than "of the world."

The Yiddish Perets, with his own neo-Romantic views and concern for the survival of the Jewish people, sought a going back to the people, but with a broad modernist and internationalist perspective. In German, Perets becomes closely associated with German "völkisch" ideology, which also explains why the translator found it necessary to produce a more humane Brisker Rov, moving him and his adherents in the process closer to the Hasidim.[62]

V

The translational problems raised and strategies employed here are not an isolated instance. Like the term "kol yisroel," the Yiddish word "Yid," for which the apparent linguistic equivalent, "Jew," would appear unproblematic, becomes indeed much more problematic when translational issues are viewed in terms of cultural ideologies, a point revealed by the way different translators have approached the opening passage in Perets's story, "A shmues" ("A Conversation"). The story depicts the meeting one Passover of two elderly, once embattled, Hasidim, whose conversation soon turns into a dialogue on Jewish ethics, stressing the importance of empathy with one's opponents. By placing in the mouth of an elderly Hasid this universalist ethical message, which however appears only at the end of the story, Perets undermines stereotypes about traditional and modern secularized society, thereby playing ironically with readers' expectations about the relationship of Hasidism—and hence at least one strand of Jewish tradition—to the surrounding world.

"A shmues" opens with the following description:

> Es iz a varemer, emes-yom-tovdiker tog un reb Shakhne—a hoykher, darer yid, a sorid u-polit fun di alte Kotsker,—un reb Zerakh, oykh a darer, nor a kleyn-gevaksener yid, a nishar fun di alte Belzer—lozn zikh hinter der shtot, aroys shpatsirn.
>
> (It is a warm, truly festive day and Reb Shakhne—a tall, thin figure/Jew, a remnant and survivor from the old Kotsk [sect],—and Reb Zerakh—also a thin man/Jew, but small in growth, a remnant of the old Belz [sect]—go for a walk outside of town.)[63]

The word *Yid,* as in this passage, differs from the English word *Jew* or the German *Jude,* which immediately mark the person so described as belonging to a specific group, the Jews. *Yid* is generally unmarked in Yiddish and does not draw attention to the fact that the person referred to is a *Jew,* but frequently means simply "person" or "figure." The different ways translators approach and appropriate this passage thus point to the image of Perets's work (and of Yiddish literature) they sought to produce in German, whether and in what sense, for instance, that work was about Jews and what it was trying to say about their relationship to the non-Jewish world.

Alexander Eliasberg, for instance, translates *Yid* with the German *Jude:*

> An einem langen Frühlingstage, einem richtigen warmen Pessachtage, gehen Reb Schachno, ein langer, magerer Jude, der letzte Überrest der alten Kotsker Chassidim-Gemeinde, und Reb Sorach, ein ebenso magerer, doch kleingewachsener Jude, der letzte Überrest der alten Belzer' Gemeinde, vor der Stadt spazieren.
>
> (On a long Spring day, a truly warm Passover day, Reb Shakhne, a long, thin Jew, the last remnant of the old Kotsk Hasidic community, and Reb Zerakh, an equally thin Jew, though small in growth, the last of the old Belz community go for a walk outside of (literally, "before") the town.)[64]

This translation contrasts with that of Baal Makhshoves who uses the word *Gestalt* (or "figure"):

> Ein warmer, echt festlicher Pessachtag. Reb Schachno,—eine lang aufgeschlossene, spindeldürre Gestalt, einer von den wenigen noch am

> Leben gebliebenen echten Kotzkern—und Reb Sorach,—gleichfalls mager, doch klein von Wuchs, ein verwaistes Ueberbliebsel der alten, echten Belsern—machen einen gemeinsamen Spaziergang ausserhalb der Stadt.
>
> (A warm, truly festive Passover day. Reb Shakhne,—a long, langy and spindly figure, one of the few genuine Kotsk [Hasidim] remaining alive—and Reb Zerakh,—also thin, but small in growth, an orphaned remnant of the old genuine Belz [Hasidim]—take a walk together outside of town.)[65]

Eliasberg rewrites the story's opening so as to situate it immediately in a culture marked as foreign to the mainstream German audience for which it was clearly intended, since it was published by Insel Verlag in an inexpensive edition. That same volume of Perets stories bears the title *Jüdische Geschichten* (*Jewish Stories*), a title that transforms Perets from one of several important East European Jewish writers into an icon of Jewish literature, and which, in turn, transforms his idiosyncratic view of Hasidism, the subject of most stories in the volume, into the central image of Jewish life.

As the title and opening sentence suggest, Eliasberg sought in his translation to direct attention to the foreignness of the Perets stories and figures, while, at the same time, acculturating them for a German audience. Eliasberg's elegant prose, in this story as well as others, invests Perets's work with high literary status in German,[66] but he simultaneously retains a few Hebrew terms, words designating forms of literature like *Haggadah* and *Midrash,* or describing specific and frequently referred to cultural phenomena: eating Matzoh balls (*Mazzeknödel,* in German) at Passover in this story, or, in other stories, references to a *Melamed, Schoifer* or the hybrid Hebrew-German *Selichoszeit* (= *selikhestsayt,* i.e. the period when the *seliḥot* are said)—terms that Eliasberg then explains in a footnote.[67] At the didactic conclusion of the story, the translation makes clear this intention to explain the customs of a foreign people. In the Yiddish text, Reb Shakhne, citing the Kotsk Rebbe's citing of a Midrash, explains that the Rebbe "revealed the secret why one reads the Haggạdah . . . with a mournful Sinai-melody" ("hot er megola geven dem sod, farvos men leyent die hagoda . . . mit a troyerik sinay-nign").[68] Eliasberg removes the *sod* ("secret") from this sentence, supplanting it with the German *Sitte* ("custom"), thus removing the sentence from the language of mysticism and rewriting it in that of ethnology. Eliasberg's translation, in effect, announces to the reader her presence in an exotic Jewish world, but seeks further to show that this world lends itself to ethnological explanation provided by the translator who thereby moves it closer to the reader.

By establishing this tension between the presentation of an exotic, even mystifying, world and its rational explanation, the translation also effaces a central component of Perets's own reading of Hasidism. In that reading, the Kotsk Rebbe possesses unique interpretative powers that enable him to reveal a secret code of ethics embedded in Jewish religious practice. By effacing this reference to the "secret," Eliasberg undermines his own attempt to clarify the Eastern Jewish world, as represented by Perets, for a German audience, even as he presents an image of that world that challenges stereotypes of the "mysterious" world of Eastern Jewry.

If Eliasberg rewrites secrecy out of the exotic, Baal Makhshoves seeks to inscribe it in the language of his translation which, having appeared in the magazine *Ost und West,* was clearly targeted for a Jewish audience. Like Eliasberg, Baal Makhshoves retains a number of Hebraic terms; unlike Eliasberg, he includes far more terms and expressions, including those not generally found in common German-language texts on Judaism. In this way, his translational strategy resembles that of Nathan Birnbaum, but unlike Birnbaum, Baal Makhshoves eschews footnotes, often, but *not* always, providing the translation for a Hebrew expression in the text itself. He thus retains *Beit-Hamidrash* for *bes medresh* in the Yiddish text, which Eliasberg translates as German *Bethaus* ("house of prayer"); he provides no explanation for the word Haggadah, which his Jewish readers would readily understand, and retains less well-known Hebrew or Aramaic terms, like the words *tume* (impurity) and *galgalim* (wheels), and the Hebrew phrase *lo tasgir eved el adonav,* which he then translates, though in a lower register and somewhat less elegantly than Eliasberg who, however, did not provide the Hebrew.[69] In the case of *galgalim,* Baal Makhshoves provides *no* translation, whereas Eliasberg first translates the word as *Räder* (wheels), and then explains it as a reference to God's throne.

Unlike Eliasberg, Baal Makhshoves does not announce at the outset that the characters are Jews, but, instead, represents a Jewish world that accepts its culture and everyday existence as commonplace facts, even when this culture appears foreign or esoteric. By writing many Hebrew words into the text, Baal Makhshoves produces an exoticizing effect on the language itself, producing a form of German unfamiliar by 1900 even to most Jewish readers in Germany.[70] He simultaneously constructs a language composed of a Germanic and a Hebrew-Aramaic component, thereby partially replicating what Max Weinreich called the "fusion" structure of Yiddish, and producing a sound-image resonant of, but not, Yiddish.

When, for instance, in the description of the stars and heavens rejoicing over Pharaoh's death, Baal Makhshoves leaves the word "galgalim" untranslated, he allows the reader access only to the sound of the word, rendering its meaning impenetrable to all those unfamiliar with Hebrew. In contrast to Eliasberg's explanatory tendency, Baal Makhshoves seeks to transmit a sense of the power and esoteric meanings lurking in Jewish literature, while simultaneously investing Jewish life with the status of norm rather than presenting it as a special case of foreign culture, as Eliasberg did by rewriting *Yid* as Jew. Thus, where Eliasberg substitutes "customs" for *sod,* Baal Makhshoves writes "secret meaning" ("geheimen Sinn") emphasizing, unlike Perets, that the Rebbe revealed this meaning "in his reference to the Midrash" ("mit seiner Bezugnahme auf den Midrash)."[71] Baal Makhshoves's translation thereby refuses to move the text closer to him, requiring, instead, that the reader seek a deeper submergence in Jewish culture and literature. Whereas Eliasberg sought to clarify the meanings of terms, but lost much of their effect as a result, Baal Makhshoves's esoteric translation in turn recovers part of that effect, but mystifies the reader unfamiliar with Hebrew and Hasidism.

At the same time, this translation corresponds to Baal Makhshoves's attempt in an article, published in *Ost und West* not long before the translation of "A shmues," to read Perets as the Jewish *national* poet or writer *par excellence,* a role to be filled a few years later in Eastern Europe by Bialik, but never by Perets. Seeking to elevate Perets's status, Baal Makhshoves reads him as both a "sharp-eyed realist" and a "romantic," writing of and for the Jewish people.[72] He proceeds to evoke a symbol not from Yiddish or specifically Jewish culture, but from German Romanticism, the mysterious *blaue*

Blume ("blue flower"), made famous by Friedrich von Hardenberg (better known by the pseudonym Novalis), among others, in his visionary novel, *Heinrich von Ofterdingen* (1802).[73] Using this symbol, suggestive of the mysterious powers of the imagination, Baal Makhshoves links the romantic notion of poet as oracle bearing special knowledge to another invention of Romanticism, that of the national poet who embodies the spirit of the nation. Perets's simultaneous interest in contemporary ideas and in Hasidism help him fulfill his "national task, like every national poet, by bringing his people into living contact with the general ideas of a new era."[74]

Like his contemporary Nathan Birnbaum, Baal Makhshoves thus transformed Perets into the leading Jewish national poet in German by rewriting him as such. These rewritings of Perets were opposed by a critic who reviewed another Eliasberg translation of Perets stories, *Chassidische Geschichten* (Berlin, 1917), for the *Neue Jüdische Monatshefte.* The critic, Alfred Lemm, argues instead that Perets's work embodies the "Jewish-oriental quality of the soul" ("der jüdisch-orientalischen Seelenbeschaffenheit").[75] The language of what Edward Said has called "orientalism" serves here less to take "control" of Eastern Jews, than to appropriate a quality imagined as part of Eastern Jewish culture for a critique of Western society. The reviewer performs a transvaluation of the "despised Eastern Jews," to discover among them an "ethos" and "spiritual life," which can reinvigorate an increasingly soulless Western society.[76] At a time when awareness of the devastation of the First World War was on the rise, Lemm takes care to sunder this neoromantic impulse, symptomatic of the widespread disillusion in modern industrialized society which preceded the war, from "nationalist" imagery. Perets writes out of "sympathy with his fellow people [*Volksgenossen*] living under those terrible economic conditions [in Eastern Europe]," but the "religious renewal of Judaism" must not occur from any "völkisch" impulse, since, in Lemm's somewhat idealized image, "the peoples living in the European cultural sphere share too many of the same ideals of God and the world to allow for the unity of nationhood with religion."[77]

Lemm's reading of Eliasberg's rewriting of Perets, which concurs with positions voiced by Eliasberg in reviews he also apparently wrote for the *Neue Jüdische Monatshefte,* represents a response to the (diaspora) national readings of Birnbaum, Baal Makhshoves and the circle around *Ost und West,* images of Jewish life that also found their way into the more liberal *Neue Jüdische Monatshefte,* where one posthumous tribute to Hermann Cohen praised the philosopher's mind and humanity, but reproached his negation of "*völkisch* individuality," "national continuity" ["das *nationale* Forbestehen"] and "the future of Israel."[78]

VI

The translation of Perets in early twentieth-century Germany became ultimately a rewriting of Perets and the image of Eastern Jewish culture in his texts, whereby translators appropriated those aspects of his work that would generate the "Perets" most suited to their needs and ideological aims. Where the liberal Eliasberg ethnologized and clarified, Baal Makhshoves exoticized and mystified; where Eliasberg dressed Perets in elegant German of a high register and poetic style, Baal Makhshoves and Nathan Birnbaum "Yiddishized" the text to promote Jewish national-cultural renewal; and where Eliasberg sought to Germanize the text according to liberal values while integrating East European Judaism into the post-Enlightenment West European tradition of "science" (*Wissenschaft*) and "universalistic" ethics, Baal Makhshoves and Nathan Birnbaum pursued the forging of a specific Jewish cultural nuance, even as they sought to appeal to a readership increasingly focused on "modern" literary and cultural movements; and, where Perets wrote of disunity and conflict, while upholding the *pietistic* element of Hasidism, the "going back to the people," the anonymous translator of "Tsvishn tsvey berg" translated that *pietism* into a *völkisch* discourse that eliminated the image of internal conflict marking Jewish life, and Perets's work, in the nineteenth and twentieth centuries.

Yet, for all their differences, translations of Perets relate to the source texts in certain common ways relevant for understanding how translations can function in certain contexts. Recent work on translation frequently places greater emphasis on the liberty of the translator or rewriter and puts in question the primacy of originals. It is not possible here to consider all the arguments related to the issue of originals, but some of the more influential arguments can be mentioned.[79] Much writing on translation, for instance, now also rejects the notion that translations ever achieve "linguistic equivalence" with the original source texts, whose meanings are generated in specific historical and cultural contexts, and whose language thus evokes different images or "scenes" for readers across those different contexts.[80] It becomes more productive, then, to focus on how translations extend the function of the text by rewriting it for a new context, where the translation, like other kinds of rewriting, and not the "original," acquires the primary function in determining the image of the text for its readers. The critique of the original also derives not least from Walter Benjamin's essay "The Task of the Translator." For Benjamin, "a translation comes later than the original, and since the important works of world literature never find their chosen translators at the time of their origin, their translation marks their stage of continued life."[81] Translation becomes for Benjamin a transformative process that generates a new language and new text, thus producing innovation in its new context. In Susan Bassnett's words: "Translation is therefore a particularly special activity, since it enables a text to continue life in another context, and the translated text becomes an original by virtue of its continued existence in that new context."[82] Benjamin also serves as the basis for deconstruction's radical critique of the original, a critique that has influenced certain feminist approaches to translation.[83] In his essay "Des Tours de Babel," Derrida argues that all writing, all efforts to express ideas or events or experiences are ultimately translations: "the letter ceases to oppress insofar as it is no longer the exterior body or the corset of meaning. The letter also translates itself of itself, and it is in this self-relation of the sacred body that the task of the translator finds itself engaged,"[84] a formulation that no longer allows for the notion of the original.

In a somewhat different approach, André Lefevere focuses concretely on the function of translations in practice, and citing countless instances of rewritings in context, concludes "that for the reader who cannot check the translation against the original, the translation, quite simply is the original," a remark that prompted another student of translation to cast doubt on whether "the matter is as simple as that," despite his general agreement with Lefevere's approach.[85]

The problem with asserting that the translation *is* the original for the reader is not that the assertion has no validity whatsoever, but that, as Theo Hermans suggests, it does not really address the complexity of the problem. Many readers, not only naive ones, especially in places where major European languages are the first spoken language, frequently take little note of the fact that they are reading translations at all, and many teachers of the standard "Introduction to World Literature" courses offered at American universities spend little time addressing such issues, a state of affairs that would seem to confirm Lefevere's remark. Yet, for all their differences, Perets's German translators developed certain similar translational strategies for alerting the reader to the fact that the translated text was precisely that. Such was clearly the case with Nathan Birnbaum who, as a proponent of a diaspora national view of Jewry, hoped to incite readers to acquire the Yiddish language and thus inundated his translations with Hebrew-Aramaic and other Yiddish expressions, which he explained with footnotes. It was also the case, if to a lesser degree, with Alexander Eliasberg, whose translations became a means for explaining a foreign culture to a German-speaking audience. Birnbaum and Eliasberg both sought through footnotes to make the original texts and culture more accessible to their audience, and sought as well to change the audience's reading habits. The use of footnotes is significant, since, as Umberto Eco's English translator, William Weaver, noted not long ago, footnotes "are an intrusive reminder to the reader that what he is reading is not the original," which is why he and Eco "hate this" solution to translational problems, but which also suggests that the strategies for translating from Yiddish to German constantly reminded readers that they were not reading the original, a reminder apparently done by design.[86]

It remains nonetheless the case that for the German reader unable to read Yiddish texts in Yiddish, these translations, like other rewritings, became the image of Perets. More importantly, perhaps, translators appropriated Perets for their own purposes, rewriting his work according to their own image of what Yiddish literature and Perets should be for German audiences, and how they should function ideologically in that context. The translators's rewritings thus innovated, producing original texts that were not identical with those written by Perets, and their rewritings proceeded to introduce changes into the German and German Jewish cultural sphere, not only altering the image of Yiddish speakers in Germany, but also helping, by their very presence, to shape the literacy and culture of the German and German Jewish population.[87]

German translations of Perets thus acquired a dual function, operating as a primary or "original" source for German-language readers, but also serving to remind the readers that they referred back to a Yiddish source. Yet their originality or innovative effects ultimately depended on their masquerade as "faithful" translations of the Yiddish. Yiddish translations of Perets were thus in one sense, in one of their functions, "originals," but originals whose textual and social power depended on their reference to a prior "original" text that they purported to represent *in translation*.

NOTES

I would like to thank Avrom Novershtern of the Yiddish Department at the Hebrew University for his helpful comments on a draft of this article.

1. I am transliterating Perets according to the YIVO system, rather than using the more common English spelling, I. L. Peretz, since this spelling simplifies the problem of negotiating between the most common spelling in German, which is also "Perets," and the English spellings.

2. Mendelssohn, *Gesammelte Schriften* (Stuttgart, 1971), 13: 80.

3. Various studies have referred to this image: see, especially, Steven Aschheim, *Brothers and Strangers: The East European Jew in German and German Jewish Consciousness* (Madison, 1982), 8–11, 63–64; Sander Gilman, *Jewish Self-Hatred: Anti-Semitism and the Hidden Language of the Jews* (Baltimore, 1986), esp. 71–85, 102–107, 155–158, 254–258.

4. Dan Miron, *A Traveler Disguised: A Study in the Rise of Modern Yiddish Fiction in the Nineteenth Century* (New York, 1973), e.g. 60–63, 240–241, 267–268.

5. The case of the notorious antisemitic play *Unser Verkehr* (1813) by a little known playwright, K.A.B. Sessa, and featuring the popular actor Albert Wurm depicted Jews aspiring to German culture and *Bildung* (cultivation), but unable to refrain from lapsing in their speech from German into Yiddish, thereby exposing, as it were, the backward ghetto Jew "hidden" within the German Jew. A revealing

twist in this history, which shows the complexity of German and East European Jewish relations, is a story called "Esterka Regina" by the once popular, but today largely forgotten, nineteenth-century writer Karl Emil Franzos. At one point in Franzos's story, two enlightened German-acculturated Jews mock the behavior of an Eastern Jewish woman who harbors pretensions to enlightened rationalist culture, but who cannot escape the "provincial" mentality of her traditional East European upbringing. While she feigns literacy in German, she can in fact not read the alphabet, a fact that amuses the German Jews, who as already mentioned, bore the brunt of a similar joke in the earlier part of the century and could still be made the object of such derision. See "Esterka Regina" *Die Juden von Barnow* (Reinbek bei Hamburg, 1990), 164–165. *Unser Verkehr* was first performed on 13 February 1813 and published in 1814. The best account of the play and its performance Hans-Joachim Neubauer's article, "Auf Begehr/Unser Verkehr," *Antisemitismus und Jüdische Geschichte: Studien zu Ehren von Hebert A. Strauss,* ed. Rainer Erb and Michael Schmidt (Berlin, 1987), 313–327.

6. In the research of Yiddish language and literature up to the end of the nineteenth century, Novershtern notes, for instance, that the "interest of individuals did not lead to the permanent recognition of Yiddish as a field of learning in any Western university" ("From the Folk to the Academics: Study and Research of Yiddish after the Holocaust," *Encyclopedia Judaica Yearbook* [1988/9], 17).

7. Israel Isidor Elyashev, who wrote under the name Baal Makhshoves (1873–1924), was the most important Yiddish literary critic of his time; see, e.g., the entry in Zalman Rejzen, *Leksikon fun yidisher literatur, prese un filologye* (Vilna, 1927), 2: 744–766. The name appears as J. Eliaschoff in German. I am adhering to the pseudonym to avoid confusion between the names Eliasberg and Elyashev.

8. On Birnbaum, see Emanual Goldsmith, *Architects of Yiddishism at the Beginning of the Twentieth Century* (Rutherford, N.J., 1976), 99–119; and Joshua Fishman, *Ideology, Society and Language: The Odyssey of Nathan Birnbaum* (Ann Arbor, 1987); on the Czernovitz conference, see Joshua Fishman, "Attracting a Following to High-Culture Functions for a Language of Everyday Life: The Role of the Tshernovits Language Conference in the 'Rise of Yiddish,'" in *Never Say Die! A Thousand Years of Yiddish in Jewish Life and Letters,* ed. Joshua A. Fishman (The Hague, 1981), 369–394.

9. Martin Buber's *Der Jude,* of course, also played an important mediating role between east and west, but it did not publish works of fiction or poetry by Yiddish writers.

10. Aschheim, *Brothers and Strangers,* 157–169.

11. André Lefevere, "'Beyond Interpretation' Or the Business of (Re)Writing" *Comparative Literature Studies* 24, 1 (1987), 17–39, 30.

12. André Lefevere, *Translation, Rewriting and the Manipulation of Literary Frame* (London, 1992), 14.

13. Terry Eagleton, *Ideology: An Introduction* (London, 1991), 221.

14. Lefevere, *Translation,* 150–160.

15. Alfred Ivry, "Philosophical Translations from the Arabic in Hebrew during the Middle Ages," in *Recontres de Cultures dans la Philosophie Médiévale: Traductions et Traducteurs de l'Antiquité Tardine au XIV Siècle* (Louvain-la-Neuve, 1990), 167–188, esp. 173–174.

16. Ivry, "Philosophical Translations," 176.

17. Lefevere, *Translation,* 26.

18. Preface (1802) to *Lyrical Ballads,* ed. Michael Mason (London, 1992), 57.

19. *Ost und West* 1, 1 (1901), 1.

20. "Es ist eine der wesentlichsten Aufgaben unserer Zeitschrift, zwischen dem jüdischen Osten und dem westlichen Judentum Brücken zu schlagen . . . ," in "Die Transformation der russischen Juden," *Ost und West* 1, 9 (1901), 673–674. The author of the article was given by the abbreviation "B . . . d," which may refer to the historian and literary critic Simon Bernfeld who occasionally published articles in *Ost und West.*

21. Perets, "Vier Testamente," trans. A. Brümann, *Ost und West* 1, 9 (1901), 698–702.

22. Cf. David Roskies, *A Bridge of Longing: The Lost Art of Yiddish Storytelling* (Cambridge, Mass., 1995), 107–108.

23. Perets, "Mekubolim" in *Ale verk fun Y. L. Perets* (New York, 1947), 4: 20.

24. The German Jewish reception of Kabbalah is more complicated than the view Gershom Scholem once argued, as Moshe Idel has shown in his discussion of the subject. Scholars like Heinrich Graetz and Moritz Steinschneider made important contributions to the study of Kabbalah, even as they proceeded to de-value that part of Jewish tradition; see M. Idel, *Kabbalah: New Perspectives* (New Haven, 1988), 7–10.

25. Perets, "Jonathan und David," trans. Albert Katz, *Allgemeine Zeitung des* Judenthums 59 (1895), 406–408.

26. Perets, "Kabbalisten," in *Erzählungen und Skizzen,* trans. Matthias Acher [= Nathan Birnbaum] (Berlin: Jüdischer Verlag), 275–282, 275.

27. Perets, "Die Kabbalisten," trans. Theodor Zlocisti, *Ost und West* 8, 8 (1908), 459–464, 459.

28. Perets, "Die Kabbalisten," in *Jüdische Geschichten,* trans. Alexander Eliasberg (Leipzig: Insel Verlag, n.d. [1920?]), 11–17, 11.

29. Perets, "Die Kabbalisten," in *Musikalische Novellen,* trans. Alexander Elaisberg (Berlin: Verlag für jüdische Kunst und Kultur Fritz Gurlitt, 1920), 45–50, 45.

30. Ismar Schorsch describes the advent of German scholarship as a radical rupture in Jewish thought: "To rethink Judaism in terms of the historical canons of the German university was no less of a rupture in Jewish continuity than it had once been to rethink Judaism in terms of Greek philosophy under the impetus of Islam. " See "The Ethos of Modern Jewish Scholarship," *Leo Baeck Institute Yearbook* 35 (1990), 60.

31. It would be worth examining how the concept of translation as "rewriting" relates to Roger Chartier's use of the term "appropriation" for studying popular culture, for while Lefevere and Bassnett are concerned with the ways that translators manipulate and "take control" of texts, like Chartier, they also seek to stress the productive socio-cultural practices that translation entails. Compare, for instance, Chartier's "reformulation of the concept of appropriation" to "accentuate [. . .] plural uses and diverse understandings and diverge [. . .] from the meaning Michel Foucault gives appropriation when he holds 'the social appropriation of discourse' to be one of the primary procedures for gaining control of discourses and putting them beyond the reach of those who were denied access," and his interest in the "various uses (which are not necessarily interpretations) of discourses and models, brought back to their fundamental social and institutional determinants and lodged in the specific practices that produce them" with Susan Bassnett's discussion of Brazilian and feminist approaches to translation: "Haraldo and Augusto de Campos use translation as a way of affirming their right as Brazilians to reread and repossess canonical European literature, while the Canadian women see translation as fundamental to their existence as bilinguals and as feminists struggling against phallo/logocentric values. Both groups are concerned to find a translation practice and terminology that will convey the rupture with the dominance of the European heritage even as it is transmitted" (Susan Bassnett, *Comparative Literature: A Critical Introduction* [Oxford, 1993], 157; Roger Chartier, *Forms and Meanings: Texts, Performances, and Audiences from Codex to Computer* [Philadelphia, 1995], 89).

32. Birnbaum's translation of the story "Nilo," for instance, contains 43 explanatory footnotes in about 15 pages of largely printed text, notes explaining expressions ranging from "Jissgadal" ("yisgadal") to "Lichtbenschen" ("likht bentshen") to "Cheder" ("kheder") and so on; see Perets, *Erzählungen und Skizzen,* 157–173.

33. Perets, "Kabbalisten," trans. Birnbaum, 275; Perets, "Jonathan und David," trans. Katz, 406.

34. Perets, "Die Kabbalisten," *Jüdische Geschichten,* trans. Eliasberg, 11.

35. Perets, "Kabbalisten," trans. Birnbaum, 275.

36. "Einleitung" to Perets, *Skizzen und Erzählungen* 9–10.

37. Nathan Birnbaum, "Die Juden und das Drama," *Ausgewählte Schriften zur jüdischen Frage,* (Czernowitz: Verlag der Buchhandlung Dr. Birnbaum & Dr. Kohut, 1910), 2: 256.

38. Perets first collected a number of stories including "Mekubolim" and "Tsvishn tsvey berg" under the title *Khsidish* in *Shriften: yubileum oysgabe* (Warsaw, 1901); cf. Roskies 367, n. 15.

39. Cf. Roskies, 118–120.

40. Perets, "Tsvishn tsvey berg" in *Ale verk,* 4: 103–117, 106.

41. Perets, "Tsvishn tsvey berg," 4: 106; "Der Rabbi und der Zaddik," trans. anonymous, *Ost und West* 1, 1 (1901), 41–48, 43.

42. Perets, "Tsvishn tsvey," 4: 103; "Der Rabbi und der Zaddik," 41.

43. On East European Jewish immigrants, see Jack Wertheimer *Unwelcome Strangers: East European Jews in Imperial Germany* (New York, 1987), especially the chapters on "Public Debates over Eastern Jews" (23–41), and "Social and Cultural Tensions" among Eastern and German Jews (143–161).

44. Two other attributes of the German version, related but not central to the argument here, contribute to this collapsing of conflict and difference. First is the change in the title, which in Yiddish suggests an unbridgeable gulf between Hasidism and Mitnagdism and is replaced in German by the connecting conjunction "und." Second, while Reb Yekhiel's son, an adherent of the Brisker Rov, remains unnamed in the Yiddish, he is given the name Jonatan in German, an attribute that makes him appear less like an abstract principle or stereotyped version of anti-Hasidism and invests him with an element of personal definition.

45. See Max Weinreich's discussion of the relationship of Yiddish and *loshn koydesh* in chapter 4 of his *Geshikhte fun der yidisher shprakh* (New York, 1973), e.g. 1:310–321; cf. Benjamin Harshav, *The Meaning of Yiddish* (Berkeley, 1990), 32–49.

46. While there is little doubt that a larger component of Yiddish derives from Germanic language, Max Weinreich cautions against seeking to fix specific percentages to the various components, suggesting that one can, at best, approximate the quantities of source languages on a local level, e.g. in a given writer's texts. The literary historian, Leo Wiener, had suggested in 1904 that 70% of Yiddish vocabu-

lary derives from German, 20% from Hebrew and Aramaic, and 10% from Slavic languages. Weinreich, *Geshikhte* 1: 37.

47. André Lefevere and Susan Bassnett, "Introduction: Proust's Grandmother and the Thousand and One Nights: The Cultural Turn in Translation Studies," in *Translation, History and Culture,* ed. Susan Bassnett and André Lefevere (London, 1990), 1–13.

48. Perets, "Tsvishn tsvey berg," 4: 103.

49. bYom 23a; I would like to thank Paul Mandel for helping me locate this reference.

50. See, for example Heinrich Graetz, *Geschichte der Juden.* 3rd rev. ed. (Leipzig, 1897), 10: 56–57.

51. The stereotype of the deceptive or casuistic Jewish intellect has often been discussed; see, e.g. Stefan Rohrbacher, *Judenbilder: Kulturgeschichte antijudischer Mythen und antisemitischer Vorurteile* (Reinbek bei Hamburg, 1991), 343–344.

52. Perets, "Tsvishn tsvey," 4: 105.

53. Perets, "Der Rabbi und der Zaddik," 42.

54. George Mosse, *Germans and Jews: The Right, the Left and the Search for a "Third Force" in Pre-Nazi Germany* (New York, 1970); see chapter 4, esp. 88, where the author comments on Martin Buber's emphasis on "the shared inner experience of the Volk as a vehicle for the transformation of modern man."

55. Perets, "Tsvishn tsvey berg," 4: 106.

56. Perets, "Der Rabbi und der Zaddik," 43.

57. Perets, "Tsvishn tsvey berg," 4: 106.

58. Perets, "Der Rabbi und der Zaddik," 43; emphasis added to indicate text found in the German, but not in the Yiddish.

59. Perets, "Tsvishn tsvey berg," 4:117.

60. Roskies, *Bridge of Longing,* 22.

61. Perets, "Der Rabbi und der Zaddik," 48.

62. Contending with contemporary criticism of Perets, the Yiddish writer Hirsh Dovid Nomberg sought in his own way to recuperate the Brisker Rov, arguing that Perets "unconsciously" constructed him as a more positive "universalist" type, though Nomberg at the same time recognized that it is the Hasid who, at least ostensibly, seeks to leave the crystal palace to be among *all* the people; H. D. Nomberg, *Y. L. Perets* (Buenos Aires, 1946), 113–115.

63. Perets, "A shmues," in *Ale verk,* 4: 141–144, 141.

64. Perets, "Ein Zwiegespräch," in *Jüdische Geshichten,* 3–7, 3.

65. Perets, "Ein Pessach-Gespräch," trans. Isidor Elyashev [= Eliaschoff = Baal Makhshoves], *Ost und West* 2, 4 (1902), 263–266, 263.

66. Compare, for instance, the following passage with that of Baal Makhshoves's rendition of the same passage: "An einem Wintertage, an der Ofenbank im Bethause haben sie Frieden geschlossen, und nun gehen sie am dritten Pessachfeiertage spazieren. Am weiten, blauen Himmel strahlt die Sonne . . ." ("Ein Zwiegespräch," trans. Eliasberg, 3); "Im Beth-Ha-Midrash trafen sie sich wieder. Winters am Ofen schlossen sie Frieden mit einander und heute, zum erstenmal nach langer Zeit der Fehde, an einem der Zwischenfesttage von Pessach nutzten sie das schöne Wetter zu einem gemeinsamen Spaziergange aus" ("Ein Pessach-Gespräch," trans. Baal Makhshoves, 263).

67. The words are translated as follows: *Melamed* = "Jüdischer Kleinkindlehrer" ("Jewish teacher of small children"); *Schoifer* = "Widderhorn, das am jüdischen Neujahrstage geblasen wird (ram's horn blown on the Jewish New Year"); Selichoszeit = "Drei Tage vor dem Neujahrsfeste, an denen die Juden vor Morgengraue geweckt werden, um in den Bethäusern Selichos (Buspsalmen) zu beten" (Three days before the New Year's Holiday, when Jews are awakened before dawn in order to say *Selichot* [prayers of repentance] in the prayer house"); see Perets, *Jüdische Geschichten,* trans. A. Eliasberg, 23, 22 and 7, respectively.

68. Perets, "A shmues," 4: 144.

69. Cf.: "Du sollst den Knecht nicht seinem Herrn überantworten" (trans. Eliasberg, "Zwiegespräch," 3); "Du sollst den Sklaven seinem Herrn nicht ausliefern (trans. Baal Makhshoves, "Pessach-Gespräch," 263).

70. While some Yiddish words entered the German language, especially among German Jewish speakers, these tended to include more common everyday words like "mishpokhe" and "meshugge," though a more strongly Yiddish-inflected vocabulary was to be found among Jews from a more traditional background; see e.g. Werner Weinberg, *Die Reste des Jüdischdeutschen,* 2nd exp. ed. (Stuttgart, 1969).

71. Perets, "Pessach-Gespräch," 266.

72. J. Eliaschoff [= Elyashev = Baal Makhshoves], "Leon Perez: Ein moderner jüdischer Volksdichter," *Ost und West* 1, 4 (1901), 296–306, here 303.

73. Elyashev, "Leon Perez," 303.

74. Elyashev, "Leon Perez," 303.

75. Alfred Lemm, "Bemerkungen zu den chassidischen Geschichten des Jizchok Leib Perez," *Neue Jüdische Monatshefte: Zeitschrift für Politik, Wirtschaft und Literatur in Ost und West* 1, 17 (1917), 502–505, 503.

76. Ibid., 504–505.

77. Ibid., 504, 502.

78. M. Glückson, "Hermann Cohen und das nationale Judentum," *Neue Jüdische Monatshefte* 3, 9/12 (1919), 231–235; here 234.

79. For a more detailed account of these issues, see Edwin Gentzler, *Contemporary Translation Theories* (London, 1993), especially the section on deconstruction, 149–180, and the concluding chapter on "The Future of Translation Studies," 181–199; and S. Bassnett's comments on the status of originals and its relevance for the study of comparative literature and translation in *Comparative Literature,* 146–159.

80. Cf. Lefevere, *Translation,* 103–104.

81. Walter Benjamin, "The Task of the Translator," in *Illuminations* (London, 1973), 69–83; cited in Bassnett, *Comparative Literature,* 151.

82. Bassnet, *Comparative Literature,* 151.

83. Cf. Barbara Godard, "Theorizing Feminist Discourse/Translation," in Bassnett and Lefevere, 87–96; Bassnett, *Comparative Literature,* 156–168.

84. Jacques Derrida, "Des Tours de Babel," trans. Joseph F. Graham, in *Difference in Translation,* ed. Joseph F. Graham (Ithaca, 1985), 205; cf. Derrida's comments on 195 and 202–204.

85. Theo Hermans, "Translation between Poetics and Ideology," Review Article, *Translation and Literature* 3 (1994), 138–145, here 142.

86. William Weaver, "In Other Words: A Translator's Journal," *New York Times Book Review,* 19 November 1995, p. 16.

87. One could claim that translations of Yiddish literature had *no* impact on German and German Jewish culture only if one discounted as completely negligible the role of German Jewish magazines from the *Allgemeine Zeitung des Judentums* to *Ost und West* and *Neue Jüdische Monatshefte,* not to mention the numerous German editions of Perets, Shalom Asch, Scholem Aleichem and others. To claim that the translations of Yiddish literature had an impact is, however, not to claim that they dominated or controlled the German or German Jewish cultural scene. Readers of these works would no doubt do with them as they pleased, including subordinating them, as did the translators, to their own interests, but the Yiddish works in German translation nonetheless left their mark on the culture, and, since many of these translations are currently reprinted in Germany to meet the demands of readers, continue to do so.

NINE

The Kinnus *Project:* Wissenschaft des Judentums *and the Fashioning of a "National Culture" in Palestine*

ISRAEL BARTAL

Of all the disciplines of our literature, from every corner and angle, wherever a trace of the nation's "holy spirit" lurks, wherever a little of the creative force of its finest people resides, we must extract and fan the dying and distant flickers of them all, connect and unify them, and make them a whole in the nation's hands.

—H. N. Bialik, *from address upon the inauguration of the Hebrew University of Jerusalem, Mount Scopus, April 1, 1925*[1]

When the modern Jewish national movement awakened in the late nineteenth century, the question arose in full fury: what complexion would the Jews' future "national culture" acquire? The *kultur* question itself was not at all new: every innovative current in European Jewish society since the dawn of the Haskalah movement in the late eighteenth century had pondered it. However, the adjective "national" totally transformed the contours of the

kultur debate and endowed it with political and social implications of a new and, to that point, unfamiliar type. The urge to achieve a continuity of cultural values from the past and to apply those values to the nation's realities of life exacerbated contrasts between the divergent currents of national thinking. The question of culture gave rise to education, research, and publishing projects that stressed different aspects of the heritage, each in its distinct way; and it fused the Jewish intellectual world with the world of the new Jewish politics. For adherents of traditional society in the Ashkenazi Diaspora, the concept of "national culture" was alien and bizarre. Not until the advent of the national movements in Europe was the all-embracing world of Jewish religion—its generations and communities linked by the chain of halakhic and kabbalistic texts—defined in romantic, anachronistic terms such as these. However, even nationalist thinkers who absorbed the influences of the new currents struggled to define the all-inclusive religious world of their society of origin in terms of the new nationalism. The Haskalah heritage had divorced them from the old community's spiritual world, and the romantic nationalist return to the past was not a re-assumption of the faith—*ḥazara bi-teshuva*—but the rediscovery of an old spiritual world through new lenses. The rule in these matters—applied (for example) by a radical Jewish intellectual who for years has been disgusted with every manifestation of the "exilic" Jewish reality—was to seek "national culture" in this reality, select elements deemed worthy of preservation, and consign the rest to deep oblivion. The new "national culture" should be discovered within the old world and redeemed from its midst. Its genesis is bound up with the claim of continuity but entails an act of dislodging, change, and banishment from memory.

One of the horizons in the creation of "national culture" was the project of *kinnus* ("ingathering"), the collection, editing, and preservation of the nation's cultural creative assets. This project, like other manifestations of European nationalism, blended influences of the European Haskalah movement with the Romantic spirit. On the one hand, the project, the likes of which have occurred in many national movements, was profoundly and substantively connected with several of the most distinct manifestations of the eighteenth-century Haskalah movement: a scholarly approach that preaches the possibility of sorting and categorizing spiritual phenomena, i.e., the systematization of texts, works of art, and so on; the aspiration to create a complete encyclopedia of the fullness of human creative endeavor through the use of rational sorting principles; and the ambition to compile a "dictionary" of values and definitions for the various scholarly disciplines. By the same token, the nationalist romantics gave the *kinnus* endeavor a totally subjective complexion and linked it to the particularistic aspirations of ethnic groups.

The genesis of the modern Jewish *kinnus* endeavor, in which the aforementioned dualism was already evident, preceded the ascendancy of the modern national movement by decades. It was rooted in the dawn of *Wissenschaft des Judentums*. Leopold Zunz's programmatic lecture, "Remarks on Rabbinical Literature," delivered to the *Verein für Kultur und Wissenschaft der Juden* in 1819, already presents several of the major guidelines of the *kinnus* project, including the irresolvable dualism of the universal and the particular. The engineers of *Wissenschaft des Judentums* envisaged the gathering of material buried in prior generations' bookcases as the construction of a great monument to a past forever gone. However, their enterprise also contained a strong element of continuity. Gershom Scholem, who drew up his reckoning with the national *kinnus* movement on the twentieth anniversary of the inauguration of the Hebrew University of Jerusalem, used almost demonic terms to describe Y. L. Zunz's and M. Steinschneider's *kinnus* enterprise as an act of entombment:

> Your eyes behold giants who, for reasons known only to them, function as undertakers, embalmers, and even eulogizers, who costume themselves as dwarfs, who gather blades of grass in the fields of yore, dry them until their vitality is gone, and place them in a dubious book-grave.[2]

These scholars' *kinnus* project exuded a tremendous potential of romantic national energy—in Scholem's own words, "a seed for enthusiasm for the Jewish national values that they had inadvertently discovered."[3]

Practitioners of *Wissenschaft des Judentums* in various European countries, from France in the west to the Russian Empire in the east, initiated and carried out several segments of the great project: gathering and editing the midrashic literature, anthologizing and publishing segments of community records, copying inscriptions from tombstones, and so on. Not until the late nineteenth century, however, did these efforts—although clearly endowed with national consciousness—coalesce into a totality of political and institutional national activity. The national ideology lifted everything that had preceded nationalism from its concrete historical context and—in both senses of the *double entendre*—"nationalized" the *kinnus* enterprise of *Wissenschaft des Judentums* to mold the future. For example, the Jewish-Russian historian Simon Dubnow harnessed the great enterprise of gathering documents and papers for research on Eastern European Jewish history in order to promote a new Jewish historical consciousness. In a manifesto called *Naḥpesa ve-naḥqora* ("Let us search and investigate"—cf. Lamentations 3:40), published in three languages in the Jewish press in Russia in 1891, Dubnow urged Jews to gather their historical sources in order to study their past and develop a sense of history. In the opinion of this nationalist historian, the previous generations of *Wissenschaft des Judentums* in Germany and Galicia had probed their people's past for years, while Jews in the Russian Empire lacked a similar historical consciousness:

> Only among us, Jews of Russia and Poland, has the craving to reveal the mysteries of our history—to know what we lived, how we arrived at our present situation, and how our forebears lived during the eight hundred years since Polish Jewry began to form—not awakened, and sometimes my emotions convince me that we shall be totally bereft of a sense of history. . . .[4]

The ingathering, study, and publication of the historical material equipped this national historian with tools for his political endeavors. Dubnow, a supporter of Autonomism, derived inspiration from studying the community and committee records that he gathered, researched, and published for decades. For Dubnow, gathering different versions of the *Record of the Council of Lithuania,* editing the old text, and publishing it in Russian seemed not only a mere scholarly enterprise but the restoration of lost political material to the forefront of public debate on the future of Eastern European Jewry. In his introduction to the Hebrew edition of the *Record,* Dubnow wrote:

> To peruse and study this trove, the *Record of Lithuania,* to discover in it how the previous generations lived, and foremost, the spirit of national life that wafts from every page of the record [. . .] a whole record reminiscent of the most enlightened of collections of decisions of world parliaments has become available to us in manuscript and in various versions, urging us to explore![5]

A similar fusion — collecting various kinds of popular-level Jewish creative endeavors and integrating these works into the invigoration of a new national culture — occurred in the great collection projects of Jewish ethnographers and musicologists in the Russian empire in the years preceding World War I. These collectors, nearly all possessed by the idea of the new Jewish nationalism, carried out their collection missions in a new reality. Within a few decades, ramified and large-scale activity erupted in cultural societies, nationalist students' circles, political parties, trade unions, book publishers, and the editorial boards of newspapers and journals. Centers of new Jewish culture had coalesced in Moscow, St. Petersburg, Kiev, Vilna and Odessa, Warsaw and Berlin, and the fusion effected there occurred among Jewish students, members of the intelligentsia who lacked formal higher schooling, political functionaries, and patrons of the literary arts. The entire plan of this *kinnus* project was never set forth in clear and uniform strokes. Instead, publication was incremental: from the collection of Yiddish folk songs, edited by S. Ginsburg and P. Marek, to the Russian-language *Jewish Encyclopaedia,* to which the most prominent members of the nationalist intelligentsia in Eastern Europe contributed. These people, including the folklore researcher S. Rapoport, better known by his *nom de plume,* S. An-Ski; S. Z. Rubashov (subsequently Zalman Shazar, the third president of the State of Israel); and the musicologist and composer Joel Angel, deeply internalized the spirit of Russian populism. Their cultural worldview placed the masses at the forefront as the primary source of creative endeavor and national renewal. Political radicalism and romanticism converged in their consciousness, surfaced in various works, and produced a portrait of Jewish culture in which everything good and vital in the "old" domain, preserved among the Jewish masses in the great Eastern European Diaspora, would flow and cross into the reawakening national consciousness. However, in making the transition from the traditional Jewish context, the national material would exchange its antiquated garb and adjust to the modern world. The members of this group, although prone to disagreements about minutiae and ideological nuances, certainly agreed about a matter clear and self-evident to all champions of the national worldview: that traditional Jewish society and the society fated to evolve are, in fact, *one* society, unchanged in its basic cultural complexion. For the nationalist collectors, the organic continuity that has characterized Jewish civilization from time immemorial—the chain of halakhic endeavor and extension of the axis between the spirit of erstwhile values to that of the new national essence—is an absolute prerequisite for Jewish nationhood in the future. After all, every national culture dislodges the prenational past to invent the national future. To fulfill this concurrence of cultural continuity and change and improvement, as postulated by much of the Eastern European Jewish intelligentsia between 1880 and 1914, alternatives to the traditional channels of information transmission must be created. The *kinnus* project, inspired by the Jewish national movement, was one of these paths. Thus, various shades of Jewish cultural creative endeavor flourished shortly before World War I among Eastern European Jewry and its new offshoots in the United States and Palestine, and within this endeavor the *kinnus* project was an important avenue that linked the past to the present and the future.

One of the principal paths of the *kinnus* idea branched to Palestine and converged there with the nascent Hebrew-speaking secular culture. The idea of establishing a "spiritual center" in Palestine, as bruited by Ahad Ha'am and Bialik—a new cultural center for Diaspora Jewry—fused with the first coalescence of a new type of Jewish society in the land of the Patriarchs. The leading discussants of the question of the future culture of the Yishuv, as the community in Palestine was known, sought to link the cultural reality that had developed in the Yishuv with the heritage of the past. The impact of secularization and abandonment of the traditional social reality on the one hand, and the innovative ideologies embraced by many of the new settlers on the other, turned the changeover from traditional culture to the future national culture into a pressing issue. The spontaneous historical process enacted over the generations in transmission, selection, and canonization of texts no longer seemed to correspond with the new reality.

The masterminds of the Zionist *kinnus* project wished to intervene non-traditionally in metamorphosing the old texts into the new reality, i.e., to *create* a culture. As Bialik put it:

> The concept of "culture," in its comprehensive and pan-human sense, has now overtaken the theological concept of "torah" in the nation's consciousness. We have come to acknowledge that any people that wishes to exist without shame and disgrace must *create* a culture; not just to use it but to create it, literally to create it with its own hands, with its own tools and materials, and under its own imprimatur.[6]

The "tools and materials," according to Bialik, are the Jewish people's singular methods of creative endeavor and, indeed, its traditional creativity over the generations. These two essentials in fashioning the new national culture were supposed to relocate to the new center in Palestine in a textual "ingathering of exiles," written and oral. Here they should be re-examined with pronouncedly modern tools, cleansed of the foreign influences that had adhered to them during their generations in exile, and fused with the living, creative population carrying out the Zionist settlement enterprise.

It is no coincidence that the idea of establishing a Jewish national university, which captured several of the conceptual forebears of Zionism back in the 1880s, was associated with the *kinnus* endeavor. In Zionism, as in other national movements, academic institutions created in the context of national resurrection were given a central role in fashioning the national culture. The convergence of ostensibly objective science and the treasures of the nation's generations of creative output was to take place between the walls of academia. Some proponents of the idea of a new "spiritual center" for the Jewish people in Palestine had this in mind. Bialik maintained that a Hebrew university embracing all the humanities and the natural and social sciences, with an institute for Jewish studies as its spine, would signal the first efflorescence of this spiritual center in Palestine. In his congratulatory remarks upon the inauguration of the Hebrew University and the Institute for Jewish Studies in 1925, Bialik stressed the importance of the national university as a creator of culture:

> I prefer one small university entirely my own, made entirely by my own hand, from bottom to top, over thousands of halls of learning in which I reap the benefits but have no visible portion in their upbuilding.[7]

Bialik's remarks referred to the new Jewish cultural upbuilding on the foundations of old sources bequeathed from the past. At the Institute for Jewish Studies on Mount Scopus, Bialik thought, the old books would fuse with the new Hebrew literature and give rise to a new corpus of texts incorporating the finest of each. What Bialik did in conjunction with Yehoshua Khone Ravnitzki in *Sefer ha-Aggadah* is what he expected the university to accomplish: they re-created an old corpus and tailored it to the new era and the new reality being fashioned in Palestine. Bialik wrote and lectured extensively on the *kinnus* idea and even enumerated its five phases: a) seeking, locating, and gathering texts from the innumerable written and oral sources; b) sorting and classifying the texts; c) arranging and editing them scientifically, separating the portion fit for deep-burial and keeping that worthy of preservation for posterity; d) translating and interpreting the texts, to make them accessible to the nascent Yishuv *and* to return them to the old-new national language, Hebrew; e) publishing and disseminating the material so it may influence the new life being fashioned in Palestine. The *kinnus* project, on the magnitude and of the quality envisioned by Bialik, needed an organizational system and financial resources that would allow its practitioners to locate, copy or transfer, study, and publish the material.

Most importantly, however, these scholars were to adopt the national-culture perspective that underlies the very idea of *kinnus*. The right setting for the most effective implementation of such a massive national project, in the absence of a state and a government, was the Hebrew University on Mount Scopus. A group of Zionist creative artists and writers from Russia that relocated to Palestine after the Bolshevik Revolution and the civil war enriched the small Yishuv with top-notch research and creative talent. Among these immigrants, apart from Bialik himself, were the educator and historian Ben Zion Dinaburg (Dinur) and the author Alter Druyanov—two central figures in the *kinnus* idea and its fulfillment. Scholarly societies of pronounced nationalist complexion came into being in Palestine and became active in carrying out various parts of the enterprise.

Surprisingly, however, the Institute for Jewish Studies did not become a motive force in this field. A series of books prepared before the move to Palestine, research projects, and source anthologies — all, practically speaking, segments of this project — were brought over from Europe. Other segments were performed in Palestine in the 1920s and 1930s, but most of these efforts were made by scholarly societies, political organizations, or individuals who devoted themselves to the matter. Thus, for example, the pronouncedly Zionist effort that elicited *Sefer ha-Yishuv* — that monumental enterprise that gathered everything known about Jews in Palestine from the Arab occupation in the seventh century to the dawn of modern settlement in the late nineteenth century — was not undertaken at the Institute for Jewish Studies, although several professors at the Hebrew University, such as Shmuel Klein, were active in it. Neither Alter Druyanov's projects in gathering documents on the history of the Hibbat Tsiyyon movement and the early history of modern agrarian settlement in Palestine, nor *Sefer ha-Tsiyyonut,* conceived and initially prepared by B. Z. Dinur, were performed under the University's auspices. Why did this happen? Was it the paucity of professors who received positions at the new institution, as most of the Zionist intelligentsia made its living elsewhere? Did a dearth of funding sources make it impossible to marshal the sums needed to compile and publish anthologies of documents? Or was it the discrepancy between the secular-national *kinnus* idea and the religious and scholastic *weltanschauung* of the formative generation at the Institute for Jewish Studies? Berl Katznelson, a prominent leader and major intellectual in the Zionist Labour Movement who participated actively in the 1930s in meetings of the Hebrew University board of governors and executive committee, scathingly criticized academia's hands-off attitude toward the new reality taking shape in Palestine. Thus he explained the disengagement that, he believed, had come about between academia and the nascent national culture in Palestine. He cited the state of research and teaching of Jewish history on Mount Scopus as an example:

> The university has been growing for ten years but still does not offer a full program in Jewish history. Ancient history is not taught — out of fear of the Orthodox — and modern history is also not taught, but for

what reason? Perhaps the rabbinical seminaries and the higher institutes of *Wissenschaft des Judentums* do not consider modern Jewish history "studies"; they are not ancient enough. Hasidism and misnaggedism, the Haskalah, the Emancipation, assimilation, Hibbat Tsiyyon, socialism, the decline of erstwhile Jewish centers and the ascendancy of new ones — for the masters of *Wissenschaft des Judentums,* all of these express nothing but journalistic grist and living for the moment. However, for a Hebrew university meant to bring forth not only scholars of antiquities but also enlightened Jews who are active in their people's life, this is a matter of the utmost importance. In no nation and language can one imagine a national intelligentsia that is not lavishly versed in the life of the past few generations.[8]

In other words, the tradition of the rabbinical seminaries in Germany, which relocated to Mount Scopus and left its imprint on the Institute of Jewish Studies, preached a cautious scholarly "objectivity." This attitude tended to eschew involvement in creating a new national culture and ingathering past assets, for such involvement amounted to taking a stance and dictating future directions of development. Thus, even though the National Library, one of the pinnacles of the *kinnus* endeavor, moved to the summit of Mount Scopus, the University rejected another *kinnus* idea — the Jewish Studies Collection (*Otsar Mad'ey Hayahadut*) that Bialik conceived and Dinur planned. Nor did the university accommodate Dinur's venture in gathering Jewish historical sources, *Israel in Exile,* the virtues of which Dinur described in his introduction to the second edition of the 1958 anthology:

> [. . .] A historical presentation that converges with direct testimony of the sources that preserves an ennobling diversity, that pulses with the spirit of their time, and is set in the climate of the historical events — can insert the reader into the entire reality of the past and may also attract him intimately toward historical research in all its diverse elements: review of sources and establishing facts, linking events and probing their motives, examining circumstances and reconstructing a world of yore on the basis of its surviving vestiges.[9]

In gathering material on Jewish mysticism, in contrast, much of the work did take place at the Hebrew University, at the initiative and through the efforts of Gershom Scholem, who was influenced to no small extent by Bialik and Zalman Rubashov (Shazar). Scholem proposed his main role in *kinnus* — gathering, publishing, and studying kabbalistic writings — in a letter to Bialik in 1925, an excerpt of which follows:

> It is definitely possible to obtain information on the creation of kabbalah and its offshoots, since *seventy percent* of the important texts are available in manuscripts scattered across the Diaspora. I am confident that research on kabbalah is hopeless and a dead letter unless people devote themselves to researching these manuscripts: to *publish* everything of importance that they contain (and yes, they contain much of importance!) in critical and analytical forums, to anthologize them, and to extract from them the truth about the development and antiquity of kabbalah.[10]

Thus the Hebrew University, which Ḥayyim Naḥman Bialik envisaged as a center and focal point in the fulfillment of the *kinnus* project idea, accommodated several parts of a project that began elsewhere. All of Ben Zion Dinur's ingathering and research projects, including the monumental amassing of sources on Jewish history (*Israel in Exile*), the anthology on Jewish history in the Land of Israel (*Sefer ha-Yishuv*), and the collection of documents on the history of Zionism (*Sefer ha-Tsiyyonut*) began outside the academic institute established on Mount Scopus. The same occurred with respect to Isaiah Tishby's *Mishnat ha-Zohar* — also a *kinnus* endeavor in the spirit of Bialik and the literary researcher Fischel Lachower. Their influence percolated into the Hebrew University chiefly when several directors of *kinnus* enterprises in the national spirit obtained professorships at the university and organized their departments' research and teaching activities under the *kinnus* principles. We consider Isaiah Tishby, who deemed himself one of Bialik's loyal successors in *kinnus* efforts, a reliable commentator:

> [. . .] Might it not seem presumptuous if I am praised for having had the privilege of being Bialik's loyal disciple and servant in my scholarly work in teaching and research? From the day I took the lectern in

> the Department of Hebrew Literature in Jerusalem and established a new section in the department—that of philosophical and ethical literature—more than twenty years ago [these remarks were made in 1973], I have done everything I could to promote the fulfillment of the *kinnus* idea in the literary-continuity format that Bialik explicitly set forth.[11]

Dinur, a fervent Zionist historian, also bequeathed to his many students at the Hebrew University Department of Jewish History his Zionist construction of *naḥpesa ve-naḥqora*. It is anything but a coincidence that Dinur chose this expression, the title of Dubnow's 1891 manifesto on the ingathering of the Jewish national documents, to encapsulate his outlook on the current national value of Jewish historical research. Neither is it a coincidence that his programmatic article in this vein was published in an extra-university ideological journal, *The* Davar *Collection, Marking the Thirtieth Anniversary of the Palestine Workers' Newspaper,* edited by D. Zakai and Z. Shazar. Thus, about twenty years after he began to teach Jewish history at the Hebrew University and sire generations of disciples-successors, Dinur wrote:

> We are living in one of the most crucial periods in our history, and we are duty-bound to uphold the principle of *naḥpesa derakheynu ve-naḥqora*. It is our life's blood. Not only can historical experience teach us to re-examine the formation of values of the past, but it is also a mighty lever that can reinforce and develop a renewed historical awareness, a prerequisite for a historical endeavor of mighty vigor that the fate of history has imposed on us and that propels us forward, whether we wish it or not.[12]

Interest in the scholarly, critical ingathering of Jewish texts, first evinced in Germany in the early nineteenth century in the context of the political struggle for Jewish emancipation, metamorphosed by the end of that century into a fixture of cultural activity in the Jewish national movement. To put it differently, the latter incarnation of the *kinnus* enterprise, the "national" one, did not modify the scientific-critical posture but gave it a new ideological infrastructure. Instead of anticipating the Jews' political and social integration in their countries of residence, it hoped to create an autonomous Jewish society with singular cultural indicators. When it moved from Europe to Palestine, an impressive cultural attempt was made to carry this great cultural project to fruition. Its two intentions, the scholarly and the national, did not always march hand-in-hand, but the cooperation forged between the Hebrew University and non-academic organizations and associations in certain parts of the *kinnus* project resulted in several impressive endeavors in various dominions of the Jewish cultural heritage.

What has become of this national ingathering endeavor today, as modern Jewish nationalism is being pulled apart by an all-demanding Orthodoxy at one extreme and hostile estrangement from Jewish tradition, in the name of universalism, at the other? I shall not address myself to this question, which oversteps the historical discussion and pertains to current Israeli political and cultural realities. I shall say only this: unless the dialectic essence of the continuum of Jewish creative endeavor is acknowledged, and unless the various currents that permeate it and the upbuilding and "down-building" trends that typify it are given a meaningful role, the enterprise of national cultural revival will return to its point of departure: an ahistorical harmonization that derives its justification from an irrational source. If that day comes, the national *kinnus* project will have become superfluous and "Jewish studies" will obviously have become unnecessary.

NOTES

This chapter is an expanded version of a lecture given at the Hebrew University of Jerusalem on Mount Scopus in June 1997.

1. "Le-Petiḥat ha-Universitah ha-Ivrit be-Yerushalayim," in *Kol Kitve H.N. Bialik* (Tel Aviv, 1938), 241–243.
2. G. Scholem, "Mi-tokh hirhurim 'al ḥokhmat yisrael" (From Thoughts on *Wissenschaft des Judentums*), in *Devarim bego* (Tel Aviv, 1975), 392.
3. Ibid., p. 393.
4. S. Dubnow, *Naḥpesa ve-naḥqora, qol gore el ha-nevonim ba-'am, ha-mitnadvim le'esof ḥomer le-vinyan toledot benei yisrael be-Polin u-ve Rusya* (Let us

search and investigate, a call to the Jewish intelligentsia, volunteers in gathering material to construct the history of the Jews in Poland and Russia), *Pardes,* 1892, p. 226.

5. *Pinqas ha-medina, o pinqas va'ad ha-qehilot ha-rashiyot be-medinat Lite* (Country record or record of the council of main communities in Lithuania), edited, with introduction and notes, by S. Dubnow (Berlin, 1925), xi, xxix.

6. *Kol Kitve H.N. Bialik,* 242.

7. Ibid.

8. B. Katznelson, *Divrei Berl Katznelson 'al ha-universita ha-'ivrit* (Remarks by Berl Katznelson concerning the Hebrew University) (Jerusalem, 1948), 4–5.

9. B. Z. Dinur, *Yisrael ba-gola* (The Jews in exile), 2nd edition (Tel Aviv, 1958), 1: 47.

10. G. Scholem, "*Mikhtav le-H.N. Bialik*" (Letter to H. N. Bialik), in *Devarim bego,* 60.

11. I. Tishby, "*Be'ayat ha-retsifut ba-sifrut ha-'ivrit be-haguto shel Bialik u-ve-yamenu*" (The problem of continuity in Hebrew literature in Bialik's thought and in our times), *Ha'aretz,* 27 December 1972.

12. B. Z. Dinur, *Be'ayot ha-yesod shel ha-meḥqar ha-histori ha-yehudi be-yamenu* (Basic problems of Jewish historical research in our times), *Dorot u-reshumot* (Generations and records) (Jerusalem, 1978), 159.

TEN

"Secondary Intellectuals," Readers, and Readership as Agents of National-Cultural Reproduction in Modern Egypt

ISRAEL GERSHONI

National culture in modern Egypt was the handiwork of intellectuals. Philosophers, authors, poets, playwrights, artists, journalists and educators (*Udaba, Mufakkirun, Muthaqqafun* in Arabic) — not politicians, technocrats, bureaucrats or military leaders — began molding it in the late nineteenth century, and gave it its definitive contours between the two World Wars. It was they who compiled its repertoire and invented Egypt's national self-image, fashioning the constituent genres, themes and representations. It was also they who, via the print media, disseminated and conventionalized the culture throughout the various layers of the Egyptian public. Moreover, they were responsible for enlisting the political elites and bureaucrats and, indeed, the state apparatus itself for purposes of institutionalizing their cultural output, formalizing its status as the modern national culture of Egypt.[1]

In the historical narrative which treats the formative process of Egyptian national culture, it is standard to distinguish two discrete developmental periods.[2] In the first, spanning the last quarter of the nineteenth century and the late 1920s (approximately 1882–1929), intellectuals based their output on an exclusivist vision of Egypt as culturally bounded by the Nile Valley, heir to the unique civilization and history of the "nation" dwelling there since time immemorial. The antique pharaonic legacy, Hellenistic-Roman influences and age-old traditions, myths, customs and folk-tales, derived primarily from the rural milieu, served as the reservoirs from which producers of modern national culture drew. A fundamental principle of these producer-intellectuals was the credo that the Nile Valley and its singular culture are a subset of the Mediterranean cultural array, quite distinct from the Islamic, Arabic or Eastern. Hence, they saw their mission as two-fold: the recovery of particularist Egyptian cultural strands and their extrusion as modern literate culture, "the culture of a revived nation," on the one hand, and the identification of close links between it and modern national European cultures, on the other. Islamic, Arab and Eastern elements, such as the majority religion of Egypt's inhabitants, their shared language and their history over the prior millenium, were represented as foreign intrusions impeding the project of creating authentic national culture for modern Egypt.

In the second period, spanning the 1930s, 40s, and 50s (approximately 1930 to the consolidation of the Nasserite regime near the end of the 1950s), a profound shift occurred in the processes of national cultural production and consequently in the repertoire, resulting in its Islamicization and Arabization. The intellectuals identified or rediscovered the Islamic, Arab and Eastern reservoirs which were now assumed to be the "authentic" legacy of the Nile Valley. From this, they derived an alternative repertoire for creating modern national culture based on Islamic history and culture, Arabic language and literature, and on sentiments of Egyptian solidarity with the peoples of the East. The mission of these producers of culture was to relocate Egypt within the vast cultural sphere of the speakers of Arabic. The attempts of their predecessors to detach Egypt from its supposed "natural" milieu was now seen as having been motivated not by a sincere reckoning of Egyptian cultural identity, but rather by a will to innovate a modernity for its own sake. Such alienation from Egypt's putatively "true" cultural roots was fated to fail, due to its lack of foundation, they asserted. The new cultural producers, of course, did all they could to stage the prior national culture as irrelevant by portraying pharaonicism as anachronistic and pagan, and European affiliation as a foreign admixture incompatible with the civilization of the Middle East. Claims of Egypt's European affiliation were also discredited by stressing the imperialist nature of Europe's political relations with Egypt, whose cultural consequence was the suppression of the so-called native Islamic-Arabic culture.

Why did this shift occur? What agents were responsible? Who had an interest in effecting such a shift? This paper is an attempt to answer these questions, not by resorting to the received strategies tried by the History of Ideas, Intellectual History, or the theory of "crisis" among luminary intellectuals, but instead by offering a history of cultural consumption and reading. The paper sets out to account for the changed shape of the repertoire of Egyptian national culture in terms of changes in modes of transmission and patterns of reception in Egypt during this period. The protagonists in this story will be *secondary intellectuals* and *their readership.*

Efforts to explain the shift in cultural production have occupied a central place in the historical study of modern Egypt. For the last half-century the topic has been surveyed in fine detail by various historiographic schools, which have focused on intellectual developments in the inter-war period, especially during the transition from the 1920s to the 1930s. All these schools shared a trickle-down understanding of cultural change as transpiring "from top to bottom": the production of national culture, the dynamics of its evolution, and controlling mechanisms over the repertoires were all viewed as monopolized by small groups of cultural elites. Scholars concentrated on these select groups, studying their strategies and texts for disseminating their ideas. To a lesser extent, attention was devoted to modes by which the intellectuals manipulated political systems like the political parties, the Palace, Parliament, the various administrations, and the Ministry of Education, exploiting their resources to promote and institutionalize the national culture which they designed and circulated. On this plane as well, discussion remained restricted to the elites.

Using the more traditional method of "History of Ideas" as expounded by A. Lovejoy, some scholars in the 1940s, 1950s, and 1960s tried to comprehend national cultural evolution either as the unfolding of elitist ideas, as the inner dynamic of high belief-systems, or as the record of mutations in constellations of abstruse theory. Later, with the adoption of more fashionable contextualist Intellectual History methodologies in the 1970s and 1980s, especially the social history of ideas and discourse analysis, an attempt was made to explain the socio-cultural background of the intellectual producers, to locate the texts in their fluctuating Egyptian socio-political contexts, and to decode their meanings for a specific discourse that emerged in a particular historical context. This contextualist method offered means to trace Egypt's intellectual change by recovering the motivations and intentions of writers, and to correlate these authorial intentions as projected in their texts with the actual progress of cultural change outside of the texts in the everyday life of Egypt.

In the early applications of these interpretive frameworks, there was a decided tendency to rely on value judgments, moralism, and Orientalism as explanatory factors. They were used to account for cultural change as the consequence of a "deep intellectual crisis" which propelled national cultural producers to embrace Islamic-Arab themes and subjects. H. A. R. Gibb criticized the modernist intellectuals for fashioning a cult of personality for the Prophet and his way of life, as well as for idealizing other classic Islamic heroes.[3] He reasoned that this led them down an intellectual and moral blind alley, into "sterile apologetics," "confusion of principles," and a "paralyzing romanticism," which, he averred, challenged and wrecked the foundations of the modern Muslim culture rather than shored it up.[4] N. Safran, the star pupil of Gibb and heir to his narrative, presented this permutation as a "crisis of orientation."[5] Blaming the writers for "*trahison de clerks,*" Safran concluded that "the writers had surrendered their previous guide and bearing—rationalism and a Western cultural orientation—without being able to produce viable Muslim-inspired alternatives."[6]

Earlier efforts, culminating in the 1920s, to shape a national, progressive, Western-oriented community failed miserably, mostly because of the intellectuals' unwillingness to weather the recriminations of the orthodox religious establishment. In the 1930s and 1940s, its proponents retreated amidst their own conceptual confusion and ideological anarchy into a "reactionary phase," ultimately encouraging the ascent of the deleterious "Mahdiist mentality" over the entire cultural field.[7] In the mid-1960s, B. Johansen interpreted the intellectual crisis in Egypt as a direct reflection of the crisis of liberalism and positivism in intellectual circles in Europe in the late 1920s and 1930s. Egyptian intellectuals resorted to Islam in order to find an harmonious blend of reason and revelation, science and religious belief.[8] D. Semah, in the early 1970s, suggested a less dramatic, less crisis-ridden interpretation of the shift. He ascribed the ideological shift to the intellectuals' quest for cultural authenticity. Pharaonicism and Western, positivist models for progress through Westernization and secularization were newly regarded as artificial and sterile experiments by repentant intellectuals who now saw in Islamic, Eastern and Arab orientations a more authentic basis for national culture.[9]

C. Smith has performed the most significant revision of the early interpretive methods.[10] Through a contextualist approach to intellectual history, he tries to retrieve the political-cultural foundations of the intellectual movement and explain the motivations of the writers for prompting the changes. He construes the shift to an Islamic focus as a tactical, instrumental measure by which "the intellectuals were trying to achieve their previous goals by different means because of the resurgence of Islamic sentiment which had occurred" in the 1930s and 1940s.[11] According to his narrative, the project of constructing a rational and secular national culture with a Westernist affiliation, promising hegemony to an enlightened intellectual avant garde, was not abandoned at all in the later period. By the purely tactical transition which involved writing about Islamic issues, manipulating religious sentiments, and appropriating classical Islamic heroes, the intellectuals undertook to create a modern society "validated by Islam" which would "incorporate the ideals of European rationalism while preserving social order."[12]

Thus, the research which tried to account for the change in the national culture concentrated exclusively on the elitist discourse of cultural producers. It almost completely disregarded the role of "consumption" and "consumers," "reception" and "receivers," as agents in the creative process and transformations of national culture. A by-product of this disregard was inattention to the interaction between cultural creation and consumption, between intellectual texts and their reading and interpretive contexts. The naive assumption, common to all these elitist approaches to the study of national culture, is that texts and other intellectual artifacts are automatically "inscribed on the minds and bodies of those to whom they are directed or on whom they are 'imposed'."[13] Consumers or readers are presumed as utterly passive and as historical entities in the field of cultural production. They have no creative function at all in the production of national culture and in its dissemination, nor share in its meanings, which are monopolized by the intellectuals.

We maintain that the uni-directional "top-to-bottom" model of cultural production is non-exhaustive and but one aspect of its manufacture, and not necessarily the most important one, in the layered dynamic of Egypt's national cultural evolution. A fuller appreciation of the cultural dynamic reveals a bi-directional, feedback mechanism in which culture also leavens from "bottom-to-top." This approach first scrutinizes procedures of national cultural transmission at various social levels in the context of a struggle for political hegemony. Secondly, it enquires into patterns of consumption and modes of reception by broad publics as they assimilate the national culture and make it their own. It assumes that consumers are not passive assimilators of culture; rather, their modes of reception are "characterized by interpretive activity that involves resistance and evasion as well as substrative, supplemental, and transformative revisions."[14]

The autonomy of consumer communities is defined by a production of meaning in the culture that is not necessarily correlative to the meaning which the intellectual producers intend.[15] In the Egyptian case under discussion, the central role of "high" intellectual groups in planning and generating national culture is demonopolized almost as soon as its production is disseminated. An "alternative production," to borrow Roger Chartier's term,[16] occupies no less central a place once consumers receive the transmissions "from on high." Intellectuals are thus forced to share control of the means of cultural production with other forces in the cultural field. Historically, in that moment of relative maturity in the making of national culture, when "alternative production" makes inroads into the cultural polysystem, the study of intellectuals alone becomes myopic and reductionist. More comprehensive cultural study is called for in order to embrace various communities of interpreters, readers and listeners, serving as central agents diligently creating and recreating the complex and expanding field of national culture. One can regard as paradoxical that as national culture becomes truly more national, that is, conquers larger sectors of the nation, it becomes less the private precinct of elite intellectuals.[17] Hence, the shift in research from producers to consumers, from writers to readers, was inevitable. This issue is critical to the thesis of our discussion. We will try to show that the essential transformation that took place in the composition of the repertoire of national culture in Egypt since the beginning of the 1930s has its basis in the fundamental change in the cultural field of consumption and readership in the 1930s and 1940s. Furthermore, without taking these changes into account, it would be impossible to adequately explain the intellectual transition to Islamic-Arab themes and the neglect of the earlier Westernizing pharaonic repertoire.

In this chapter we will attempt in broad strokes to present the historical framework in which the structure of literate culture emerged and crystallized, its subsequent changes, and the specific influences impinging on the reproduction of the national culture in its later Islamic-Arab phase of development. Within the expanding structure of written culture consumption in Egypt at the end of the nineteenth century and more emphatically in the first half of the twentieth, it is worth discerning two mechanisms in the cycle of reception. The first is a relatively narrow network of non-elite intellectuals who rendered immediate interpretation of "high" intellectual products before disseminating them throughout various levels of society and culture. The principal agents comprising this network can be defined as "secondary intellectuals" or "reproductive intellectuals." The second is the much broader system of consumption and mass reading, in which secondary intellectuals exerted strong leverage as arbiters of meaning, even among the lower strata of the reading communities.

The network of "secondary intellectuals" was a mediating mechanism between the "high caste" producer intellectuals and the network of mass consumption. The cardinal cultural function of secondary intellectual clusters—both according to their collective self-image and self-expectations and according to the expectations of the "high" intellectuals—was the diffusion of the national repertoire. Their vocation was the popularization, conventionalization, and occasional vulgarization of the authoritative texts, cultural artifacts, social perceptions and political values which initially originated mostly with the upper intellectuals.[18]

This activity was especially intense when it came to the operation of the print media, which was the single most important organ of written culture within national culture. In the period in question, print journalism was dominant and flourished in its sundry branches: dailies, weeklies, and monthlies with their own political, cultural, and religious platforms, as well as papers which introduced the use of artistic sketches and caricatures, some dedicated solely to entertainment. As the historiographic cliché indicates, "Egyptians read papers, not books." Indeed, the journalistic print-media were the most intense arenas for the cycle of production, distribution, and reception of national culture. High, producer intellectuals generally served as chief editors on the papers. They would decide a paper's general strategy and its topical orientation. But it was the secondary intellectuals who gave the papers their ambience by serving as investigative reporters, publicists, columnists and hands-on administrators and editors. Premier journals like *al-Jarida* before the First World War, *al-Siyasa al-Usbu'iyya, al-Balagh al-Usbu'i* and *al-'Usur* in the 1920s, and *Mulhaq al-Siyasa, al-Majalla al-Jadida, al-Risala* and *al-Thaqafa* in the 1930s and 1940s, provide excellent examples of this type of activity. The respective editors-in-chief, Ahmed Lutfi al-Sayyid, Muhammad Husayn Haykal, 'Abd al-Qadir Hamza, Isma'il Mazhar, Ibrahim 'Abd al-Qadir al-Mazini, Salama Musa, Ahmad Hasan al-Zayyat, Taha Husayn and Ahmad Amin, all belonged to the high intellectual set. They were vastly outnumbered, however, by the members of their staffs numbering hundreds of journalists and publicists. The disseminators of the product who were its ultimate shapers were these staff members. Journalists and publicists at this second tier who were conspicuous between the wars included Mahmud 'Azmi, Muhammad Lutfi Jum'a, Ibrahim al-Misri, Hafiz Mahmud, Muhammad 'Abdallah 'Inan, Niqula Yusuf, Ibrahim Ibrahim Jum'a, 'Abd al-Wahhab 'Azzam, Zaki Mubarak, Muhamad Zaki 'Abd al-Qadir, Isma'il Adham, Mirrit Butrus Ghali, Husayn Fawzi, Sayyid Qutb, Muhammad Amin Hussuna, Mahmud Izzat Musa, Salah Dhuhni, and two women, Nabawiya Musa and Aster Wisa.[19] Political magazines illustrated with photos or cartoons such as *al-Kashkul, al-Musawwar, Ruz al-Yusuf* and *al-Ithnayn,* which became exceedingly popular in the interwar era, were also run by journalists and intellectuals of the second order.[20]

A survey of the activities of the Ministry of Education, especially from the time it became an independent office with a generous budget in the 1920s and after, reveals a similar pattern. Several "high" pedagogic personalities were surrounded by a vast majority of secondary intellectuals serving in both official and unofficial capacities: tens of thousands of teachers, educators, supervisors, bureaucrats and so forth, who replicated, distributed and implemented national culture through the available media in education. They also compiled and amended school textbooks and curricula.[21]

From a social standpoint, secondary intellectuals all derived from the ranks of the *effendiyya:* a middle-stratum which had been evolving since the end of the nineteenth century, but which only realized a distinct cultural character and a degree of political autonomy between the two world wars. Trading in its mostly rural roots as it underwent urban, literate and modern professional acculturization in the framework of Western-oriented state education, the *effendiyya* constituted the intermediate, urban, lettered class which gradually became the de facto guides of public opinion and political-cultural tendencies. This class included the "professionals" in the broad sense of the term, among whom were counted the secondary intellectuals. Since the 1920s, most political activists in all parties and movements hailed from the *effendiyya*. The secondary intellectuals as a discrete group within the *effendiyya* worked professionally as journalists, authors, poets, educators, government officials, attorneys, physicians, engineers, lecturers at universities and other institutions of higher learning, heads of sporting organizations, religious preachers, and directors of cultural and artistic clubs.[22]

As the *effendiyya* gained in self-assurance and assertiveness, its autonomous intermediary powers in the field of production and reproduction of national culture burgeoned. The secondary intellectuals, as the ideologists of their *effendiyya* class, were increasingly able to determine the cultural repertoire independently and dictate the dynamics and transformations of its unfolding. Particularly following World War I and the popular national revolution of 1919 in Egypt, and in an even more mature fashion from the early 1930s, their activity as dispensers of cultural products shaded over into actual cultural creation. In transmitting the texts and artifacts of national culture, they transformed them, adapting them for mass consumption by the less modern, less Westernized reading publics.

Constituting the junction where intellectual luminaries and broad sectors of society converged, the secondary intellectuals conducted the cultural feedback from elite to popular minds and vice-versa. As the principal agents of a mutually reinforcing loop of cultural circulation, they oversaw the confection of a "common culture" incorporating elements of both "high" and "low" culture. In their approach to less literate audiences, these secondary intellectuals also penetrated mosques, cafes, and street demonstrations, translating concepts of national culture into traditionalist terms and images in order to render them more readily digestible.[23]

We are now prepared to address directly the central question concerning the causes of change in the repertoire of national culture. From the end of the nineteenth century to the 1920s, the *effendiyya* and the secondary intellectuals among them had not yet crystallized into an autonomous sociocultural entity. Their dependence on groups of "high" intellectuals and political elites for their cultural diet was absolute. Although they took part in the production and dissemination of the national-pharaonic-Westernizing repertoire profferred by individual "high" intellectuals, they did not significantly impact on it, since their own cultural profile was still gestating. Thus they inclined to rather perfunctory imitations of "high" cultural products at this stage. What is more, their numbers involved in cultural production had not yet reached a critical mass. On the whole, these *effendis* did not yet sense that their role in manning the machinery of cultural production could be anything more than turning out faithful transmissions of the "high" cultural discourse. Out of a strong desire to integrate into the intellectual and political elite, they assimilated the Westernizing Egyptian culture.[24]

However, from the end of the 1920s into the 1930s and 1940s, profound structural changes occurred in the cultural and social standing of the *effendiyya* in general and of the secondary intellectuals in particular. First and foremost, their numbers proliferated dramatically. Overproduction at the primary, secondary and university levels of education turned out tens of thousands, perhaps hundreds of thousands of graduates, only a fraction of whom the job market could accommodate. Numbering in the mere hundreds during the First World War, the *effendiyya* grew to thousands by the 1920s, tens of thousands by the 1930s, and hundreds of thousands, if not a million, by the 1940s. The pool of journalists and publicists alone rose from approximately one thousand in the late 1920s to about eight thousand in the 1940s. A qualitative change was discernible as well. The *effendiyya* devolved into a lower social stratum, deriving increasingly from humbler precincts of society, without reasonable prospect of merging with the old intellectual, political or bureaucratic elites. Alienation and disappointment replaced the expectation of easy upward mobility. As a result, hostility rationalized itself into a strategy of dismantling the old elite structures of national culture, and replacing them with their own alternatives. The *effendiyya* profile was also becoming younger and more politicized. By the 1930s, the *effendiyya,* and its secondary intellectuals in particular, spearheaded the young generation's expressions of rage. It became the socio-cultural breeding ground for ideological and religious protest movements and political opposition groups voicing the estrangement of masses of Egyptian youth and challenging the political establishment. The *effendiyya* also grew more and more antipathetic to the West. The continuing presence of British colonial rule, the failure of Egyptian governments to deliver national independence, and the perceived association of Western culture with the political and military practice of Western imperialism, prompted the sundry blocs of *effendiyya* to resort to militant and even violent methods in a nationalist struggle for political liberation and cultural autonomy.[25]

An important expression of the growing autonomy of the *effendiyya* was its construction during the 1930s of its own political associations such as the Young Men's Muslim Association, the Muslim Brothers, Young Egypt and some ad hoc students' organizations. All of these expressed the new militant, anti-establishment *effendi* political counter-culture, directed against older nationalist parties such as the Wafd, the Liberal Constitutionalists, and even the Palace. The ideological and doctrinaire activity of youth-oriented *effendiyya* organizations exerted a marked influence on the political arena. They introduced a new national discourse redefining collective identity in Islamic-Arab or Egyptian integral-nationalist terms. In their rejection of "pharaonicism" (*al-Fir'awniyya*) as a Western imperialist implant, and in their critique of Egypt's "cultural isolation" from its "natural" Eastern context, they formulated an alternative national agenda in which Egypt was imagined as the locomotive of the Arab nation and Islamic community. Egypt's national destiny, they insisted, was to catalyze the movement toward Arab unity and the larger project of general Islamic amalgamation. Such radical *effendi* forces thus constituted a significant factor in institutionalizing national cultural transition and imparting it to youth and broad non-elite sectors of the public.[26]

The structural metamorphosis in the *effendiyya* induced the secondary intellectuals to see themselves more and more as representatives and spokesmen for the new urban masses, bound to the nationalist ideals of the young militants. From then on, they reworked national culture in a more populist and nativist direction, adjusting the repertoire to the new human geography. At the same time, their allegiance to the elite intellectuals and ruling political forces diminished in direct proportion. The reformulation of national culture in radical terms and the espousal of populist rhetoric became indispensible in the secondary intellectuals' outreach to the increasingly restive cultural consumers. The upshot was the Islamicization and Arabization of culture on the one hand, de-pharaonicization and de-Westernization on the other. They were thenceforth committed to assembling or inventing a cultural repertoire founded on Egypt's Islamic-Arab heritage: on the language and literature of Arabic and on the faith, history and civilization of Islam. Islam, Arabism and Easternist sentiments became reservoirs to draw on for producing a new common culture, whose reception was to be ensured by fitting itself to the contours of the urban masses and the ascendent *effendiyya*. These processes ravaged the confidence of the veteran intellectuals promoting a pharaonist and Westernizing repertoire, and threatened to make them socially and culturally irrelevant. Given the intense pressures for change coming from below, and given their wish to maintain their status, the luminary intellectuals began writing on Islamic and Arab themes as well. They concluded that their survival as major players in the field of cultural production mandated their conversion into enthusiasts of the new cultural reality of the 1930s and 1940s.[27] Many of them, realizing that their former repertoire was no longer relevant, sincerely overhauled their cultural orientation for the sake of the larger cause of avoiding a *Kulturkampf* by preserving common cultural ground for the disparate social sectors.

The most salient demonstration of this process was the explosion of *Islamiyyat* literature: the composition of dozens, perhaps hundreds, of biographies of the Prophet Muhammad, the Four Orthodox Caliphs (*al-Khulafa' al-Rashidun*), and other Muslim and Arab heroes of the classical era. Production of this literature occupied a great many of the leading intellectuals of the 1930s, and 1940s: Taha Husayn wrote *'Ala Hamish al-Sira* (On the Margin of the Prophet's Life, 3 volumes appearing in 1934, 1937 and 1943); Muhammad Husayn Haykal penned *Hayat Muhammad* (The Life of Muhammad, 1935) and *Fi Manzil al-Wahy* (At the Site of Revelation, 1937); Tawfiq al-Hakim composed the monumental drama *Muhammad* (1936); 'Abbas Mahmud al-'Aqqad turned out serial biographical volumes, the *'Abqariyyat,* throughout the 1940s, commencing with the most popular in the series, *'Abqariyyat Muhammad* (The Genius of Muhammad, 1942); and Mahmud Taymur rounds out the list of authors whose works set the tone for the *Islamiyyat* genre with his *al-Nabiy al-Insan* (The Prophet as Human Being, 1945). Via this Islamic literature, such luminary writers—all erstwhile acolytes of the pharaonicist, Westernizing repertoire—consciously sought to reach the new mass audience by pandering to its literary expectations and cultural norms.

As far as the public was concerned, these were the de facto guardians of the historical Islamic heritage and simultaneously the shapers of a new and modern image for the foundational heroes of this heritage, starting with the Prophet. They succeeded in making Islam seem newly relevant and attractive to the average reader with primary or secondary education. They were regarded as making sincere efforts to engage in a popular discourse with the new *effendiyya* strata and beyond them with the newly literate masses. The unprecedented commercial success of the *Islamiyyat* literary industry, with biographies of the Prophet, particularly those by Haykal, Taha Husayn, and 'Aqqad, selling in the tens of thousands per edition and running through many editions as they were read by hundreds of thousands of enthusiasts, demonstrates the success of the intellectuals' outreach to lower sectors of society. Their marketing triumph stood in diametric opposition to the comparatively anemic circulation of their own earlier intellectual products of a Westernizing, pharaonic nature, created mostly in the 1920s, which sold only in the low thousands and never ran more than one edition which itself usually did not sell out.

These older intellectuals who overhauled and Islamicized their output did, at the same time, subtly modernize and even liberalize Islam in their presentation of it. Approaching the history of the Prophet and the *Rashidun* of the seventh century with less of the traditional pieties and more contemporary openness, they portrayed their subjects in a new, dynamic light as models not just for Muslims but for universal emulation by all moderns. Thus they were fighting a two-front campaign, waged on the one hand to evince Islam's virtues to their contemporaries in the West, and on the other, to challenge the Orthodox Islamic establishment (the '*ulama*') and its conservative, uninspiring, and putatively distorted versions of the lives of Islam's founders. Committed to the scientific methods of historiography which they gleaned during their studies in Europe, these intellectuals mustered critical and rational tools to analyze Islamic traditions by submitting them to scientific, empirical enquiry. For example, they dismissed stories of miracles and supernatural events surrounding the revelations to the Prophet as figments of an overactive religious imagination in the centuries following the Prophet's death, and they constructed a rational and historicistic narrative of the *sira*. Given their status and authority as creators of the dominant modern culture, their alternative readings of the Prophet's life indeed threatened the orthodox interpretations rendered by the '*ulama*'.

For the most part, the newfangled interpretations of Islam and particularly of events in the lives of its founders, were welcomed warmly by the secondary, *effendi* intellectuals. Less interested in the specific novelties of presentation, the *effendiyya* made much of the conversion of luminary intellectuals from Westernizing to Islamicist orientations, describing it as a recognition and admission of the necessity of Islamic-Arab culture for modern Egypt. They praised the high intellectuals for their defense of the Prophet from perceived enemies both abroad and at home. They called for a struggle to revive the ideals and precepts of early Islam and to install them as the basis for modern culture in Egypt and the Arab world.

However, the process of reception of the *Islamiyyat* literature by the *effendiyya* was not passive. They projected autonomous interpretations over the *Islamiyyat* output, and even offered their own texts addressing the same issues. Thus they responded to the *Islamiyyat* at several levels. Firstly, they issued direct replies to the works by writing dozens of essays and reviews in the press. The Islamicist publications of Haykal, Taha Husayn, Hakim and 'Aqqad received special notice by the *effendi* critics. The *effendi* intellectuals proffered their opinions and passed judgment on the manner in which luminary intellectuals formerly identified with pharaonicism and Western cultural assimilation now combed Islamic sources for modern literary and cultural inspiration. Secondary intellectuals such as Muhammad 'Ali al-Najjar, 'Abd al-Wahhab 'Azzam, Zaki Mubarak, Muhammad Ahmad al-Ghamrawi, Muhibb al-Din al-Khatib, Mustafa Sadiq al-Rafi'i, 'Ali Mahmud Taha, as well as Ahmad Husayn, the leader of Young Egypt, and Hasan al-Banna, the "General Guide" of the Muslim Brothers, churned out essays detailing their reactions to works of the *Islamiyyat.*

Secondly, the secondary intellectuals themselves composed historical biographies of the Prophet and the *Rashidun.* Examples include Rashid Rida Effendi's five biographical volumes on Muhammad, Abu Bakr, 'Umar, 'Uthman, and 'Ali which he published between 1934–1939, and the popular biographies of the Prophet and other key Islamic figures issued by Young Egypt in economy pocket book editions in the late 1930s and early 1940s. They also published works on the Islamic literary and poetic history of the Umayyad and 'Abassid periods, such as Zaki Mubarak's monographs of the 1930s, and researched the historical genesis of Islam and its development into a vast empire in the seventh century, as in the comprehensive works of 'Abd al-Wahhab al-Najjar (e.g., *Ta'rikh al-Islam: al-Khulafa' al-Rashidun,* 1930), and 'Abd al-Wahhab 'Azzam (e.g., *Mudhakkirat fi Ta'rikh al-Umma al-'Arabbiyya,* 1932).

Thirdly, and perhaps most importantly, the secondary intellectuals added a major dimension to the *Islamiyyat* discourse in their pieces in the era's literary journals. The pivotal weeklies *al-Risala* (from 1934) and *al-Thaqafa* (from 1940) each published semi-annual special editions on the occasions of the new *Hijra* year and the Prophet's birthday. These editions were double and sometimes triple the size of the regular edition, arrayed festively, and sold three times as many copies. For instance, *al-Risala*'s normal weekly circulation was 15,000, but its holiday editions reached 45,000 readers. In terms of content, the special editions were comprised of dozens of essays by secondary intellectuals on varied topics in Islamic history, including its political leaders, military commanders, the Islamic-Arab literary and poetic heritage, and other aspects of the civilization. Particular attention was devoted to the Prophet's virtues and his exemplary life, as well as the abiding legacies of the Four Orthodox Caliphs, in terms of the lessons to be derived from their military triumphs, political expansion, and social organization. If we add to this the copious articles and essays on such subjects appearing in the organs of the Young Men's Muslim Association (chiefly in the weekly *al-Fath* and the monthly *Majallat al-Shubban al-Muslimin*) or that of the Muslim Brothers (*Jaridat al-Ikhwan al-Muslimin, al-Nadhir,* and *al-Khulud*), the full scope of secondary intellectuals' participation in the production of *Islamiyyat* discourse becomes evident. Needless to say, their journalistic output was consumed by the more popular social strata, and thus reached hundreds of thousands if not over a million readers. In this sense, the texts of the secondary intellectuals significantly facilitated the penetration and popularization of the *Islamiyyat* among the lower social tiers which remained impervious to works by Haykal, Taha Husayn, or 'Aqqad.

Despite the variety of readings and interpretations of Islam and its historical protagonists offered by the secondary intellectuals, several commonalities are discernible. In stark contrast to the tendency of the luminary intellectuals to ascribe modernist, liberal, and rational qualities to early Islamic society, the secondary intellectuals read the founders' society with an eye to picking up on revivalist, fundamentalist, and nationalist themes. The ideal Muslim society of the seventh century which they yearned to restore differed markedly from that portrayed by Haykal, Taha Husayn, Hakim, or 'Aqqad. Among the Prophet and his immediate successors they sought and found models for strength, unity, prestige and dignity, grounds for superiority, expansion and hegemony, and sources of authenticity, identity, and cultural self-sufficiency. In their representations, the Prophet and the *Rashidun* not only embodied universal virtues to be emulated by all mankind, as for Haykal and 'Aqqad, but primarily served as national heroes whose example would galvanize a national political liberation movement and serve as the paradigm for constructing a vigorous and independent Islamic community in the here and now.[28]

In considering the processes of the *Islamiyyat*'s diffusion to broad publics, it is important to examine how the Islamicist texts of the secondary intellectuals were received and consumed by their broad audience. As already noted, the secondary intellectuals functioned as agents of dissemination and inculcation of elite intellectual products for mass reception. They reworked these products as they passed them on so as to adapt them to the tastes and faculties of their prospective consumers. This does not mean, however, that consumers of these "secondary" products assimilated them passively. At this "tertiary" level of the cultural dynamic, patterns of reception and strategies of assimilation evolved, in light of which one can speak of a third stratum of cultural "production." The cultural historian's ability to reconstruct specific hermeneutic procedures and propensities of mass reception of national culture in the 1930s is understandably limited. Nonetheless, the available evidence clearly indicates that at this tertiary layer of production-cum-consumption, the vast reading audience was comprised of a number of interpretive communities which synthesized "another production," using the texts and messages of secondary intellectuals as their raw material.

An example of this cultural dynamic can be found in the system of production and consumption of written products that developed among the Muslim Brothers in the 1930s and 1940s. Hasan al-Banna, the seemingly omnipotent "General Guide" of the movement, also served as its authoritative ideologue; from the standpoint of our discussion, he is a quintessential secondary intellectual. Almost singlehandedly, he formulated the Muslim Brothers' program on matters of religion, society, politics, education, culture, ethics and even aesthetics. He also took a clear stance regarding the *Islamiyyat* literature of the luminary intellectuals. His response to Haykal's *Hayat Muhammad*, for instance, was to be the official reaction of the Brothers. Al-Banna, like so many of the *effendi* intellectuals, expressed a qualified approval of the work. In bringing his own revivalist, fundamentalist, and nationalist horizons of expectations to bear on his reading of the work, he discerned in it a modernist intellectual call to return to Islamic sources and recognition that only such sources afford the requisite resources for building the most suitable modern culture for Egypt. He interpreted *Hayat Muhammad* as a summons to adopt principles, norms, and ideals of the Islamic Golden Age in order to rehabilitate the contemporary Islamic community. At the same time, al-Banna rejected the liberal, rationalist overtones of Haykal's *sira* of Muhammad, and took exception to Haykal's dismissal of miracles in the Prophet's life and in the preternatural events surrounding the emergence of the prophecy.[29]

This "official interpretation" by al-Banna was by and large accepted by his young adherents within the Muslim Brothers organization. They immediately consumed the opinions and texts of the General Guide, as they regarded themselves as his devout and loyal disciples. However, even among them, the process of digesting ideological products from "on high" was not automatic or mechanical. They, too, could often not help but perform "another production" as they imbibed the General Guide's words. For example, one young member of the Brothers, Muhammad 'Abduh, a high school pupil, wrote his own independent-minded critique of Haykal's Islamicist writings of the 1930s. In the official political journal of the Muslim Brothers in 1939, 'Abduh proffered his own analysis of the shift by Haykal and other prominent intellectuals toward Islamic subjects. Despite a clear foundation in al-Banna's perspective, 'Abduh's essay exhibits ample autonomy of thought. Thus he writes,

> No one could have imagined that Dr. Muhammad Husayn Haykal Pasha—one of those who was indebted to the civilization of Europe... and who assigned themselves the task of creating a European intellectual renaissance in Egypt which derived its teachings from Western thought and philosophy, would make the life of the great Prophet the subject of an extended study. Nor could anyone have imagined that Dr. Muhammad Husayn Haykal Pasha would go to the Holy Places of Pilgrimage . . . All this no one could imagine. Yet, all of it transpired. Haykal wrote on the life of the Prophet [*sirat al-nabiy*] . . . And Haykal went on Pilgrimage to the House of God and stood in the place where Muhammad had stood and thus realized the Islamic ideal in his soul and committed himself to strive as Muhammad and his Companions strove.[30]

One instantly observes that what interests ‘Abduh is the victory of Islam’s eternal truth over the “truths” of European culture, now exposed as transitory and misleading. He represents Haykal as publicly confessing, via his Islamicist writings, that the attempt by modernist intellectuals to import cultural products from Europe and graft them onto Egypt’s Islamic “reality” had failed miserably. At the time, Haykal served as Egypt’s Minister of Education, and thus ‘Abduh regarded such a confession as carrying far-reaching implications for Egyptian cultural sensibilities. ‘Abduh stresses that the idealization of the life of the Prophet in *Hayat Muhammad* and the discussion of personal transformation in Haykal’s account of his pilgrimage to the holy sites in *Fi Manzil al-Wahy* are typical of the new consciousness of the luminary intellectuals. ‘Abduh’s reading of Haykal differs from al-Banna’s in his concentration on the personal religious dimension: where al-Banna contemplates the advantages of retrieving political, social, and military aspects of early Islam, ‘Abduh focuses on rigorous obedience to Islamic law (culminating in the *hajj*), as the key for modern Egypt to actualize its authentic self and to thrive.[31]

We may assume that such autonomy of interpretation of the *Islamiyyat* was common at the tertiary level. The masses of new readers seem to have apprehended the intellectual-cultural shift of the 1930s and 1940s as proof of Islam’s triumph in Egypt. Thus, many at the tertiary level may have had a primarily religious focus similar to ‘Abduh’s as they considered the significance of the explosion of *Islamiyyat* literature.

Finally, in order to understand how communities of readers from lower social strata entered the market of consumption of written cultural products and towards the 1930s became a decisive agency fomenting cultural transition, we must briefly review the transformations in the more general system of written cultural consumption in Egypt. Until the First World War, patterns of written cultural consumption, mostly in journalism and education, were elitist. Reader communities were still circumscribed and selective. Readership did not yet exercise a palpable interpretive counterweight in the cultural field. Elitist modes of planning and, in effect, coercive implementation “from top-to-bottom” of its program of modern national culture, went unchallenged. The national revolution of 1919 and its deep impact on social, political and cultural structures in Egypt facilitated the participation of urban masses in the political and cultural arenas. Reading publics expanded swiftly, as did agents mediating their reception of cultural products by coating them with populist interpretation before dispensing them. This was felt most strongly in journalism, education, intellectual salons, ideological movements and political organizations.[32]

The process gathered momentum toward the close of the 1920s, and culminated in the 1930s and 1940s, as changes in patterns of reception were intimately linked to massive urbanization and the consequently steep growth in the urban population. The entry of huge rural masses into the socio-political urban arena and their socialization into a new urban, literate society greatly widened, and thereby altered, the markets that consumed literate products. This process was played out on three interrelated planes. The first consisted of a large-scale acquisition of literate urban culture. Fluency in written Arabic became a virtual "ticket" into urban life, as Arabic became a major focus of cultural identity. The second plane entailed participation in the shaping of a new collective sense of belonging to the urban Islamic-Arab community as a political, social and cultural identity framework. For the newly urbanized masses, literate urban, Islamic-Arab culture became a substitute loyalty framework for the oral, popular Islamic (or folk-Egyptian) culture of the now abandoned rural community. The third plane consisted of the formation of a new human milieu of a more populist and traditionalist nature that was incapable of assimilating symbols and values of a Westernizing, secular national culture carrying an implicit anti-Islamic and anti-Arab message.

Therefore, in these sociocultural processes, which peaked in the 1940s and 1950s, the uprooted masses that had abandoned traditional rural communities and crowded into the big cities (especially Cairo and Alexandria) rejected as alien most of the products of the Egyptianist repertoire of national culture, with its secular, Westernist and pharaonic trappings. At the same time, through their very urbanization, the newcomers to the cities lost, once and for all, their traditional oral culture, with its underpinnings in popular Islam, and their previous rural foci of loyalty.

This mass incorporation into urban life was made difficult because of severe economic conditions reflecting the world depression in the 1930s, a loss of confidence in the political system given chronic parliamentary crises, and corruption and intrigues afflicting the Palace, political parties and governments. Aggravating the general mood of disarray and the increasing political radicalization was the infiltration into Egypt of European fascist tendencies. At this moment of "crisis of urbanization" and "search for identity," only Islamic-Arab culture could offer both adequate compensation for forsaken traditional patterns of life, and a functional system of neo-traditional symbols based on Islam and Arabic with which to identify and through which to interpret and experience the rapidly changing world.

The very processes entailed by a mass reception of written national culture that were involved in its formulation vis-à-vis a mass-market audience—and the correspondingly heightened receptivity to Islamic-Arab cultural products within the now dominant urban literate community—played a decisive role in the Islamic-Arabic repertoire's takeover of the sociocultural center. Toward the end of the era under study, this sort of national cultural system achieved hegemony within the cultural polysystem and, more generally, throughout the entire urban society.[33] Hence, national culture in modern Egypt underwent Islamic and Arabic metamorphosis not because of an independent change of heart among the upper stratum of luminary intellectuals, but rather because new agents of cultural transmission and a new dynamic of reception had transformed both the constitution and operation of the machinery of cultural production.

NOTES

1. For a systematic treatment of the evolution of national culture in modern Egypt, see I. Gershoni, "The Evolution of National Culture in Modern Egypt: Intellectual Formation and Social Diffusion, 1892–1945," *Poetics Today* 13, 2 (1992), 325–350.

2. See P. J. Vatikiotis, *The Modern History of Egypt* (London, 1969), 204–373.

3. H. A. R. Gibb, *Modern Trends in Islam* (Chicago, 1947), 63–105.

4. Ibid., 68–69, 77, 105.

5. Nadav Safran, *Egypt in Search of Political Community* (Cambridge, Mass., 1961), 165–180.

6. Ibid., 140.

7. Ibid., 209–244.

8. Baber Johansen, *Muhammad Husain Haikal: Europa und der Orient im Weltbild eines Egyptischen Liberalen* (Beirut, 1967), 125–212.

9. David Semah, *Four Egyptian Literary Critics* (Leiden, 1974), 96–100.

10. Charles D. Smith, "The 'Crisis of Orientation': The Shift of Egyptian Intellectuals to Islamic Subjects in the 1930's," *International Journal of Middle East Studies* 4/3 (1973), 382–410.

11. Ibid., 384.

12. Charles D. Smith, *Islam and the Search for Social Order in Modern Egypt: A Biography of Muhammad Husayn Haykal* (Albany, 1983), 5, 130; see also ibid., 89–129.

13. John E. Toews, "Intellectual History after the Linguistic Turn: The Autonomy of Meaning and the Irreducibility of Experience," *The American Historical Review* 92 (1987), 884.

14. Ibid.

15. For further discussion of this issue, see D. La Capra, *History and Criticism* (Ithaca, N.Y., 1985), 71–114, 135–142. See also, D. La Capra, *Soundings in Critical Theory* (Ithaca, N.Y., 1989); R. Darnton, "Readers Respond to Rousseau: The Fabrication of Romantic Sensitivity," in his *The Great Cat Massacre and Other Episodes in French Cultural History* (London, 1984), 215–256. For the approach of literary criticism to the subject, see S. Fish, *Is There a Text in This Class? The Authority of Interpretive Communities* (Cambridge, Mass., 1980); S. R. Suleiman and I. Crosman, eds., *The Reader in the Text: Essays on Audience and Interpretation* (Princeton, 1980); W. Iser, *The Act of Reading: A Theory of Aesthetic Response* (Baltimore, 1978); R. C. Holub, *Reception Theory: A Critical Introduction* (London, 1984); J. Culler, *On Deconstruction: Theory and Criticism after Structuralism* (Ithaca, N.Y., 1985), 31–83; J. P. Tompkins, ed., *Reader-Response Criticism: From Formalism to Post-Structuralism* (Baltimore, 1988).

16. Roger Chartier, "Intellectual History or Sociocultural History? The French Trajectories," in *Modern European Intellectual History: Reappraisals and New Perspectives,* ed. D. La Capra and S. L. Kaplan (Ithaca, 1982), 37.

17. I. Gershoni, "The Evolution of National Culture," 325–331.

18. For a discussion of the secondary intellectuals' cultural function, see I. Gershoni and J. P. Jankowski, *Egypt, Islam, and the Arabs: The Search for Egyptian Nationhood, 1900–1930* (New York, 1987), 77–95.

19. For biographical information on these intellectuals and their cultural and

journalistic activities, see G. Eliraz, "Egyptian Intellectuals in the Face of Tradition and Change, 1919–1939" (Hebrew), Ph.D. diss., Hebrew University of Jerusalem, 1980; Gershoni and Jankowski, *Egypt, Islam, and the Arabs,* 77–95.

20. Beth Baron, "Nationalist Iconography: Egypt as a Woman," in *Rethinking Nationalism in the Arab Middle East,* ed. I. Gershoni and J. P. Jankowski (New York: Columbia University Press, forthcoming); see also Gershoni, "The Evolution of National Culture," 329–346.

21. Gershoni and Jankowski, *Egypt, Islam, and the Arabs,* 136–138.

22. For a comprehensive discussion of the Egyptian *effendiyya,* see I. Gershoni and J. P. Jankowski, *Redefining the Egyptian Nation, 1930–1945* (Cambridge, 1995), 1–31. For the *effendiyya*'s role in Egyptian politics since 1919, see M. Deeb, *Party Politics in Egypt: The Wafd and Its Rivals, 1919–1939* (London, 1979).

23. Gershoni, "The Evolution of National Culture," 331–336.

24. Deeb, *Party Politics in Egypt,* 1–15; Z. M. Quraishi, *Liberal Nationalism in Egypt: Rise and Fall of the Wafd Party* (Delhi, 1967), 36–37.

25. For details, see Gershoni and Jankowski, *Redefining the Egyptian Nation,* 7–116.

26. About these organizations and their activities, see R. P. Mitchell, *The Society of the Muslim Brothers* (London, 1969); A. Shalabi, *Misr al-Fatah wa-Dawruha fi al-Siyasa al-Misriyya, 1933–1941* (Cairo, 1982); J. P. Jankowski, *Egypt's Young Rebels: "Young Egypt," 1933–1952* (Stanford, 1975); J. Heyworth-Dunne, *Religious and Political Trends in Modern Egypt* (Washington, 1950).

27. Gershoni, "The Evolution of National Culture," 333–341.

28. For a detailed discussion of the *Islamiyyat* phenomenon, see Gershoni and Jankowski, *Redefining the Egyptian Nation,* 54–96; See also A. Wessels, *A Modern Arabic Biography of Muhammad: A Critical Study of Muhammad Husayn Haykal's "Hayat Muhammad"* (Leiden, 1972), 1–48; C. D. Smith, *Islam and the Search for Social Order,* 109–157. On the *Islammiyat*'s public reception in the 1930s, see I. Gershoni, "The Reader, 'Another Production': The Reception of Haykal's Biography of Muhammad and the Shift of Egyptian Intellectuals to Islamic Subjects in the 1930s," *Poetics Today* 15, 2 (1994), 241–277.

29. Hasan al-Banna, "Al-Duktur Haykal wa-Kitab Hayat Muhammad," *Jaridat al-Ikhwan al-Muslimin,* 21 May 1935, 30.

30. Muhammad 'Abduh, "al-Duktur Muhammad Husayn Haykal Bayna al-Ams wa-al-Yawm," *al-Nadhir,* 29 Jumada al-Ula 1358 (1939), 3.

31. Ibid., 3–4.

32. B. Baron, *The Women's Awakening in Egypt: Culture, Society, and the Press*

(New Haven, 1994); J. S. Beinin and Z. Lockman, *Workers on the Nile: Nationalism, Communism, Islam and the Egyptian Working Class, 1882–1954* (Princeton, 1987); Gershoni and Jankowski, *Egypt, Islam, and the Arabs;* Gershoni and Jankowski, *Redefining the Egyptian Nation.*

33. See in Gershoni and Jankowski, *Redefining the Egyptian Nation.*

Index